THE BALLAD OF AMERICA

The History of the United States In Song and Story

John Anthony Scott

Southern Illinois University Press
Carbondale and Edwardsville

Library of Congress Cataloging in Publication Data

Scott, John Anthony, 1916–
    The Ballad of America.

    Reprint. Originally published: New York: Bantam Books, 1966. With new afterword.
    Bibliography: p.
    Discography: p.
    Includes songs and index.
    1. Folk music-United States—History and criticism. 2. Ballads—United States—History and criticism. 3. Folk songs—United States—History and criticism. 4. Ballads—United States. 5. Folk songs—United States.
I. Title.
ML3551.S35   1983   784.4'973   82-3180
ISBN 0-8093-1061-9   781.599   AACR2

For Anne, and to the memory of Frank, Warner. As partners they traveled this country, making friends, listening to the people's songs, learning, recording, transcribing. By their scholarship they have helped to preserve the American song heritage; by their singing and teaching they have passed it on to others, and have enriched it.

Contents

Immigrants   **284**

The Negro People   **301**

VII BETWEEN TWO WORLD WARS   **324**

VIII SINCE THE WAR   **362**

Introduction

During the past ten years, there has been a great revival of interest in traditional music in America. Sales of folk song records run into the millions. Guitars today are as numerous on college campuses as bicycles, sometimes more so. The Newport Folk Festival of 1964 impressed its organizers with attendance of seventy thousand enthusiasts, mostly young, at its sessions. Magazines dealing with folk songs and their performers have burgeoned. *Sing Out* alone, which appears five times a year, has a circulation of approximately forty thousand. Itinerant singers find large and receptive audiences on college campuses, in high school and elementary school assemblies, and in summer camps. The coffee house has both reflected and promoted the folk song revival. College students, playing to packed audiences, have begun to stage their own folk festivals and "hoots." "Folk" is invading the academic curriculum: Several major universities now offer courses and degrees in folklore.

The passion for folk music is manifested primarily among young people, but it would be wrong to dismiss it as merely a youthful craze, a new fad, or as a form of youthful protest. In fact, the revival is a search for roots, for a sense of identity, for a concept of the world we live in, for a vision of the future. The meaning of American nationality, of American ideals, of dedication to America, are all involved.

This book is an attempt to show how the story of the American people is revealed in their song; to provide an introduction to this national song heritage, and to indicate its extent, variety, and beauty; to make some little-known singing materials easily and cheaply available; and, in response to many requests, to provide historical songs for use at various levels of the educational system.

The book had its origins in a course given by Bill Bonyun and the author at the 16th Annual Seminars on American Culture under the sponsorship of the New York State Historical Association, Cooperstown 1963. It represents an expansion of the thoughts presented at Cooperstown, together with a transcription of a number of the songs used by way of illustration.

The songs in this book, chosen from literally thousands, had to pass rather rigid selection tests. I sought songs that conveyed most clearly, most *typically,* a given national mood or experience; that were examples of the finest melodies and lyrics available; and that had proved their effectiveness and their popularity with modern audiences and modern singers, both student and adult.

A person is, ethically and nationally speaking, cultivated, when he learns to love and cherish the songs of his people; such a person may lack formal education, but he will yet be, in a human sense, an educated being. This fact struck Cecil J. Sharp, the great English musician and teacher, with great force when he visited the Southern Appalachians during the years 1916–1918. Sharp found the mountain people largely illiterate and lacking in formal education; but they were deeply versed in their own musical tradition and deeply attached to it. "I have no doubt," he wrote, "but that this delightful habit of making beautiful music at all times and in all places largely compensates for any deficiencies in the matter of reading and writing."*

As a people, we have, most of us, lost this precious ability "to make music at all times and in all places." Many Americans possess a fund of songs, but can only be induced to sing them on rare occasions; and the number of traditional songs known to and sung by all of us without exception is astonishingly small. Like Sharp's mountaineers, we Americans have a remarkable song heritage *available* to all of us, but we do not *utilize* it fully; we do not learn it, cherish it, teach it to our children, and sing it in our daily lives. But perhaps the folk song revival will help to change this situation; perhaps the day will come when every child will learn, as he grows up, hundreds of songs that tell the American story with fullness, feeling, and depth, and that constitute the essence of the national song heritage.

It was with the thought that it might help, just a little, to bring that day nearer, that this book was prepared. It is only a very small beginning in the musical approach to our national story. It can only suggest tentatively the wonders of this musical heritage and help arouse a curiosity to explore it further.

My indebtedness to singers, scholars, and musical collections is indicated throughout this book and in the bibliography. Beyond this, my chief debt is to Bill Bonyun. Few insights in this field are as rich as his, and I have benefited from his friendship more than I can say. Thanks also go to Dr. Louis Jones, President of the New York State Historical Association, and to the members of the Cooperstown seminar for the collective enthusiasm and wisdom which they contributed to the shap-

*English Folk Songs from the Southern Appalachians, Cecil J. Sharp. (London and New York: Oxford, 1960), xxv.

ing of this project; and to my own students, who have sung
many of the songs reproduced here, and have taught me much
about them.

JOHN ANTHONY SCOTT
HOLLAND, MASSACHUSETTS

Note on the Music

The songs included in this book are pitched in keys suitable for the ordinary voice and are easy for the average guitarist to play. For most of them, simple chord progressions have been given. But there are some songs to which any kind of conventional musical accompaniment is a hindrance rather than a help. In the case of laments, instrumentation may often be a barrier between the singer's utterance of sorrow and the listener. Work songs and "shouts," for example, often need either no accompaniment, or only an elementary rhythmic one, such as hand-clapping. A few songs included in this collection, mostly work songs and laments, have no accompaniment. Marked in the index with an asterisk (*), they are, hopefully, an introduction to the beauties of unaccompanied singing.

I

THE

COLONIAL

PERIOD

WHAT KIND OF SONGS did the people of this country sing
during the colonial period? The majority of the settlers who
arrived here during the seventeenth and eighteenth centuries
came from the British Isles—from England, Scotland, Wales,
and Ireland. They brought with them a vast heritage of British
and Irish melodies and lyrics, dance tunes, marches, and sacred
songs. This store constituted the starting point for the development of American national music. It would be transformed and modified, as time went on, both by the contributions of other immigrant peoples and by the nature of
American experience itself; but it would remain an influence
of major proportions in shaping American musical expression.
Americans, throughout their history, would draw upon this
British heritage as they strove to develop and create a unique,
American national song and music.

What was the nature of this heritage? British song itself had
been evolving for centuries. A rich and many-sided expression
of the life of an island people, it included courting songs,
love songs, and laments; pipe and fiddle tunes for dancing

1

and marching; songs of work and songs of the sea; psalms and carols; and ballads relating great events in the life of the people, and their struggles, triumphs, and disasters. All of this material united melody of extraordinary simplicity and beauty to lyrics of vivid imagery and imaginative power.

Accordingly, the first section of the chapter that follows is devoted to "the British Heritage." It contains a small selection of British songs chosen to give some idea of the variety of musical material brought by the colonists from their native land. All of the songs reproduced here were actually sung on the colonial seaboard during the seventeenth and eighteenth centuries. Dance and bagpipe tunes are not included here, since they fall beyond the scope of this book; and some of the sea songs will be found further on when we come to discuss seafaring (see pp. 126-147 below). Only one Irish song, "The Bonny Boy," is included; even this is only half-Irish, since it represents the wedding of an English lyric to an Irish melody. Irish songs will receive fuller attention as we go on. Irish immigrants who came here during the colonial period were Gaelic rather than English in language and culture; Irish song was the product of a proud and independent civiliation, and it possessed marvelous poetic and melodic qualities all its own. It has been, as much as English song, an influence of first-rate importance in the shaping of the American musical tradition —an aspect not given separate treatment, but woven into our story throughout.

When these British songs arrived at our shores, a process of change and transformation set in. This process, from the start of our history, reflected and gave expression to the emergence of a separate American identity. The colonists had crossed three thousand miles of ocean; they had severed the living, day-to-day bond with the motherland. They had come to a new country in which entirely new problems were to occupy their full attention. From the very beginning, therefore, they were developing a new style of living, and with it new and appropriate forms of expression. So it is not surprising that the colonists began to sing the old songs in a new way, with various changes of plot, lyric, and music. Since thousands of Americans, scattered throughout a huge area along the colonial seaboard, were singing the same songs, hundreds of *variants,* or new ways of singing the old songs, arose. In other words, the old songs began to be Americanized; but not, at first, through radical or far-reaching changes,

2

but through endless minor shifts in expression, emphasis, rhythm, melody, and vocabulary.

That Americans took their traditional songs wherever they went provides a partial answer to another question: What kind of songs did pioneers and frontier people sing? The answer is rooted in the colonial period, but takes us far beyond it. The pioneers sang the traditional songs wherever the frontier went, from New England to the plains of Texas, to the wilds of Michigan, to the coast of California. These songs have been traced and recorded throughout the Union; they bear witness to the fantastic extent of the diffusion of the original British heritage and of its enduring appeal to the pioneers, loggers, cowboys, farmers, Indian fighters, trappers, rivermen and canaleeers who opened up the continent. The traditional songs have been sung continuously on this side of the Atlantic in an ever-expanding area from the time of the first settlements in Massachusetts to the final elimination of the frontier two and one-half centuries later.

For this reason, too, it is not surprising that British enthusiasts studying their own song heritage have found a trail leading them to Canada and to the United States; for this heritage has been preserved in North America more fully than in Britain itself. The Industrial Revolution hit Great Britain with full force at the opening of the nineteenth century, and swept the rural population rapidly and completely off the land and into the industrial centers. Traditional singing was severely affected, and survived mainly in remote and outlying rural districts. But in America, at this very same time, the Revolution had just been won and the West was being opened up in an era of unprecedented expansion. Thus, the vitality of rural singing in America was retained well into the twentieth century—time enough for song enthusiasts, both British and American, to collect, record, and transcribe the heritage, one of the major achievements of modern scholarship.

The traditional songs were an important element in the creation of the American nation, for they provided Americans with knowledge of a common tradition, a common literature, and a common morality. They gave a scattered and struggling people a sense of unity and common destiny amidst new and difficult problems. To provide unity and spiritual bonds between people of the same nationality has been, immemorially, one of the central functions of song. Because this is so, we use throughout this book the term "national song" to denote

3

music that deals with our common past, our common destiny, our common experience, and our common values. This, in my opinion, is preferable to the much-abused term "folk song"; the latter has vague and even mystical overtones that we ought to try to avoid in a precise discussion of the subject. It is helpful to think of national song as a spectrum of musical expression ranging from hymns and sacred song to, for example, rock 'n' roll. This spectrum is vast in extent precisely because it reflects all aspects and varieties of our people's thought, life, and common experience.

As time went by, a second kind of variation crept into American singing; new lyrics were written and set to traditional tunes—a more fundamental variation than the first. Americans now began to produce songs that were not merely variants of the old ones, but that were actually new, that reflected and gave expression to the radically new issues and conflicts of colonial life. As this began to happen, a native, distinctively American song music took its first giant step forward.

Accordingly, the second section of the chapter that follows, entitled "Colonial Songs and Ballads," is devoted to a selection of these first national songs. Some of these followed the English models closely, but added new verses born of the experience of frontier life. "The Old Man Who Lived in the Woods," and "Sweet William" are good examples. Others, such as "The Death of General Wolfe," "Springfield Mountain," or "The Young Man Who Wouldn't Hoe Corn," were altogether new, and the lyrics were native American products from start to finish. All of these songs illustrate a principle of continuity and of differentiation in the making of national music; they exemplify the art of mastering a tradition and at the same time adding to it and making it over. This process has been fundamental in the creation of American national song, and its roots lie deep in the colonial era. We shall find it repeated over and over and illustrated many times in the pages of this book.

We talk of "songs and ballads." How, precisely, are these terms to be differentiated? There are no precise lines dividing songs and ballads, and we need not worry about an exact definition. The ballad is often thought of as telling a story, and in this it is contrasted with songs that are more lyrical, more personal in their expression of human emotion. Ballads recount a calamity, a feat of heroism, the fighting of a battle, the sink-ing of a ship, a natural disaster, an act of violence or treachery,

4

and they convey their message somewhat as a movie does, by linking a succession of brilliant and evocative images that the mind sees with a musical dialogue that the ear hears. Many ballads, furthermore, include highly personal and lyrical elements, as when they give ecstatic utterance to delight in the beauty of nature, or when they comment on the tragedy which they unfold. "Song and ballad" must not, therefore, be contrasted or differentiated too mechanically or rigidly. It is helpful to think of national song, in this connection, as a spectrum of human expression ranging from a stark, impersonal narration of calamitous events to the profoundly personal, lyrical utterance found in the blues or in the traditional Irish lament, the *chaoine*.

The first colonists sang the traditional ballads and songs from memory and transmitted them to their children by word of mouth. New ballads, by contrast, whether indigenously American or imported from the motherland, were in most cases written down; it was natural and inevitable that the printing press should become a powerful instrument for the diffusion of such material. Such printed ballads—broadside ballads, as they are called—provide the raw material for the study of many of our historical songs. These broadsides, providing news in verse form and appropriate editorial comment, were in effect singing newspapers. The classic example of such a ballad given in this chapter is "The Death of General Wolfe" (see p. 36).

Some people have argued that there is a distinction between the "pure" art of the traditional ballads of the type of "Bawbee Allen" or "Sir Patrick Spens" and the "vulgar" outpourings of the topical or broadside ballads. Both historically and artistically, the distinction appears to us invalid. We are not concerned with all the broadside ballads, but only with the best of them, those that most clearly and fully convey to us the meaning of a past age. The best of these songs have extraordinary literary qualities, of which the pages of this book will provide eloquent proof. These broadside ballads are indispensable to an understanding of our national history, and our song heritage would be vastly poorer without them.

How did the colonists sing their songs? For the most part they sang unaccompanied, using no instruments at all; and this, not because they did not prize musical accompaniment, but simply because the conditions under which they sang did not permit the use of instrumentation. People in colonial days and throughout the greater part of American history, sang under every conceivable kind of circumstance and on every occa-

5

sion. They had songs for work, washing dishes, seafaring, logging, hunting, war, mourning, and love. There was a time for everything, and there was a song for everything. The very omnipresence of song in people's lives guaranteed that the human voice itself and the human voice alone should be the supreme vehicle for musical expression. You cannot play a guitar, nor even a mouth organ, while you are plowing a field, washing dishes, changing a baby's diaper, or cutting a tree down. Out of necessity, therefore, the people relied upon the unaided power of the voice; they came to cherish it as the most marvelous instrument of all. The imagery of the traditional songs, their melodic power, their sheer humanity, these more than compensated for a lack of accompaniment.

Thus, we do the past wrong if, when we sing its songs today, we overlard them with instrumental accompaniment so emphatic that it stands between the song itself and the audience. Accompaniment must be used, if at all, with subtlety and great discrimination—to accent rhythm, provide harmonic color, and connect verses while the singer catches his breath. And nothing more. For the rest, the style of traditional singers from rural areas both in the United States and Canada has been abundantly recorded; we can study it from the life. In singing traditional songs, we must be guided not only by a grasp of traditional style, but, finally, by our own understanding of the meaning of the songs we sing, by our own sense of integrity in conveying meaning. The important thing is not to strive for a fake "authenticity" but to grasp and convey by singing the essence of the mood, experience, and event, about which we are singing. In this way, the past is recreated imaginatively and emotionally in our singing, and comes to life.

We have said that traditionally the American people sang their songs without accompaniment. But this does not mean that they did not possess instruments, and did not use them skilfully and effectively. On the crew of a square-rigger, there would likely be a fiddler or harmonica player; Negro slaves developed the fretless banjo, the banjo, and the washtub bass; Scottish highlanders brought the skirl of the bagpipe to North Carolina and New York; colonial militia paraded and marched away to war to the sound of fife and drum; country people created a variety of "folk" instruments, including the incomparable dulcimer. But there was always an appointed time for the playing of instruments, and it was usually when men and women were at leisure, or marching to war, or dancing. Such times, in the life of a hard-working people, were relatively few.

The British Heritage

Bawbee Allen

"Barbara Allen" is a ballad that has been sung for three centuries, at the very least, in all parts of the British Isles and Eire. Its wide diffusion throughout the United States, and the endless variety of melody and lyric found, are evidence that it was brought to the colonies in the earliest days.

The version reproduced here comes from Scotland, and is given to us from the family tradition of the great Scottish folk singer, Ewan MacColl. It has been included here, from the hundreds of American and British versions that might have been chosen, for a number of reasons. Sir John Graeme, in the first place, is shown as a flesh-and-blood man who fought a duel and died for love. This is much truer to life than the common and generally accepted version of "a spineless lover who gave up the ghost without a struggle." In the second place, MacColl's melody is, in this editor's judgment, among the most perfect that we inherit. And finally, melody and lyric combined provide a classic example of the great and passionate art of the ballad at its best.

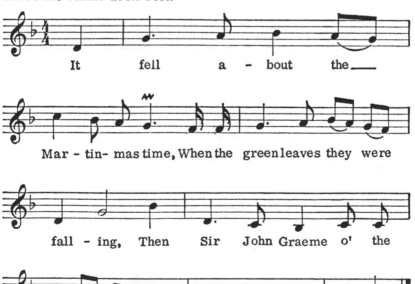

It fell a - bout the ___
Mar - tin- mas time, When the green leaves they were
fall - ing, Then Sir John Graeme o' the
North Coun-try Fell in love with Baw-bee All -en.

7

2. He's sent his man all through the town,
   To the place where she was dwelling,
   "Come down, come down to my master dear,
   If your name be Bawbee Allen."

3. O slowly slowly rose she up,
   And slowly she went to him;
   And when she came to his bedside:
   "Young man, I think you're dying."

4. " 'Tis I am sick and very sick,
   And it's a' for Bawbee Allen."
   "It's better for me ye'll never be,
   For bonnie Bawbee Allen.

5. "When ye were in the tavern, sir,
   And at the wine was swilling,
   Ye made the toasts go round and round,
   But slighted Bawbee Allen."

6. He's turned his face unto the wall,
   And death was with him dealing,
   "Then fare ye well my kind friends all,
   But be kind to Bawbee Allen.

7. "Then put your hand unto the wall,
   And there you'll find a token,
   With my gold watch and my gold ring,
   Give that to Bawbee Allen.

8. "Then put your hand unto my side,
   And there you'll find a warrant;
   And there you'll get my blood-red shirt,
   It bled for Bawbee Allen."

9. She had not gone a step, a step,
   When she heard the death bell knelling,
   And every clap the death bell gave,
   Said "Woe to Bawbee Allen."

10. "O mother dear, you'll make my bed,
    You'll make it soft and narrow;
    My love has died for me this day,
    I'll die for him tomorrow."

I Will Give My Love an Apple

This song illustrates well the extraordinary lyrical qualities so often to be found in the old ballads. The version given here has been collected in both England and Nova Scotia with practically identical words and melody. Other versions have been popular in the United States, but none of these, in the opinion of the editor, compare with the Nova Scotian version given here, and which deserves to be more widely known.

2. How can there be an apple without e'er a core?
   How can there be a dwelling without e'er a door?
   How can there be a palace wherein she may be,
   That she may unlock it without e'er a key?

3. My head is an apple without e'er a core,
   My mind is a dwelling without e'er a door,
   My heart is the palace wherein she may be,
   And she may unlock it without e'er a key.

4. I will give my love a cherry without e'er a stone,
   I will give my love a chicken without e'er a bone,
   I will give my love a ring, not a rent to be seen,
   I will give my love a baby and no crying.

5. How can there be a cherry without e'er a stone?
   How can there be a chicken without e'er a bone?
   How can there be a ring, not a rent to be seen?
   How can there be a baby and no crying?

6. When the cherry's in blossom it has no stone,
   When the chicken's in the egg it has no bone,
   When the ring's a-running, there's not a rent to be seer
   When the baby's a-getting, there's no crying.

The Keys of Canterbury

The old songs were often cast in dialogue form, as a conversation between lovers, or between father and daughter, mother and son, etc. The dramatic possibilities of the song, the sense of reality conveyed by it, were in this way vastly enhanced.

"The Keys of Canterbury," a classic example of a courting song in dialogue, is found in practically identical form on both sides of the Atlantic and is also widely known in a number of parodies. In the Southern version given here, the dialogue form is emphasized by an alternation of major and minor keys, and also by a change of beat. English versions of the song are uniformly in minor key and 6/8 time.

"Mad - am I will give to you the
keys of Can - ter - bur - y, And
all the bells of Lon - don Town shall
ring and make you mer - ry; If
you will be my dar - ling, my

11

joy— and my dear, If you will go a-walk-ing with me an - y - where."

"Sir, I'll not ac - cept of you the keys of Can - ter - bur - y, Though all the bells of Lon - don Town should ring and make me mer - ry, And I'll not be your bride, your joy, and your dear, And I'll not take a walk with you an - y - where."

"Madam, I will give to you a little ivory comb,
To fasten up your golden locks when I am not at home;
If you will be my darling, my joy, and my dear,
If you will go a-walking with me anywhere."

    "Sir, I'll not accept from you a little ivory comb
    To fasten up my golden locks when I am not at home;
    And I'll not be your bride, your joy, and your dear,
    And I'll not take a walk with you anywhere."

"Madam, I will give to you a pair of boots of cork,
One was made in London, the other made in York;
If you will be my darling, my joy, and my dear,
If you will go a-walking with me anywhere."

    "Sir, I'll not accept of you a pair of boots of cork,
    Though one was made in London, the other made in
      York;
    And I'll not be your bride, your joy, and your dear,
    And I'll not take a walk with you anywhere."

"Madam, I will give to you the keys to my heart,
And all my sacred promises that we shall never part;
If you will be my darling, my joy, and my dear,
If you will go a-walking with me anywhere."

    "Sir, I will accept of you the keys to your heart,
    To lock it up for ever that we never more may part,
    And I will be your bride, your joy, and your dear,
    And I will take a walk with you anywhere."

The Sycamore Tree

Over the centuries, this song has achieved an extraordinary popularity on both sides of the Atlantic, particularly among children. During slavery days, Negro people in the South appropriated it as their own (see pp. 207-8). Pioneers carried it throughout the length and breadth of the United States. The version given here, chosen for its delightful vitality and the lilting beauty of the melody, comes from Florida.

"Oh, hang - man, hang - man, slack-en your rope, And wait a lit - tle while;__ I think I see my fa - ther com - ing, A - rid - ing from man - y a mile." "Oh, have you come with sil - ver and gold__ And mon - ey to buy me free,__ Or

14

have you come to see me hung Upon the syc-a-more tree?"__ "No
gold nor sil-ver have__ I here, Nor
mon-ey to buy__ you free;__ But
I have come to see__ you hang Upon the syc-a-more tree."__

*Repeat with mother, brother, sister, and
finally lover, who replies:*

"Yes gold and silver have I here,
And money to buy you free;
But I've not come to see you hang
Nor hung you shall not be."

From *Folk Songs of Florida,* by Alton C. Morris. Published by the
University of Florida Press, 1950. Used by permission.

15

The Trees They Grow So High

This ballad exercises an almost uncanny influence over the singer: it communicates a seemingly inexhaustible sense of the mystery of life, its joy and its sadness. Many versions have been collected in the British Isles, and the number of fine melodies to which the lyric has been set is altogether remarkable. Robert Burns tried his hand at "improving" this song, with indifferent success. Irish variants were brought by immigrants to Canada and the United States to provide the basis for two unique and indigenous American songs, "The Jam on Gerry's Rock," and "Peter Emberley" (see pp. 175 and 270).

To understand this song it is only necessary to know that child marriages in Europe, either for the consolidation of family estates or for the alliance of royal dynasties, were not at all uncommon during the feudal period and until quite recently. Scottish tradition links the ballad to the marriage arranged in 1634 between Elizabeth Innes of Craigston and the boy heir to the Urquhart estates. The child husband died while still at school.

We reproduce two beautiful versions from widely separated parts of the British Isles: from Somerset and Devon, in the west of England; and from Eire, where the version given is entitled "The Bonny Boy."

(West of England)

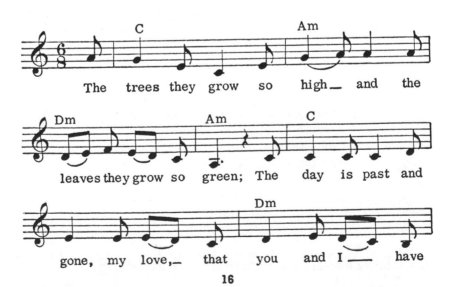

The trees they grow so high — and the leaves they grow so green; The day is past and gone, my love, — that you and I — have

16

seen. It's a cold__ win- ter's night, my love, when
I __ must bide__ a - lone, For my
bon - ny lad is long, long a - grow- ing. _____

2. "Oh father, dearest father, you've done to me much wrong;
   You've tied me to a boy when you know he is too young;
   For he is but sixteen, and I am twenty-one,
   And my bonny lad is long, long a-growing."

3. "Oh daughter, dearest daughter, I've done to you no wrong,
   For I have wedded you to a noble lord's son.
   And he shall be the lord, and you shall wait upon,
   And your bonny lad is young, but he's growing.

4. "We'll send your love to college all for a year or two,
   And then perhaps in time the boy will do for you;
   I'l buy you white ribbons to tie about his waist,
   To let the ladies know that he's married."

5. As she went a-walking by yonder churchyard wall,
   She saw four and twenty young men a-playing at the ball;
   She called for her own true love, but they would not let
       him come,
   They said the lad was young, but a-growing.

6. And at the age of sixteen he was a married man,
   And at the age of seventeen the father to a son;
   And at the age of eighteen, on his grave the grass grew
       green,
   For death had put an end to his growing.

7. So now her love is dead, and in his grave does lie,
    The green grass will grow over him so very, very high;
    And this poor girl will mourn for him until the day she
        dies,
    A-watching o'er his son while he's growing.

The Bonny Boy (Eire)

The __ trees are grow-ing tall __ and the leaves are grow-ing green; And man-y a day __ and night have __ gone since __ you and I have seen: The win-ter nights are com ing, and __ I must bide a - lone, For my bon-ny boy is long, long a - grow - ing.

2. "O father, dear father, you've done what's very wrong,
   To marry me to this bonny boy and he so very young,
   He being sixteen years and I being twenty-one,
   He's my bonny boy, he's young, but he's growing."

3. "O daughter, dear daughter, don't mind what people say,
   He will be a man to you when you are old and gray,
   He will be a man to you when I am dead and gone,
   He's your bonny boy, he's young, but he's growing."

4. At the age of sixteen he was a married man,
   And at the age of seventeen the father of a son,
   And at the age of eighteen on his grave the grass grew
        green,
   Cruel death had put an end to his growing.

5. "I will buy my love a shroud of the ornamental brown,
   And while they are weaving it the tears they will run down;
   For once I had a true love and now he's dead and gone
   And I lost this bonny boy while he was growing."

6. Come all you pretty fair maids, a warning take from me,
   And never build your nest on the top of any tree,
   For the green leaves they will wither, and the roots they
        will decay,
   And the blushes of your bonny boy will soon fade away.

19

The Bonnie Lass o' Fyvie

This ballad with its passionate and lyrical overtones has been sung in Scotland since the eighteenth century. English versions, possibly of greater age, are also known, though the relationship of these to the Scottish song is far from clear. The "Bonnie Lass o' Fyvie" was most probably brought to the New World by Scottish immigrants who settled in North Carolina during colonial times; the song has been found primarily in the South. In the American versions, "Fyvie" becomes "'Ivory" or "Ireo," and Ned, the captain's name, becomes "Wade." He is buried not "in the lowlands of Fyvie," but in "the lowlands of Louisiana." The lyrics reproduced here were published in Buchan, Scotland in 1906 by Gavin Greig, the great Scots song collector. The melody is traditional.

There was — a — troop of
I - rish dra-goons Came march-ing — down through —
Fy - rie O; The — Cap-tain's fallen in
love with a bon-nie, bon-nie lass, Her
name it is called — pret - ty Peg - gy O.

20

2. "O come down the stairs, pretty Peggy," he said,
   "O come down the stairs pretty Peggy, O,
   O come down the stairs, comb aside your yellow hair,
   Take the last farewell of your daddy, O.

3. "It's I'll give ye ribbons, love, I'll give ye rings,
   And I'll give ye necklaces of lammer, O,
   And I'll give ye silken gowns flounced to your knees,
   If ye would come down to my chamber, O."

4. "I thank you for your ribbons, love, I thank you for your
          rings,
   I thank you for your necklace of lammer, O.
   I do not want gowns to suit my degree,
   I would scorn to be seen in your chamber, O.

5. "A soldier's wife I never shall be,
   A soldier shall never enjoy me, O;
   For I never do intend to go to a foreign land,
   So I never shall marry a soldier, O."

6. The colonel cries "Mount boys, mount boys, mount,"
   But the captain he cries "Tarry, O,
   O tarry, O tarry another day or two,
   Till we see if this bonnie lass will marry, O.

7. "There is many a bonnie lass into bonnie Auchterless,
   And many a bonnie lass in the Carioch, O,
   There's many a bonnie Jean in the town of Aberdeen,
   But the flower of them all lies in Fyvie, O."

8. "I'll drink no more of your claret wine,
   I'll break no more of your glasses, O;
   But tomorrow is the day that I must go away,
   So farewell to Fyvie's lasses, O."

9. Early next morning we all marched away,
   And O, but the captain he was sorry, O,
   For the drums they did beat, o'er the bonnie bogs of Gight,
   And the band played the Lowlands of Fyvie, O.

10. Long, long ere they came to old Meldrum town
    Their captain they had to carry, O,

And long long ere they came to bonnie Aberdeen,
They had their captain to bury, O.

11. Green grow the birches on bonnie Ythanside,
And low lie the Lowlands of Fyvie, O;
Our captain's name was Ned, and he died for the maid,
He died for the chambermaid of Fyvie, O.

Lord Ronald

A brooding sense of the world's evil and a passionate cry of pain and weariness are embodied in "Lord Ronald," one of the starkest and loveliest of the classic ballads. Long a favorite in the British Isles, the United States, and Canada, the story is unfolded by a dramatic use of the dialogue form. Many of us get our first introduction to this song when as children we sing a parody of it, "Billy Boy." The version chosen for reproduction here was selected for the special beauty of its melody, which is Scottish.

"Where hae you been a' day, Lord Ron-ald, my son? Where hae you been a' day, my hand-some young one?" "I've been in the wood hunt-ing; moth-er, make my bed soon, For I'm wea-ry, wea-ry hunt-ing, and fain would lie down."

2. "O where did you dine, Lord Ronald my son?
O where did you dine, my handsome young one?"
"I dined with my sweetheart; mother, make my bed soon,
For I am weary, weary hunting, and fain would lie down."

3. "What got you to dine on, Lord Ronald my son?
What got you to dine on, my handsome young one?"
"I got eels boiled in water that in heather doth run,
And I am weary, weary hunting, and fain would lie down."

4. "What did she wi' the brew o' them, Lord Ronald my son?
What did she wi' the brew o' them, my handsome young
    one?"
"She gave it to my hounds for to live upon,
And I am weary, weary hunting, and fain would lie down."

5. "Where are your hounds now, Lord Ronald my son?
Where are your hounds now, my handsome young one?"
"They are all swelled and bursted, and so will I soon,
And I am weary, weary hunting, and fain would lie down."

6. "What will you leave your father, Lord Ronald my son?
What will you leave your father, my handsome young
    one?"
"I'll leave him my lands for to live upon,
And I am weary, weary hunting, and fain would lie down."

7. "What will you leave your mother, Lord Ronald my son?
What will you leave your mother, my handsome young
    one?"
"I'll leave her my Bible for to read upon,
And I'm weary, weary hunting, and fain would lie down."

8. "What will you leave your sweetheart, Lord Ronald my
    son?
What will you leave your sweetheart, my handsome young
    one?"
"I'll leave her the gallows-tree for to hang upon,
And I'm weary, weary hunting, and fain would lie down."

Sir Patrick Spens

This ballad is included here as an example of folk poetry and the ballad art at its very greatest. The lyric is reproduced, with minor changes in spelling, from the first published version of the song that appeared in 1765. This is rounded out by the addition of verses 8–10 which appear in one form or another in other published versions and are necessary for the dramatic continuity of the story. The age of this ballad, the extent and nature of any factual basis for it, are unknown; there is certainly no record of Sir Patrick Spens as a great Scottish mariner. Though we may be reasonably certain that the ballad came to Virginia and North Carolina with Scottish settlers in colonial times, it has evidently been little sung in the United States. The majestic melody with which the lyric is here linked comes to us through the singing of Ewan MacColl.

The king sits in Dum-fer-line town, Drink-ing the blood-red wine: "O where will I get a good sail-or To sail this ship of mine?"

2. Up and spoke an eldern knight,
    Sat at the king's right knee:
   "Sir Patrick Spens is the best sailor
    That sails upon the sea."

25

3. The king has written a broad letter,
   And signed it with his hand,
   And sent it to Sir Patrick Spens
   Was walking on Leith sand.

4. The first line that Sir Patrick read,
   A loud laugh laughed he;
   The next line that Sir Patrick read,
   The tear blinded his eye.

5. "O who has done this ill deed,
   This ill deed done to me,
   To send me out this time of the year,
   To sail upon the sea?

6. "Make haste, make haste, my merry men all,
   Our good ship sails the morn:"
   "O say not so my master dear,
   For I fear a deadly storm.

7. "Late, late yester e'en I saw the new moon,
   With the old moon in her arm,
   And I fear, I fear, my dear master,
   That we will come to harm."

8. They had not sailed a league, a league,
   A league but barely three,
   When the sky grew dark and the wind blew loud,
   And angry grew the sea.

9. "O where will I get a good sailor,
   To take my helm in hand,
   Till I get up to the tall topmast,
   To see if I can spy land?"

10. He had not gone a step, a step,
    A step but barely one,
    When the bows of our goodly ship did break,
    And the salt sea it came in.

11. O our Scots nobles were right loath
    To wet their cork-heeled shoon;
    But long e'er all the play was played
    Their hats they swam aboon.

12. O long, long may their ladies sit
        With their fans into their hands,
    Or ere they see Sir Patrick Spens
        Come sailing to the land.

13. And long, long may their ladies stand,
        With their gold combs in their hair,
    Waiting for their own dear lords,
        For they'll see them no more.

14. Half o'er, half o'er to Aberdour,
        It's fifty fathoms deep;
    And there lies good Sir Patrick Spens
        With the Scots lords at his feet.

Psalm 100
(A Psalm of Praise)

From the beginning of American history there has been an intimate connection between "spiritual" or sacred song, and popular song. The first thing that the Puritans did, musically speaking, was to translate the Psalms from the original Hebrew and set them to folk melodies, or, as they put it, to "the graver sort of tunes of our own country songs." The psalms so set were put to many uses; for worship on the Sabbath, private devotionals, work in the field, marching into battle, and other time of trial. "Old Hundred," or "Psalm 100," was one of the best known and most sung of the old devotional songs. We reproduce the lyric as given in the Bay Psalm Book of 1640, together with the melodic line as given in Ravenscroft's Psalter of 1621.

Make ye a joy-ful sound-ing noise,

Un-to Je-ho-vah, all the earth:

Serve ye Je-ho-vah with glad-ness:

Be-fore his pres-ence come with mirth.

Know that Jehovah he is God,
Who hath us formed it is he,
And not ourselves: his own people
And sheep of his pasture are we.

Enter into his gates with praise,
Into his courts with thankfulness:
Make ye confession unto him,
And his name reverently bless.

Because Jehovah he is good
For evermore is his mercy:
And unto generations all
Continue doth his verity.

Colonial Songs
and Ballads

Soldier, Soldier, Won't You Marry Me?

This charming dialogue song is undoubtedly of English origin, but its widespread popularity in the United States and the variety of forms in which it has been sung entitle it to be considered as a traditional American song. The dialogue is amusing to act out, and furthermore it makes a sharp point. Colonial militiamen were responsible for their own outfitting with clothes, guns, and boots. The government in those days, in sharp contrast to our own times, assumed no responsibility in such matters. Militiamen often went ragged and when on active duty picked up what they could where they could. They had a reputation, evidently, as a down-at-heel, thieving lot.

The variant of the song as reproduced here was transcribed by Cecil J. Sharp from the singing of Mrs. Carrie Ford in North Carolina. The melody is sung on the five-tone, or pentatonic scale.

"Sol - dier, sol - dier, won't you mar - ry me?" It's_ O a fife and drum: "How can I mar - ry such a pret - ty girl as you, When I've

got no hat to put on, When I've

got no hat to put on?"

Off to the tailor she did go,
As hard as she could run,
Brought him back the finest that was there,
"Now soldier, put it on."

"Soldier, soldier, won't you marry me?"
It's O a fife and drum:
"How can I marry such a pretty girl as you
When I've got no coat to put on?"

Off to the tailor she did go,
As hard as she could run,
Brought him back the finest that was there,
"Now soldier, put it on."

"Soldier, soldier, won't you marry me?"
It's O a fife and drum:
"How can I marry such a pretty girl as you
When I've got no shoes to put on?"

Off to the shoe shop she did go,
As hard as she could run,
Brought him back the finest that was there,
"Now soldier, put them on."

"Soldier, soldier, won't you marry me?"
It's O a fife and drum:
"How can I marry such a pretty girl as you
With a wife and two babies at home?"

Reprinted by permission of Oxford University Press from *English Folk Songs from the Southern Appalachians*, collected by Cecil J. Sharp and edited by Maud Karpeles. Copyright © by Oxford University Press, London and New York, 1932.

Siubhail a Gradh

This song is a fine example of a lament that has been sung continuously on both sides of the Atlantic since the late seventeenth century, and that has also developed in the United States in a distinctively American form.

"Siubhail a Gradh" arose out of the agonies of Irish struggle against British rule. In 1688, rebellion broke out and was crushed by the English king, William of Orange. The Treaty of Limerick, which terminated hostilities in 1691, provided honorable terms for the Irish warriors: they might take the oath of allegiance to England, or they might leave their native land for exile and for military service on the continent. The majority of Eire's leaders, the flower of her aristocracy, chose exile. There remained to them hope that they might one day come home, sword in hand, under the leadership of a "King's son from across the sea," to deliver their country from the hated British rule.

"Siubhail a Gradh" records a nation's desolation and the glimmering spark of its hope, still lingering in defeat. Irish immigrants to the New World brought this song with them. In time, it rooted itself in American soil, and became a lament for militiamen departed to fight the French or the British. The Gaelic refrain dropped away, or survived only as a nonsense rhyme; the melody became Americanized. We reproduce here the Irish lyric and one of the beautiful melodies to which it was set; and an American version found originally among Irish settlers in the Hudson Valley, and transmitted to us through the family tradition of the New York song collector, John Allison.

Come, My Love (Eire)

I wish I were on yon green hill, 'Tis there I'd sit and cry my fill, And___

ev - er- y tear would turn a mill. My— dar - ling and my life, I love you so. Come, come, come, my love, Now death a - lone can end my woe, Don't— leave me— here to mourn a - lone, My— dar - ling and my life, I love you so.

I'll sell my rack, I'll sell my reel,
I'll sell my only spinning wheel,
To buy my love a sword of steel,
My darling and my life, I love you so.

Refrain

But now my love has gone to France,
To try his fortune to advance,
If he come back, 'tis but a chance,
My darling and my life, I love you so.

The refrain is translated from the Gaelic by Samuel Preston Bayard and John Anthony Scott.

I'll dye my petticoat, I'll dye it red,
And round the world I'll beg my bread,
For the lad that I love from me is fled,
My darling and my life, I love you so.

Refrain

*   *   *

*The Gaelic refrain, often still sung by Irish singers along
with the English verses, goes as follows:*

Siubhail, siubhail, siubhail a gradh,
Ní leigheas le fagháil acht leigheas an bháis.
Ó d'fhág tu mise, is bocht mo chás,
Is go dteidhidh tu a mhúirnin slán.

Johnny Has Gone for a Soldier (Hudson Valley)

Sad I sit on But-ter-nut Hill,
Who could blame me cry my fill? And
ev-ery tear would turn a mill,
John-ny has gone for a sol-dier.

Me oh my, I loved him so,
Broke my heart to see him go,
And only time can heal my woe,
Johnny has gone for a soldier.

I'll sell my clock, I'll sell my reel,
Likewise I'll sell my spinning wheel,
To buy my love a sword of steel,
Johnny has gone for a soldier.

Sad I sit on Butternut Hill,
Who can blame me cry my fill?
And every tear would turn a mill,
Johnny has gone for a soldier.

The Death of General Wolfe

The ballad of the death of General Wolfe is a historical song of unusual importance, and also one of the first American broadside ballads of which we have a record.

In the colonial period, British settlers were moving slowly and painfully westward from their coastal beach heads between the Appalachian barrier and the sea. In the race for empire and for the interior of the American continent, they had been outflanked by the French. From the days of Champlain to those of Montcalm, a series of brilliant explorations had brought the entire Mississippi valley under French control. Britain's mainland colonies thus grew up in the shadow of French power and with an acute awareness of French rivalry. In colonial days, the military conflict between Britain and France erupted time and again—all along the frontier, in New Brunswick and New Scotia, in the valleys of the Hudson and the St. Lawrence.

The climax of the battle for North American dominion came with the French and Indian Wars which began in 1754 in the Ohio valley, and culminated with the siege of Quebec in 1759. British victory in this struggle obliterated French power in the New World and opened a new chapter in the history of the North American continent.

The hero of the siege of Quebec and the victor of September 13, 1759 was the young British commander General James Wolfe, who died in the hour of triumph. It was understandable that he should become an American national hero whose great exploit in storming the Heights of Abraham should find enduring expression in song.

The version of the great ballad in celebration of Wolfe that is reproduced here is a composite of two broadsides in the Harris Collection of the University of Rhode Island, and one in the Isaiah Thomas Collection of the American Antiquarian Society. Other versions printed in early American songbooks testify to the widespread popularity of this song. It was, of course, also well known in Canada. The wonderful Dorian melody to which the words are here set was collected from Canadian singers in Newfoundland.

Come all ye young men — all, let — this de - light you; — Cheer up, ye young men — all, let — noth -ing — fright you. — Nev - er let your — cour - age — fail when you're brought to tri - al, — Nor let your fan - cy — move at the first de - ni - al. ——

2. Bad news is come to town, bad news is carried,
   Bad news is whispered round, my love is married.
   Bad news is come to town, I fell a-weeping,
   They stole my love from me while I lay sleeping.

3. "Love, here's a diamond ring, if you'll accept it,
   'Tis for your sake alone, long time I've kept it;
   When you this posy read think on the giver,
   Madam, remember me, or I'm undone for ever."

4. So then this gallant youth did cross the ocean,
   To free America from her invasion;
   He landed at Quebec with all his party,
   The city to attack, being brave and hearty.

5. Brave Wolfe drew up his men, in a line so pretty,
   On the plains of Abraham before the city;
   A distance from the town the French did meet him,
   With a double number they resolved to beat him.

6. The French drew up their men, for death prepared;
   In one another's face the armies stared,
   While Wolfe and Montcalm together walked
   Between their armies they like brothers talked.

7. Each man then took his post at their retire,
   So then these numerous hosts began to fire—
   The cannon on each side did roar like thunder,
   And youths in all their pride were torn asunder.

8. The drums did loudly beat, colors were flying,
   The purple gore did stream, and men lay dying,
   When shot off from his horse fell this brave hero,
   And we lament his loss in weeds of sorrow.

9. The French began to break, their ranks were flying,
   Wolfe seemed to revive while he lay dying.
   He lifted up his head while guns did rattle,
   And to his army said, "How goes the battle?"

10. His aide-de-camp replied, " 'Tis in our favor;
    Quebec with all her pride, nothing can save her;
    She falls into our hands with all her treasure,"
    "O then," brave Wolfe replied, "I die with pleasure."

11. Bad news is come to town, bad news is carried,
    Some say my love is dead, some say he's married.
    As I was a pondering on this, I feel a-weeping,
    They stole my love from me while I lay sleeping.

Melody from Elisabeth B. Greenleaf and Grace Y. Mansfield, *Ballads and Sea Songs of Newfoundland*, Harvard University Press. Copyright 1933 by The President and Fellows of Harvard College; c. 1961 by Elisabeth B. Greenleaf and Grace Y. Mansfield. Reprinted by permission.

Sweet William

This song came to America from Britain in colonial days. Taken by pioneers all the way from the east coast to California, it underwent many changes of lyric, and was used as a commentary on all kinds of tragic experiences in American life. In wartime, it became a lament over a fate that robbed young women of their lovers. On the frontier and in the logging camps, under the title "The Pinery Boy," it bewailed the hard, dangerous life of the lumberman. During the gold rush, it became a commentary on the craze for quick riches that snatched men from their sweethearts and lured them to death in Panamanian swamps or on desert trails. The uniquely American melody given here is from North Carolina; the mode is Aeolian (A to A on the white keys of the piano). The lyric is a composite, put together from dozens of partial and corrupted texts that have been left to us.

It was ear - ly, ear - ly all in_ the spring, That my boy Wil - lie went to serve the King; The_ night was dark and the wind blew_ high, It was then that I lost my dear sol -dier boy.

2. The night is long and I can find no rest,
   The thought of Willie runs in my breast;
   I'll search the green woods and village wide
   Still hoping my true love for to find.

3. A soldier's life is a cruel life,
   It robs young ladies of their heart's delight,
   Causes them to weep and causes them to mourn
   The loss of their true love never to return.

4. "Father, father build me a boat,
   That on the ocean I may float,
   I'll hail every vessel that passes by,
   There to inquire for my sweet soldier boy."

5. She had not been sailing far on the main,
   When she spied a ship coming in from Spain:
   "Captain, oh captain, tell me true,
   If my sweet William is with your crew."

6. "What was the color of your true love's hair?
   What kind of rig did your true love wear?"
   "His eyes were blue, his lips like wine,
   Ten thousand thousand times they've met with mine."

7. "Lady, lady, he is not here;
   He was killed in battle, my dear.
   At the head of Rocky Island, as we passed by,
   There we left your sweet soldier boy."

8. She wrung her hands, she tore her hair,
   She sobbed and sighed in her despair,
   She run her boat against a rock,
   I thought, in my soul, her heart it would break.

9. "Go dig my grave both wide and deep,
   Put a marble stone at my head and feet;
   And above my breast carve a turtle dove
   To let the world know I died for love."

Melody reproduced by permission of Oxford University Press from *English Folk Songs from the Southern Appalachians,* collected by Cecil J. Sharp and edited by Maud Karpeles. Copyright © by Oxford University Press, London and New York, 1932.

The Old Man Who Lived in the Woods

The story of the man who competed with his wife to see which of them could do more work came from the Old World. Evidently, it was a favorite of the American settlers, for it has been found everywhere—in the North, South, and Midwest. During its travels, the song picked up unique and original American lyrics, loading upon the wretched husband's shoulders as many chores as there were in a woman's day. Such versions are of great length, but they give a vivid impression of the endless toil that fell to a woman's lot on the average pioneer farm: washing the dirty laundry, churning the cream, milking the cow, feeding the animals, spinning and winding the yarn. The melody given here is taken from the singing of the New England folklorist Bill Bonyun.

There was an old man who lived in the woods, As you shall plain-ly see, Who said he could do more work in a day, Than his wife could do in three. "With all my heart!" the old wom-an said, "But

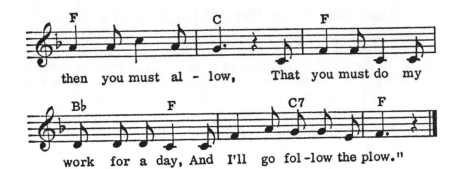

then you must al - low, That you must do my

work for a day, And I'll go fol -low the plow."

3. "You must milk the tiny cow,
    Lest she should go quite dry,
And you must feed the little pigs
    That live in yonder sty.

4. "You must watch the speckled hen,
    For fear she lays astray,
And not forget the spool of yarn
    That I spin every day."

5. The old woman took the staff in her hand,
    And went to follow the plow;
And the old man took the pail on his head
    And went to milk the cow.

6. But Tiny she winked and Tiny she blinked,
    And Tiny she tossed her nose,
And Tiny she gave him a kick on the shins
    Till the blood ran down to his toes.

7. Then "Whoa, Tiny!" and "So, Tiny!
    My pretty little cow, stand still!
If ever I milk you again," he said,
    "It will be against my will."

8. And then he went to feed the pigs
    That lived within the sty;
The old sow ran against his legs
    And threw him in the mire.

9. And then he watched the speckled hen
    Lest she might lay astray;
But he quite forgot the spool of yarn
    That his wife spun every day.

10. Then the old man swore by the sun and the moon,
       And the green leaves on the trees,
    That his wife could do more work in a day
       Than he could do in three.

11. And when he saw how well she plowed,
       And ran the furrows even,
    He swore she could do more work in a day
       Than he could do in seven.

Springfield Mountain

The life of a frontier farmer in colonial days was a harsh, dangerous, and precarious one. Death might strike without warning in many different ways: disease or epidemic, forest accident, Indian raid, the attack of a wild animal, or the bite of a poisonous snake. These perils gave an urgent significance to the theme of religious revivalism that kept pace with westward-moving settlement. Repent now, and give your soul to God, while there is time: tomorrow may be too late.

"Springfield Mountain" is a classic example of this revivalist message and its expression in song. The version given here is traditional in New England, and tells the story of an accidental death that actually occurred at Wilbraham, Massachusetts, in the middle of the eighteenth century. This song has been found in one form or another throughout the Union, which attests to the universality of the experience with which it deals. The simple yet beautiful melody is sung on five notes of the scale and is of mixed modality, that is, it has no dominant emphasis in either major or minor key. It is harmonized with two chords, a major chord and its relative minor.

"Springfield Mountain" has been called the first truly American folk song. This statement really does not have very much meaning, since the Americanization of British song was so gradual and continuous a process. It is a good example of traditional ballad form, and the melody slightly resembles Psalm 100. For "The Pesky Sarpent," a comic version of "Springfield Mountain," and its significance in New England history, see page 156.

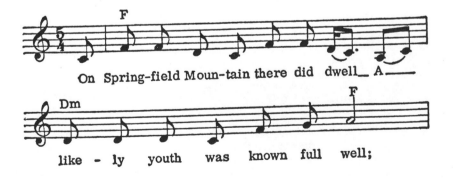

On Spring-field Moun-tain there did dwell_ A_ like - ly youth was known full well;

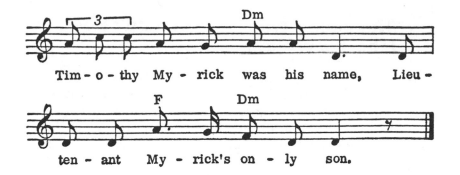

Tim-o-thy My-rick was his name, Lieu-
ten-ant My-rick's on-ly son.

2. On Friday morning he did go
   Down to the meadow for to mow;
   He mowed and mowed around the field
   Till a poisonous serpent bit his heel.

3. When he received his deathly wound
   He laid his scythe down on the ground;
   For to return was his intent
   Crying out loud long as he went.

4. His cries were heard both near and far,
   But no friend to him did appear;
   They thought he did some workman call,
   And so poor boy alone did fall.

5. Day being done, now, and night coming on,
   The father went to seek his son,
   And soon his only son he found
   Cold as a stone, dead on the ground.

6. He took him up and bore him home,
   And all the time did cry and mourn,
   Saying "I heard, but did not come,
   And now I'm left alone to mourn."

7. 'Twas the seventh of August in seventeen sixty-one,
   That this sad accident was done;
   Let this a warning be to all,
   To be prepared when God doth call.

Transcribed from the singing of Bill Bonyun, by permission.

The Young Man Who Couldn't Hoe Corn
(The Lazy Man)

A song about corn could only be a native American product, something arising out of American experience alone. Corn was, and is, not grown in Western Europe. In the Queen's English, it denotes "wheat," and this is a crop that by no stretch of the imagination can be hoed, or cultivated, as American corn has to be. So a song that deals with the hoeing of corn is natively and indubitably American.

The wide distribution of this song in all the Atlantic seaboard states, both North and South, indicates its age and colonial origins. In its own way it makes the same point as "Springfield Mountain" and "The Old Man Who Lived in the Woods"—that colonial life was an unending battle with nature, and that a man who couldn't or wouldn't work in the fields was no man at all.

As one would expect, this song went westward with the pioneers. Versions of it have been found in Iowa and Nebraska.

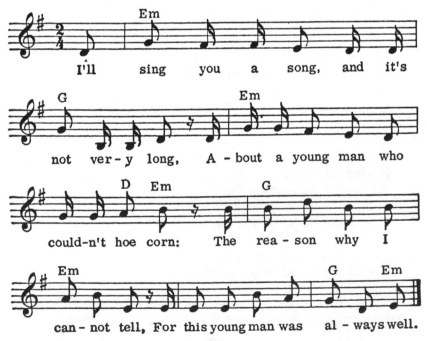

2. He planted by the moon in the month of June,
   And in July it was knee high;
   But in September there came a frost,
   And all this young man's corn was lost.

3. He went to the corn field and peeped in,
   The careless weeds had grown to his chin,
   The careless weeds had grown so high,
   They caused this young man for to cry.

4. He went to his nearest neighbor's door,
   Where ofttimes he had been before;
   And when his courtship he'd begun,
   She asked him if he'd hoed his corn?

5. He hung his head and drew a sigh,
   "Oh no, dear madam, no not I;
   I've tried and tried but all in vain,
   I fear I shall not raise a grain."

6. "Then why do you ask me for to wed,
   When you can't even raise your own cornbread?
   Single I am and single I'll remain,
   For a lazy man I won't maintain."

Jenny Jenkins

"Jenny Jenkins" is a courting song that in colonial days enjoyed a widespread popularity. It has none of the stateliness of "The Keys of Canterbury," but exhibits instead a typical American bounce. It is based upon traditional color symbolism: red stands for sin, blue for faithfulness, white for purity, and so on; by asking the girl what dress she intends to wear, the young man hopes to learn something of her attitude toward him. But some of the colors used are merely an excuse for a nonsense rhyme, which makes it immediately appealing to children. Bill Bonyun and I have sung this song for years at Old Sturbridge Village: it is a continuing favorite of young and old alike.

seek - a dou - ble, us - a - caus - a roll,____ Jen-ny Jen-kins roll".____

2. "Will you wear green, oh my dear, oh my dear,
   Will you wear green, Jenny Jenkins?"
   "No I won't wear green, it's a shame to be seen,"
   I'll buy me a fol-de-rol-de, etc.

3. "Will you wear white, oh my dear, oh my dear,
   Will you wear white, Jenny Jenkins?"
   "No I won't wear white, 'cause the color's too bright,"
   I'll buy me a fol-de-rol-de, etc.

4. "Will you wear yellow, oh my dear, oh my dear,
   Will you wear yellow, Jenny Jenkins?"
   "No I won't wear yellow, might be chased by a fellow,"
   I'll buy me a fol-de-rol-de, etc.

5. "Will you wear pink, oh my dear, oh my dear,
   Will you wear pink, Jenny Jenkins?"
   "Well, I might wear pink, but I'd still have to think,"
   I'll buy me a fol-de-rol-de, etc.

6. "Now will you wear blue, oh my dear, oh my dear,
   Will you wear blue, Jenny Jenkins?"
   "No, I won't wear blue 'cause the color's too true,"
   I'll buy me a fol-de-rol-de, etc.

7. "Then *what* will you wear, oh my dear, oh my dear,
   What will you wear, Jenny Jenkins?"
   "Now what do you care, so I don't go bare?"
   I'll buy me a fol-de-rol-de, etc.

Katie Cruel

"Katie Cruel" originated in New England in colonial times, and has been sung there continuously from the eighteenth century until today. Colonial militiamen used it as a marching song; children sang it as a jingle and speeded the tempo to a skipping pace; for women it was either a lullaby or a lament that captured well the dreaming loneliness and pain of love. Peggy Seeger sings a children's version which is reproduced in the *Young Folk Song Book* (New York: Simon and Schuster, 1963) as one of her most requested songs. Bill Bonyun and I have been singing the more serious version to audiences at Old Sturbridge Village for a number of years; it seems to have an instant and universal appeal.

When I first came to town, They called me the rov - ing jew - el; Now they've changed their tune, And call me Ka - ty Cru - el, O lit - tle lol - ly - day, O the lit - tle li - o day. O that I were where I

would be, Then would I be where I am not,

But I am where I must be, Where I

would be I can-not, O lit-tle lol-ly-

day, O the lit-tle li-o day.

I know who I love,
And I know who does love me;
I know where I'll go,
And I know who'll go with me,
 O little lolly day,
 O the little lioday.

O that I were where I would be,
Then would I be where I am not,
But I am where I must be,
Where I would be I cannot,
 O little lolly day,
 O the little lioday.

Through the woods I'll go,
And through the bogs and mire,
Straightway down the road,
Till I come to my heart's desire,
 O little lolly day,
 O the little lioday.

O that I were where I would be,
Then would I be where I am not,

But I am where I must be,
Where I would be I cannot,
O little lolly day,
O the little lioday.

Eyes as bright as coal,
Lips as red as cherry,
And 'tis her delight
To make the young folks merry,
    O little lolly day,
    O the little lioday.

Printed with the permission of Eloise Hubbard Linscott and Archon
Books from *Folk Songs of Old New England*, second edition, copyright
1962.

II

THE AMERICAN REVOLUTION

THE UNITED STATES grew up in an age of empires—a whole epoch of European history stretching from the fifteenth to the end of the nineteenth century. During this period, Europeans explored and mapped the entire globe and erected great overseas empires. The theory underlying such empire-building was called the mercantile theory and was, with appropriate variations, common to all the colonizing powers. In general terms, the theory stated that colonies existed and should be exploited principally for the military, naval, and commercial advancement of the "mother country" and her citizens; that colonies must be held subordinate in every way; and that their main purpose was to provide raw materials, shipping, markets, manpower, and bullion necessary to the European nations in their race for supremacy.

The hard facts of American life soon conflicted with British rule in both theory and practice, for from the very first days of settlement the colonists were slowly but surely developing as an independent nation with objectives and interests all of their own. A nation is a group of people bound over a long period of time by powerful and permanent ties: a common land, common traditions, common beliefs, a common culture, a common system of law, and self-rule. All of these Americans either inherited or created during the colonial periods. They cleared, settled, and made their own the great and beautiful land lying between the Atlantic Ocean and the Appalachians; brought all the people, by means of the great "awakenings" or revivals of the late seventeenth and eighteenth centuries, into the fold of a common Protestant religion; inherited a common English culture which they adapted to their own uses; underwent common trials and experiences in the struggle to settle a new land and create a new society; and developed institutions and laws to regulate local affairs.

By the middle of the eighteenth century, the growing initiative and independence of the colonies became clear to the English; the elimination of French power from the Western Hemisphere by the French and Indian Wars and the Treaty of Paris of 1763 brought into the open the divergence of British and colonial interests. England, if she wished to use to her advantage the French Empire she had just won, could not hesitate to impose her authority on the refractory colonies. The colonies, too, had ideas about the development of the continent, and they differed not a little from those of England.

From 1763 to 1774 the struggle by the colonies against complete submission to British imperial control was fought openly. The story is familiar. As we know, the Revolution came because it was clear to the colonials that Britain sought to impose upon them a sweeping political and military control; they could either fight for their freedom or submit to vassalage.

But the Revolution that broke out in 1775 had world significance. It was the first occasion in the modern age a colony challenged a mother country's claim to absolute sovereignty over it and succeeded in absolutely extinguishing that claim. Of all the pioneering that Americans have ever done, this is perhaps the most notable. From that day to this, over the course of nearly two centuries, colonial nations have continued to press this challenge to colonizing powers. America took the first great step in an ongoing battle to rid the world of nations that rule and nations that are ruled, to create an international community of free, equal, and independent peoples.

Song played an important role in the struggles of the American Revolution. As we have seen, broadside ballads were brought to America from England during colonial times, and in the eighteenth century American writers began to create and publish broadsides of their own. But it was not until the Revolution that broadside balladry came of age in this country. The revolutionary crisis witnessed an extraordinary outpouring of topical songs, many of which first appeared either as broadsides or in newspaper columns. They satisfied a number of needs arising from the war itself: to convey news of battles and naval engagements, to celebrate triumphs, to poke fun at the enemy, to promote an understanding of war aims, and to arouse the courage of men and women.

Many of the songs of the Revolution have vanished from popular tradition, and have been preserved only in written form. Our chief sources are the files of contemporary newspapers, broadside ballad collections such as the Isaiah Thomas Collection of the American Antiquarian Society, and song books published for the most part after the fighting was over.

The songs of the American Revolution are of great value to us today. The story of that struggle may be told vividly and accurately through its songs; from the considerable material left us, it is possible to select a group that will provide a stirring and eloquent narrative of almost epic dimension. Moreover, these songs provide us with insight into both the mood of the revolutionary era and the meaning of the revolutionary struggle, seen from the viewpoint of those individuals who were actually engaged in it. Their songs help us discover our own historical roots and traditions in the American Revolution, and to identify with those people whose sacrifices made the existence of America possible. Finally, these songs have an international significance. To the extent that we understand our own Revolution we can understand the liberation movements currently taking place in Africa, Asia, India, Latin America, and Indonesia.*

*Part of the commentary accompanying the songs in this chapter first appeared in *The American Revolution through Its Songs and Ballads*, by Bill Bonyun and John Anthony Scott: and is reproduced here by permission of Heirloom Records, Brookhaven, N. Y.

Young Ladies in Town

In 1763, with the end of the war against France, the British took swift steps to make certain the colonists interfered in no way with the empire won from the French, confined their activities to the Atlantic seaboard, and maintained the subordinate political position from which they were so obviously threatening to break away. A standing army was established in America with its commander, General Thomas Gage, as imperial viceroy. Colonial movement into the Mississippi Valley was prohibited by royal proclamation. Plans were made for a stricter enforcement of the Navigation Laws and for the raising of a colonial revenue that would flow directly into the imperial treasury.

Colonial resistance to this "new imperial policy," as it was called, was so widespread that it may be termed national. It took the form of mass demonstrations against measures like the Stamp Act, the evasion of import duties by smuggling, the boycott of British goods, and the refusal to vote supplies for the use of the British occupation troops.

The new spirit of militant opposition to Great Britain is excellently illustrated by "Young Ladies in Town." This song came into being as a result of the Townshend Acts of 1767 which decreed that Americans must pay duties on imported British lead, paint, glass, and tea. The American reaction was to boycott all British imported goods, with the hope that the loss of the American market would bring the British authorities to their senses.

This boycott was in effect for two years and inflicted staggering losses upon British trade. The song, which first appeared in the New England newspapers in 1767, appealed to American women to foreswear the use of British textiles and British tea, and to make homespun a symbol of dedication to the national cause; the song is noteworthy for its impassioned appeal to women to place love of country above love of finery. Mahatma Gandhi was to make a similar appeal to the people of India a century and a half later; he too, made the village spinning wheel a symbol of national independence.

once it is known, 'tis much worn in town, One and
all will cry out, 'tis the fash – ion!

And as one all agree that you'll not married be
    To such as will wear London factory;
But at first sight refuse, tell 'em you will choose
    As encourage our own manufactory.
No more ribbons wear, nor in rich silks appear,
    Love your country much better than fine things;
Begin without passion, 'twill soon be the fashion
    To grace your smooth locks with a twine string.

Throw away your bohea, and your green hyson tea
    And all things of a new-fashioned duty;
Get in a good store of the choice Labrador
    There'll soon be enough here to suit ye.
These do without fear, and to all you'll appear
    Fair, charming, true, lovely, and clever;
Though the times remain darkish, young men will be sparkish,
    And love you much stronger than ever.

The Rich Lady over the Sea

As everyone knows, the tea tax was the spark that set off the revolutionary explosion. In 1770, Britain withdrew all of the obnoxious Townshend duties except the tax on tea. Three years later, British interests moved to dump quantities of Indian tea on the American market at prices which would have destroyed the colonists' own trade and established a British monopoly of the market. This threat led to the famous Boston act of defiance of December 16, 1773.

Britain reacted to the Boston Tea Party in the spring of 1774 by suspending Boston's town meeting, closing its port to commerce, and establishing direct military rule under General Gage himself. Three British generals, Henry Clinton, John Burgoyne, and William Howe, were dispatched across the Atlantic with reinforcements to put down the rebellion.

These measures led to the Revolution because it was clear to all the colonists what was intended for them, as well as for Boston, should they be rash enough to incur the royal displeasure. Thus, Boston's cause became the national cause, the Continental Congress was convened in Philadelphia in September 1774, and measures to organize resistance were initiated. The war began in earnest the following year with the skirmishes at Lexington and Concord. By May 1775, all of New England was in arms, and the British found themselves besieged in Boston.

"The Rich Lady over the Sea" is perhaps the best of many songs about the tea party; its message is expressed in vivid terms that even a child can understand. The little girl has grown up. She is going to assume a position of equality and independence in relation to her mother.

There was a rich la - dy lived o - ver the sea, And she was an is - land queen; Her

59

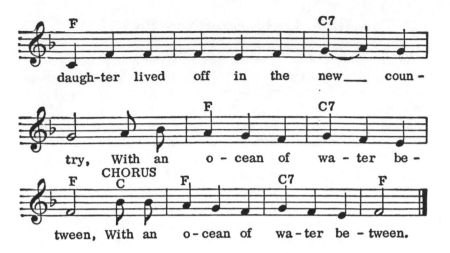

daugh-ter lived off in the new___ coun -
try, With an o - cean of wa - ter be -
CHORUS
tween, With an o-cean of wa-ter be - tween.

2. The old lady's pockets were fillèd with gold,
      Yet never contented was she;
  So she ordered her daughter to pay her a tax
      Of thruppence a pound on the tea.
Chorus: repeat the last line of each verse.

3. "O mother, dear mother," the daughter replied,
      "I'll not do the thing that you ask;
  I'm willing to pay a fair price on the tea,
      But never the thruppeny tax."
Chorus

4. "You shall!" cried the mother, and reddened with rage,
      "For you're my own daughter, you see;
  And it's only proper that daughter should pay
      Her mother a tax on the tea."
Chorus

5. She ordered her servant to be called up
      To wrap up a package of tea;
  And eager for threepence a pound, she put in
      Enough for a large family.
Chorus

6. She ordered her servant to bring home the tax,
      Declaring her child must obey,
  Or, old as she was, and woman most grown,
      She'd half whip her life away.
Chorus

7. The tea was conveyed to her daughter's own door,
        All down by the oceanside;
  But the bouncing girl poured out every pound
        On the dark and boiling tide.
Chorus

8. And then she called out to the island queen,
        "O mother, dear mother," called she,
  "Your tea you may have when 'tis stepped enough,
        But never a tax from me."
Chorus

The Folks on t'Other Side the Wave

Having first appeared in England in 1776, this little song was published the following year as a broadside. A warning to His Majesty's government of the consequences of undertaking a war to suppress the colonial revolt, it is marked by an almost uncanny sense of the realities of life. It foreshadows clearly the grim nature of the struggle that Britain would encounter in the effort to put down a rebellion three thousand miles from her own shores. America, the song hints, is not a second Ireland—a tiny country that may be overridden with impunity by British military might: it is a vast continent, whose permanent occupation in the face of American resistance will be impossible. The patriotic ferver of the Americans, plus the vast spaces and natural wealth of the country, will make conquest impossible. Clearly embodied in the song is the concept of a people's war against a foreign invader, and, beyond that, a whole new era of colonial struggle against foreign domination and exploitation.

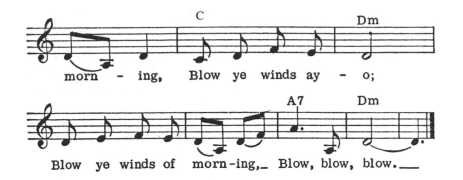

morn - ing, Blow ye winds ay - o;
Blow ye winds of morn-ing,_ Blow, blow, blow.__

What though your cannon raze their towns,
 And tumble down their houses;
They'll fight like devils, blood and bones,
 For children and for spouses.
Chorus

Another truth, nay, 'tis no boast,
 Nor yet the lie o' the day, sirs;
The saints on Massachusetts' coast
 Gain if they run away, sirs.
Chorus

For further than your bullets fly
 A common man may run, sirs;
And wheat will grow beneath a sky
 Where cannot reach a gun, sirs.
Chorus

Sir Peter Parker

In the winter of 1775–1776, British power in the rebellious colonies was limited to Boston, where the British troops under Cornwallis were tightly hemmed in by General Washington. Beyond the port, all of New England was in arms against the invader. In the spring of 1776, the British, acknowledging the hopelessness of their situation, withdrew by sea to Halifax. Clearly, if the defiant Americans were to be reconquered, other bases, further to the south and among a population some portion of which was friendlier to the British cause, had to be sought. Accordingly, the plan of campaign for 1776 called for the invasion and occupation of the port of New York. In addition, an expedition was dispatched in June, under the joint command of Sir Henry Clinton and Admiral Sir Peter Parker, with instructions to occupy Charleston, South Carolina.

The approach to Charleston harbor was dominated by Fort Moultrie, on Sullivan's Island. The British plan of attack provided that Sir Henry Clinton and his marines would land on Sullivan's Island and attack the fort from the north, while Sir Peter Parker used his naval artillery to pound the American installation from the sea.

Matters did not work out as the British had planned. Clinton landed on Long Island, just adjacent to Sullivan's Island, but failed to take his troops across the narrow inlet dividing the two; Parker had to attack Fort Moultrie unaided. The American defenders gave a good acount of themselves, and on June 28, 1776, drove off the British nine ship flotilla with heavy losses. Sir Peter's temper, already frayed by Clinton's failure, was not improved when, as he stood on the quarterdeck of his flagship, the *Bristol,* an American shot blew off his pants.

An observer with the British fleet gave the following account of the American defense:

Our ships, lying nine hours before the battery, were obliged to retire with great loss. The provincials reserved their fire until the shipping were advanced within point blank shot. Their artillery was surprisingly well served, it is said under the command of a Mr. Masson and De Brahm. It was slow, but decisive indeed. They were very cool, and took great care not to fire except their guns were exceedingly well directed: but there was a time when the battery appeared to be silenced for more than an hour. The navy say, had the troops been ready to land at this time, they could have taken possession; how that is, I will not pretend to say. I will rather suppose it; but the fire became exceedingly severe when it was renewed again, and did amazing execution, after the battery had been supposed to have been silenced. This will not be believed when it is first reported in England. I can scarcely believe what I saw on that day; a day to me one of the most distressing of my life.

Sir Peter Parker and Sir Henry Clinton were obliged to sail away again for New York, arguing bitterly over who was to blame for this fiasco. The American victory occasioned the appearance of the sparkling propaganda piece printed below, which put the tale of woe into Sir Peter's own mouth. This song set the whole country laughing. Beneath the witty thrusts lay an exhilarating thought: How do the British expect to take an entire continent when they cannot even capture a small island?

My lords, with your leave, An account I will give that de - serves to be
writ - ten in me - tre; For the
reb - els and I have— been pret - ty nigh, Faith
al-most too nigh for Sir Pe - ter! Ti-mi-
al - der-ry O, ti - mi - al - der-ry ay, Faith,

al - most too nigh for Sir Pe - ter!

2. With much labor and toil
   Unto Sullivan's Isle,
   I came firm as Falstaff or Pistol;
   But the Yankees, God rot 'em,
   I could not get at 'em;
   They most terribly mauled my poor *Bristol.*
Chorus

3. Bold Clinton by land
   Did quietly stand,
   While I made a thundering clatter.
   But the channel was deep,
   So he only could peep
   And not venture over the water.
Chorus

4. Devil take 'em, their shot
   Came so swift and so hot,
   And the cowardly dogs stood so stiff, sirs!
   That I put ship about
   And was glad to get out
   Or they would not have left me a skiff, sirs!
Chorus

5. Now, bold as a Turk,
   I proceed to New York,
   Where with Clinton and Howe you may find me.
   I've the wind in my tail, and am hoisting sail,
   To leave Sullivan's Island behind me.
Chorus

6. But, my lords, do not fear,
   For before the next year,
   Although a small island could fret us,
   The continent whole,
   We shall take, by my soul,
   If the cowardly Yankees will let us.
Chorus

Nathan Hale

The Yankees might laugh at Sir Peter Parker, but the New York campaign was no laughing matter. In July, 1776, Howe's fleet sailed up the East River and landed British troops in Brooklyn, where they came within a hair's breadth of destroying Washington's forces. Washington slipped away to Manhattan and retreated helter-skelter up the island and into Westchester, with the British in hot pursuit.

Nathan Hale gave his life for his country on September 22, 1776, during the retreat of the American forces from New York City. Descended from an old, established New England family, Hale was born in Coventry, Connecticut, and graduated from Yale College in 1773 with distinction. When the war broke out, he took a commission in the Continental army and was sent on a mission by General Washington behind the British lines. Attempting to regain his own command via the King's Bridge connecting Manhattan with the Bronx, he was arrested and hanged as a spy. According to the *Freeman's Journal,* Hale, when at the gallows, ". . . made a sensible and spirited speech, among other things told them they were shedding the blood of the innocent, and that if he had ten thousand lives, he would lay them all down, if called to it, in defence of this injured, bleeding country."

The lyric for "Nathan Hale" was printed by Frank Moore in *Songs and Ballads of the American Revolution,* but he gives no information as to its origins. It is probably of earlier date than the melody to which it is here set, which was composed after the end of the Revolution. The melody, as given here, is transcribed from the singing of Bill Bonyun.

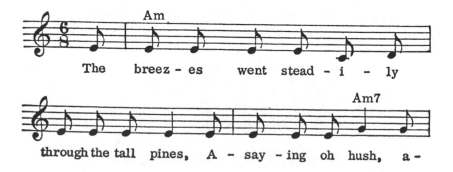

The breez - es went stead - i - ly

through the tall pines, A - say - ing oh hush, a -

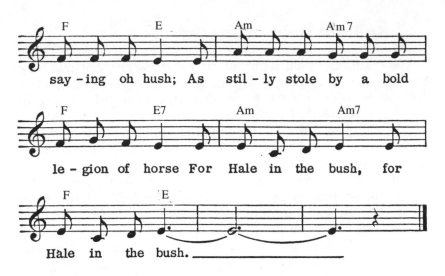

say – ing oh hush; As stil – ly stole by a bold

le – gion of horse For Hale in the bush, for

Hale in the bush. _____

Cooling shades of the night were a-coming apace,
    The tattoo had beat, the tattoo had beat;
The noble one sprang from his dark lurking place,
    To make his retreat, to make his retreat.

The guard of the camp on that dark dreary night
    Had a murderous will, had a murderous will;
They took him and bore him afar from the shore
    To a hut on the hill, to a hut on the hill.

They took him and bound him and bore him away
    Down the hill's grassy side, down the hill's grassy side;
'Twas there the base hirelings in royal array
    His cause did deride, his cause did deride.

The fate of a martyr the tragedy showed,
    As he trod the last stage, as he trod the last stage;
And Briton's will shudder at gallant Hale's blood,
    As his words do presage, as his words do presage.

The Dying Redcoat

This is a song of extraordinary significance in the study of the American Revolution. A broadside ballad of unknown authorship, it relates the experience of a British soldier from his embarkation from England in December 1773 until his death in the New York campaign in September 1776.

The ballad is said to have been written by a British sergeant fatally wounded in the fierce conflict resulting from the British landing on Manhattan on September 16; but whether this is true or not, the song was evidently popular with Americans, and it enables us to see how those actually involved in the revolutionary struggle viewed themselves: Patriots rise up "like grasshoppers" to defend their country; the land is a garden place full of "bitter weeds," that is, men who spread death and destruction from their rifles and are not afraid to die for their freedom. The British soldier finds that he has met his end as the result of a campaign far different from the type for which he was trained, or which he might have expected to fight in Europe. His antagonists are a people in arms. The song, further, is as remarkable for its insistence on the righteousness of the American cause as for the compassion which it expresses for the British soldier wrongly torn from his home to die a futile death in an alien land.

The lyric reproduced here is a composite of several broadsides that have survived in the collections of the University of Rhode Island and the American Antiquarian Society. The song has remained in oral tradition until recent times. Helen Hartness Flanders collected a version from Mrs. Ellen Nye Lawrence of Vermont in 1931.

on that dark and dis-mal day, When
we set__ sail__ for A - mer - i - ca. 'Twas
on that dark and____ dis-mal time,__ When
we set sail for the North-ern clime, Where
drums do beat and trum-pets sound, And
un - to__ Bos - ton__ we__ were bound.

And when to Boston we did come,
We thought by the aid of our British guns,
To drive the rebels from that place,

To fill their hearts with sore disgrace.
But to our sorrow and surprise,
We saw men like grasshoppers rise;
They fought like heroes much enraged,
Which did affright old General Gage.

Like lions roaring for their prey,
They feared no danger or dismay;
Bold British blood runs through their veins,
And still with courage they sustain.
We saw those bold Columbia's sons
Spread death and slaughter from their guns:
Freedom or death! these heroes cry,
They did not seem afraid to die.

We sailed to York, as you've been told,
With the loss of many a Briton bold,
For to make those rebels own our King,
And daily tribute to him bring.
They said it was a garden place,
And that our armies could, with ease,
Pull down their town, lay waste their lands,
In spite of all their boasted bands.

A garden place it was indeed,
And in it grew many a bitter weed,
Which will pull down our highest hopes
And sorely wound our British troops.
'Tis now September the seventeenth day,
I wish I'd never come to America;
Full fifteen thousand has been slain,
Bold British heroes every one.

Now I've received my mortal wound,
I bid farewell to Old England's ground;
My wife and children will mourn for me,
Whilst I lie cold in America.
Fight on America's noble sons,
Fear not Britannia's thundering guns;
Maintain your cause from year to year,
God's on your side, you need not fear.

The melody given here was learned by Frank Warner from the singing of John Galusha of Minerva, N. Y., and is transcribed by permission.

The Battle of Trenton

Britain's major thrust against the colonists was centered upon New York in 1776. As we have seen, the experience proved to be a disastrous one for the Americans. In the summer and fall of this year, Sir William Howe occupied New York and New Jersey with only token opposition. And, as the British armies advanced, the American forces melted away. By the end of 1776, Washington retained command of only a few hundred men; he had withdrawn far to the south, beyond the Delaware.

But on Christmas Day, amid ice and freezing sleet and snow, the American commander-in-chief staged a justly famous and totally unexpected counterattack. Crossing the Delaware, he drove out the Hessian mercenaries occupying the outposts of Trenton and Princeton, regained control of New Jersey, and immensely boosted the morale of the colonists and their will to continue resistance. "The Battle of Trenton," a song of uncertain date and composition, is a stirring march song that successfully captures the mood of a great turning point in the national struggle.

A contemporary account, from the *Freeman's Journal* of January 21, 1777, provides the following information about the action of Christmas Day:

General Washington, finding it absolutely necessary to rouse the spirits of the army, which have been sorely depressed by the long series of disasters which have attended us for almost the whole of this month, resolved to attempt surprising a considerable body of Hessians, quartered at Trenton, consisting of about nineteen hundred, and a detachment of British light horse. The plan was as spiritedly executed as it was judiciously concerted, and terminated in fully answering the warmest expectations of its projectors. December 25, orders were given for a large part of the army to have three days provisions ready cooked, and forty rounds a man, and to be ready to march by three o'clock in the afternoon; accordingly the farthest brigades marched by two oclock. About eleven o'clock at night it began snowing, and continued so until daybreak, when a most violent northeast storm came on, of snow, rain, and hail together. Early the American army, which did not exceed twenty-four hundred men, crossed the Delaware with several companies of artillery, and thirteen field pieces, and formed in two divisions; one commanded by General Greene, the other by General Sullivan, and the whole by General Washington. The attack began about seven o'clock by the vanguard of Sullivan's division, who attacked the Hessians' advance guard, about a mile from the town. These they soon drove off, when the whole pushed with the utmost vigor for the town, which they immediately entered. General Greene's division attacked the town on the other side at the same time. The Hessians did as much as could be expected from people so surprised, but the impetuosity of our men was irresistible; fifteen minutes decided the action, and the enemy threw down their arms and surrendered as prisoners of war.

On Christ-mas day in sev-en-ty-six, Our rag-ged troops with bay-o-nets fixed For Tren-ton marched a-way. The Del-a-ware see! the boats be-low! The light ob-scured by hail and snow: But no signs of dis-may.

2. Our object was the Hessian band,
That dared invade fair freedom's land,
And quarter in that place.
Great Washington he led us on,
Whose streaming flag in storm or sun,
Had never known disgrace.

3. In silent march we passed the night,
Each soldier panting for the fight,
Though quite benumbed with frost.
Greene, on the left, at six began,
The right was led by Sullivan,
Who never a moment lost.

4. Their pickets stormed, the alarm was spread,
    That rebels risen from the dead,
    Were marching into town.
    Some scampered here, some scampered there,
    And some for action did prepare,
    But soon their arms laid down.

5. Now, brothers of the patriot bands,
    Let's sing deliverance from the hands
    Of arbitrary sway.
    And as our life is but a span,
    Let's touch the tankard while we can,
    In memory of that day.

The Fate of John Burgoyne

Spring, 1777. Two years had passed since Lexington and Concord. Yet the British could boast only the occupation of Manhattan—a hollow boast, since they dared not venture far from the port. Supply lines were cut, foraging parties ambushed. Out of reach, elusive, Washington held his forces in the New Jersey hills, watching, waiting.

The British Government, rubbing its face in surprise, prepared for a decisive campaign against the rebels in the summer of 1777. Burgoyne, one of the trio of generals sent to Boston in 1775, the dandy who carried wine, women, and song with him on his campaigns, Gentleman Johnny, was ordered to push down the Hudson Valley and to cut off New England from the rest of the colonies. Sir William Howe's role, this year, was to occupy Philadelphia, a second important base.

Everything went wrong for Gentleman Johnny on his invasion from Canada via the familiar Lake Champlain-Hudson route. Guerrillas in his rear cut off his supplies. Gates, Arnold, and Morgan blocked his advance. By October 1777, his own mistakes and his enemy's valor had brought Burgoyne to surrender at Saratoga, for the British one of the most colossal disasters of the war. But all was not lost, for they still controlled New York; and, while Burgoyne was fighting his last battles, Howe had slipped off by sea, invaded Philadelphia, and settled down comfortably in the colonists' capital.

This delightful song, "The Fate of John Burgoyne," tells of the general's humiliation. With appropriately satiric humor, it is here set to the tune of "The Girl I Left Behind Me."

When_ Jack, the King's com - mand-er_ bold, Was

go - ing to _ his_ du - ty, He_

smiled and bowed through all _ the_ crowd At

ev - ery bloom - ing beau - ty. The

Low - er House sat mute as mouse To

hear his grand o - ra - tion, And—

all the peers with loud - est cheers, Pro -

claimed him to the na - tion.

Then off he went to Canada,
    Next to Ticonderoga,
And quitting those, away he goes
    Straightway to Saratoga.
But the sons of freedom gathered round,
    His hostile bands surrounded,
And when they'd fain have turned their backs
    They found themselves surrounded.

In vain they fought, in vain they fled,
    Their chief, humane and tender,
To save the rest soon thought it best
    His forces to surrender.
Thus may America's brave sons
    With honor be rewarded,
And be the fate of all her foes
    The same as here recorded.

The Battle of the Kegs

In October 1778, the British occupied Philadelphia, and Washington went into winter quarters close by, at Valley Forge. The sufferings of that winter are well known. Not so familiar is the fact that the Americans then began to experiment with floating mines (floating kegs, primed to explode on contact) to harass British shipping on the Delaware. The British, understandably, took steps to neutralize these weapons; on January 5, 1778, they fired at and exploded a number of these kegs as they floated down river.

These circumstances gave rise to the following delightful ballad by the American poet Francis Hopkinson. It is one of the wittiest and most telling satires in the entire American literary heritage. The events which occasioned the poet's mockery were related in the *New Jersey Gazette,* January 21, 1778, with a certain amount of pardonable exaggeration:

Philadelphia has been entertained with the most astonishing instance of the activity, bravery, and military skill of the royal navy of Great Britain. The affair is somewhat particular, and deserves notice. Some time last week, two boys observed a keg of singular construction, floating in the river opposite the city; they got into a small boat, and attempted to take up the keg, it burst with a great explosion, and blew up the unfortunate boys.

Yesterday, January 5, several kegs of a like construction made their appearance. An alarm was immediately spread through the city; various reports prevailed, filling the city and the royal troops with consternation. Some reported that the kegs were filled with armed rebels, who were to issue forth in the dead of night, as the Grecians did of old from their wooden horse at the siege of Troy, and take the city by surprise; asserting that they had seen the points of their bayonets through the bungholes of the kegs.

Others said they were charged with the most inveterate combustibles, to be kindled by secret machinery, and, setting the whole Delaware in flames, were to consume all the shipping in the harbor; whilst others asserted that they were constructed by magic art, would of themselves ascend the wharves in the night time, and roll all flaming through the streets of the city, destroying everything in their way.

Be this as it may, certain it is that the shipping in the harbor, and all the wharves in the city, were fully manned, the battle began, and it was surprising to behold the incessant blaze that was kept up against the enemy, the kegs. Both officers and men exhibited the most unparalleled skill and bravery on the occasion; whilst the citizens stood gazing as solemn witnesses of their prowess. From the *Roebuck* and other ships of war, whole broadsides were poured into the Delaware. In short, not a wandering ship, stick or drift log but felt the vigor of the British arms.

The action began about sunrise, and would have been completed with great success by noon, had not an old market woman coming down the river with provisions, let a small keg of butter fall overboard, which (as it was then ebb) floated down to the scene of action. At sight of this unexpected reinforcement of the enemy, the battle was renewed with fresh fury, and the firing was incessant till the evening closed the affair. The kegs were totally demolished or obliged to fly, as none of them have shown their *heads* since.

It is said his Excellency, Lord Howe, has despatched a swift sailing packet with an account of this victory, to the court of London. In a word, Monday, the fifth of January, 1778, must ever be distinguished in history for the memorable *Battle of the Kegs.*

2. As in a maze, he stood to gaze,
       The truth can't be denied, sir,
   He spied a score—of kegs, or more,
       Come floating down the tide, sir.

A sailor too, in jerkin blue,
    The strange appearance viewing,
First damned his eyes, in great surprise,
    Then said, "Some mischief's brewing.

3. "These kegs now hold the rebels bold,
    Pack'd up like pickled herring:
And they're come down to attack the town,
    In this new way of ferrying."
The soldier flew, the sailor too,
    And, scared almost to death, sir,
Wore out their shoes, to spread the news,
    And ran till out of breath, sir.

4. Now up and down throughout the town,
    Most frantic scenes were acted:
And some ran here, and some ran there
    Like men almost distracted,
Some fire cried, which some denied,
    But said the earth had quaked:
And girls and boys, with hideous noise,
    Ran through the town half naked.

5. Sir William he, snug as a flea,
    Lay all this time a-snoring,
Nor dreamed of harm, as he lay warm
    In bed with Mrs. Loring.
Now in a fright he starts upright,
    Awaked by such a clatter;
He rubs his eyes, and boldly cries,
    "For God's sake what's the matter?"

6. At his bedside, he then espied
    Sir Erskine in command, sir,
Upon one foot he had one boot,
    And t' other in his hand, sir.
"Arise! Arise!" Sir Erskine cries;
    "The rebels—more's the pity—
Without a boat, are all on float,
    And ranged before the city.

7. "The motley crew, in vessels new,
    With Satan for their guide, sir,

Packed up in bags or wooden kegs,
    Come driving down the tide, sir.
Therefore prepare for bloody war;
    These kegs must all be routed;
Or surely we despised shall be,
    And British courage doubted."

8. The royal band now ready stand,
    All ranged in dread array, sir,
With stomach stout to see it out,
    And make a bloody day, sir.
The cannons roar, from shore to shore,
    The small arms make a rattle:
Since wars began I'm sure no man
    E'er saw so strange a battle.

9. The fish below swam to and fro,
    Attacked from every quarter;
Why sure, thought they, the devil's to pay,
    'Mongst folk above the water.
These kegs 'tis said, tho' strongly made,
    Of rebel staves and hoops, sir,
Could not oppose their powerful foes,
    The conquering British troops, sir.

10. From morn to night, these men of might
    Displayed amazing courage;
And when the sun was fairly down,
    Retired to sup their porridge:
An hundred men with each a pen,
    Or more upon my word, sir,
It is most true, would be too few,
    Their valor to record, sir.

11. Such feats did they perform that day
    Upon these wicked kegs, sir,
That years to come, if they get home,
    They'll make their boasts and brags, sir.

Paul Jones's Victory
(Poor Richard and the Serapis and Alliance)

In April 1778, good news arrived from France. A French-American alliance that promised aid to the revolutionary cause in men, money, and arms had been signed. It was a black day for the British. Sir Henry Clinton, now commander-in-chief, fearing the intervention of the French fleet, abandoned Philadelphia and drew his forces back to New York. A line of troops wound across the Jersey flats, harassed and pursued by the patriot forces. Then the British set to work to fortify Manhattan, still their only refuge in the colonies.

But the bright promise which the French alliance seemed to hold for the Americans was, for various reasons, not immediately realized, and in the years 1778–1779 a stalemate set in. The British forces were too small to conquer so huge a country whose hostile population was so scattered; and the colonists lacked the naval power that held the key to victory.

Lacking the strength to build a navy, the colonists resorted to harassing tactics. Privateers were authorized by government commission to scour the seas and to capture British merchantmen. After the conclusion of the treaty with France, these privateers fitted out in French ports and sailed brazenly about in British waters; they became a menace to British commerce.

John Paul Jones, an American sea captain, commanded a small squadron of fourth- or fifth-rate frigates provided by the French. A dramatic duel took place off Flamborough Head on September 23, 1779 when Jones encountered the *Serapis* and the *Scarborough*, English men o' war, commanded by Captain Pearson, which were convoying the Baltic merchant fleet home to London. After a fierce battle between the *Serapis* and Jones' leaky tub, the *Bonhomme Richard*, Pearson surrendered and his ship sank. Paul Jones was obliged to abandon his ship too, but he had established a new tradition.

This naval epic found expression in one of the most famous broadside ballads of the times. Often reprinted, it has remained in oral tradition until our own days.

An A - mer - i - can frig-ate, a frig-ate of fame, With guns mount-ed for-ty, the Rich-ard by name,— For to cruise in the chan-nel of old Eng - land, And a val-iant com-mand-er, Paul Jones is the man.

We had not sailed long before we did spy
A large forty-four, and a twenty so nigh,
With fifty bold seamen well laid in with store,
In consort pursued us from the old English shore.

About twelve at noon Percy came alongside,
With a speaking trumpet; "Whence came you?" he cried,
"It's now give an answer, I hail'd you before,
Or this moment a broadside into you I will pour."

Paul Jones then he says to his men every one,
"Let every bold seaman stand true to his gun;
We'll receive a broadside from these bold Englishmen,
And like true Yankee heroes return it again."

The melody given here was learned by Frank Warner from the singing of C. K. Tillett of Wanchese, North Carolina. Transcribed by permission.

The contest was bloody, both decks ran with gore,
The sea seemed to blaze when the cannon did roar;
"Fight on my brave boys," then Paul Jones he cried,
"We will soon humble this bold Englishman's pride."

We fought them eight glasses, eight glasses so hot,
Till seventy bold seamen lay dead on the spot,
And ninety bold seamen lay bleeding in gore,
While the pieces of cannon most wretched did roar.

Our gunner in a fright to Paul Jones he came;
"We make water quite fast, and our side's in a flame;"
Then brave Jones he said in the height of his pride
"If we can't do no better boys, sink alongside."

The *Alliance* bore down while the *Richard* did rake,
Which caused the heart of poor Percy to ache;
Our shot flew so hot they could not stand us long,
And the flag of proud Britain was forced to come down.

So now my brave boys, you have taken a prize,
A large forty-four and a twenty likewise;
Both noble vessels well laden with store,
We'll bend on all canvas for New England once more.

God bless the widows who shortly must weep
For the loss of their husbands now sunk in the deep;
Here's a health to Paul Jones, a sword in his hand,
Who led us to battle and gave the command!

The Ballad of Major André

Paul Jones' exploit was one bright flash in the long winter of stalemate, the winter of 1779–1780—a time to test a man's soul. Washington and his rebel band was encamped in New Jersey and the New York highland, watching Clinton, waiting in the snow that lay feet deep upon the frozen ground in a winter that seemed eternal.

General Benedict Arnold spent these winter months in Philadelphia, as Commandant of the American forces in the capital. One of the most heroic of Washington's officers, he had acquitted himself brilliantly in the grim winter invasion of Canada (1775–1776) and in the Saratoga campaign. He had gained a reputation second to none as a brave and patriotic soldier. Assigned to the Philadelphia post when the British withdrew in 1778, he gave himself over to luxury and entered into relations with loyalists. He was reprimanded by Washington, passed over for promotion, and became disgruntled. Worse than this, he fell simultaneously into debt and into doubt. Was it really possible for a few bickering and ragged colonials to win a war against the mightiest Empire in the world?

A desperate need for money did the rest. Arnold entered into communication with Sir Henry Clinton, British commander-in-chief. The latter instructed him to obtain from Washington the command of West Point. Construction of the fort on the west bank of the Hudson River had just been completed. It commanded the approach to the New York highlands from the south, was the key to Washington's defensive position, and assured contact between New England and the rest of the colonies.

Washington reluctantly yielded to Arnold's request (he felt that a good field commander was wasted in such a post). Arnold assumed his new command in the spring of 1780.

The man whom Sir Henry Clinton had assigned to maintain connection with the commander of West Point and to perfect the plot for the surrender of the fort was his adjutant, young Major John André. On September 20, 1780, a British man o' war, the *Vulture,* sailed up the Hudson and dropped anchor off Croton Point. John André rowed ashore and met with Arnold among the trees foresting the west bank of the river. The general had the plans of the fort with him. The discussion was prolonged by some tedious bartering over the price of treason.

The *Vulture* came under the fire of American shore batteries, and dropped back down river without André. The young adjutant had no alternative but to make his way back to the British lines by land. In West Haverstraw, an accomplice provided him with civilian clothes and a horse. Armed with a pass from Arnold "to go to the lines of White Plains or lower if he thought proper, he being on public business," André set out for Manhattan. He crossed the Hudson at King's Ferry, headed east to Yorktown, and then south through the no-man's-land of Westchester county. Traveling all night, he reached Tarrytown by mid morning, September 23. There he was arrested by a group of American militiamen headed by John Paulding. A search discovered the plans of West Point concealed in his boot.

Arnold got wind of the arrest and fled to New York City on the *Vulture* which, providentially, had returned. André went on trial on September 29 at Washington's headquarters in Tappan, N. Y., was found guilty of espionage, and sentenced to die. On October 2, he was hanged on the hill that bears his name in the presence of a sad and troubled crowd of American soldiers and civilians.

The magnificent Hudson Valley ballad that is reproduced below immortalizes the soldier who was hung and pillories the traitor who fled. This uniquely American ballad comes down to us through the family tradition and the singing of John Allison, noted New York song collector.

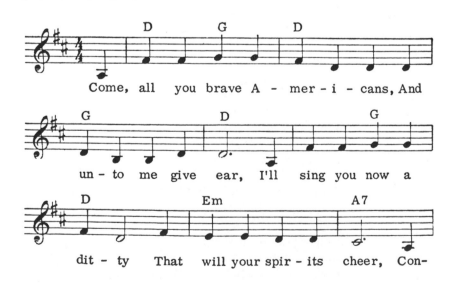

Come, all you brave A - mer - i - cans, And
un - to me give ear, I'll sing you now a
dit - ty That will your spir - its cheer, Con-

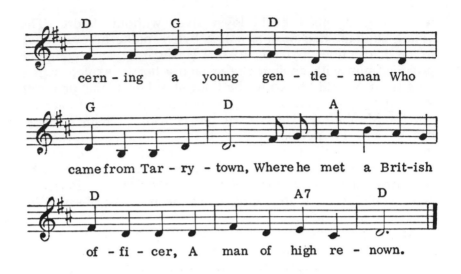

cern - ing a young gen - tle - man Who
came from Tar - ry - town, Where he met a Brit-ish
of - fi - cer, A man of high re - nown.

2. Then up spoke this young hero,
   Young Paulding was his name;
   "O tell us where you're going, sir,
   And also whence you came."
   "I bear the British flag, sir,"
   Up answered bold André,
   "I have a pass that takes me through,
   I have no time to stay."

3. Then others came around him,
   And bade him to dismount:
   "Come tell us where you're going,
   Give us a strict account;"
   Young Paulding said, "We are resolved
   That you shall ne'er pass by";
   And so the evidence did prove
   The prisoner a spy.

4. He begged for his liberty,
   He pled for his discharge,
   And oftentimes he told them,
   If they'd set him at large,
   "Of all the gold and silver
   I have laid up in store,
   But when I reach the city
   I will send you ten times more."

5. "We scorn this gold and silver
   You have laid up in store,"
   Van Vert and Paulding both did cry,
   "You need not send us more."
   He saw that his conspiracy
   Would soon be brought to light,
   He begged for pen and paper
   And he asked for to write.

6. The story came to Arnold
   Commanding at the Fort:
   He called for the Vulture
   And sailed for New York;
   Now Arnold to New York has gone,
   A-fighting for his King,
   And left poor Major André
   On the gallows for to swing.

7. André was executed,
   He looked both meek and mild,
   His face was fair and handsome,
   And pleasantly he smiled.
   It moved each eye with pity,
   And every heart there bled,
   And everyone wished him released
   And Arnold in his stead.

8. He was a man of honor!
   In Britain he was born,
   To die upon the gallows
   Most highly he did scorn.
   And now his life has reached its end
   So young and blooming still—
   In Tappan's quiet countryside
   He sleeps upon the hill.

Lord Cornwallis's Surrender

In 1780, the decisive campaign of the war got under way. Lord Charles Cornwallis, sent from England to launch a full scale invasion of the South, planned to drive up through the Southern states, summon the loyalists to his standard, and conquer Georgia, the Carolinas, and Virginia one by one.

England's experience in other parts of the country repeated itself, but on a vaster scale. Southern patriots rose against the invader. Southern forest and swamp fighters under Marion, Sumter, and Davidson ambushed foraging parties and cut off supply trains. Nathanael Greene's army remained in the field, battered but unbeaten. Cornwallis found himself among a hostile people. He could win battles, but he could not win the war. Caught up at Yorktown between Washington and his troops by land and de Grasse and the French fleet by sea, he thus came to the same end as Burgoyne. On October 19, 1881, Cornwallis surrendered with his entire army. This catastrophe in effect ended the war. The British army, about six thousand strong, marched out between two lines of American and French troops, grounded arms, and was placed under guard. An American officer described the scene in the New Jersey *Gazette* (November 7) as follows:

The British officers in general behaved like boys who had been whipped at school; some bit their lips, some pouted, others cried; their round, broad-brimmed hats were well adapted to the occasion, hiding those faces they were ashamed to show. The foreign regiments made a much more military appearance, and the conduct of their officers was far more becoming men of fortitude.

"Lord Cornwallis's Surrender" is a famous contemporary broadside which gives an accurate picture of the scene and captures the mood of American elation. The melody makes the humiliation of the British more complete: it is "The British Grenadiers," one of the proudest marching songs of the British army.

Come all you brave A - mer-i - cans, the

truth to you I'll tell, 'Tis of a sad mis-
for - tune, to Bri - tain late be -
fell; 'Twas all in the heights of York — town, where
can-nons loud did roar; They sum-moned Lord Corn-
wal - lis to fight or else give o'er.

Come all you brave Americans,
    The truth to you I'll tell,
'Tis of a sad misfortune,
    To Britain late befell;
'Twas all in the heights of Yorktown,
    Where cannons loud did roar;
They summoned Lord Cornwallis
    To fight or else give o'er.

The summons then to be served,
    Was sent unto my Lord,
Which made him feel like poor Burgoyne,
    And quickly draw his sword,
Say, must I give these glittering troops,
    These ships and Hessians too,
And yield to General Washington,
    And his bold rebel crew?

A grand council then was called,
    His Lordship gave command,
Say, what think you now my heroes,
    To yield you may depend—
For don't you see the bombshells fly,
    And cannons loud do roar,
Count de Grasse lies in the harbour,
    And Washington's on shore.

'Twas the nineteenth of October,
    In the year of eighty-one,
Lord Cornwallis he surrendered
    To General Washington.
They marched from their posts, brave boys,
    And quickly grounded arms,
Rejoice you brave Americans,
    With music's sweetest charms.

Six thousand chosen British troops
    To Washington resigned,
Besides some ships and Hessians
    That could not stay behind;
With refugees and blackamores,
    Oh, what a direful crew!
It was then he had some thousands,
    But now he's got but few.

Here's a health to great Washington,
    And his brave army too,
And likewise to our worthy Greene,
    To him much honor's due.
May we subdue those English troops,
    And clear the eastern shore,
That we may live in peace, my boys,
    While wars they are no more.

III
THE
EARLY
NATIONAL
PERIOD

THE UNITED STATES, after having achieved independence, did not isolate itself from the European civilization of which it was a product. "Isolation" as a traditional American ideal originally expressed by Washington and Hamilton meant isolation only from the *military* conflicts of Europe. As the young nation matured, its links—spiritual, cultural, economic, and technological—with the parent civilization did not diminish, but increased.

The first years of independence, from 1790 to 1814, have been termed by historians "the early national period." American experience during this time vividly illustrates the country's profound involvement with Europe. The United States was then involved in the crisis in which the whole Western world found itself, and its life and thinking reflected that crisis. Only in the context of the international community within which American nationality was developing can we appreciate the meaning of the songs Americans were then writing and singing.

What was this context? In 1789, George Washington was inaugurated first President of the United States in New York City, and in that year the French Revolution began. In 1793, the Bourbon monarchy, symbol of a cruel and dying feudal order, came crashing down, and thrones throughout Europe began to shake. Throughout the Western World, the peoples had begun to glimpse a vision of republican democracy and of freedom from the tyranny of kings; and everywhere they were marching passionately toward their ideal.

Many of the great national songs of this time reflect this new mood, and the songs of the United States are no exception. A new nation had been born in freedom. Its songs in this period were characterized by an exalted national tone, a sometimes boastful self-assurance, and the confidence of youth. Lyrical, passionate, even flowery, they expressed the new style in literature and politics that we call romanticism.

But in Europe, the early dawn was soon darkened by clouds. The French Revolution fell victim to a new monarchist tyranny when Napoleon became first consul in 1800 and made himself Emperor in 1802. A man of boundless ambition, he sought to build an empire through the enslavement of millions of his fellows; and he brought all of Europe under his control or influence. First, he conquered the Germanys and Italy; then, he advanced into Spain, Poland, and Russia. For 13 years, he engaged Great Britain in a life-and-death struggle.

American reaction to this crisis followed a pattern born of the revolutionary experience in the years 1776-1783. France, traditionally, had been America's friend, and Britain its foe. Britain's involvement, furthermore, in an all-out struggle for survival gave the United States a golden opportunity to wrest from the British Empire advantages which the latter was in no position to withhold; the War of 1812 was undertaken precisely for such objectives. The latter included land acquisitions in Canada and Florida, the destruction of British influence among the Indians of the Old Northwest, and the elimination of British interference with American shipping on the high seas, which was considered to be an intolerable affront to an independent power.

Below we reproduce some of the great songs that arose from this war, in which the United States was fighting on Napoleon's side, though not allied with him. The songs reflect not only the national reaction to incidents in the struggle, but also an unabashed admiration of Napoleon, the military genius who had toppled thrones and twisted the British lion's tail with, one might say, an almost American impudence.

The early national era not only produced songs about war-but also songs of protest against the senseless slaughter of human life, which blasted the hopes of youth and wasted a people's most precious resources. One of the very greatest of such songs was an Irish broadside ballad brought to the New World by immigrants; it provides the last song in our selection for this period. The dream of peace it expressed was to be the keynote of American national policy for nearly half a century. America, in the era of construction that was to come, must isolate herself from the brutal realities of European war; she must pursue a policy of peace that would enable her to devote her mighty resources to the building of a strong and civilized state.

Caitilín Ní Uallacháin
(Cathaleen Ni Houlihan)

The American Revolution was an event of international significance, the first successful action by a colonial people in the modern world against a foreign power. The Revolution's world-wide impact was both immediate and continuing.

This fact is vividly illustrated by the almost immediate reaction in Eire. The Irish, a people whose land, religion, and national traditions were distinctly their own, had for centuries suffered under and resisted British occupation. By the eighteenth century, Britain's long struggle to fasten her rule upon the entire country had met with final and complete success. Eire was reduced to a colonial dependency, a land whose wealth and vitality were drained by an absentee aristocracy. The poverty and misery in which the mass of her landless people dwelt were, in 1776, eloquent proof of the disheartening effect of colonial status and despotic rule.

But the Irish, though beaten, nursed a stubborn dream of freedom, of deliverance from tyranny. They remembered when Patrick Sarsfield and his warriors had fought Britain with the aid of the Catholic King, James, and the French. One day, they believed, the King's son, James, would return from France across the sea. Then all of Eire would respond to his call, would rise to battle for freedom.

The shot fired at Bunker Hill in 1775, heard around the world, echoed nowhere more loudly than in Eire. In 1798, it triggered a great uprising led by Wolfe Tone, protestant, patriot, and visionary. This struggle ended in failure, but it produced one of the most famous and beautiful of Eire's national songs—*Caitilín ní Uallacháin*. Once there had been a woman so-named, and a love song for her. *Caitilín* now came to symbolize the country, Eire herself. It is a song noteworthy for its flaming spirit, its exalted vision of freedom, its readiness to accept death rather than shame, its identification of the Catholic Irish with the oppressed of all the world as symbolized by Israel.

The Irish failure of 1798 was closely bound up with the destiny of the United States; thereafter, many Irish would emigrate to the New World with the love of liberty in their hearts. Thus, this song, *Caitilín*, casts its luster over the history of the United States in the early national period. For, more than most songs of this time, it reveals to us the exalted national mood then prevailing, the value and the meaning that people then attached to life, and the cause for which a man might sacrifice it.

Our— hopes run high, the— time is nigh To—
make the test of war, Our— plans are laid,— our—
weap - ons made, And—— soon our guns will—
roar. Let oth - ers sleep! We watch will
keep To hail— a — new day's dawn, When the
king's son shall be seen with
Cath - a - leen Ni — Houl - i - han.

Our hated foes must not suppose
    That we shall fear to die,
Though the clouds are dark we still can mark
    God's rainbow in the sky.
As the Red Sea sand became dry land
    When Moses led Israel on,
May Jesus save thee, Cathaleen
    Ni Houlihan!

Green Grow the Rushes O

Robert Burns has an extraordinary importance in the history of American song. This Scotsman was one of the world's great song writers, who expressed his love of man and life in a host of incomparable lyrics which he wedded to traditional Scots melodies. Burns' creative work and thought illuminate the struggle for freedom in the modern era. Many of his songs—he wrote more than six hundred—were widely sung in the United States during the nineteenth century; they have left an enduring imprint upon American national music.

Burns was born in 1759, the son of an impoverished Ayrshire farmer. He spent his youth toiling on the farm; there burned in his soul a fierce desire for knowledge and a passion for his people's songs. Years of bleak labor were lightened for this hungry youth by the melodies that chased through his head as he followed the plough.

Rejected in love and living in dire poverty, Burns was, in 1786, at the point of emigrating to the New World. But then his first book of poetry was published, and it took his countrymen by storm. For them, Burns epitomized the most exalted aspects of the national, romantic, revolutionary movement of his day: the deep love of country and of man, the simplicity of life, the lyrical apotheosis of the human condition, the hatred of human bondage, and the sense of human equality.

We reproduce here a song, "Green Grow the Rushes O" which represents, in its perfection, the best that Burns ever wrote. As with most of his songs, the lyrics are his own, and the melody is traditional.

sig - ni - fies the life of man, And
'twere not for the las - ses, O?

REFRAIN

Green__ grow the rush - es, O,
Green__ grow the rush - es, O, The
sweet - est hours__ that e'er are spent, Are
spent a - mong the las - ses, O.

The worldly race may riches chase,
　　And riches still may fly them, O;
And though at last they catch them fast,
　　Their hearts may ne'er enjoy them, O.
Refrain

Give me a quiet hour at even,
　　My arms about my dearie, O;
And worldly cares and worldly men,
　　May all go topsyturvy, O.
Refrain

For you so prim you sneer at this,
      You're naught but senseless asses, O;
The wisest man the world e'er saw,
      He dearly loved the lasses, O.
Refrain

Old Nature swears the lovely dears
      Her noblest works she classes, O;
Her prentice hand she tried on man—
      And then she made the lasses, O.
Refrain

Jefferson and Liberty

The Federalist Party, of which George Washington was titular head, made important contributions to American life in the years following the Revolution. The Federalists elaborated the Constitution, secured its ratification, and organized the machinery of the new national government. But in the last decade of the eighteenth century, when they enjoyed uninterrupted control of the presidency and of Congress, the Federalists pursued policies that made them unpopular with large numbers of Americans. Their financial and foreign policies in particular, it was charged, were governed by a narrow and selfishly exclusive class interest.

By 1798, the tide was running strong against the Federalists. In that year, they brought the country to the brink of war with its traditional ally, France; and they passed the Alien and Sedition Acts in order to muzzle opposition to the conflict when it should break out. One of these acts at the very least (the Sedition Act) was unconstitutional and an obvious flouting of the Bill of Rights.

All in all, there was not a little to be said for the charge that Federalist rule had brought down upon the American people those dire evils which Jefferson's followers had predicted would be the consequence of Federalist control of the National government.

"Jefferson and Liberty" is a campaign song that first appeared during the elections of 1800, and it remains one of the most popular campaign songs of American history. It celebrates the simple virtues of Jeffersonian philosophy, elation at the approaching end of Federalist rule, and boundless confidence in the nation's destiny as a free and democratic Republic. This great vision of the American dream is appropriately set to an Irish jig tune with a majestic sweep all its own.

The gloom-y night be-fore us flies, The reign of ter-ror now is o'er;Its gags, in-quis-i-

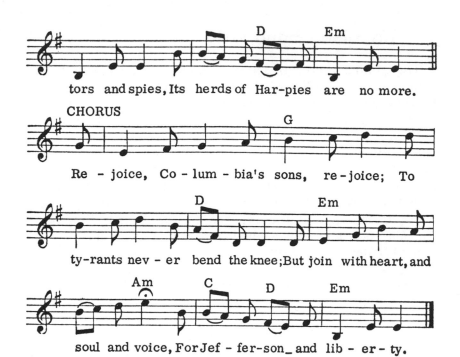

tors and spies, Its herds of Har-pies are no more.

CHORUS

Re - joice, Co - lum - bia's sons, re - joice; To

ty-rants nev - er bend the knee; But join with heart, and

soul and voice, For Jef - fer-son_ and lib - er - ty.

No lordling here with gorging jaws
Shall wring from industry the food,
Nor fiery bigot's holy laws
Lay waste our fields and streets in blood!
Chorus

Here strangers from a thousand shores
Compelled by tyranny to roam,
Shall find, amidst abundant stores
A nobler and a happier home.
Chorus

Here Art shall lift her laurel'd head,
Wealth, Industry, and Peace divine;
And where dark, pathless forests spread,
Rich fields and lofty cities shine.
Chorus

Napoleon Bonaparte

The administrations of Jefferson and Madison (1800–1816) witnessed the unfolding, and the final climax, of Napoleon Bonaparte's struggle to dominate Europe and the world. His titanic struggle against England in this period could not fail to influence American thinking and conduct profoundly.

Hostility toward Great Britain and a feeling of friendship toward France was, by 1800, a firmly rooted American tradition. Furthermore, England's predicament, her death grapple with Napoleon, gave the United States an opportunity to expand its territory at the expense of the British Empire in Canada and of its ally Spain in Florida. When, in 1812, the United States declared war against England in pursuit of these territorial objectives, it was not formally allied with France; but both Napoleon and the American Republic were simultaneously fighting the same enemy, England, and were thus, in effect, allies. Accordingly, Napoleon became a continuing symbol of America's traditional feeling of friendship for France, a feeling reinforced by the fact that the French dictator had renounced his territorial claims to lands beyond the Mississippi by the Louisiana Purchase agreement of 1803.

In Europe itself, furthermore, Napoleon Bonaparte had been a strangely contradictory force. Wherever his conquering armies marched, tyranny and oppression followed in their wake; but with them had come, almost like an infection, the ideas of the French Revolution. From the safe distance of three thousand miles, Americans might be pardoned if they saw this cruel and dangerous dictator through a romantic haze, if they saw in him no more than the symbol of a revolutionary nation, France, resisting its traditional foe.

It is, therefore, not surprising that the song, "Napoleon Bonaparte," with its sumptuous melody, has been found widespread in North America: in Newfoundland, New England, New York, the South, and the Midwest. It probably originated as a broadside ballad in Eire. Irish admiration for Great Britain's mighty antagonist and the Irish lament for his fallen greatness could not fail, for the reasons given above, to find an echo in the hearts of many Americans.

Now Na - po - leon_ he has done with his
wars and his fight - ing. He has gone to the
land he can take no de - light in. He may
set him down and tell of the bat - tles
he has been in,_ While for - lorn he does
mourn on the isle of St. Hel - e - na.

Louisa does weep for her husband's departing;
She dreams when she sleeps and she wakens broken-hearted.
Not a friend to console or even those who might be with her,
While forlorn she does mourn on the Isle of St. Helena.

The rude rushing waves all around the shores are washing;
Now the high billows roar, on the rough rocks are dashing.
He may look to the moon, to the great mount of Diana,
While forlorn he does mourn on the Isle of St. Helena.

All you that have wealth beware of ambition,
Lest in some degree of health you should change your condition.
Be steadfast in time, for what's to come you know not,
And your days they may end on the Isle of St. Helena.

You Parliaments of war, and your Holy Alliance,
To the prisoner of war you may now bid defiance.
For your base intrigues and your baser misdemeanors,
Have caused him to die on the Isle of St. Helena.

The Bonny Bunch of Roses O

This song originated as a broadside and is still sung in England, Scotland, and Eire. The fine melody to which it is here set was recorded by Elisabeth B. Greenleaf in Newfoundland in 1929 from the singing of Mrs. Patrick Lahey of Fortune Harbor. That it was highly popular in the United States as well as in Britain is evidenced by its having been reproduced in many songbooks of the early national period, though it apparently has not survived in this country in oral tradition. The lyric reproduced here, a composite of many partial and corrupted texts, illustrates the high quality of poetic feeling and imaginative sweep which the broadside ballad sometimes achieved.

"The Bonny Bunch of Roses O" is cast in the form of a dialogue between Napoleon Bonaparte's son, the Duke of Reichstadt (1811–1832), and his wife, the Empress Marie Louise, after the Emperor's fall from power and exile to St. Helena. The princeling dreams of his future glory, of when he will follow in his father's footsteps and one day take the field against Great Britain, referred to symbolically here as "the bonny bunch of roses." Reichstadt's mother, dreaming wistfully of the glory that was, and will never be again, speaks of the fallen Emperor almost in the same vein that Cleopatra spoke of Mark Anthony:

> In his livery
> Walkt crowns and crownets; realms and islands were
> As plates dropt from his pocket.

By a few swift verses, this song brilliantly condensed the Napoleonic saga, and, for Americans, vividly crystallized the central events of the times in which they lived.

By the bor - der of the o - cean One

morn-ing in the month of June, A__ feath - ered

song-ster His cheer-ful notes did sweet-ly tune. There I o-ver-heard a la-dy Who seemed to be in grief and woe, Con-ver-sing with young Bo-na-parte A-bout the Bon-ny Bunch of Ros-es, O.

Then up spoke young Napoleon
   And takes his mother by the hand,
Saying "Mother dear have patience,
   Til I am able to command.
Then I will raise an army
   And through tremendous dangers go,
And I never will return again
   Til I have conquered the Bonny Bunch of Roses O."

"O son, don't be so venturesome,
   For England has a heart of oak:
England, Ireland, Scotland—
   Their unity may not be broke.
Remember your brave father,
   In St. Helena he lies low,
And if you follow after,
   Beware the Bonny Bunch of Roses O."

"When first you saw great Bonaparte,
   You fell upon your bended knee,
You asked your father's blessing,
   He granted it right manfully.
'Dear son,' says he, 'I'll take an army,
   Over the frozen Alps I'll go;
Then I will conquer Moscow
   And return to the Bonny Bunch of Roses O.'

"Your father raised great armies,
   Likewise kings to bear his train,
He was so well provided he
   Could sweep the world for gain.
But when he came to Moscow
   Nigh overpowered by the driving snow,
All Moscow was a-blazing.
   And he lost the Bonny Bunch of Roses O."

"Now do believe me mother,
   For I'm on my dying bed,
If I had lived, I would have been brave,
   Now I droop my youthful head.
But while our bones lie moldering,
   And weeping willows o'er us grow,
The fame of great Napoleon
   Shall shame the Bonny Bunch of Roses O."

Melody from Elisabeth B. Greenleaf and Grace Y. Mansfield, *Ballads and Sea Songs of Newfoundland,* Harvard University Press. Copyright 1933 by The President and Fellows of Harvard College; c. 1961 by Elisabeth B. Greenleaf and Grace Y. Mansfield. Reprinted by permission.

The Constitution and Guerrière

The War of 1812 broke out, ostensibly, over the issue of British interference with American commerce and the need to enforce the fundamental right to freedom of the seas. In permitting this conflict to break out and failing to neutralize United States hostility, British diplomacy committed a serious error; England was, at the time, engaged in a life-and-death struggle with Napoleon and could ill afford another foe. From the American point of view, Madison's declaration of war in July 1812 was equally ill-advised. It rested upon an estimate of the country's preparedness which had no basis in fact; the territorial ambitions of the War Hawks who precipitated the adventure far exceeded their abilities. The inevitable result was two and one-half years of see-saw conflict that humiliated both sides and ended in a stalemate.

The war was indecisive by land, and both sides found solace in the events that occurred at sea. Because the American navy had made considerable progress since the days of Paul Jones, the war at sea was marked by a series of duels between British and American men o' war. These dramatic and colorful engagements, although absolutely indecisive, were diverting, at least to the onlookers. As one commentator has aptly observed:

The engagements between British and American frigates did little or nothing to settle the final issue of the war. As sporting events, testing the skill and the courage of the combatants and arousing the emotions of the supporters of the ships engaged, they were without equal.*

In early August 1812, Captain Isaac Hull, commanding the U.S. frigate *Constitution,* was cruising in mid-Atlantic, with the general mission of harrying British commerce. When he encountered the English frigate *Guerrière,* commanded by Captain James Dacres, he decided to stand and fight. Dacres unlimbered his guns and fired upon the *Constitution,* but Hull, much to the disgust of his crew, refused to return fire until literally within hailing distance of his antagonist. He then fired a series of broadsides with crushing effect. The *Guerrière* was completely disabled and obliged to surrender. The American vessel was superior to its rival in tonnage and firepower, but news of the victory sent American morale sky high.

*H. F. Beirne, *The War of 1812* (New York: Dutton, 1949), 124.

This was the first time that a British man o' war had struck its colors to an American since the time of Paul Jones.

The Boston broadside commemorating Hull's triumph is one of the best known and remembered of the songs to which the War of 1812 gave rise. Set to the tune of a rousing English drinking song, it expresses to perfection the cocksure Yankee boastfulness of that time.

It oft - times has been told, that the
Brit - ish sea - men bold Could flog the tars of
France so neat and hand - y, O; But they
nev - er met their match till the Yan-kees did them
catch, O the Yan-kee boys for fight-ing are the
dan-dy, O! (*Whistle*) _____ O the
Yan-kee boys for fight-ing are the dan-dy, O!

2. The *Guerrière*, a frigate bold, on the foaming ocean rolled,
    Commanded by Dacres the grandee, O;
    With as proud a British crew as a rammer ever drew,
    They could flog the tars of France so neat and handy, O!

3. Then Dacres loudly cries, "Make this Yankee ship your
        prize,
    You can do it in thirty minutes so neat and handy, O;
    Twenty-five's enough, I'm sure, and if you'll do it in a score,
    I'll treat you to a double tot of brandy, O!"

4. The British shot flew hot, which the Yankees answered not,
    'Til they got within a space they thought was handy, O;
    "Now," Hull says to his crew, "Boys, let's see what you
        can do,
    If we take this boasting Briton we're the dandy, O!"

5. The first broadside we poured swept their mainmast over-
        board,
    Which made this lofty frigate look abandoned, O;
    Then Dacres he did sigh, and to his officers did cry,
    "I did not think these Yankees were so handy, O!"

6. Our second told so well, that their fore and mizzen fell,
    Which doused the royal ensign so neat and handy, O;
    "By George!" says he, "We're done!" and they fired a lee
        gun,·
    And the Yankees struck up Yankee Doodle Dandy, O!

7. Now fill your glasses full, let's drink a toast to Captain
        Hull,
    So merrily we'll push around the brandy, O;
    For John Bull may drink his fill, and the world say what
        it will,
    The Yankee tars for fighting are the dandy, O!

The Chesapeake and the Shannon

Not all these naval engagements turned out so well. In May 1813, Captain Philip Broke, commanding the British frigate *Shannon* then blockading Boston, issued this challenge to Captain James Lawrence, commanding the *Chesapeake:*

As the *Chesapeake* appears now ready for sea, I request you will do me the favor to meet the *Shannon* with her, ship for ship, to try the fortunes of our respective flags.

News of the challenge spread rapidly. On June 1, the day appointed for the contest, crowds thronged the Boston waterfront. By early evening, the two vessels were engaged at point-blank range. Lawrence, mortally wounded, was carried below, and gave his never-forgotten last order, "Don't give up the ship." But the British boarded the *Chesapeake,* struck its colors, and took the prize in tow to Halifax.

Now it was Britain's turn to sing a boastful song, which is reproduced below, to the same tune as "The Constitution and the Guerrière." But the people of Nova Scotia who saw the two vessels coming into port on July 6 did not talk or sing of the engagement. The scenes of mutilation and death which they were obliged to witness had been too frightful.

1. The Chesapeake so bold, out of Boston as we're told,
   Came to take the British frigate neat and handy, O.
   The people in the port all came out to see the sport
   And the bands played Yankee Doodle Dandy, O.

2. Before this fight begun, the Yankees made such fun,
   Saying "We'll tow her up to Boston so neat and handy, O;
   And after that we'll dine, treat our sweethearts all with
      wine,
   And we'll dance a jig of Yankee Doodle Dandy, O."

3. Our British frigate's name that for the purpose came
   To cool the Yankees' courage so neat and handy, O
   Was the Shannon—Captain Broke, all his crew had hearts
      of oak
   And in fighting were allowed to be the dandy, O.

4. The action scarce begun when they flinchèd from their
    guns,
   They thought that they had worked us neat and handy, O;
   But Broke he moved his sword saying "Come, my boys,
    we'll board,
   And we'll stop them playing Yankee Doodle Dandy, O."

5. When the Britons heard this word, they quickly sprang on
    board,
   And seized the Yankees' ensign neat and handy, O;
   Notwithstanding all their brags the British raised their
    flags;
   On the Yankees' mizzen-peak they flew so dandy, O.

6. Here's to Broke and all his crew who with courage stout
    and true
   Fought against the Yankee frigate neat and handy, O;
   O may they ever prove, in fighting or in love,
   That the British tars will always be the dandy, O!

The Hunters of Kentucky

This famous ballad tells the story of the greatest American military triumph of the War of 1812, Andrew Jackson's defeat of the hard-bitten British veterans at the battle of New Orleans on January 8, 1815. Written by Samuel Woodworth shortly after the conclusion of the war, "The Hunters of Kentucky" served as a campaign song during Jackson's first effort to win the presidency in 1824. It became immensely popular during the actual years of Jackson's presidency, 1829–1837. Since this victory was decisive in sending Jackson to the White House, the song also had its share in the making of a President.

Napoleon's defeat in 1814 boded no good for the United States. Britain was now freed from her military commitment in Europe and could therefore give her undivided attention to the American foe. Accordingly, in the summer of 1814, a thrust against Louisiana was planned: to close the mouth of the Mississippi, tie up American commerce, and attempt to re-establish England's territorial power in the heart of the North American continent.

Andrew Jackson, commander of the Seventh Military District, with headquarters at Mobile, was in charge of the military forces in that area. In November, he arrived at New Orleans and personally directed the city's defenses. Fort St. Philip, near the mouth of the Mississippi, was manned; batteries were erected, and a defensive force was assembled. Tennessee and Kentucky riflemen began to arrive shortly before Christmas.

The British, meanwhile, massed at Jamaica for the invasion. A striking force of 10,000 men was stiffened by a corps of hardened veterans from the campaign against Napoleon in Portugal and Spain; Major General Sir Edward Pakenham, a hero of that same Peninsular war, was sent from England to assume command.

The main British thrust toward New Orleans came from the south, up along the bank of the Mississippi between the river and the cypress swamps to the east. Jackson drew up his forces along the Rodriguez Canal, below the city, on a line a little more than half a mile in extent, running east and west, and anchored on one flank by the river and on the other by the swamps. He fortified this line with gun batteries, and awaited the enemy. Jackson's forces were thus disposed squarely across Pakenham's line of march, between the British army and New Orleans.

A series of minor skirmishes was climaxed by Pakenham's frontal attack upon the American position at dawn on January 8, 1815. As the morning mists lifted, an unforgettable sight met the eyes of the defenders:

Across the wide plain, in the river haze, moved the British regiments in solid front, their red and white uniforms giving a bold touch of color to the somber lowlands. It was a sight that only a few men in Jackson's army . . . had ever before witnessed. A shout broke from Carroll's troops and was taken up by the Kentuckians. No one could tell whether it was a shout of confidence or one of delight over the spectacle presented by the advancing columns. They came silently, without drumbeat, without firing, into artillery range.*

Armed with Kentucky rifles, the Western marksmen wrought terrible destruction upon these advancing troops. Jackson inflicted over 2,000 casualties upon the British at a cost of only 21 dead to himself. The ballad reproduced here is a masterpiece of understatement which gives little hint of the grimness of the engagement. But as a serious account of the experience from the viewpoint of the victor, it is not very far from the truth. Men who had survived the inconceivable hardships and horrors of Wellington's Peninsular campaign were broken by the small arms fire of the Tennessee and Kentucky militia.

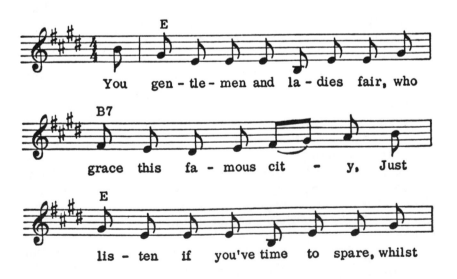

You gen-tle-men and la-dies fair, who
grace this fa-mous cit - y, Just
lis-ten if you've time to spare, whilst

*Glenn Tucker, *Poltroons and Patriots* (New York: Bobbs, Merrill, 1954), II, 699.

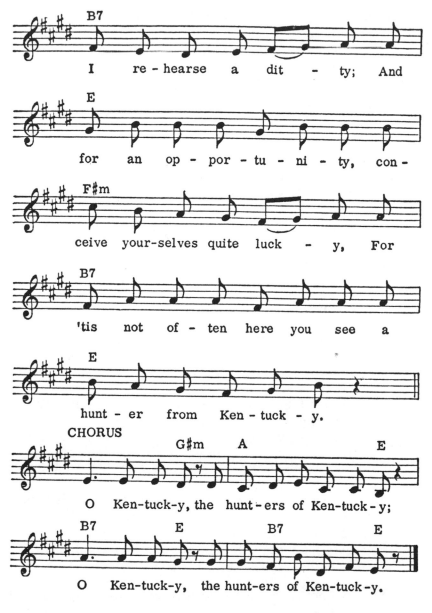

I re-hearse a dit - ty; And
for an op - por - tu - ni - ty, con -
ceive your-selves quite luck - y, For
'tis not of - ten here you see a
hunt - er from Ken - tuck - y.

CHORUS

O Ken-tuck-y, the hunt - ers of Ken-tuck - y;
O Ken-tuck-y, the hunt-ers of Ken-tuck - y.

2. We are a hardy freeborn race, each man to fear a stranger,
   Whate'er the game we join the chase, despising toil and
      danger;
   And if a daring foe annoys, whatever his strength and
      forces,
   We'll show him that Kentucky boys are "alligator horses."
      O Kentucky, etc.

115

3. I suppose you've read it in the prints, how Pakenham attempted
   To make old Hickory Jackson wince, but soon his schemes repented,
   For we with rifles ready cocked, thought such occasion lucky,
   And soon around the hero flocked the hunters of Kentucky,
      O Kentucky, etc.

4. You've heard I suppose how New Orleans is famed for wealth and beauty.
   There's girls of every hue it seems, from snowy white to sooty,
   So Pakenham he mad his brag, if he in fight was lucky,
   He'd have their girls and cotton bags in spite of old Kentucky,
      O Kentucky, etc.

5. But Jackson he was wide awake, and wasn't scared at trifles,
   For well he knew what aim we'd take with our Kentucky rifles;
   So he led us down to Cypress swamp, the ground was low and mucky,
   There stood John Bull in martial pomp, and here was old Kentucky,
      O Kentucky, etc.

6. A bank was raised to hide our breast, not that we thought of dying,
   But that we always like to rest, unless the game is flying:
   Behind it stood our little force: none wished it to be greater,
   For every man was half a horse, and half an alligator,
      O Kentucky, etc.

7. They did not let our patience tire before they showed their faces—
   We did not choose to waste our fire, but snugly kept our places;
   And when so near to see them wink, we thought 'twas time to stop 'em;
   And 'twould have done you good, I think, to see Kentuckians drop 'em.
      O Kentucky, etc.

8. They found at last 'twas vain to fight when lead was all
       their booty,
    And so they wisely took to flight, and left us all our beauty,
    And now if danger e'er annoys, remember what our trade
       is,
    Just send for us Kentucky boys, and we'll protect you,
       ladies,
        O Kentucky, etc.

Johnny Bull, My Jo, John

"Johnny Bull" began life as a broadside ballad shortly after the termination of the War of 1812. That it was reprinted and appeared in a number of collections in succeeding years indicates that the song enjoyed a measure of popularity. We may think of it as a brilliant recapitulation of the war from the American viewpoint; it stresses the American national achievement, puts the best face possible on disgraceful episodes like the British occupation of Washington, D. C., in 1813, and quietly omits any reference to the less glorious aspects of the military effort.

The melody to which "Johnny Bull" is set is perhaps one of the loveliest that has come down to us from the olden days. Robert Burns composed a poem which he set to this tune, and the two were published together for the first time in the *Scots Musical Museum* in 1790 under the title "John Anderson My Jo, John." Burns's version ran as follows:

> John Anderson my jo, John,
>   When we were first acquent,
> Your locks were like the raven,
>   Your bonny brow was brent;
> But now your brow is bald, John,
>   Your locks are like the snow,
> But blessings on your frosty pow,
>   John Anderson my jo!
>
> John Anderson my jo, John,
>   We clamb the hill together;
> And many a cantie [merry] day, John,
>   We've had wi' ane another:
> But we maun totter down, John,
>   And hand in hand we'll go,
> And sleep together at the foot,
>   John Anderson, my jo!

Such was the musical and lyrical inspiration for the American version of the song.

118

won - der what you mean; Are__ you on for-eign con-quest bent, or what am - bi -tious scheme? Now list to broth - er Jon - a - than, your fruit - less plans fore - go, Re - main on your fast-an-chored isle, O__ John - ny Bull, my jo.

O Johnny Bull, my jo, John, don't come across the main;
Our fathers bled and suffered, John, our freedom to maintain,
And him who in the cradle, John, repelled the ruthless foe,
Provoke not when to manhood grown, O Johnny Bull, my jo.

O Johnny Bull, my jo, John, on Erie's distant shores,
See how the battle rages, and loud the cannon roars;
But Perry taught our seamen to crush the assailing foe,
He met and made them ours, O Johnny Bull, my jo.

What though at Washington a base marauding band,
Our monuments of art, John, destroyed with ruthless hand?
It was a savage warfare, beneath a generous foe,
And brings the more disgrace on you, O Johnny Bull my jo.

O Johnny Bull my jo, John, when all your schemes have failed,
To wipe away the stigmas, John, for New Orleans you sailed;

Far heavier woes await thee John, for Jackson meets the foe,
Whose name and fame's immortal, O Johnny Bull, my jo.

Your schemes to gather laurels here I guess were badly planned;
We have whipped you on the ocean, jo, we have bothered you
    on land:
Then hie thee to old England, John, thy fruitless plans forego,
And haste to thy fast-anchored isle, O Johnny Bull, my jo.

Mrs. McGrath

During the Napoleonic Era, war was practically continuous. Everywhere in the Western world the cruelty, waste, and inhumanity of war was borne home to millions of people; and it is no accident that a movement for the abolition of war as an instrument of national policy arose in the years immediately following the conclusion of peace in 1815. The peace movement of that day was to constitute an important part of the humanitarian crusade for social reform that gave dignity and meaning to the Jacksonian era.

One of the most poignant judgments upon war and all its works was delivered in the broadside ballad. "Mrs. McGrath," that appeared upon the Dublin streets as early as 1815 and has been sung in Eire ever since. In these years of British rule, poverty-stricken Irish—landless, starving, and oppressed—were forced to become mercenaries of many European powers, including, ironically enough, England, the national enemy. "Mrs. McGrath" expresses the tragedy of a young man mutilated while fighting for the King of England with Wellington in the famous Peninsular Campaign of 1808–1814. This campaign, it will be remembered, was one phase of the huge struggle then being waged with Napoleon.

The dramatic irony, the human sympathy, and the simple lyric of "Mrs. McGrath" illustrate the effectiveness of the broadside ballad at its very best.

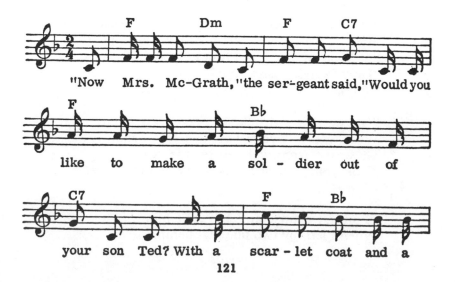

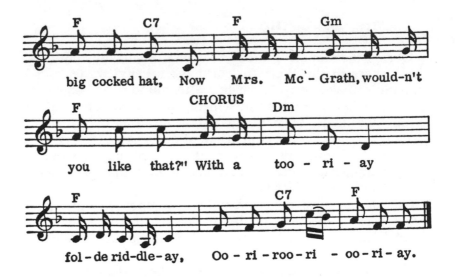

big cocked hat, Now Mrs. Mc'- Grath, would-n't you like that?" With a too - ri - ay CHORUS fol - de rid-dle-ay, Oo - ri - roo - ri - oo - ri - ay.

So Mrs. McGrath lived by the seashore
For the space of seven long years or more,
Till a great big ship came a-sailing in the bay:
"Oh it's my son Ted who's been so long away!"
Chorus

"Oh captain dear, where have you been,
Have you been a-sailing on the Mediterreen?
And have you any news of my son Ted,
Is the poor boy living, or is he dead?"
Chorus

Then up stepped Ted without any legs,
And in their place were two wooden pegs;
She kissed him a dozen times or two,
"Holy Moses, it isn't you!"
Chorus

"Oh were you drunk, or were you blind,
When you left your two fine legs behind:
Or was it from walking on the seas,
Took your two fine legs away at the knees?"
Chorus

"I wasn't drunk, and I wasn't blind,
When I left my two fine legs behind;

But a cannon ball on the fifth of May
Tore my two fine legs at the knees away."
Chorus

"Teddy my dear," the widow cried,
"Your two fine legs were your mother's pride;
These two stumps of a tree won't do at all,
Why didn't you flee from the big cannon ball?"
Chorus

"All foreign wars I do proclaim
Against Napoleon and the King of Spain;
And by Heaven, I'll make them rue the time,
When they took the legs from a child of mine,"
Chorus

IV

JACKSONIAN

AMERICA

THE END OF THE WAR OF 1812 marked the beginning of a new period in American history. The American people could now devote their full energies and attention to settling and developing the continent which they had won. Thus, 1815 marks the start of an era of unprecedented expansion, which continued in full swing until 1848. This period, 1815–1848, had a unity and a quality of its own, which entitle us to label it "Jacksonian." It possessed many of the attributes associated with Jacksonian democracy: raw materialism, driving expansion, but also generous enthusiasms and reforming zeals. Americans achieved a sense of stability derived from pride in their past and a feeling of abounding confidence in the future. This, of course, would change after 1848 and give way to a vastly different mood. For in the fifties, there was a growing preoccupation with the slavery crisis and a growing conviction of the inevitability of civil war.

In Jacksonian America, national development assumed a sectional form. A single nation was growing, developing, evolving; but it was organized into three clearly differentiated sections, or regions, each with its own distinct patterns of social, political, and economic life.

In the Northeast, the first decisive steps were taken, during this period, toward industrialization. The countryside was beginning to be transformed. Factories were established, canals dug, and railroads built; swarms of immigrants were brought in to do construction work and to man the new machines. In the West, pioneers began to move rapidly toward the Mississippi Valley, pushing back the Indians and founding new states as they went, then leaping across the High Plains into California and Oregon. A new community of free farmers was coming into being to provide wheat for the industrial East and for the world.

In the South, slavery reached its height. Jefferson, years earlier, had dreamed of the day when the slaves would be emancipated and sent back to Africa, leaving the Southland, even as the West, for settlement by free and prosperous white farmers. But with the industrial revolution and its bottomless demand for raw cotton, slavery acquired a new lease on life as slaveowners hastened to move their black chattels into the rich new lands of the Southwest.

The Jacksonian period achieved a deep and abiding expression in the singing of the American people. Each main region—North, West, South—produced new songs which reflected and gave expression to the distinctive features of its own sectional life. America was singing now of its experience and destiny in accents unmistakably American. The old songs, of course, continued to be sung, but new lyrics were being composed, and the nation's musical resources were being marvelously enriched. Immigrants, pouring in, brought their own special contributions with them; and, in the South, the Negro people were creating a new and uniquely American musical idiom that was already beginning to feed back into the singing of white America.

In the following chapter, we shall be concerned with the development of the different aspects of national singing in each of the great sections of the country, taken one by one.

125

Sea and Immigration

The period 1814–1860 was the climactic age of sail, an epoch in which American square riggers scoured the world in pursuit of trade and established a reputation for being the swiftest and loveliest vessels afloat. The great opportunities which opened up for the merchant marine during this period were a direct result of the Revolution, which had freed United States commerce from the straitjacket of British domination and laid the globe itself open to American searfaring enterprise. Northerners were not slow to exploit this opportunity. British mercantile policy had fostered the shipbuilding industry in colonial days; a hardy race of skilled seamen, whalermen, and shipbuilders had developed as a result of dozens of harbors sprung up along the navigable rivers and coasts of New England and New York.

Young people, in the age of the square rigger, were lured to sea by the glittering image of adventure and romance which it presented. Here is the testimony of Richard Henry Dana, a Harvard student who served as an ordinary seaman on the merchant ships *Pilgrim* and *Alert* in the years 1834–1836 and recorded his experiences in the classic *Two Years before the Mast*:

There is a witchery in the sea, its songs and stories, and in the mere sight of a ship, and the sailor's dress, especially to a young mind, which has done more to man navies, and fill merchantmen, than all the press-gangs of Europe. I have known a young man with such passion for the sea that the very creaking of a block stirred up his imagination so that he could hardly keep his feet on dry ground; and many are the boys, in every seaport, who are drawn away, as by an almost irresistible attraction, from their work and schools, and hang about the decks and yards of vessels, with a fondness which, it is plain, will have its way.

But the beauty of sail, the grace of a ship's motion, and the boundless expanse of sea and stars and sky—all this was a painted veil. Beyond it lay agonies of toil and heartbreak. "No sooner," continued Dana, "has the young sailor begun his life in earnest, then all this fine drapery falls off, and he learns that it is but work and hardship, after all. *This is the true light in which a sailor's life is to be viewed.*"*

Two Years before the Mast (New York: Bantam Books, 1959), 320. Italics not in original.

Manning the great sailing vessels of Dana's time was back-breaking toil. The seaman's calling was especially dangerous, and the whalerman faced a whole series of additional perils inseparable from the hunting of whales and the processing of their carcasses. Voyages lasted for months, sometimes for years. Men had to cope with the despair and homesickness engendered by prolonged periods of exile from native land and loved ones.

Life at sea, as we might expect, produced songs fulfilling a central function in the existence of the people involved. The songs these men created and sang and taught to each other helped them to face and overcome dire, daily peril, to undergo backbreaking toil, to cope with monotony and boredom, to summon inspiration for life from the bottom of their souls, and, above all, to work together.

Again, as might be expected, British and American sea songs had a close affinity to each other, and many of the same ones, with appropriate variations, were sung on board both British and American ships. Though the age of sail has vanished many of the songs to which it gave rise have come down to us. Many seem to possess a mysterious inner life all of their own. They are imbued with a strange sense of the surge of the sea, and of its vastness. Often, they express the sailor's deep inner sadness, the yearning for home, the bitterness that a man feels at scorn and abuse, the immediacy of death.

Seamen sang many songs, and many different kinds of song. Although some were reserved for special occasions or for certain types of work, there were, for the most part, no hard and fast barriers: The same song might be pressed into different kinds of service at different times. But, once this is clearly understood, it is still helpful to divide sea songs, in the most general kind of way, into *shanties* and *fo'c'sle* (forecastle) songs. The shanties are that very large group of songs used as work songs, to help in the performance of a sailor's tasks on, above, or below decks, and at the rowing of the ship's boats. Fo'c'sle songs—or forebitters—were sung in the crew's quarters during watch below, on deck during dogwatches, or during other spells of leisure time. Their purpose was recreational.

The shanties, or work songs, arose out of the requirements of hard physical labor. Such work, if steadily and rhythmically performed, does not exhaust to nearly the same degree as labor devoid of rhythmic flow. Rhythm, when the work is undertaken by gangs, plays the additional role of enabling the group to pull together as one.

An incredible amount of backbreaking labor had to be performed in the course of a single sea voyage. Cargo and supplies had to be loaded, stowed below decks, and unloaded, and this was done by the crew working as a gang with block and tackle. Ballast had to be taken on and dumped off; the heavy cast-iron anchors had to be hove up and let down, a job that, before the coming of steam, could only be performed by gang labor at the capstan. Much work had to be done high above the deck, in the ship's rigging: Sails had to be set, reefed, furled, and bunted in an endless, Sisyphean labor, as the wind conditions changed. The deck itself had to be sanded daily and swabbed for an hour or so at daybreak; the pumps had to be manned and the bilge pumped out both in fair weather and foul. Here again, in the days before steam, the energy was provided by gangs of men pulling at the long pump handles or hauling on ropes attached to the pump's twin flywheels; sails had to be bent on and hauled into position by means of a complex array of sheets, halyards, bowlines, buntlines, and downhauls. All of this work was physically exhausting, and much of it was difficult and dangerous—like hauling on the sheet on the leeward side of a heeling ship with decks awash, or furling the topgallants in an icy gale.

In the course of a long voyage, not only the ship itself, but also the ship's *boats* absorbed vast amounts of labor. This was almost as true for regular merchant ships as it was for whalers. In both situations, the crew was obliged to spend days, weeks, and even months at the oars. Here, again, songs were indispensable, and these boatsongs were as much shanties as anything sung on board the ship itself. Telling of the collection and unloading of hides on the California coast, Dana says:

> The next day the *California* began unloading her cargo; and her boats' crews, in coming and going, sang their boatsongs, keeping time with their oars. This they did all day long for several days, until their hides were all discharged. . . .

Shanties were sung, almost without exception, without instrumental accompaniment. The human voice and the human soul stood unaided against the elements. But the same did not hold for the sailor's recreational songs. On the old sailing vessels, the entire crew was divided into two watches. All hands would be on deck between noon and 8:00 p.m.; thereafter, they would have "watch and watch," that is, alternate spells of deck duty and "watch below." During "watch below," a man was not off duty. He might be called on deck any moment for an emergency in which his help was needed; but, if all went well, the men would have leisure then, on Sundays, and during twilight hours on deck, for sleep, mending of clothes, reading, and singing.

The songs used on such occasions have been called fo'c'sle songs. A sailor's repertoire might include shanties, with whatever modifications seemed appropriate, but also ballads, sentimental ditties, love songs, or anything else that Jack might have learned on shore and brought to sea with him for diversion. The usual instrumental accompaniment was a fiddle or harmonica.

Below we reproduce a small selection of the great and beautiful heritage of song left us from the era of sail, as an introduction to the nature and meaning of seafaring life at that time.

* * * *

One of the major achievements of the American merchant marine in this period, seconded by the British, was the transportation of some four million immigrants to North America. The speed of this operation, the numbers of people involved, and the distance they moved characterize it as one of the greatest movements of peoples which history, until that time, had seen.

This period of immigration is known to historians as "the old immigration" to distinguish it from the even greater flood of humanity that arrived upon American shores in the period 1885–1917. The peoples of the old immigration came from Western Europe, primarily from the British Isles, Eire, Western Germany, and Scandinavia. The musical implications of this were, in the long run, to prove significant. The American musical heritage began to receive a massive infusion of materials not only in English but in other European tongues.

We have chosen to focus upon the Irish as a people whose story is in many ways representative of that of other immigrant peoples, in many ways *typical* of people whose musical contribution was created in a foreign tongue. And, as we have seen, Eire's story, her people, and her music, had become intertwined with American history almost from the beginning.

The Irish, at the opening of the nineteenth century, faced

a bleak future. They might starve slowly on their miserable plots, seek jobs in British textile factories, join the British Army—or they might emigrate. The new Republic in America, the United States, had kicked over the British traces. It was a symbol of equality and freedom. Above all, it offered jobs and bread. Thus, when peace came in 1815, Irish began to stream to New York and New England to dig canals, build railroads, and man cotton factories.

In 1846, famine came to Eire and the stream of emigration turned into a flood. The mass of the Irish people were so poor that only the potato patch stood between them and starvation. But the potato's yield was uncertain. In 1845, the rot set in and did not run its course until 1850. In that five year period, over one and one-quarter million Irish died of cold, hunger, and disease. Over one and one-half million Irish left their native land forever; most of them came to Canada and to the United States. In the following pages, we reproduce a few of the exquisite songs that these people brought with them in the steerage, which express the beauty of their heritage, the sorrow of their life, and the yearning for a happier future. These Irish songs, as we shall see later, were destined to find their way to the remotest corners of the Union.

Haul on the Bowline

This is one of the oldest, best-known, and best-loved, of the "short haul" shanties, used whenever a short, sharp, powerful pull was needed. The bowline was a rope with an important function on the square sails of medieval ships, but it retained its popularity, over the years, for other short hauls. Simple as it is, the melody conveys a powerful rhythmic thrust. Accent and action are both concentrated on the final *"haul!"*

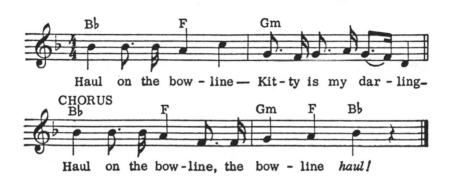

Haul on the bowline—Kitty comes from Liverpool
Chorus
Haul on the bowline—so early in the morning
Chorus
Haul on the bowline—the bully mate is snarling
Chorus
Haul on the bowline—haul for better weather
Chorus
Haul on the bowline—we'll either break or bend her
Chorus
Haul on the bowline—the bully ship's a-rolling
Chorus
Haul on the bowline—it's a long time to pay day
Chorus

Blood-red Roses

This is a halyard shanty, a type of song used when a steady, intermittent pull was needed, as in hoisting the heavy yards (spars) upon which many of a square-rigger's sails were bent. The hands took their places at the rope, the shantyman, or leader, yelled out the solo, and, as the men came in on the refrain, they hauled with a will. There were two hauls to each refrain. Before the men had finished hauling and singing, the high-pitched cry of the leader would again be heard, giving out on the next line of the song.

SOLO
Our boots and clothes are all in pawn,

CHORUS
Go down, you blood - red ros - es,

SOLO
go down! And it's might - y draft - y

CHORUS
round Cape Horn, Go down, you blood - red ros - es,

SOLO
go down! Oh, you pinks and po - sies,

CHORUS
Go down, you blood-red ros - es, go down!

Solo
1. Our boots and clothes are all in pawn
   Chorus
   Go down, you blood-red roses, go down!
   Solo
   And it's mighty drafty round Cape Horn
   Chorus
   Go down, you blood-red roses, go down!
   Solo
   Oh, you pinks and posies
   Chorus
   Go down, you blood-red roses, go down!
   Solo
   Oh, you pinks and posies
   Chorus
   Go down, you blood-red roses, go down!

2. You've had your advance and to sea must go
   Chorus
   Chasing whales through the frost and snow
   Chorus
   Oh, you pinks and posies
   Chorus
   Oh, you pinks and posies
   Chorus

3. My old mother, she wrote to me
   Chorus
   "My dearest son, come home from sea."
   Chorus
   Oh, you pinks and posies
   Chorus
   Oh, you pinks and posies
   Chorus

4. But around Cape Horn we all must go
   Chorus
   Round Cape Horn through the ice and snow
   Chorus
   Oh, you pinks and posies
   Chorus
   Oh, you pinks and posies
   Chorus

5. Round Cape Horn we all must go
   Chorus
   For that is where the whalefish blow
   Chorus
   Oh, you pinks and posies
   Chorus
   Oh, you pinks and posies
   Chorus

6. Just one more pull and that will do
   Chorus
   For we're the bullies to kick her through
   Chorus

Leave Her, Johnny, Leave Her

This song, with its soaring chorus, was usually sung as a capstan shanty at the end of a voyage. While entering port and "warping" the vessel alongside the dock, the sailor had the privilege of unloading his feelings about the captain, the mates, the owners, the ship, and the treatment that he had received aboard. Such sentiments, uttered during the course of the voyage itself, would have earned him a flogging or irons. "Leave Her, Johnny, Leave Her," provided the musical form for the seaman's final gripes. It is reproduced here with a few of the seemingly endless verses. Without the full chorus and using only the more discreet verses, the song might also be sung at sea as a halyard shanty.

An immigrant version, evidently inspired by the sailor's, is given on page 150.

SOLO   D

Now the times were hard, and the wag-es were low,

CHORUS / A7

Leave her, John - ny, leave her!

D   SOLO   Bm   F♯m

And now once more a-

F♯7   Bm   CHORUS / D   A7   D

shore we'll go, It's time for us to leave her.

A7   D

Leave her, John - ny, leave her, Oh,—

leave her, John - ny, leave her! For the
voy-age is done, and the winds don't blow, And it's
time for us to leave _____ her.

She would not wear, and she would not stay,
Chorus   Leave her, Johnny, leave her!
She shipped great seas both night and day,
Chorus   And it's time for us to leave her.

Full Chorus

It was rotten meat and weevily bread
Chorus   Leave her, Johnny, leave her!
Eat it or starve, the Old Man said,
Chorus   And it's time for us to leave her.

Full Chorus

Oh the winds were foul and the work was hard,
Chorus   Leave her, Johnny, leave her!
From Liverpool dock to the Brooklyn yard,
Chorus   And it's time for us to leave her.

Full Chorus

The sails are all furled and the work is all done,
Chorus   Leave her, Johnny, leave her!
And homeward now we've made our run,
Chorus   And it's time for us to leave her.

Full Chorus

I thought I heard the Old Man say,
Chorus   Leave her, Johnny, leave her!
Tomorrow you will get your pay,
Chorus   And it's time for us to leave her.

Full Chorus

Now it's time for us to say goodbye,
Chorus   Leave her, Johnny, leave her!
The old pierhead is drawing nigh,
Chorus   And it's time for us to leave her.

Full Chorus

The Golden Vanity

One of the oldest and most familiar of the traditional songs, "The Golden Vanity" survives on both sides of the Atlantic in dozens of variants. Among ordinary seamen, it was a favorite at both capstan and pump, for it expressed the truth of life at sea: the heroism of sailors, the tyranny of command, the ever-present mystery of the ocean.

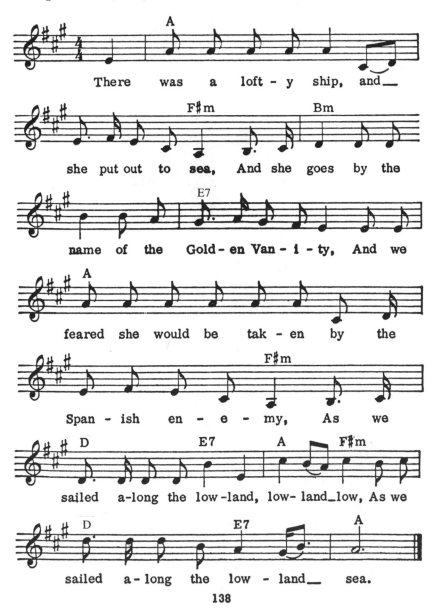

Oh, we had a little cabin boy, and boldly up spoke he,
And he said to the captain, "What will you give me,
If I'll swim alongside of the Spanish enemy,
And I sink her in the lowland, lowland low,
    If I sink her in the lowland sea?"

"Of gold and silver I will give you fee,
And my only daughter your bonny bride to be,
If you'll swim alongside of the Spanish enemy
And you sink them in the lowland, lowland, low,
    If you sink them in the lowland sea."

Then the boy bared his breast and overboard sprang he,
And he swam til he came to the Spanish enemy,
Then with his auger sharp in her sides he bored holes three,
And he sank her in the lowland, lowland low,
    He sank her in the lowland sea.

Now some were playing at cards and some were playing at dice,
And some were sitting by giving very good advice,
Until the salt water it flashed into their eyes,
And it sank them in the lowland, lowland low,
    It sank them in the lowland sea.

Then the boy swam back to the cheering of the crew
But the captain would not heed him, for his promise he did rue,
And he scorned his proud entreaties, though full loudly he did
    sue,
And he left him in the lowland, lowland low,
    He left him in the lowland sea.

So the boy swam round til he came to the larboard side,
And to his messmates bitterly he cried,
"Oh messmates pick me up, for I'm drifting with the tide,
And I'm sinking in the lowland, lowland low,
    I'm sinking in the lowland sea."

Then his messmates took him up, and upon the deck he died,
And they sewed him in his hammock, which was so large and
    wide,
And they lowered him overboard, and he drifted with the tide,
And he sank beneath the lowland, lowland low,
    He sank beneath the lowland sea.

Off to Sea Once More

In the whole range of sea songs that have survived from the age of sail few capture the sailor's mood more effectively than "Off to Sea Once More." Ashore at the end of a long voyage, the sailor has fallen prey to landsharks, both male and female, who have battened upon him and stripped him of his hard-earned, meager pay. In a strange port, without money or friends, he has only one recourse: to go to sea once more. The song, like those of a later day that recount the miner's woes, ends on a theme of warning.

The surge of the sea and the motion of the ship's deck, which do not leave the sailor, even when he is ashore, are echoed here. "Off to Sea Once More" has been found in many variations among British and American seamen, and has been collected on both sides of the Atlantic—in Nova Scotia, Maine, England, and Scotland.

When first I came to Liv - er - pool, I went up - on the spree, My mon-ey at last I spent it fast, got drunk as drunk could be; And when my mon-ey it was all gone, ah, then I want-ed more, For a man must be blind to

make up his mind to go to sea once more.

2. That night I slept with Angeline, too drunk to roll in bed;
   Me watch was new, and me money too, in the morning
      with 'em she'd fled;
   And as I roamed the streets about, the whores they all
      did roar,
   "There goes Jack Rack, poor sailor lad, he must go to sea
      once more!"

3. I shipped on board of a whaling ship bound for the
      Arctic seas,
   Where the cold wind blows through the frost and snow,
      and Jamaica rum would freeze;
   And worst of all I had no gear, for I'd lost all me
      money ashore,
   Oh, it's then that I wished that I was dead so I'd go
      to sea no more.

4. Some days we were catching whales, me lads, and some
      days we were catching none,
   With a twenty foot oar stuck into our hands from four
      o'clock in the morn,
   And when the shades of night come on, we'd rest on
      our weary oars,
   It was then that I wished that I was dead or safe
      with the gals ashore.

5. Come all ye bold seafaring men, and listen to my song;
   When you come off from your long trips, I'd have you
      not go wrong,
   Take my advice, drink no strong drink, don't
      go roaming on the shore,
   But get married lads, and have all night in, and go
      to sea no more!

The Greenland Whale Fishery

Nantucket, a sandspit in the Atlantic, 25 miles south of Cape Cod, was settled by English colonists in the seventeenth century. There was no wealth in its barren soil: for two centuries, from the time the English first came there until the Civil War, Nantucket's life was linked with seafaring and the whale fishery. The whale was the island's sole source of livelihood and wealth. Its Quaker people became famous the world over as among the most daring and resourceful seamen the world has seen.

First they killed stranded whales washed up upon their shores—an art the Indians taught them. Then they built schooners and ventured into the seas around; then they cruised north to Greenland and south to the Falklands and ranged the wide Atlantic for their quarry. After the Revolution, they rounded Cape Horn and roamed the vast Pacific from the Bering Strait to the Antarctic, from the Sea of Japan to 'Frisco Bay.

What led the whalemen to the Pacific was the search for the aristocrat of whales, the leviathan of the seas, the sperm. Sperm whales might grow to as much as 100 feet in length, and might weigh as much as ten tons. Killing this monster was a risky business, but the profits were proportionately high. Until the Civil War, the sperm was our principal source of artificial light. Sperm candles, veritable jewels of light, were made from the limpid oil found by the hundred gallons in the whale's head. From his blubber, the casing of fat around the body, huge quantities of oil were extracted to light lamps, lubricate machinery, and process leather.

Until the Revolution, England provided the principal market for Nantucket's oil and candles, but by 1820 the American demand had skyrocketed. Other New England ports, of which the greatest was New Bedford, rushed in to compete with the islanders for the fortunes to be made from this trade. The great age of American whaling had begun.

Once a ship arrived at the hunting grounds, a lookout was set, and the mastheads were manned from sunrise to sundown. Turn and turn about, the crew members stood at the crosstrees, far above the deck and scanned the wide circle of the sea for the telltale spout of the whale when he surfaced, the fluke flung heavenward when he breached. When a whale was sighted, the ship's boats were lowered from their davits. The men took their appointed places and rowed off with harpoons and lances ready for the fray. Indians and Negroes made the most skilled and daring harpooners. The steel barb, mounted on a hardwood shaft, had to be hurled 20 or 30 feet into the side of the whale.

A struck whale might race off across the sea, dragging the boat behind him; or he might turn upon his tormentors and smash their cockleshell in his jaws. Once the whale was killed, in a horrible flurry of gushing blood and boiling spray, and towed alongside, the ship was converted into a factory at sea. The blubber was removed from the carcass, cut up and "tried out"; the precious oil was poured into barrels and stowed away in the hold. An average whale might yield 40 or 50 barrels; the whole process might have to be repeated many times, over a period of months, before the hold was filled, and the ship could weigh anchor and head for home.

"The Greenland Whale Fishery" is a fo'c'sle ballad of English origin, evidently old, since British whalemen were fishing in Greenland waters centuries before Yankees headed for the Pacific. A swift and dramatic statement of whaling life, the song was much loved by American whalemen, who sang it with their own modifications of verse and melody.

way, brave boys, For_ Green-land bound a - way.

The lookout at the crosstrees stood,
With a spyglass to his eye,
"There's a whale, there's a whale, there's a whalefish,"
    he cried
"She blows on every hand, brave boys,
    She blows on every hand."

The captain stood at the quarter deck,
And the ice was in his eye,
"Overhaul, overhaul, let your davit tackles fall,
And lower your boats to the seas, brave boys,
    And lower your boats to the seas."

Now the boats got down and the men aboard,
And that whale was still in view,
Resolved, resolved was each whalerman bold,
To steer where that whalefish blew, brave boys,
    To steer where that whalefish blew.

Now the harpoon struck, and the line played out,
But she gave such a flourish with her tail,
That the boat capsized, and we lost four men,
And we never caught that whale, brave boys,
    We never caught that whale.

"To lose those men," the captain cried,
"It grieves my heart full sore,"
"But to lose a hundred barrel whale,
It grieves me ten times more, brave boys,
    It grieves me ten times more."

"Up anchor now," the captain said,
"For the winter star doth appear,
"And it's time to leave this cold cold place,
And for New England steer, brave boys,
    And for New England steer."

144

The Banks of Newfoundland

This magnificent foc's'le song and capstan shanty is a saga of the hardships of the North Atlantic passage, of its howling gales and storms that inflicted dreadful suffering upon immigrant and sailor alike. Irish sailors, like those mentioned in the song, served on both the British and the American packet ships that plied from Liverpool and were in stiff competition with each other for the transatlantic immigrant trade. "The Banks of Newfoundland," as might be expected, was popular on both British and American ships. It captures the spirit of the roaring winds blowing incessantly through the mountainous spray and the shrouds.

My bul - ly boys of Liv - er - pool, I'd have you to be - ware,_ When you sail on a Yan - kee pack - et ship, no_ dun - ga - ree jump - ers wear;_ But have a big mon - key jack - et_ al - ways at your_ com - mand,_ For there blows some cold nor'- west - ers on the_ Banks_of New - found - land._

We'll scrape her and we'll scrub her__ With ho - ly-stone and sand,_ And we'll think of the cold nor'- west - ers on the _ Banks_ of New-found - land._

2. We had Mike Lynch from Ballynahinch, Pat Murphy
      and some more;
   In the year of eighteen forty-four those seaboys
      suffered sore:
   They pawned their gear in Liverpool and sailed as they
      did stand,
   And there blows some cold nor'westers on the Banks
      of Newfoundland.
Chorus

3. We had on board an Irish girl, Bridget Reilly was her name,
   To her I'd promised marriage, on me she had a claim:
   She tore up her flannel petticoat to make mittens for
      my hands,
   Before she'd see her true love freeze on the Banks of
      Newfoundland.
Chorus

4. So now it's reef and reef me boys with the canvas frozen
      hard,
   And it's mount and pass every mother's son on a
      ninety foot topsail yard,
   Never mind about boots and oilskins, and haul or you'll
      be damned,
   For there blows some cold nor'westers on the Banks of
      Newfoundland.
Chorus

5. I dreamed a dream the other night, I dreamed that
      I was home,
   I dreamed that me and my true love, we was back in
      old Dublin town;
   That we were back on Erin's shore with a jug of ale in hand,
   But then I awoke and my heart was broke on the Banks of
      Newfoundland.
Chorus

6. And now we're off the Hook, me boys, ana the land's all
      white with snow,
   And soon we'll see the paytable and have all night below;
   And on the docks, come down in flocks, the pretty
      girls will stand,
   "It's snugger with me than it is at sea on the Banks of
      Newfoundland."
Chorus

The Praties They Grow Small

In 1846, in the greatest catastrophe of its long and tragic history, famine came to Eire. Ragged skeletons with staring eyes roamed the countryside, holding out skinny hands for a crust or a blessing. The people died, from exhaustion, starvation, and disease, on the roads, in the fields, and in their cabins. The British Government, which was ultimately responsible for the welfare of its Irish subjects, averted its gaze from this scene of incredible mass suffering with cold indifference.

Mr. Nicholas Cummins, an Irish magistrate, published the following eyewitness account of conditions at Skibbereen, in the County of Cork, in the *London Times* of December 24, 1846:

Being aware that I should have to witness scenes of frightful hunger, I provided myself with as much bread as five men could carry, and on reaching the spot I was surprised to find the wretched hamlet apparently deserted. I entered some of the hovels to ascertain the cause, and the scenes which presented themselves were such as no tongue or pen can convey the slightest idea of. In the first, six famished and ghastly skeletons, to all appearances dead, were huddled in a corner on some filthy straw, their sole covering what seemed a ragged horsecloth, their wretched legs hanging about, naked above the knees. I approached with horror, and found by a low moaning they were alive—they were in fever, four children, a woman, and what had once been a man.

It is impossible to go through the detail. Suffice it to say, that in a few minutes I was surrounded by at least two hundred such phantoms, such frightful spectres as no words can describe, either from famine or from fever. Their demoniac yells are still ringing in my ears, and their horrible images are fixed upon my brain.

In another case, decency would forbid what follows, but it must be told. . . . I found myself grasped by a woman with an infant just born in her arms and the remains of a filthy sack across her loins—the sole covering of herself and her baby. The same morning the police opened a house on the adjoining lands, which was observed shut for many days, and two frozen corpses were found, lying upon the mud floor, half devoured by rats.

In the years that followed, such scenes would become all too familiar in many parts of Eire.

"The Praties They Grow Small" arose out of sufferings such as these, in the years 1846–1848. Perhaps this song rivals as a lament "Lay This Body Down" (see p. 209 below) in its simplicity and power, its capacity to convey the terrible meaning of agony, oppression, and death in three short stanzas.

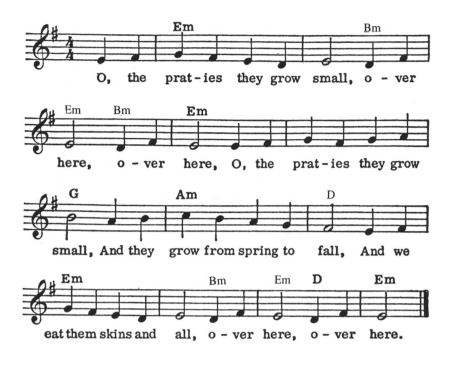

O, the prat-ies they grow small, o-ver here, o-ver here, O, the prat-ies they grow small, And they grow from spring to fall, And we eat them skins and all, o-ver here, o-ver here.

O, I wish that we were geese, night and morn, night and morn,
O, I wish that we were geese,
For they fly and take their ease,
And they live and die in peace, over here, over here.

O, we're trampled in the dust, over here, over here,
O, we're trampled in the dust,
But the Lord in whom we trust,
Will give us crumb for crust, over here, over here.

Across the Western Ocean

Between 1846 and 1850, one and one-half million Irish people emigrated to the New World. Most were the penniless victims of natural calamity and governmental indifference. Incredible though it may seem, their passage was, for the most part, paid by relatives already in America who saved the needed sum of money out of their own often pitiably low wages. In some cases, the money came from landlords who cynically calculated that it was cheaper to pay the passage and rid the county of paupers than to pay the poor-rate necessary for their support at home.

Many emigrants sailed from Irish ports, but most crossed to England and took ship from Liverpool. American ships were preferred, because they usually were faster than the British. Passage, too, was very cheap, both because shippers who had been delivering bulky goods in Europe preferred to return with people rather than ballast, and because of the British-American competition for the trade.

At best, the Atlantic crossing took six weeks and was a cruel and dangerous experience. At worst, the crossing was a hell on earth, an ordeal of famine, overcrowding, disease, and shipwreck. In those days, neither Washington nor London exercised the least control over conditions prevailing on immigrant boats. In 1847 alone, 17,000 Irish immigrants—one out of every five who embarked upon the transatlantic voyage—died at sea.

"Across the Western Ocean" is an immigrant song set to the tune of "Leave Her, Johnny, Leave Her" (see p. 135 above). Immigrants evidently learned the melody from the sailors.

Oh, the times are hard and the wages are low,
    Amelia, where you bound for?
The Rocky Mountains is my home,
    Across the Western Ocean.

Beware these packet ships I say,
    Amelia, where you bound for?
They'll steal your stores and clothes away,
    Across the Western Ocean.

There's Liverpool Pat with his tarpaulin hat,
    Amelia, where you bound for?
And Yankee John the packet rat,
    Across the Western Ocean.

Father and Mother, say good bye,
    Amelia, where you bound for?
Brother and sister, don't you cry,
    Across the Western Ocean.

The Farmer's Curst Wife
(The Devil and the Farmer)

Crossing the Atlantic on the packet ships was, at best, a weary business. Time hung heavy at sea, and in the cramped space between decks the young people sang and danced as best they might. "The Farmer's Curst Wife" was a favorite jig. Widely known throughout the British Isles in one form or another, this song was taken by British and Irish immigrants to all parts of the United States.

A farm-er was plough-ing his field one day, Rite-ful, rite-ful, tit-ty fie day, A farm-er was plough-ing his field_ one day When the dev-il came up, and to him he did say, With a rite-ful la, tit-ty fie day, Rite-ful, rite-ful, tit-ty fie day.

2. "See here my good man, I have come for your wife
    Riteful, riteful, titty fie day,
   See here my good man I have come for your wife,
   For she's the bane and torment of your life,"
    With a riteful la, etc.

3. So the Devil he hoisted her up on his hump,
    Riteful, riteful, titty fie day,
   So the Devil he hoisted her up his hump,
   And down to Hell with her he did jump,
    With a riteful la, etc.

4. When they got there the gates they were shut,
    Riteful, riteful, titty fie day,
   When they got there the gates they were shut,
   With a blow of her hand she laid open his nut,
    Riteful la, etc.

5. Two little devils were playing handball,
    Riteful, riteful, titty fie day,
   Two little devils were playing handball,
   "Take her back Daddy, she'll be the death of us all!"
    Riteful la, etc.

6. So the Devil he hoisted her up on his hump,
    Riteful, riteful, titty fie day,
   So the Devil he hoisted her up on his hump,
   And back to earth with her he did jump,
    With a riteful la, etc.

7. "See here my good man, I have come with your wife,"
    Riteful, riteful, titty fie day,
   "See here my good man, I have come with your wife,
   For she's the bane and torment of my life,"
    Riteful la, etc.

8. Now they say that the women are worse than the men,
    Riteful, riteful, titty fie day,
   They say that the women are worse than the men,
   They went down to Hell and got kicked out again,
    Riteful la, etc.

The Castle of Dromore
(Caislean Droim an Oir)

"The Castle of Dromore" is a lullaby which people of Irish descent still sing in New England. Traditionally, it is one of the most ancient of Irish songs, dating back to the early middle ages. In Eire, it is still sung in the native Gaelic, but during the nineteenth century, like so many other Gaelic songs, it was translated into English; in this form, it has found its way to England and to the United States.

hush - a - bye, lou lo lan. (Hum)

Bring no ill will to hinder us, my helpless babe and me,
Dread spirits of the black water, Clanowen's wild banshee;
And holy Mary pitying us, in Heaven for grace that is true,
Singing hushabye, lullabye, lou lo lan, sing hushabye lou lo lan.

Take time to thrive my ray of hope in the garden of Dromore,
Take heed young eaglet that thy wings are feathered fit to soar;
A little rest, and then the world is full of work to do,
Singing hushabye lullabye lou lo lan. sing hushabye lou lo lan.

* * *

Tá gaoth an geimread sgaolta fuair,
    Thar timpeall Droim an Óir,
Ach ins an halla taob istigh,
    Ta síochain ann go leor.
Ta gach sean-duilliúr, dul ar crith,
    Ach is óg an leanán thú,
Seinn lóitin is lú lá lú lá ló,
    Seinn lóitin is lú lá ló.

A Róis mo chroi a shlaitin óir
    As garra Droim an Óir,
Bi ag fás go mbeidh gach cleite beag
    Mar sgíatan iolrea mhór.
Is leim ansan ar fuaid an tsaol,
    Oibrig is saothraig clú,
Seinn lóitin is lú lá lú lá ló,
    Seinn lóitin is lú lá ló.

The Pesky Sarpent

From the end of the War of 1812 to the early fifties, Irish immigrants were streaming into New England to build railroads, dig canals, and man cotton factories. The traditional New England farmer of Yankee stock was on the way out, abandoning his native soil and seeking more fertile land in New York State and points west.

The changing times, the transition of New England from rural to industrial economy, are clearly reflected in the evolution of "Springfield Mountain." We first encountered this song (p. 44 above) as a funeral elegy for a young farmer of Protestant, Anglo-Saxon origin. But in the Jacksonian period, Protestants were being replaced by Catholics, Anglo-Saxons by Gaels, farmers by workers. To these newly arrived Americans, the traditional New Englander was a strange phenomenon. Caricatures, on the Boston stage, of the sanctimonious, high-pitched Yankee hayseeds were sure to evoke hilarious laughter.

Accordingly, "Springfield Mountain" was material made to order for stage comedians seeking to entertain Irish Catholic audiences. The old elegy was cleverly reworked and made its appearance on the Boston music-hall stage in the 1830's under the title "The Pesky Sarpent." The date of its first publication as sheet music was 1840. In one or another version, the story of Timothy Myrick spread across the country and became one of America's most popular songs.

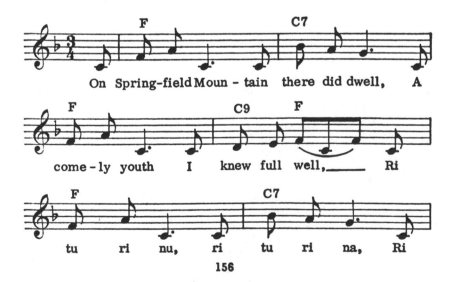

On Spring-field Moun - tain there did dwell, A
come - ly youth I knew full well,____ Ri
tu ri nu, ri tu ri na, Ri

156

tu ri nu, ri tu ri na.

2. One Monday morning he did go,
   Down in the meadow for to mow,
       Ri tu ri nu, etc.

3. He scarce had mowed half round the field,
   When a pesky sarpent bit his heel,
       Ri tu ri nu, etc.

4. He took his scythe and with a blow,
   He laid the pesky sarpent low,
       Ri tu ri nu, etc.

5. He took the sarpent in his hand,
   And straitway went to Molly Bland.
       Ri tu ri nu, etc.

6. "Oh, Molly, Molly here you see
   The pesky sarpent what bit me."
       Ri tu ri nu, etc.

7. Now Molly had a ruby lip,
   With which the pizen she did sip.
       Ri tu ri nu, etc.

8. But Molly had a rotten tooth,
   Which the pizen struck and killed 'em both.
       Ri tu ri nu, etc.

9. The neighbours found that they were dead,
   So laid them both upon one bed.
       Ri tu ri nu, etc.

10. And all their friends both far and near,
    Did cry and howl they were so dear.
        Ri tu ri nu, etc.

11. Now all you maids a warning take
    From Molly Bland and Tommy Blake.
        Ri tu ri nu, etc.

12. And mind when you're in love, don't pass,
    Too near to patches of high grass.
        Ri tu ri nu, etc.

The Westward Movement

In the period between the War of 1812 and the outbreak of the Civil War, westward advance proceeded with impressive speed. Settlers poured through the mountain gaps into the mighty central valley lying between the Appalachians and the Rockies, carried white civilization beyond the Mississippi into Texas, Kansas, Missouri and Iowa, and moved through the last huge barrier of western mountain and desert to found new states in California and Oregon.

In the Jacksonian age, frontiering was a complex and many-sided activity. Far ahead of the main advance ranged the hunter, the lumberman, and the miner, for the first valuable products of the wilderness were furs, timber, and precious metals. Such men were professional pioneers; some were rude farmers, while others were prospectors or land surveyors. They blazed the trails and cleared a path for the advance of the main army of settlers, the mass of small farmers who came west to raise crops, build communities, and found states. These were drawn from the South, the East, and the far corners of Europe not mainly by the lust for gold or quick wealth, but by the most powerful magnet of all, virgin land.

What kind of songs did these pioneers—hunters, lumbermen, and farmfolk—sing? They sang everything which Americans had created or inherited: lullabies, colonial and revolutionary songs, ancient European ballads, sea songs, psalms, and spirituals. This fact is well illustrated in the manuscript song books in which the pioneers painfully copied down for themselves and their children the songs which they treasured. All of our American songs were frontier songs simply because Americans sang them on the frontier.

But the frontier was not only a place where people sang. Frontiering was also an occupation which produced songs that expressed specific aspects of pioneer life and experience. During the Jacksonian period, the frontier produced its own special and unique songs telling of lumbering, hunting, Indian fighting, overlanding, and the gold rush. The body of songs produced by such experiences in this period was very rich: in this section, we shall try to suggest through a small sampling something of its beauty and profundity.

Over the course of time, an idealized image of the frontier has become embodied in literature and raised to the status of a folk myth that exercises a continuing and extraordinary

159

influence. The frontier as embodied in myth is a rich and complex bundle of associations. It represents the simple, unaffected life compared to the complexity and sophistication of civilization, closeness to the serenity of nature—trees, rivers, earth, and stars—compared to the raucous urban community from which the wilderness has been forever banished. The frontier is free in the narrow sense from the endless petty restraints of modern life, and free in the broadest spiritual sense conceivable; for we like to think that this country was settled by free men, and not a few of these were small farmers fleeing westward from the blight of slavery as it advanced through the rich river bottoms of the South. The frontier, we have been taught, is American national identity itself. American experience, for close to three hundred years, has been synonymous with the on-going process of Western movement, with the never-ending struggle to clear, tame, and settle the continent Americans have come to believe that pioneering—with its symbols of ax, cap, cabin, and gun—constituted a uniquely American way of life. This way of life has vanished, but we cling tenaciously to its symbols.

In short, the frontier as crystallized in myth gives form to an American dream of freedom, equality, and happiness that has been sought through all our past and yet remains to be realized. The songs of the frontier do not neglect this dream, but they also emphasize another aspect of frontier life. They tell us that frontiering was a harsh, dangerous, and cruel existence; that its unrelieved toil robbed women of youth, beauty, and even sanity; that it was a brutal battle with the elements, with Indians, with sickness, and with disease; and that it was a moral catastrophe which enslaved men to false and wicked appetites and lured them to their destruction. In song, the settlement of the wilderness appears to be not only a story of epic dimension, but also an American tragedy. There is a deeply human message in this music, for it emphasizes the immense cost involved in clearing the continent and the senseless wastage of a frenzied, hectic, competitive race for wealth.

The Wisconsin Emigrant

After the War of 1812, the face of New England changed as industrialization advanced. Pioneering fever gripped the boldest and most adventurous; they loaded the wagons, hitched up the oxen, and started West toward New York state and the Northwestern Territory.

Both those who stayed and those who left faced and made a serious decision. In the West lay the promise of virgin fields and rich harvests; toils and hazards still unknown would have to be undergone before the dream of prosperity became a fact. At home, in New England, the soil was undeniably poor and stony, daily labor was hard, and a man's bread was earned by the sweat of his brow; but there was also security. Generations had toiled to make New England productive and beautiful; children grew up in settled surroundings, amid the beloved sights and sounds of home.

"The Wisconsin Emigrant" was collected in Vermont and Massachusetts in the early 1930's by Helen Hartness Flanders; the source for the lyric was A. L. Stewart of West Springfield, Massachusetts, a man then in his nineties who had learned the song in the years before the Civil War. "The Wisconsin Emigrant" is delightful for the frankness and clarity with which it expresses the alternatives between which the New England pioneer of that day was torn.

"Since times are so hard,— I've thought, my true heart, Of— leav - ing my ox - en, my plough, and my cart, And a - way to Wis - con - sin, a jour - ney we'd

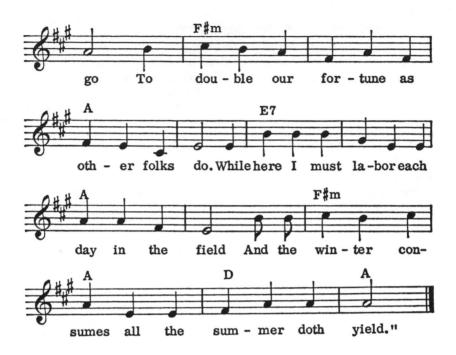

go To dou - ble our for - tune as

oth - er folks do. While here I must la - bor each

day in the field And the win - ter con-

sumes all the sum - mer doth yield."

2. "Oh husband I've noticed with sorrowful heart
    You've neglected your oxen, your plough, and your cart.
    Your sheep are disordered; at random they run,
    And your new Sunday suit is now every day on.
    Oh, stay on the farm and you'll suffer no loss,
    For the stone that keeps rolling will gather no moss." } *bis*

3. "Oh wife, let's go. Oh, don't let us wait.
    Oh, I long to be there. Oh, I long to be great!
    While you some rich lady—and who knows but I
    Some governor may be before that I die?
    While here I must labor each day in the field,
    And the winter consumes all the summer doth yield." } *bis*

4. "Oh husband, remember that land is to clear,
   Which will cost you the labor of many a year,
   Where horses, sheep, cattle, and hogs are to buy—
   And you'll scarcely get settled before you must die.
   Oh, stay on your farm and you'll suffer no loss, ⎫ *bis*
   For the stone that keeps rolling will gather no moss."⎭

5. "Oh wife, let's go. Oh, don't let us stay.
   I will buy me a farm that is cleared by the way,
   Where horses, sheep, cattle, and hogs are not dear,
   And we'll feast on fat buffalo half of the year.
   While here I must labor each day in the field, ⎫ *bis*
   And the winter consumes all the summer doth yield."⎭

6. "Oh husband, remember, that land of delight
   Is surrounded by Indians who murder by night.
   Your house they will plunder and burn to the ground,
   While your wife and your children lie murdered around.
   Oh, stay on the farm, and you'll suffer no loss, ⎫ *bis*
   For the stone that keeps rolling will gather no moss."⎭

7. "Now, wife, you've convinced me. I'll argue no more.
   I never had thought of your dying before;
   I love my dear children, although they are small,—
   But you, my dear wife, are more precious than all.
   We'll stay on the farm, and suffer no loss ⎫ *bis*
   For the stone that keeps rolling will gather no moss."⎭

Hush, Little Baby

"Hush, Little Baby" is one of the most widely loved, and widely used, American lullabies. Generations of children have been lulled to sleep with it. The version given here was collected by the late John A. Lomax in Alabama.

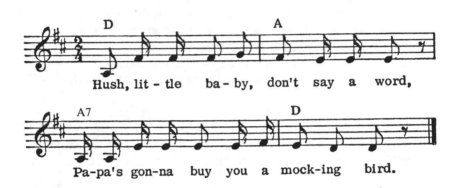

Hush, lit - tle ba - by, don't say a word,

Pa-pa's gon-na buy you a mock-ing bird.

If that mocking bird won't sing,
Papa's gonna buy you a diamond ring.

If that diamond ring turns brass,
Papa's gonna buy you a looking glass.

If that looking glass gets broke,
Papa's gonna buy you a billy goat.

If that billy goat won't pull,
Papa's gonna buy you a cart and bull.

If that cart and bull turn over,
Papa's gonna buy you a dog named Rover.

If that dog named Rover won't bark,
Papa's gonna buy you a horse and cart.

If that horse and cart fall down,
You'll still be the sweetest little baby in town.

Hush little baby don't say a word,
Papa's gonna buy you a mocking bird.

Let's Go α-Huntin'

This song is as old as the country and followed the frontier all the way to Texas, wherever little boys went out in the woods to hunt. The charming melody of the version given here was recorded by John A. Lomax in Fort Spunky, Texas. The lyric is substantially as it is sung by Bill Bonyun, the New England folksinger. Bill has sung this song to literally thousands of elementary school children in the past decade and tells me that it ranks as "one of the all-time children's favorites." The English "Cutty Wren," from which "Let's Go a-Huntin'" is derived, is a peasant song of elaborate symbolism dating back to a period several hundred years before the founding of the American colonies. Thus, in one form or another, this song has been in continuous oral tradition for the better part of seven centuries and is one of the very oldest in our heritage.

Let's go a - hunt - in', said Risk - y Rob,

Let's go a - hunt - in', said Rob-in to Bob,

Let's go a - hunt- in', said Dan' - l to Jo,

Let's go a - hunt- in', said Bil - ly Bar - low.

2. What shall we hunt for? said Risky Rob,
   What shall we hunt for? said Robin to Bob,
   What shall we hunt for? said Dan'l to Jo,
      Let's hunt for a rat, said Billy Barlow.

3. How shall we kill him? said Risky Rob,
   How shall we kill him? said Robin to Bob,
   How shall we kill him? said Dan'l to Jo,
      Borrow a gun, said Billy Barlow.

4. How shall we haul him? said Risky Rob,
   How shall we haul him? said Robin to Bob,
   How shall we haul him? said Dan'l to Jo,
      Borrow a cart, said Billy Barlow.

5. How shall we divide him? said Risky Rob,
   How shall we divide him? said Robin to Bob,
   How shall we divide him? said Dan'l to Jo,
      Borrow a knife, said Billy Barlow.

6. How shall we cook him? said Risky Rob,
   How shall we cook him? said Robin to Bob,
   How shall we cook him? said Dan'l to Jo,
      Over a fire, said Billy Barlow.

7. I'll roast shoulder, said Risky Rob,
   I'll boil legs, said Robin to Bob,
   I'll bake back, said Dan'l to Jo,
      Tail bone raw, said Billy Barlow.

8. I feel sick, said Risky Rob,
   I gotta bellyache, said Robin to Bob,
   OOOOOOps!! said Dan'l to Jo,
      I feel fine, said Billy Barlow.

"Billy Barlow" ("Let's Go a' Huntin'"). Collected, adapted and arranged by John A. Lomax and Alan Lomax. TRO - © Copyright 1941 and renewed 1969 by Ludlow Music, Inc., New York, N.Y. Used by permission.

Skip to My Lou

This was one of the most popular play-party songs in days gone by, and was known throughout the country. To this day, children still skip to it in the streets and playgrounds. Such songs had a special use in frontier communities where revivalist influences were strong. In such communities, says one authority:

> . . . they got around the churches' opposition to square and round dancing by holding play parties, in which they took over the singing games of children, with their skipping, dancing, and marching movements. In these, boys and girls swung one another by the hand and not by the waist, which was forbidden. And thus, since the fiddle was considered the devil's instrument and other musical instruments were scarce, they got along without musicians and callers, giving their own directions for the dance movements by means of the words of the song.*

In "Skip to My Lou," all couples join hands, skip left or right singing the chorus; a lone boy in the center of the ring sings "Lost my partner, what'll I do?" as the group circles, then picks a girl and takes her hand; her first partner goes to the center of the ring as the group sings the chorus, etc.

Lost my part - ner, what-'ll I do?

Lost my part - ner, what-'ll I do?

Lost my part - ner, what-'ll I do?

*Russell Ames, *The Story of American Folk Song* (New York: Grosset & Dunlap, 1955), 65-66.

167

Skip to my Lou, my dar - ling.

CHORUS

Lou, Lou, skip to my Lou, Lou, Lou,

skip to my Lou, Lou, Lou, skip to my Lou,

Skip to my Lou, my dar - ling.

2. I'll get another one prettier than you (three times)
   Skip to my lou, my darling.
Chorus

3. Little red wagon, painted blue (three times)
   Skip to my lou, my darling.
Chorus

4. Fly in the sugar-bowl, shoo shoo shoo (three times)
   Skip to my lou, my darling.
Chorus

5. Cows in the cornfield, two by two (three times)
   Skip to my lou, my darling.
Chorus

6. Skip, skip, skip to my lou (three times)
   Skip to my lou, my darling.
Chorus

7. Skip a little faster, that won't do (three times)
   Skip to my lou, my darling.
Chorus

When I Was Single

Romance vanished early among pioneer couples. For the woman, it gave way to scouring, cooking, making and mending clothes, caring for children, fetching water, washing dishes, building fires, and tending livestock. It was a life of much toil and little joy that soon robbed a girl of her charms and speeded the process of disillusionment between husband and wife.

Both of the songs reproduced here have been very widely collected. "The Single Girl" has been reported primarily from the South, and is interesting as an early form of the blues. The melody is pentatonic (sung on five notes of the scale) and harmonized with a major chord and the relative minor.

When I Was Single

I married me a wife, O then,
I married me a wife, O then,
I married me a wife, she's the plague of my life,
And I wish I was single again.
Chorus

My wife she died, and O then,
My wife she died, and O then,
My wife she died, and I laughed till I cried,
To think I was single again.
Chorus

I married me another, O then,
I married me another, O then,
I married me another, she's the devil's grandmother,
And I wish I was single again.
Chorus

Now gather round you young men,
Now gather round you young men,
Be kind to the first, for the next will be worse,
And you'll wish you was single again.
Chorus

The Single Girl

When I was sin-gle, dressed up so fine,

Now I am mar-ried, go rag-ged all the time,

Lord, I wish I was a sin-gle girl a - gain.

When I was single, my shoes they did screek,
Now I am married, Lord, all they do is leak,
Oh Lord, don't I wish I was a single girl again.

Three little babies, crying for bread,
Nothing to give them, I'd rather be dead,
Lord, I wish I was a single girl again.

Dishes to wash, and spring to go to,
When you get married, girls, you got it all to do
Lord I wish I was a single girl again.

When I was single, I lived at my ease,
Now I am married, have a drunkard to please
Lord, I wish I was a single girl again!

The Lumberman's Alphabet
The Jam on Gerry's Rock

From early colonial days until the end of the nineteenth century, one of the most necessary and most dangerous of frontier occupations was the felling of huge stands of timber in the forests that covered much of America. Wood, in those days, was a raw material even more indispensable than it is now; from it were made homes, furniture, ships, weapons, and tools. Loggers, the professional timbermen, were pioneers among the pioneers. They ranged ahead, at the very outskirts of civilization, to clear the forests and provide abundant logs for the saw mills down river to convert into boards and beams.

The loggers lived in forest camps and worked in gangs. Their home all winter was a rude cabin chinked with moss, and their food was cooked on an open fire. All day they would work in freezing temperatures, felling and topping the pine, and hauling the logs with sled and ox to the river landings. And on the seventh day, if all went well, the time was theirs to patch their clothes, sleep, play cards and drink, or sing. When the thaw set in, in the spring, the loggers brought their rolling, twisting cargo down river to the mills, riding the logs with steel-shod boots, steering them and heading off jams with a peavey—perhaps the most dangerous work that a man might ever do.

The logger's first frontier was New England, New York, and Pennsylvania; from there it leaped to the Lake States, where the huge stands of pine in Wisconsin, Michigan, and Minnesota provided all the lumber the East needed until the end of the nineteenth century, and brought fame to Albany, New York, as the world's greatest lumber market.

We give here two of the best loved of the many lumbermen's songs, both of which have been sung by pioneers clear across the continent. "The Lumberman's Alphabet" is reproduced with a melody transcribed from the singing of Gus Schaffer at Greenland, Michigan in 1938, and recorded by Alan Lomax for the Library of Congress. It probably derives from earlier "Sailor's Alphabet" songs and is to this day an instant favorite with children.

"The Jam on Gerry's Rock" ranks among the most widely sung and deeply felt native American ballads. From a specific accident occurring in the woods—precisely when and where we do not know—it fashions a commentary of universal application on the lumberman's calling. Not only was this song

172

sung in every logging camp in the country, but after the Civil War it migrated to the High Plains to be warbled by cowboys riding the prairie with never a tree in sight. The lyric reproduced here is a composite of many versions; the first melody given, one of the most attractive of many to which the song has been set, is transcribed from the singing of Bill McBride as recorded by Alan Lomax at Mount Pleasant, Michigan; the second melody comes from George Edwards, as collected by Norman Cazden in the Catskills. It is a variant of the Irish "Bonny Boy" (see page 18 above); many of the best singers among the lumbermen were Irish.

The Lumberman's Alphabet

A is for axe and that we all know,

B is for boy who can use it al - so,

C is for chop-ping we first do be - gin,

D is for dan - ger we of - ten fall in.

CHORUS

Then so mer-ry, so mer-ry, so

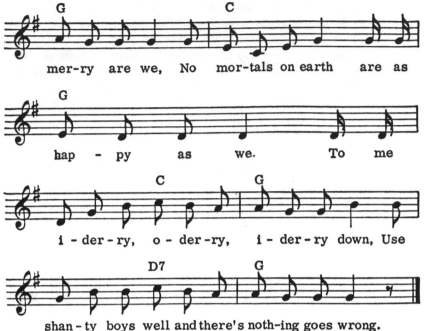

mer-ry are we, No mor-tals on earth are as

hap - py as we. To me

i - der - ry, o - der -ry, i - der - ry down, Use

shan - ty boys well and there's noth-ing goes wrong.

E is for echo that through the woods rang,
And F is for foreman the head of our gang,
G is for grindstone at night we do turn,
And H is for handle that's so smoothly worn.
Chorus

I is for iron with which we mark pine,
And J is for jolly boys, all in a line,
K is for keen edge that on our axes we keep,
And L is for lice that keep us from sleep.
Chorus

M is for moss that chinks up our camp,
And N is for needle for mending our pants,
O is for owl a-hooting by night,
And P is for pine that we always fall right.
Chorus

Q is for quickness we put ourselves to,
And R is for river we haul our logs to,
S is for sled that we haul our logs on,
And T is for team that pulls them along.
Chorus

U is for uses we set ourselves to,
And V is for valley we haul our logs through,
W is for woods that we leave in the spring,
And now I have sung all that I'm going to sing.
Chorus

The Jam on Gerry's Rock

(1)

Come all of you bold shan - ty boys__ and list while I re - late The__ tale of one__ young shan - ty boy__ and his un - time - ly fate; The__ tale of one__ young riv - er man,__ so man - ly, true and brave, 'Twas

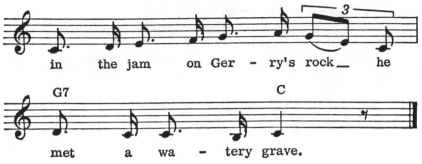

in the jam on Ger - ry's rock ___ he met a wa - tery grave.

(2)

Come, all you jol-ly riv-er lads I'll ___ have you to draw near, And lis-ten un-to the dan-ger which you are going to hear It's of six jol-ly Ca - na - dian boys who in vol-un-teer did go For to break the jam on Ger-ry's rock with their fore-man young Mon-roe.

2. It was on a Sunday morning, in the springtime of the year,
   The logs were piling mountain high; we could not keep
      them clear.
   "Turn out, turn out," our foreman cried, "no reason
      at all to fear,
   We'll break the jam on Gerry's Rock and for Saginaw
      we'll steer."

3. Now some of them were willing, and some of them
      were not;
   To work on jams on Sunday they did not think they
      ought—
   But six of our Canadian boys did volunteer to go
   To break the jam on Gerry's Rock with their foreman,
      young Monroe.

4. They had not rolled off many logs, when the foreman
      he did say,
   "I'll have you boys be on your guard, for the jam will
      soon give way."
   These words were scarcely spoken, when the jam
      did break and go
   And with it went those six brave youths with their
      foreman, young Monroe.

5. Now when the rest of the shanty-boys the sad news came
      to hear,
   In search of their lost comrades to the riverside did steer;
   Six of the mangled bodies a-floating down did go,
   While crushed and bleeding near the bank was that of
      young Monroe.

6. We dragged him from his drowning place, brushed back
      his raven hair
   There was one girl among them, whose sad cries rent
      the air,
   There was one girl among them, a maid from
      Saginaw town,
   Whose moans and cries now rent the skies for her lover
      who was drowned.

7. Miss Clara was a noble girl, the riverman's true friend,
Who with her widowed mother, lived near the river's bend,
The wages of her own true love the boss to her did pay,
And the shanty-boys for her made up a generous purse
    next day.

8. They buried him with sorrow deep, 'twas on the first
    of May—
Come all of you bold shanty-boys, and for your comrades
    pray,
Engraved upon a hemlock tree, that by the grave did grow,
Was the day and the date of the drowning of the
    shanty-boy Monroe.

"The Lumberman's Alphabet" is transcribed by permission from Record AFS L56 in
the Archive of Folk Song, Library of Congress. "The Jam on Gerry's Rock" (1) is
from the same source. "The Jam at Gerry's Rock" ("The Jam on Gerry's Rock" [2]) is
collected, edited and arranged by Norman Cazden. TRO - © Copyright 1958 World-
wide Music Services, Inc., New York, N.Y. Used by permission.

Sioux Indians

The vast stretch of land lying between Canada and the Rio Grande, between the Rockies and the hundredth meridian of longitude, was known before the Civil War as the Great Prairie Wilderness. Grass-covered, arid, and largely treeless, it was inhabited at that time only by nomadic Indians—Sioux, Dakota, Blackfoot, Cheyenne, Arapahoe—and by the buffalo herds which provided their existence. Beyond this sea of grass, to the west, lay the wall of the Rockies; and beyond them, again, huge expanses of desert intervened between the mountains and the Pacific.

The Westward Movement, faced with this formidable barrier to settlement, simply skipped over it. The path to the far West, opened up by the explorations of fur traders, led from Missouri up the Platte River, through South Pass, and down the Snake to the Columbia. It became famous as the Oregon Trail. The magnet that lured immigrants was first the lush, wooded slopes of the Pacific Northwest, and then the prospect of gold in California. During the forties and fifties, settlement of the Far West went rapidly forward in response to both these stimuli.

Emigrant parties assembled at St. Louis or Independence, were provisioned, and moved out along the trail on their 2000-mile journey. Unimaginable hardships attended the travelers. Day after day the sun beat down from a cloudless sky; storms of hail and sleet swept down from the hills. When streams had to be forded, animals were swept away, or wagons sank axle-deep in mud and had to be dragged out by teams of oxen and sweating men. With neither doctor nor remedy at hand, sickness took a heavy toll of children's lives. Indian bands prowled around the caravans and sometimes attacked, decimating the number of pioneers, plundering their possessions, and stampeding their cattle.

"Sioux Indians" is one of the memorable ballads that tell of this frontier ordeal. The version given here is transcribed from the singing of a cowboy as recorded by John A. Lomax for the Library of Congress. The melody is pentatonic, harmonized with minor chord and relative major.

I'll sing you a song though it may be a sad one, ___ Of tri - als and trou-bles, and where first be- gun ___ I left my dear fam - ily, my friends and my home, A - cross the wide des- erts and moun-tains to roam. ___

2. I crossed the Missouri and joined a large train,
   Which bore us o'er mountains and valleys and plains;
   And often at evening out hunting we'd go
   To shoot the fleet antelope and wild buffalo.

3. We heard of Sioux Indians all out on the plain,
   A-killing poor drivers and burning their train,
   A-killing poor drivers with arrow and bow,
   When captured by Indians no mercy they'd show.

4. We travelled three weeks til we came to the Platte,
   We pitched out our tents at the head of the flat,
   We spread out our blankets on the green grassy ground,
   While our horses and oxen were grazing all round.

5. While taking refreshments we heard a loud yell,
   The whoop of Sioux Indians coming out of the dell;
   We sprang to our rifles with a flash in each eye,
   "Boys," says our brave leader, "we'll fight til we die."

6. They made a bold dash and came near to our train,
   The arrows fall round us like hail and like rain,
   But with our long rifles we fed them cold lead,
   Till many a brave warrior around us lay dead.

7. We shot their bold chief at the head of the band,
   He died like a warrior with a gun in his hand;
   When they saw their bold chief laying dead in his gore,
   They whooped and they yelled and we saw them no more.

8. We hitched up our horses and started our train,
   Three more bloody battles this trip on the plain;
   And in our last battle three of our brave boys fell,
   And we left them to rest in a green shady dell.

9. We travelled by days, guarded camp during night,
   Till Oregon's mountains looked high in their might;
   Now at Pocahontas beside a clear stream
   Our journey is ended in the land of our dream.

From Record AAFS L49 in the Archive of Folk Song, Library of Congress.

The Fools of Forty-Nine
Santy Anno
The Dying Californian

Westward expansion was climaxed in the Jacksonian era by the war of 1846–1848, which wrested millions of acres from Mexican possession and brought the rich lands of California into the Union. The value of this act of conquest became immediately apparent when gold was discovered at Sutter's Mill in January, 1848. This was four months after Santa Anna's surrender at Mexico City and a few days before the treaty of peace was signed at Guadeloupe Hidalgo, which formally ceded California to the United States.

Among thousands of people, the discovery of gold sparked a mania for quick and easy wealth, and touched off a wild race for the Far West—overland along the Oregon and California trails, through the fever-ridden swamps of Panama, by boat around Cape Horn. En route, many fell victim to starvation, disease, exhaustion, accident, or shipwreck, and thousands more who reached their destination never found the wealth of their dreams. But so great was the influx of gold-diggers that California was soon ready for statehood. In January, 1848, this Mexican province boasted scarcely 30,000 inhabitants, of whom two-thirds were Mexican or Indian. Two years later, the population had risen to 200,000, and a state constitution had been adopted.

The following is an impressive picture of the passion for gold among the prospectors in the valley of the Sacramento in 1849:

Some, with long-handled shovels, delved among clumps of bushes, or by the side of large rocks, never raising their eyes for an instant; others, with pick and shovel, worked among stone and gravel, or with trowels searched under banks and roots of trees, where, if rewarded with small lumps of gold, the eye shone brighter for an instant, when the search was immediately and more ardently resumed. At the edge of the stream, or knee-deep and waist-deep in water, as cold as melted ice and snow could make it, some were washing gold with tin-pans, or the common cradle-rocker, while the rays of the sun were pouring down on their heads with an intensity exceeding anything we ever experienced at home, though it was but in the middle of April.

The thirst for gold, and the labor of acquisition, overruled all else, and totally absorbed every faculty. Complete silence reigned among the miners; they addressed not a word to each other, and seemed averse to all conversation. All the sympathies of our common humanity, all the finer and nobler attributes of our nature seemed lost, buried beneath the soil they were eagerly delving, or swept away with the rushing waters that revealed the shining treasure.*

The Gold Rush produced many songs; we select for reproduction here three that embody most brilliantly its reckless passions, and comment upon them. "The Fools of Forty-Nine" is a ballad telling of the race across the continent on land and water passages that merely led to death. Appearing in *Put's Original California Songster,* it might be characterized as a magnificent and native American commentary upon Macbeth's great theme:

> And all our yesterdays have lighted fools
> The road to dusty death.

—with the added implication of the chorus that the only wealth men ought to seek is in the salvation of their eternal souls.

The route around Cape Horn was the longest way to California, but it was the wisest. It is celebrated in the beautiful "Santy Anno," which originated among British sailors as a pump shanty. The American version reproduced here gloats over the United States victory over General Santa Anna "on the plains of Mexico"—a victory that laid California open to the Yankees and brought gold within their grasp. As given here, "Santy Anno" is both a shanty and a Gold Rush song. Some of the sailors who sang it were making their last voyage before the mast and would go looking for gold when they reached California.

"The Dying Californian" is a product both of our general ballad tradition and of the revivalist movement that reached its climax in the Jacksonian era. The lyric, based on a letter telling of a New Englander's death at sea while on the way to California, first appeared in the *New England Diadem* in December, 1854. The exquisite melody which we give here was one of several to which the poem was later set. It is taken from the University of Virginia Collection of Folk Music, and was originally printed by George Pullen Jackson in 1940 as No. 36 in his collection of *Down-East Spirituals and Others.* The result may stand as an example of American religious balladry at its best.

*Henry Howe, *Historical Collections of the Great West* (N. Y., 1857), 386.

The Fools of Forty-Nine

When gold was found in . for - ty-eight, the peo-ple said 'twas gas, And some were fools e - nough to think the lumps were on - ly brass, But they soon were sat - is - fied and start - ed off_ to mine, They bought a ship came round the Horn in the fall of for - ty - nine.

CHORUS

Then they thought of what they had been told, When they start - ed aft - er gold, That they

nev-er in this world would make a pile.

2. The poor, the old, the rotten scows were advertised to sail,
   To New Orleans with passengers, but they must come and bail,
   The ships were crowded more than full, but some hung on behind,
   And others dived off from the wharf and swam till they were blind.
Chorus

3. With rusty pork and stinking beef and rotten wormy bread
   With captains too that never were as high as the main-mast head,
   The steerage passengers would rave and swear they'd paid their passage
   They wanted something more to eat besides the lowly sausage.
Chorus

4. And they begun to cross the plains with oxen, holler and haul,
   And steamers they began to run as far as Panama,
   And there for months the people stayed that started after gold,
   And some returned disgusted with the lies they had been told.
Chorus

5. The people died on every route, they sickened and died like sheep,
   And those at sea before they were dead were launched into the deep,
   And those that died crossing the Plains fared not as well as that,
   For a hole was dug and they was dumped along the terrible Platte.
Chorus

Santy Anno

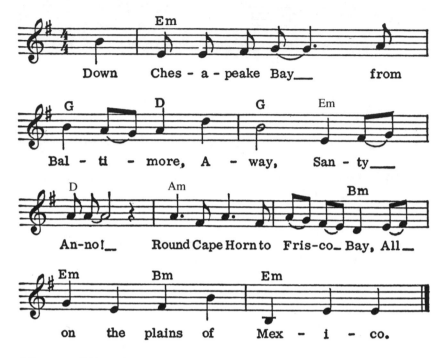

Down Ches - a - peake Bay __ from Bal - ti - more, A - way, San - ty __ An-no! __ Round Cape Horn to Fris-co __ Bay, All __ on the plains of Mex - i - co.

Chorus   Then heave her up and away we'll go
           Away, Santy Anno!
        Heave her up, and away we'll go,
          All on the Plains of Mexico.

2. She's a fast clipper ship with a bully crew,
         Away, Santy Anno!
   A down-east Yankee for a captain too
        All on the Plains of Mexico.
Chorus

3. There's plenty of gold so I've been told
         Away, Santy Anno!
   There's plenty of gold so I've been told
        All on the Plains of Mexico.
Chorus

4. Back in the days of Forty-nine,
         Away, Santy Anno!
   Those were the days of the good old times,
        All on the Plains of Mexico.

Chorus

5. When Zach Taylor gained the day,
      Away, Santy Anno!
He made poor Santy run away,
      All on the Plains of Mexico.

Chorus

6. Santy Anno was a good old man
      Away, Santy Anno!
Till he went to war with Uncle Sam
      All on the Plains of Mexico.

Chorus

7. When I leave this ship I'll settle down
      Away, Santy Anno!
Marry a girl named Sally Brown
      All on the Plains of Mexico.

Chorus

The Dying Californian

Lay up near - er, broth - er,— near - er, For my limbs are grow - ing cold, And thy pres - ence seem -eth near - er When thine arms a - round me

fold. I am dy - ing, broth - er, dy - ing, Soon you'll miss me in__ your berth; For my form will soon be__ ly - ing Be-neath the o - cean's brin-y__ surf.

Tell my father when you see him
 That in death I prayed for him,
Prayed that I might only meet him
 In a world that's free from sin.
Tell my mother, God assist her
 Now that she is growing old,
That her child would glad have kissed her
 When his lips grew pale and cold.

Listen, brother, catch each whisper
 'Tis my wife I speak of now,
Tell, oh tell her how I missed her
 When the fever burned my brow.
Tell her she must kiss my children
 Like the kiss I last impressed,
Hold them as when last I held them
 Held them closely to my breast.

It was for them I crossed the ocean,
    What my hopes were I'll not tell;
But they gained an orphan's portion,
    Yet He doeth all things well;
Tell them I have reached the haven
    Where I sought the precious dust,
But I gained a port called Heaven
    Where the gold will never rust.

Slavery Days

The majority of America's white European immigrants have always been the landless, the hungry, and the poor. That they accepted servitude, as many did in colonial days, was a temporary expedient to cross the wide Atlantic and to get a start in the New World. But black men were brought here by force from Africa, deliberately. They were sold into perpetual bondage that their labor might be used to develop the continent; that they might toil and die so that others might prosper.

To the first white settlers, America seemed a paradise, a land of boundless plenty where the skies were darkened by flocks of birds, where the rivers brimmed with fish, and the fertile earth was veined with precious ores. But, rich though it may have been in natural resources, this land was poor in people. The scattered bands of red men fought the whites, fled, or died; the boundless forests of oak and beech and elm lay silent and deserted. To white men, this absence of labor presented a problem. Some of them sought fortunes from the production and export of commercial crops—rice, sugar, tobacco, wheat, and rum; these fortunes might not be made unless there was ample labor available to clear the trees, plant the land, cultivate the crops, and harvest them.

Not to be denied in their quest for wealth, these whites turned for toilers to the unexplored continent of Africa. Thus, the slave trade arose and endured for nearly four centuries. In this time Christian civilization robbed Africa of perhaps fifty million human beings.

In the seventeenth century, slavery was introduced into all the mainland colonies, but it did not prove very profitable in the North. In the South, it spread like a blight, and a powerful and wealthy class of slaveholders arose. After the Revolution, the Southern United States became the principal source of supply of cotton to feed British, French, Belgian, and American textile factories. Slavery now moved westward by leaps and bounds, always to fresh and virgin lands, to Tennessee, Alabama, Mississippi, Arkansas, Missouri, and Texas.

From the tragic experience of the Negro people under slavery there came a music that enriched American culture immeasurably and was of world significance. Appropriating whatever materials were available—in the Bible, white spirituals, hymns, and secular songs—the genius of an enslaved people fused these with elements of its own African tradi-

190

tion to create an incomparably profound and original expression of the predicament of American man, of man enslaved.

During slavery days, the Negro people created a vast repertoire of song. Much of their secular music, in the form then played and sung, has been lost to us; the majority of the songs that have survived are spirituals. But these spirituals meant far more to the slave than the name implies; that is, devotional songs for church or other solemn occasions. Spirituals were put to the most varied uses: as laments, work songs in the fields and mills, rowing or hauling songs, war songs, lullabies, the special form of sacred dance known as the "shout," and funeral dirges. Spirituals were sung with endless variations of style and tempo, depending on the occasion. As sung by the slaves the spiritual evidently had little in common with the stylized and conventionally harmonized versions that have graced the church services and concert halls of a later age.

The development of the spiritual was linked to one of the Negro people's major cultural achievements under slavery—Christianization. Negroes had begun to move toward protestantism in the days of the great eighteenth century revival of religion known as the "Great Awakening." Jonathan Edwards, most eminent of the American leaders of this Awakening, had noted as early as 1736 the presence of New England slaves in the throngs that attended revival meeings. In 1776 the Methodist bishop, Francis Asbury, recorded that his revival meetings were attended by "hundreds of Negroes . . . with the tears streaming down their faces." After the Revolution, the tempo of this evangelical activity stepped up and continued unabated until the Civil War. White hymns and revival songs, with both music and lyrics, became available to Negro people throughout the nation.

During the eighteenth century the Puritan psalm-singing tradition had been enriched by the importation of hymns, like those of Isaac Watts, and by the beginning of native American composition of religious anthems and odes. The advance of the revivalist movement stimulated the demand for religious music with a propaganda mission and a popular approach to the problem of salvation. For the work of the revivalist movement, numbers of traditional hymns were pressed into service; ordinary folk in newly "awakened" communities began to try their own hands at religious versification.

New lyrics took a passionate approach to the question of sin, conversion, and sanctification. They warned sinners of the reality of death, and the urgent need to prepare for it; they pointed up the certainty of hellfire for the unrepentant and of everlasting damnation for the unregenerate. They told of the experience of conversion and of the raptures of the vision of the Living God. They affirmed faith in Jesus Christ and in the possibility of eternal life.

The revivalists set their lyrics to traditional tunes familiar to and loved by the common people, to tunes overwhelmingly of British folk origin.* As the frontier moved Westward during the Jacksonian era, this type of sacred popular song, or *white spiritual,* became general among frontier folk, both North and South. A vast amount of new song was thus proliferated: hymns of praise, religious ballads, revivalist songs of many types. But this material found a ready audience not only among white farmers, woodsmen, and pioneers, but also among the Negro slaves. Both white and Negro Americans utilized the same musical tradition and lyrics that were, by the 1820's, finding their way with profusion into the songsters. Inevitably, white and Negro people would use the *common* tradition in *different* ways. Both White and Negro spirituals were, as a class, appropriate, profound, and creatively beautiful expressions of the spiritual and intellectual needs of the people who produced them.

Slaveholders were, for the most part, reluctant witnesses of the great movement of religious conversion among their slaves, but they were obliged to make the best of it. It is true that Christian religion could be used, and often was, to inculcate acceptance of one's lot on earth, of obedience to slave masters, of "pie in the sky by and by" as the reward of meekness and obedience here and now. But this is only one side of the matter. Historically, the awakening of the slave to protestantism served the same purpose among Negroes as among white Americans. The religious awakening endowed them with a sense of unity, an interpretation of history, and a readiness to accept sacrifice, struggle, and death for what was right. The connection between the rise of Christianity among the slaves, the massive role played by the Negro people during the Civil War, and the disintegration of chattel bondage *is clear and demonstrable.*

The role played by the spiritual in the education of the Negro slave was unique. Focus and expression of the people's

*"All the known tunes adopted by American religious folk from sources other than British throughout the two-hundred year period under consideration could be counted on the fingers of one hand." George Pullen Jackson, *White and Negro Spirituals* (Locust Valley, N.Y.: 1943), 75.

profoundest beliefs and aspirations, the spiritual bound the race together with a consciousness of its common oppression, human dignity, and destiny. It gave the Negro strength to face the ordeals of life under slavery: the monotony of toil, humiliation, pain, flight and separation, battle, disease and death. It made it possible for human beings to accept their fate when they could do nothing else, and it summoned them to a sustained protest against that same fate whenever the hour struck.

In addition to spirituals, slavery produced many secular songs: dance tunes, corn songs, roustabout songs, and shanties. These were songs of the devil and the flesh. More than one collector has found, to his sorrow, that freedmen or the children of freedmen were reluctant to remember or communicate these pagan ditties. William Francis Allen, a pioneer collector of slave songs during the Civil War, wrote explicitly that it was ". . . no easy matter to persuade them to sing their old songs, even as a curiosity, such is the sense of dignity that has come to them with freedom.* Dorothy Scarborough, another and later collector, tried to coax such songs out of an old man in Birmingham, Alabama, and received the answer: "Yes, mistis, I knows dem. But I ain' gwine backslide by talkin' 'bout 'em. Ef you wants 'reels' you'll have to hunt up some dem young sinner folks. Not me, naw, not me!**

Sea shanties of clearly Negro origin appear elsewhere in this book. Some of the authentic secular songs that have survived slavery days are included in the selection of slave songs that follows.

Until the Civil War, there was but the faintest appreciation among white people of the extraordinary significance of Negro singing. Among the exceptions were the English actress, Frances Ann Kemble, whose comments upon slave songs are reproduced in part below; the Virginia novelist George Tucker; and blackface minstrels, who were quick to realize the extraordinary value of Negro "material" for entertainment purposes. However, Negro song transmitted by these minstrels reaches us in a stereotyped form because it has suffered the distortions that folk music undergoes when exploited for consciously commercial purposes.

The first people to appreciate the national significance of the songs of slavery, and the first to record them, were the fighters against slavery—Northern soldiers, ministers, scholars, and teachers. This work began with the capture of Port

*Slave Songs of the United States (New York, 1867), x.
**On the Trail of Negro Folk Songs (Cambridge, Mass.: 1925), 98.

Royal in 1861 by the Union forces and the liberation of the slave population on the sea islands of that area. In 1862, Secretary of the Treasury Salmon Chase launched an economic plan for these islands, and for the education of the freedman. Northern soldiers, teachers, and social workers hastened South to take part in the project. Among them were a number of skilled amateur musicians: Lucy McKim, daughter of a celebrated Philadelphia abolitionist, who married Wendell, son of William Lloyd Garrison in 1865; William Francis Allen, of Harvard University, one of America's foremost classical scholars; Charles Pickard Ware, son of Henry Ware the well known Unitarian minister of antislavery convictions from Hingham, Massachusetts; and Thomas Wentworth Higginson, also from Massachusetts, who assumed command of the First Carolina Volunteers, a regiment of freedmen who trained at Beaufort, South Carolina, in October 1862.

These people found in the spirituals sung so universally and so freely by the ex-slaves an incredibly vital, moving, and novel form of music. They busied themselves in noting down as much of it as time and other duties permitted. Higginson has left us a number of valuable lyrics and some revealing commentary on the singing of the soldiers, whom, as their commander, he was able to observe very closely. The volume of *Slave Songs* published by Lucy McKim, William Francis Allen, and Charles Pickard Ware in 1867 remains a landmark in the history of American folk music. We have drawn upon it for a number of the beautiful but little known songs that appear in the selection that follows.

Roll, Jordan, Roll

Lucy McKim called "Roll, Jordan, Roll" "one of the best known and noblest" of the spirituals. Describing the impression that the song made on her friends and herself, she wrote in 1862:

Perhaps the grandest singing we heard was at the Baptist Church, on St. Helena Island, when a congregation of three hundred men and women joined in a hymn:

> Roll, Jordan, roll, Jordan!
> Roll, Jordan, roll!

It swelled forth like a triumphal anthem. That same hymn was sung by thousands of Negroes on the Fourth of July last, when they marched in procession under the Stars and Stripes, cheering them for the first time as the "flag of *our* country." A friend, writing from there, says that the chorus was indescribably grand—"that the whole woods and world seemed joining in that rolling sound."

My broth-er sit-ting on the tree of life, And he heard when Jor-dan roll,__ Roll Jor-dan, Roll Jor-dan, Roll Jor-dan, roll!

CHORUS
O march, the an-gels march, O march, the an-gels march, O my soul a-rise in

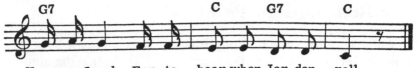

Heav-en, Lord, For to hear when Jor-dan roll.

My sister sitting on the tree of life,
And she heard when Jordan roll,
    Roll, Jordan,
    Roll, Jordan,
    Roll, Jordan, roll!

Chorus

Massa Lincoln sittin' on the tree of life,
And he heard when Jordan roll,
    Roll, Jordan,
    Roll, Jordan,
    Roll, Jordan, roll!

Chorus

Little children, learn to fear the Lord,
And let your days be long,
    Roll, Jordan,
    Roll, Jordan,
    Roll, Jordan, roll!

Chorus

O, let no false or spiteful word,
Be found upon your tongue,
    Roll, Jordan,
    Roll, Jordan,
    Roll, Jordan, roll!

Chorus

Sail, O Believer

For the Negro slave, a spiritual was something to live with, work with, pray with. American rivers and shores echoed to these melodies wherever slave stevedores worked, wherever slave oarsmen plied the longboats sailing from plantation to plantation.

Frances Ann Kemble, famous British actress, who resided in 1839 on her husband's sea island plantations at the estuary of the Altamaha river in Georgia, heard many of these boat songs. Her husband's plantations were on two islands separated by a distance of several miles, and she frequently traveled back and forth by boat. She has left the following commentary on the boat songs she heard:

My daily voyages up and down the river have introduced me to a great variety of new musical performances of our boatmen, who invariably, when the rowing is not too hard, moving up or down with the tide, accompany the stroke of their oars with the sound of their voices. . . . The way in which the chorus strikes in with the burden, between each phrase of the melody chanted by a single voice, is very curious and effective, especially with the rhythm of the rowlocks for accompaniment. The high voices all in unison, and the admirable time and true accent with which their responses are made, always makes me wish that some great musical composer could hear these semisavage performances. With a very little skillful adaptation and instrumentation, I think one or two barbaric chants and choruses might be evoked from them that would make the fortune of an opera.*

"Sail, O Believer" is a boat song that was sung by the slaves on the sea island of St. Helena; its place of origin is in the Hebrides. Changed into a spiritual, it illustrates the remarkable way in which Negro people assimilated the American musical heritage as a means to their own profound and creative expression.

Journal of a Residence on a Georgian Plantation 1838-1839 (New York: Knopf, 1961), 259-260.

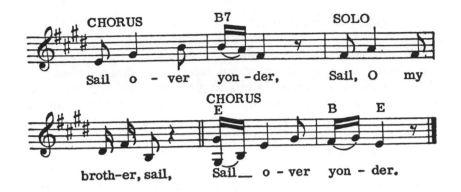

2. Come view the promised land,
    Sail over yonder,
  Come view the promised land,
    Sail over yonder.

3. O brother lend a hand,
    Sail over yonder,
  O brother lend a hand,
    Sail over yonder.

4. O Mary, weep,
    Sail over yonder,
  Bow low, Martha,
    Sail over yonder.

5. For Jesus comes,
    Sail over yonder,
  And Jesus locks the door,
    Sail over yonder.

6. For Jesus comes,
    Sail over yonder,
  And carries the keys away,
    Sail over yonder.

7. Sail, O believer, sail,
    Sail over yonder,
  Sail, O my brother, sail,
    Sail over yonder.

Poor Rosy

"Poor Rosy" is an excellent illustration of the many-sided nature and uses of the spiritual. "On the water," wrote Lucy McKim, who recorded this song among the slaves of Port Royal, "the oars dip 'Poor Rosy' to an even *andante;* a stout boy and girl at the hominy mill will make the same 'Poor Rosy' fly, to keep up with the whirling stone; and in the evening, after the day's work is done, *heaven shall-a be my home* peals up slowly and mournfully from the distant quarters." Next to "Roll, Jordan, Roll," "Poor Rosy" was evidently an all-time favorite among the sea island slaves whose feelings it so profoundly mirrors. "It can't be sung," a slave woman told Lucy, "without *a full heart and a troubled spirit.*" "Poor Rosy" possesses a deep vitality born of a combination of many moods: the contemplation of bliss, the hatred of evil and human wrong, the brooding expression of the sorrow of life, the dancing sense of tragedy and joy. American ballet, surely, will one day discover and make use of this melody.

The modality of the melody is mixed, that is, it is partly in a major, partly in a minor, key. Throughout the song, neither asserts its dominance. The scale is hexatonic, that is, with six rather than the usual seven tones.

199

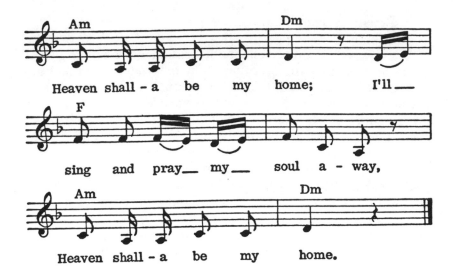

Heaven shall – a be my home; I'll —
sing and pray — my — soul a – way,
Heaven shall – a be my home.

2. Got hard trials on my way,
   Got hard trials on my way,
   Got hard trials on my way,
       Heaven shall-a be my home.
   O when I walk and talk with God
       Heaven shall-a be my home.
   O when I walk and talk with God,
       Heaven shall-a be my home.

3. I got troubles on my way,
   I got troubles on my way,
   I got troubles on my way,
       Heaven shall-a be my home;
   Before I stay in hell one day,
       Heaven shall-a be my home.
   I'll sing and pray my soul away,
       Heaven shall-a be my home.

4. River Jordan, I'm bound to go,
   River Jordan, I'm bound to go,
   River Jordan I am bound to go,
       Heaven shall-a be my home.
   Before I stay in hell one day.
       Heaven shall-a be my home.
   I'll sing and pray my soul away,
       Heaven shall-a be my home.

5. Brother Robert, I'm bound to go,
   Brother Robert, I'm bound to go,
   Brother Robert, I am bound to go,
   Heaven shall-a be my home
   O when I walk and talk with God,
   Heaven shall-a be my home,
   O when I walk and talk with God,
   Heaven shall-a be my home.

6. Sister Lucy, I'm bound to go,
   Sister Lucy, I'm bound to go,
   Sister Lucy, I am bound to go,
   Heaven shall-a be my home
   Before I stay in hell one day,
   Heaven shall-a be my home
   I'll sing and pray my soul away,
   Heaven shall-a be my home.

7. Poor Rosy, poor gal,
   Poor Rosy, poor gal,
   Rosy stole my poor heart,
   Heaven shall-a be my home.
   Oh, when I walk and talk with God
   Heaven shall-a be my home.
   Oh, when I walk and talk with God,
   Heaven shall-a be my home.

Bound to Go

"Bound to Go," collected by C. P. Ware and W. F. Allen on St. Helena Island, is another example of a spiritual that served a practical purpose both as boat song and as marching song. Its rousing melody is that of an old sea shanty, "A Long Time Ago." The combination of this with the slave lyric produces a song of great spiritual as well as rhythmic impact.

I build my house up-on the rock,
O yes, Lord! No wind, no storm can
blow it down, O yes, Lord.

CHORUS
March on, mem-ber, bound to go;
Been to the fer-ry, bound to go;.
Left St. Hel-e-na, bound to go,

Broth - er, fare you well.

2. I build my house on shifting sand,
       O yes, Lord!
   The first wind come he blow him down,
       O yes, Lord.
Chorus

3. I am not like that foolish man,
       O yes, Lord!
   Who built his house upon the sand,
       O yes, Lord.
Chorus

4. One morning as I was walkin' along,
       O yes, Lord!
   I saw the berries a-hangin' down,
       O yes, Lord.
Chorus

5. I pick the berries and I suck the juice,
       O yes, Lord!
   He sweeter than the honeycomb,
       O yes, Lord.
Chorus

6. I took them, brother, two by two,
       O yes, Lord!
   I took them, sister, three by three,
       O yes, Lord.
Chorus

Hushabye
(All the Pretty Little Horses)

During the long years of slavery, Negro women comforted and cared for white children while their own babies lay unwatched in the shacks and fields. "Hushabye" is both lullaby and lament that comes down to us from slavery days through oral tradition. It has been found in various forms in many parts of the South.

Hush - a - bye, Don't you cry, Go to sleep-y, lit - tle ba - by; When you wake You shall have All the pret-ty lit-tle hor - ses; Blacks and bays, Dap-ples and grays, Coach - a six - a lit - tle hor - ses. Hush-a - bye, Don't you cry, Go to sleep-y, lit-tle ba - by.

Hushabye,
Don't you cry,
Go to sleepy, little baby;
Way down yonder,
In the meadow,
There's a poor little lambie,
The bees and the butterflies
Pickin' out his eyes,
The poor little thing cries "Mammy!"
Hushabye,
Don't you cry,
Go to sleepy, little baby.

Sold Off to Georgy

"Sold Off to Georgy" is both lament and boat song. Conceivably it is among the very first slave songs to be noted down. George Tucker, a Virginia novelist, gave both words and music in his book, *The Valley of Shenandoah*, published in 1824. The melody uses only four tones, and is perhaps sung to best effect entirely unaccompanied. If an accompaniment is used, only one chord is required—in the setting given here, D minor. I cannot really justify the G minor chord that I have added, except that it heightens the sadness of the mood.

Farewell, ole plantation,
    Oho! Oho!
Farewell, de ole quarter,
    Oho! Oho!
An' daddy, an' mammy,
    Oho! Oho!
An' massa an' missus,
    Oho! Oho!

My dear wife and one child,
    Oho! Oho!
My poor heart is breaking,
    Oho! Oho!
No more shall I see you,
    Oho! Oho!
Oh, no more for ever,
    Oho! Oho!

Hangman, Slack on the Line

The Negro people in slavery not only borrowed the melodies and lyrics of the white spirituals and turned them to their own creative purposes, but also drew upon the rest of the song heritage which had been brought from Europe, and which belongs to all Americans. And, of course, as Negro people sang these old songs, they modified them, rhythmically, melodically, lyrically.

"Hangman" is an excellent example of this process of borrowing and creative adaptation. Compare the Negro version of this children's favorite with the traditional version given on p. 14 above. Like the white version, this one also comes from Florida.

Hang - man, hang - man, slack on the line,
Slack on the line a lit - tle while; I
think I see my fa - ther com - ing, With
mon - ey to pay my fine.

2. O father, father, did you bring me money,
   Money to pay my fine?
   Or did you come here to see me die
   On this hangman's line?

3. No, I didn't bring you money,
    Money to pay your fine,
  But I just came here, to see you die,
    Upon this hangman's line.

  *repeat sequence with mother, brother, sister,
  and lover; the last of these concludes with*

15. True love, I got gold and silver,
    Money to pay your fine;
  How could I bear to see you die
    On this hangman's line?

From Dorothy Scarborough's *On the Trail of Negro Folk Songs,* Harvard University Press. Copyright 1925 by Harvard University Press; 1953 by Mary McDaniel Parker. Reprinted by permission.

Lay This Body Down

Colonel Thomas Wentworth Higginson, commander of the First South Carolina Volunteers, took down the lyrics of this song from the singing of his freedmen soldiers during the Civil War. He termed it "a flower of poetry in that dark soil."

"Lay This Body Down" is a spiritual that was also used as a boat song and a funeral chant. It is, perhaps, one of the most consummately simple and profound laments in the whole range of our music and literature. To the high wailing notes of this song, the sea island slaves were laid to rest in graveyards without fence or mark whose very location remains to this day forgotten.

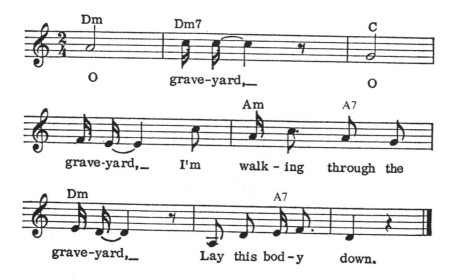

I know starlight,
I'm walking through the starlight,
Lay this body down.

I know moonlight,
I'm walking through the moonlight,
Lay this body down.

I lie in the grave,
I'm lying in the graveyard,
Lay this body down.

O graveyard, O graveyard,
I'm walking through the graveyard,
Lay this body down.

I go to judgment
In the evening of the day,
Lay this body down.

Your soul and my soul
Will meet on that day,
Lay this body down.

Graveyard, O graveyard,
I'm walking through the graveyard,
Lay this body down.

Jimmy Rose

Dorothy Scarborough learned this dance song from Dr. John A. Wyeth of Texas, who spent his childhood and youth on a large plantation during slavery days and learned much about Negro music and musical instruments from the slaves themselves.

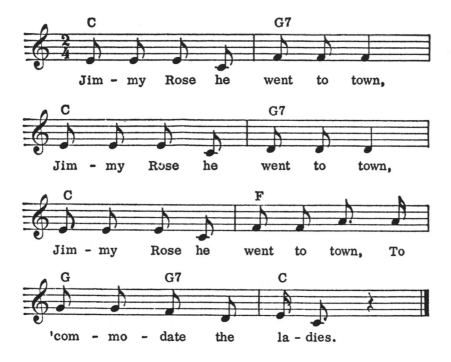

Jim - my Rose he went to town,
Jim - my Rose he went to town,
Jim - my Rose he went to town, To
'com - mo - date the la - dies.

Fare ye well, ye ladies all,
Fare ye well, ye ladies all,
Fare ye well, ye ladies all,
God Almighty bless you.

T'ain't Gonna Rain No Mo'

Dorothy Scarborough describes this as "a famous old dance song, well known especially in Texas." It was a natural for minstrel shows, and in the 1920's became popular around the world—with different lyrics—on 78 r.p.m. records. It is thus notable as one of the few dance songs of slavery days that has been in continuous oral tradition since that time.

'Tain't gon - na rain, 'Tain't gon - na snow,
'Tain't gon-na rain no mo'; Steal up, ev-ery-
bod - y, T'ain't gon-na rain no mo'.
Ole cow died at the mouth of the branch,
T'ain't gon-na rain no mo'. The buz-zards had a
pub-lic dance, 'Tain't gon-na rain no mo'.

Chorus

What did the blackbird say to the crow?
    'Tain't gonna rain no mo'.
'Tain't gonna hail and 'tain't gonna snow,
    'Tain't gonna rain no mo'.

Chorus

Gather corn in a beegum hat,
    'Tain't gonna rain no mo'.
Oh massa grumble if you eat much of that,
    'Tain't gonna rain no mo'.

Chorus

Two, two, and round up four,
    'Tain't gonna rain no mo'.
Two, two, and round up four,
    'Tain't gonna rain no mo'.

Chorus

Six, two, and round up four,
    'Tain't gonna rain no mo'.
Six, two, and round up four,
    'Tain't gonna rain no mo'.

Chorus

The Rose of Alabama

The words and music of this song were published as sheet music in Boston in 1846, after it had become part of the repertoire of a minstrel troupe known as the "Ethiopian Serenaders." The words, by Silas S. Steele, were set to a melody which was described in the *Negro Song Book* of 1848 as "a sweet and genuine plantation air, fresh from the fields." "The Rose of Alabama" remained popular for a number of years and was a favorite of Southern soldiers during the Civil War.

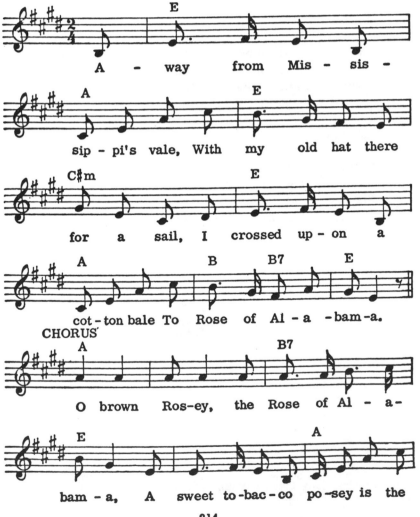

A - way from Mis - sis -
sip - pi's vale, With my old hat there
for a sail, I crossed up - on a
cot - ton bale To Rose of Al - a - bam-a.
O brown Ros-ey, the Rose of Al - a-
bam - a, A sweet to-bac-co po-sey is the

Rose of Al - a - bam-a, A sweet to-bac-co po-sey is the Rose of Al - a - bam-a.

I landed on the sandbank,
I sat upon a hollow plank,
And there I made the banjo twank,
    For Rose of Alabama.
Chorus

I asked her to set down where she please,
So cross my legs she took her ease,
"It's good to go upon the knees,"
    Says Rose of Alabama.
Chorus

The river rolled, the crickets sing,
The lightning bug he flashed his wing,
And like a rope my arms I fling
    Round Rose of Alabama.
Chorus

I hug so long I cannot tell,
For Rosey seemed to like it well,
My banjo in the river fell,
    Oh Rose of Alabama.
Chorus

Like alligator after prey,
I plunge in, but it float away,
And all the time it seemed to say,
    "Oh Rose of Alabama."
Chorus

And every night in moon or shower,
To hunt that banjo for an hour,
I meet my sweet tobacco flower,
    My Rose of Alabama.
Chorus

V

THE

CIVIL

WAR

THE CIVIL WAR resembled the Revolution and the War of 1812 in that it produced many topical songs designed to meet the urgent needs of the moment: to celebrate victory, fortify convictions, taunt the enemy, steel the soul for battle, and provide solace. It was a time when literary and musical activity flowered with a great intensity.

Thousands of ordinary, anonymous Americans—soldiers, civilians, nurses, housewives, and ministers—wrote these songs and verses, which were often sung to traditional ballad tunes. Numbers of these songs were printed as broadsides and circulated in factory, field, and camp by the tens of thousands of copies. Here, the Civil War continued and enriched the broadside ballad tradition of colonial and early national times. Professional songwriters also turned to writing war songs and found a wide and ready market for their compositions. Much money was made by publishers, especially in New York and Philadelphia, from the distribution and sale of low-priced popular songbooks and sheet music.

Notwithstanding its grandeur, much of this Civil War material has vanished from popular tradition. It is obscurely preserved in the music files, broadside, songster, and manuscript collections of public and university libraries and private homes. Yet, from a historical viewpoint, this heritage has an immense significance. The story of the Civil War may quite literally be told through its songs: there was hardly a battle that did not produce at least one major song, and many battles gave rise to several or even innumerable songs.

At a deeper level, the music of the Civil War provides a commentary on human life and fate; it gives us a key to the moods, thoughts, and agonies of a generation of Americans. The Civil War was also remarkable because for the first time hundreds of thousands of Negro Americans were fighting in it for freedom as free men. White soldiers listened to the singing of Negro troops and were deeply moved by the experience. The war, indeed, produced the first major impact of Negro singing upon the nation.

Some of the greatest freedom songs that we inherit were created in the fires of this war. Here, we reproduce a few of the songs that generally but vividly outline the story of the conflict, and that tell something of the moods and experiences which so many of the lyrics then written sought to express.

The Northern Bonny Blue Flag

When Fort Sumter fell before the cannon of the rebellious South on April 12, 1861, Northerners flocked to the colors in a blaze of passion. Though many of them felt that slavery was wrong, few foresaw that the main purpose of the war would be the ending of slavery. What most people cared about was the defense of the Union, its unity, its sovereignty, and its flag. This simple and dignified lyric by Isaac Ball, set to a traditional Irish tune, expressed the Union mood in the early months of the conflict. It also provided an answer to the popular Confederate song that boasted a single star on the "bonny blue flag" of secession, and that proclaimed, as the purpose of the war, the defense of Southern property and rights.

We're fight-ing for our Un-ion, We're fight-ing for our trust, We're fight-ing for that hap-py land, Where sleeps our fa-thers' dust. It can-not be dis-sev-ered, Though it

cost us blood-y wars, We

nev-er can give up the land Where

floats the Stripes and Stars. Hur-rah! hur-rah! For

e-qual rights, hur-rah! Hur-

rah! for the good old flag, That

bears the Stripes and Stars.

We do not want your cotton,
    We care not for your slaves,
But rather than divide this land,
    We'll fill your Southern graves.
With Lincoln for our Chieftain,
    We'll bear our country's scars,
We'll rally round the brave old flag
    That bears the Stripes and Stars.

Chorus

The Bonny Blue Flag (Southern)

We are a band of brothers,
 And native to the soil,
Fighting for the property
 We gained by honest toil;
And when our rights were threatened,
 The cry rose near and far:
"Hurrah for the Bonny Blue Flag
 That bears a single star!"
(abridged)

Song of the Southern Volunteers

In 1861, the *volunteer* was the hero, and many of the songs told of volunteering, or urged it. "The Song of the Southern Volunteers," with its sense of loneliness underlying a pose of bravado and its haunting refrain, has been widely found throughout the South. To this day, the melody is a favorite with children.

CHORUS

We go walk - ing on the green grass, thus, thus, thus: Come all ye fair and pret -ty maids, and walk a - long with us; So pret -ty and so fair as you take your-selves to be, I'll choose you for a part - ner, come walk a - long with me.

I would not marry a lawyer, who's pleading at the bar,
I'd rather marry a soldier boy who wears a Southern star,
Soldier boy, etc.

Chorus

I would not marry a doctor who tries to heal the sick,
I'd rather marry a soldier boy who marches double quick,
Soldier boy, etc.

Chorus

I would not be a lady that Southrons call a belle,
I'd rather be a soldier boy and hear the Yankees yell,
Soldier boy, etc.

Chorus

I would not be a nursemaid and hear the children squall,
I'd rather be a soldier boy and face a cannon ball,
Soldier boy, etc.

Chorus

I would not be a farmer who's toiling in the sun,
I'd rather be a soldier boy and see the Yankees run,
Soldier boy, etc.

Chorus

I would not be a miller who grinds the people's grain,
I'd rather be a soldier boy who walks through wind and
    rain,
Soldier boy, etc.

Chorus

Flag of the Free

Among the first of the Union volunteers to rush to the colors were Irish immigrants. Few brought antislavery convictions with them from the Old World; most knew little about the Negro and cared less. But they loved their adopted land, and its cause was theirs. Irish were also to be found in the Confederate forces, though to a lesser extent. One way or the other, they filled graves on every battlefield in the Civil War.

"Flag of the Free" was a recruiting song. It was set to one of the loveliest of Gaelic melodies, "Eibhleen a Ruin" (Treasure of My Heart), a love song of beauty and simplicity. In the middle of the eighteenth century, Lady Caroline Keppel had set English lyrics to "Eibhleen," and it became known to the English-speaking world, including the United States, as "Robin Adair." Then, the Civil War inspired the writing of a uniquely American lyric.

Could we de - sert you now, Flag of the Free; When we a sol - emn vow, Flag of the Free, You from all harm to save, Made when we crossed the wave, And you__ a__ wel - come gave, Flag of the Free?

2. Are we now cowards grown,
          Flag of the Free?
    Would we you now disown,
          Flag of the Free?
    You to whose folds we've fled,
    You in whose cause we've bled,
    Bearing you at our head,
          Flag of the Free?

3. Could we desert you now,
          Flag of the Free,
    And to black traitors bow,
          Flag of the Free?
    Never! through good and ill,
    Ireland her blood will spill,
    Bearing you onward still,
          Flag of the Free.

The Yankee Man o' War

The Civil War began in a light-hearted mood. The bands played, the men marched in their bright uniforms, the flags waved, and the girls flocked around. It would be easy, thought the Northerners, to teach the rebels a lesson in one summer's campaign, and be home again before winter set in. But this rosy dream was soon shattered by the Battle of Manassas, or First Bull Run, in July, 1861. The first test of strength saw the Union troops streaming back to Washington, hanging their heads in shame.

If the North was to face stern trials by land, it retained control of the navy from the very beginning of the conflict. This would prove a decisive factor in the eventual Union victory. In 1861, Abraham Lincoln threw a tight blockade around the Southern coasts; as the stranglehold tightened, overseas trade, the Confederacy's windpipe, was throttled.

"The Yankee Man o' War" is taken from the manuscript ballad book of James Ashby of Holt County, Missouri, the entry dated May 7, 1876. The theme of a young man's parting from his sweetheart was a familiar one in British broadside ballads; only minor changes were needed to produce a song appropriate to the Civil War. The ancient melody with which the lyrics are here linked is a variant of "The Lowlands of Holland," a traditional ballad that tells of a lover departed and lost at sea.

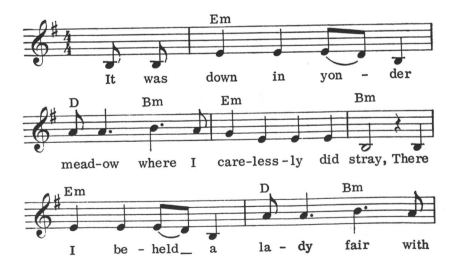

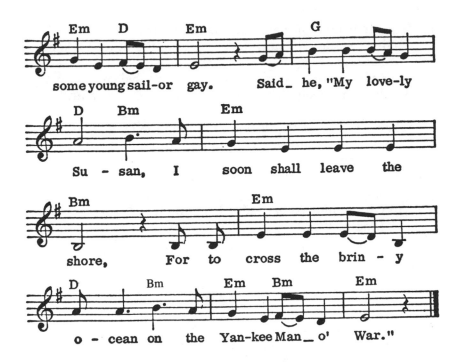

some young sail-or gay. Said he, "My love-ly
Su - san, I soon shall leave the
shore, For to cross the brin - y
o - cean on the Yan-kee Man o' War."

2. Young Susan she fell weeping, "Young sailor," she did say,
   "How can you be so venturesome and throw yourself away?
   For by the time I'm twenty-one I shall receive my store,
   So Willie, do not venture on the Yankee Man o' War."

3. "O Susan, lovely Susan, the truth to you I'll tell;
   The South she has insulted us, the North she knows it well.
   I may be crowned with laurels just like some jolly tar;
   And I'll face the forts of the rebels on the Yankee
       Man o' War."

4. "How can you be so venturesome for to face the Southern
       foes?
   When they are far in battle, love, they never take a man;
   And from some bloody weapon you might receive a scar,
   So Willie, do not venture on the Yankee Man o' War."

5. "O Susan, lovely Susan, the time will quickly pass;
   Let's go down to the ferryhouse and take the parting glass;
   My shipmates they are waiting to row me from the shore,
   And it's for America's glory on the Yankee Man o' War."

6. The sailor took his handkerchief and tore it into two,
   Saying "Susan, you may keep one half, the other I'll keep
     for you
   When bullets may surround me and the rebel cannon roar,
   I'll fight for lovely Susan on the Yankee Man o' War."

7. Then a few more words together, then she let go his hand;
   The jolly crew surrounded him and rowed him from
     the land.
   The sailor waved his handkerchief when far away from
     shore,
   And Susan blessed her sailor love on the Yankee
     Man o' War.

Reprinted from *Ballads and Songs Collected by the Missouri Folk-Lore Society*, edited by H. M. Belden, by permission of the University of Missouri Press.

The Homespun Dress

The South could and did run the blockade, could harass Northern commerce with its raiders and privateers, and could even sink battleships like the *Cumberland*. But without British help the South could not break the blockade. As the war went on, and the Northern stranglehold tightened, Southerners either had to go without, or make for themselves. Southern women took to weaving homespun, and this symbolic act of dedication to country soon found expression in song. "The Homespun Dress" was evidently popular in the South before the end of the war, and by 1865 was sufficiently well known to be published in New York. Frank Moore, famous Civil War song collector, gives the following account of how the song came into his possession:

The accompanying song was taken from a letter of a Southern girl to her lover in Lee's army, which letter was obtained from a mail captured on Sherman's march through northern Alabama. The materials of which the dress alluded to is made are of cotton and wool, and woven on the hand-loom, so commonly seen in the houses of the South. The scrap of a dress, enclosed in the letter as a sample, was of a gray color, with a stripe of crimson and green—quite pretty and creditable to the lady who made it.

The lines are not a false indication of the universal sentiment of the women of the South, who by the encouragement they have extended the soldiers and the sacrifices they have made, have exercised an influence which has proved of the greatest importance to the rebels, and have shown what can be accomplished by united effort on the part of the gentle sex.*

> O yes, I am a Southern girl,
>   And glory in the name,
> I boast of it with greater pride
>   Than glittering wealth and fame.
> I envy not the Northern girl
>   Her robes of beauty rare
> Though diamonds deck her snowy neck
>   And pearls bestud her hair.

Chorus

> Hurrah, hurrah, for the sunny South I say,
> Three cheers for the homespun dress
> The Southern ladies wear.

The Civil War in Song and Ballad (New York, 1865), 174.
For the melody, see pp. 218-9, "The Bonny Blue Flag."

Now Northern goods are out of date,
    And since old Abe's blockade,
We Southern girls can be content
    With goods that Southrons made,
We send our sweethearts to the war,
    But girls never you mind,
Your soldier love will not forget,
    The girl he left behind.

Chorus

The Southern land's a glorious land
    And has a glorious cause,
Three cheers, three cheers for Southern rights
    And for the Southern boys;
We scorn to wear a bit of silk,
    A bit of Northern lace,
But make our homespun dresses up,
    And wear them with a grace.

Chorus

And now young man a word for you
    If you would win the fair,
Go to the field where honor calls,
    And win your lady there.
Remember that our bravest smiles
    Are for the true and brave,
And that our tears are all for those
    Who fill a soldier's grave.

Chorus

On to Richmond!

In the spring of 1862, General George McClellan, the dashing commander of the Army of the Potomac, took the initiative after months of inactivity. Afraid to launch a direct attack on the Confederate capital of Richmond, McClellan instead worked out an elaborate flanking movement. He took his army by sea down the Virginia coast, and landed it between the York and James rivers. "On to Richmond!" yelled the newspapers.

As the Union troops moved ponderously forward, Robert E. Lee was placed in command of the Southern forces. At the end of June, 1862, Lee drove off McClellan in the famous and bloody series of engagements known as the Seven Days' Fight. The South rightly celebrated a brilliant victory with a very catchy song.

"Well,_ we have the na-vy an'_ we have the men, For-ward, on to Rich-mond, to storm the reb-el den, On to Rich-mond, so ear-ly in the morn-in', On to

Rich-mond!" I heard the Yan-kees say.

"We'll flank it on the North an' we'll shell it on the South,
We'll storm it on the East an' we'll run the rebels out,
On to Richmond, so early in the mornin',
On to Richmond!" I heard the Yankees say.

Lee was in the center an' Jackson in the rear,
An' on the right and left side the noble hills appear,
Longstreet he had to travel, an' branches had to cross,
An' old McGruder was about to give the Yankees grass.

It was about the first of June when the balls began to fly,
The Yankees took an' wheeled about an' changed their
        battle cry,
"Off from Richmond, so early in the mornin',
Down to the gunboats! Run boys, run."

Florida is a-hunting, an' a huntin' through the brush,
The rebels are in earnest, push boys, push,
The Louisiana Legion, Butler was the cry,
The Texas Rangers comin', fly boys, fly.

Virginia is a-comin' with her death-defying steel,
Georgia is a-chargin' across the swamps and fields,
"Off from Richmond, so early in the mornin',
Down to the gunboats, run boys, run."

"The Palmetto rebels is now upon the trail,
And the Arkansas devils want to ride us on a rail,
Never mind your knapsacks, never mind your guns,
A-fightin' these rebels it ain't no fun."

McClellan is a humbug and Lincoln is a fool,
All of them is liars of the highest greeting school,
A home was the promise, an' every man a slave,
You better run North, or you'll all find a grave.

General Lee's Wooing

By the summer of 1862, the North had scored a number of victories in the West and had taken New Orleans, but the South remained undefeated. The Union's hour of peril was at hand. Lee, having blunted McClellan's offensive in the Seven Days' Fight, began the attack. He swept northward, defeated Pope at Manassas, and placed himself astride the Potomac west of Washington. The world held its breath. If Lee could not be stopped as he headed toward Maryland and Pennsylvania, the end of the war was near.

General McClellan rallied the Union forces and met Lee at Antietam Creek in Maryland on September 17, 1862. Neither side could claim victory in the horrible carnage, but Lee suffered a severe check and was obliged to fall back. On September 24, Abraham Lincoln issued the first Emancipation Proclamation promising freedom to all slaves in States still in rebellion on January 1, 1863.

An anonymous Northern soldier wrote "General Lee's Wooing" following the battle of Antietam. These verses, among the finest penned during the war, illuminate in a single flash the meaning of the struggle at Antietam Creek. It was a battle worthy of commemoration, for it proved to be a decisive turning point in the war. Emancipation of the slaves gave the country a crusading cause, rallied the flagging energies of the North, won the sympathy of the world, and brought tens of thousands of black recruits into armies shaken by ghastly losses. British recognition of the South and her intervention in the South's behalf were alike ruled out. Confederate hopes of victory received a crushing blow.

My Mar-y-land, my Mar-y-land, I bring thee pres-ents fine, A daz-zling sword with

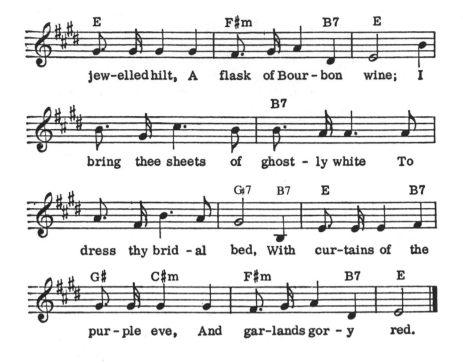

jew-elled hilt, A flask of Bour-bon wine; I bring thee sheets of ghost - ly white To dress thy brid - al bed, With cur-tains of the pur - ple eve, And gar-lands gor - y red.

My Maryland, my Maryland,
   Sweet land upon the shore,
Bring out thy stalwart yeomanry,
   Make clean the threshing floor.
My ready wains lie stretching far
   Across the fertile plain,
And I among the reapers stand
   To gather in the grain.

My Maryland, my Maryland,
   I fondly wait to see
Thy banner flaunting in the breeze,
   Beneath the trysting tree.
While all my gallant company
   Of gentlemen with spurs,
Come tramping, tramping o'er the hills,
   And tramping through the furze.

My Maryland, my Maryland,
  I feel the leaden rain,
I see the winged messenger,
  Come hurling to my brain.
I feathered with thy golden hair,
  'Tis feathered now in vain,
I spurn the hand that loosed the shaft
  And curse thee in my pain.

My Maryland, my Maryland,
  Alas the ruthless day,
That sees my gallant buttonwoods
  Ride galloping away;
And ruthless for my chivalry,
  Proud gentlemen with spurs,
Whose bones lie stark upon the hills,
  And stark among the furze.

What Gives the Wheat Fields Blades of Steel?

On January 1, 1863, the slaves were freed. This day saw the dawning of a new idea in the United States: that in this land the destinies of Negro and white are forever linked, that the white man may never be wholly free while the Negro remains a slave.

On this day, Lincoln inscribed upon the Union banners the message that slavery was the enemy and that its extinction was necessary for the survival of the Union. This, too, was the message of the great antislavery hymn, "What Gives the Wheat Fields Blades of Steel?" by John Greenleaf Whittier, composed in 1862, and set to the tune of Martin Luther's "A Mighty Fortress is our God." It mirrored the new mood and understanding that would sustain the Union soldiers to the end.

We wait beneath the furnace-blast
    The pangs of transformation:
Not painlessly doth God recast
    And mould anew the nation.
            Hot burns the fire
            Where wrongs expire;
            Nor spares the hand
            That from the land
Uproots the ancient evil.

The hand-breadth cloud the sages feared
    Its bloody rain is dropping;
The poison plant the father spared
    All else is overtopping.
            East, West, South, North,
            It curses the earth;
            All justice dies
            And fraud and lies
Live only in its shadow.

What thought the cast-out spirit tear
    The nation in his going?
We who have shared the guilt must share
    The pang of his overthrowing!
            Whate'er the loss
            Whate'er the cross
            Shall they complain
            Of present pain
Who trust in God hereafter?

                              (abridged)

Freedom Songs

Frederick Douglass, runaway slave and leader of the Negro, urged his people to rally to the Union cause and take arms to win freedom. By so doing, said he, they would win for themselves "the gratitude of our country and the best blessings of posterity through all time." The Negro people responded to his call and flocked to the colors. Over 100,000 of them actually served in the armed forces. Lincoln himself acknowledged that their contribution was decisive.

The great spirituals of slavery days went to battle with tens of thousands of Negro soldiers who fought the Confederacy and laid down their lives for the Stars and Stripes. New songs, too, were born of the new mood generated by emancipation and the war itself. We have space for only three of these here: "Many Thousand Gone" and "Oh, Freedom!" express the Negro's reaction to the end of slavery and the birth of a new vision of happiness, and rank among the great freedom songs of the modern era. "Song of the Freedmen" first appeared in the popular songsters in 1864 and was evidently a marching favorite of the Negro soldiers.

Many Thousand Gone

No more peck of corn for me,
    No more, no more;
No more peck of corn for me,
    Many thousand gone.

No more driver's lash for me,
    No more, no more;
No more driver's lash for me,
    Many thousand gone.

No more pint of salt for me,
    No more, no more;
No more pint of salt for me,
    Many thousand gone.

Oh, Freedom!

Oh, _____ free-dom! oh, _____ free-dom! Oh, free-dom o - ver me; And be-fore I'll be a slave, I'll lie bur - ied in my grave, And go home to my Lord and _____ be free.

2. No more moaning, no more moaning,
   No more moaning over me;
   And before I'll be a slave,
   I'll lie buried in my grave,
   And go home to my Lord, and be free.

3. No more mourning, no more mourning,
   No more mourning over me;
   And before I'll be a slave, etc.

4. No more weeping, no more weeping,
   No more weeping over me;
   And before I'll be a slave, etc.

5. No more sighing, no more sighing,
   No more sighing over me;
   And before I'll be a slave, etc.

6. Oh, what singing, oh, what singing,
   Oh, what singing over me;
   And before I'll be a slave, etc.

7. Oh, what shouting, oh, what shouting,
   Oh, what shouting over me;
   And before I'll be a slave, etc.

8. Oh, freedom! Oh, freedom!
   Oh, freedom over me;
   And before I'll be a slave, etc.

Song of the Freedmen

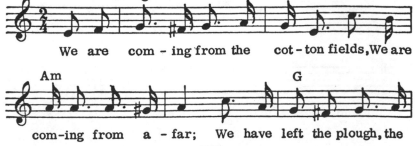

We are com - ing from the cot - ton fields, We are
com-ing from a - far; We have left the plough, the

hoe, the axe, And we are going to war. We have

left the old plan - ta - tion seat, The

sug-ar and the cane, Where we worked and toiled with

wea - ry feet, In sun and wind and rain.

CHORUS

Then __ come a - long my boys, __ O, __

come, come a - long, Then __ come a-long my

broth-ers, O __ come, come a - long. We are

com - ing from the cot - ton fields, We are

com-ing from a - far; We have left the plough, the

hoe,   the axe, And   we are going to war.

We will leave our chains behind us, boys,
    The prison and the rack;
And we'll hide beneath a soldier's coat
    The scars upon our back;
And we'll teach the world a lesson soon,
    If taken by the hand,
How night shall come before 'tis noon
    Upon old Pharaoh's land.

Chorus

A Plaint

After Antietam, the Union again took the offensive and tried to break through to Richmond, but sustained enormous losses without good result. In May, 1863, Lee stopped the Union armies at Chancellorsville and, repeating the feat of the previous year, at once passed over to the attack. Again the grey tide rolled northward, up the Shenandoah Valley, past Washington, into Pennsylvania; and again the Union braced itself for a decisive struggle. Three days of bloody conflict at Gettysburg in July, and Lee's army was broken. Long lines limped south; the wounded and the dying left bloody tracks in the dust. But Gettysburg was only a partial victory, for the Southern armies were broken, not destroyed. A long, heartbreaking struggle still lay ahead.

By spring of 1864, Lincoln was ready for the final offensive. Grant came to Washington and assumed command of all Federal forces; his plan was to pin Lee down in Virginia with the Army of the Potomac while the Army of the Cumberland slashed through Georgia deep in the Confederate rear. One of the best of the songs that told of Grant's last Virginia campaign is a Southron's lament that, as far as we know, was not set to music. A. E. Townsend's "Plaint" over the havoc of war in his native Virginia is reproduced below.

> Alas! for the pleasant peace we knew
> In the happy summers of long ago,
> When the rivers were bright and the sky was blue
> By the homes of Henrico.
> We dreamed of wars that were far away
> And read, as in fable, of blood that ran
> Where the James and Chickahominy stray,
> Through the groves of Powhatan.
>
> 'Tis a dream come true, for the afternoons,
> Blow bugles of war by our fields of grain,
> And the sabres sink as the dark dragoons
> Come galloping up the lane;
> The pigeons have flown from the eaves and tiles,
> The oat-blades have grown to blades of steel,
> And the Huns swarm down the leafy aisles
> Of the grand old commonweal.

They have torn the Indian fisher's nets
Where the gray Pamunkey goes toward the sea,
And blood runs red in the rivulets
That babbled and brawled in glee;
The corpses are strewn in Fair Oak glades,
The hoarse guns thunder from Drewry's Ridge,
The fishes that played in the cool deep shades
Are frightened from Bottom Bridge.

I would that the years were blotted away,
And the strawberries green in the hedge again;
That the scythe might swing in the tangled hay,
And the squirrels romp in the glen;
The walnuts sprinkle the clover slopes
Where graze the sheep and the spotted steer,
And the winter restore the golden hopes
That were trampled in a year.

Roll, Alabama, Roll

Throughout the war, the Confederacy with the aid of a number of cruisers built in British yards, harassed Union commerce. One of the most notorious of these raiders was the *Alabama,* which for two years roamed the high seas taking prize ships and sinking Northern craft.

The *Alabama* met her end on June 19, 1864, when the U.S. man o' war *Kearsarge* ran her down and sank her off the port of Cherbourg in Normandy. Hundreds of Southern sailors lost their lives in the brief but disastrous encounter.

William H. Cushman, chief engineer of the *Kearsarge,* wrote to his mother the following laconic description of the engagement:

We have met the celebrated "pirate Alabama" and *sunk* her, after 1 hour and 30 minutes hard fighting. She came out of Cherbourg, about 10 a.m. accompanied by the *Couronne,* a French ironclad; when at about one mile she commenced firing at 11 a.m., we waited 20 minutes until we got the range we wanted, then commenced. After firing 1 hour and 5 minutes we had the pleasure of seeing her haul down her flag (it had been twice shot down) and then surrender. Before we could launch our two good boats to get them to her, she sunk beautifully. We had hardly got warmed up and expected to fight several hours. Only 3 of our men wounded, one quarter gunner lost his arm (of the three), an officer wounded. We picked up 6 officers and 69 of the men.*

Cushman's share of the prize money given as a reward for this feat was $5,800. Officers received a disproportionate share of such bonus pay provided by the government or various American cities and this often caused resentment among the enlisted men. This is well expressed in the following anecdote that went the rounds during the war. A vessel was about to go into action, and one sailor lad was on his knees. An officer sneeringly asked him, if he was afraid?

"No, I was praying," was the response.

"Well, what were you praying for?"

"Praying," said the sailor, "that the enemy's bullets may be distributed the same way as the prize money is, *principally among the officers.*"

"Roll, Alabama, Roll" tells the story of the *Alabama* and its fate clearly, dispassionately, and concisely. The tune is that of a roustabout song and halyard shanty "Roll the Cotton Down." "Roll, Alabama, Roll" itself continued in use as a halyard

*Cherbourg. June 19, 1864. In *Letters and Papers Relating to the Sinking of the Confederate Cruiser Alabama.* Library of Congress, Division of Manuscripts.

shanty. Stan Hugill relates that he heard a variant of this song in Gisborne, New Zealand in 1925. The husband of the lady who sang it for him had been a seaman on the *Alabama*.

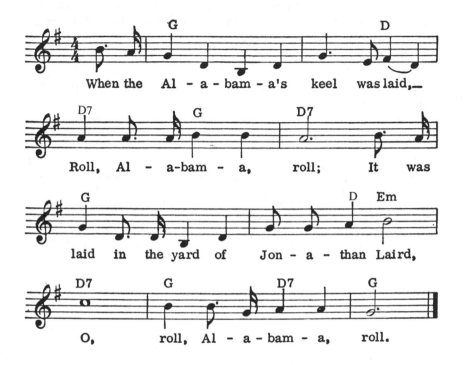

2. It was laid in the yard of Jonathan Laird,
   Roll, Alabama, roll;
   It was laid in the town of Birkenhead,
   O, roll, Alabama, roll.

3. Down the Mersey ways she rolled then,
   Roll, Alabama, roll;
   Liverpool fitted her with guns and men,
   O, roll, Alabama, roll.

4. From the Western Isles she sailed forth,
   Roll, Alabama, roll;
   To destroy the commerce of the North,
   O, roll, Alabama, roll.

5. To Cherbourg port she sailed one day,
    Roll, Alabama, roll;
   To take her count of prize monnay,
    O, roll, Alabama, roll.

6. Many a sailor lad he saw his doom,
    Roll, Alabama, roll;
   When the Kearsarge hove in view,
    O, roll, Alabama, roll.

7. A ball from the forward pivot that day,
    Roll, Alabama, roll;
   Shot the Alabama's stern away,
    O, roll, Alabama, roll.

8. Off the three mile limit in '64,
    Roll, Alabama, roll;
   The Alabama sank to the ocean floor,
    O, roll, Alabama, roll.

Sherman's March to the Sea

The two phases of Grant's plan of attack were launched simultaneously. While Grant crossed the Rapidan and headed into the wilderness, Sherman advanced down the railroad from Chattanooga to Atlanta. In September, 1864, began the famous march to the sea, cutting a swath of desolation 60 miles broad and 300 miles long through central Georgia to Savannah. Sherman reached his objective on the Georgia coast in December, 1864 and then turned north.

News of Sherman's advance preceded him. In Charleston jail, hundreds of ragged Federals eagerly awaited deliverance. One of them, Lieutenant S. H. M. Byers, composed "Sherman's March to the Sea." The simple but imaginative lyric was frequently sung to the tune of "Rosin the Beau," a much parodied Irish melody that finds in the poem here reproduced its perfect mate. This song was seized upon in the North and became a smash hit, appearing in songsters and song sheets by the hundred thousand copies.

Our camp-fires shone bright on those moun-tains That frowned on the riv-er be-low;__ While we stood by our guns in the morn-ing And ea-ger-ly watched for the foe.__ When a rid-er came out from the dark-ness That

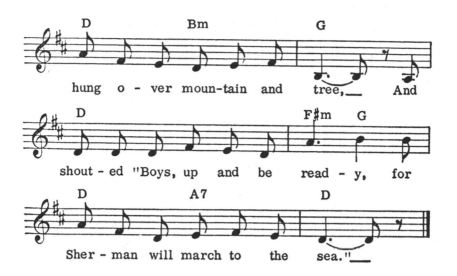

hung o - ver moun-tain and tree,__ And shout - ed "Boys, up and be read - y, for Sher - man will march to the sea."__

Then cheer upon cheer for bold Sherman
    Went up from each valley and glen,
And the bugles re-echoed the music
    That came from the lips of the men.
For we knew that the stars on our banner
    More bright in their splendor would be,
And that blessings from Northland would greet us,
    When Sherman marched down to the sea.

Then forward, boys, forward to battle,
    We marched on our wearisome way,
And we stormed the wild hills of Resaca,
    God bless those who fell on that day!
Then Kenesaw, dark in its glory
    Frowned down on the flag of the free,
But the East and the West bore our standards
    And Sherman marched down to the sea.

Still onward we pressed, til our banners
    Swept out from Atlanta's grim walls,
And the blood of the patriot dampened
    The soil where the traitor's flag falls;
But we paused not to weep for the fallen,
    Who slept by river and tree,
Yet we twined them a wreath of laurel
    As Sherman marched down to the sea.

249

O proud was our army that morning,
    That stood where the pine proudly towers,
When Sherman said "Boys, you are weary,
    This day fair Savannah is ours."
Then sung we a song for our chieftain
    That echoed o'er land and o'er lea,
And the stars on our banner shone brighter,
    When Sherman marched down to the sea.

The Southern Girl's Reply

Grant's offensive lasted for almost one year, from May 1864 to April 1865. The Federals paid in blood for every inch of Southern soil; but the more that died, the more came. Seemingly, there was no end to the blue-clad swarm seeking graves in Southern earth. Grant led his soldiers to victory, and death. They adored him and died for him. As they marched down the Southern lanes and stormed the Southern trenches, his name was on their lips.

"Our army has a leader now," they sang,
"That's gallant, true, and brave;
Though many a one we've had before
Has proved himself a knave,
And honesty's been laid aside
While scrambling after pelf,
As one by one we've found them out,
And laid them on the shelf.

"Hurrah! Hurrah! Hurrah!
For Grant's the man to lead the van,
The rest are all too slow;
But let old Grant down on them come,
Away the rebels go."

One year of bitter fighting, and the Confederacy lay in ruins. On Palm Sunday, April 9, 1865, Robert Lee, in tears, rode out to his men and told them that the war was at an end. They would ride home in defeat; at the end of the road, they would find poverty, ashes, and despair.

Slavery had divided the American people. Years would pass before a common love of freedom could reunite them. And there would be, as a Southern girl sang to her Northern wooer, a legacy of blood and bitterness in a divided land. This song, to the tune of the "Bonny Blue Flag" (see p. 218), was first published in 1865. It has been in continuous oral tradition since that time.

I cannot listen to your words,
The land's too far and wide,
Go seek some happy Northern girl
To be your loving bride.
My brothers they were soldiers;
The youngest of the three
Was slain while fighting by the side
Of General Fitzhugh Lee.

Hurrah, hurrah,
For the sunny South I say,
Three cheers for the Southern girl
And the boy that wore the Gray.

My lover was a soldier too,
    He fought at God's command;
A sabre pierced his gallant heart,
    You might have been the man;
He reeled and fell but was not dead,
    A horseman spurred his steed,
And trampled on his dying brain—
    You might have done the deed.

Hurrah, hurrah, etc.

They left his body on the field,
    Who the fight this day had won,
A horseman spurred him with his heel,
    You might have been the one.
I hold no hatred in my heart,
    Nor cold and righteous pride,
For many a gallant soldier fell
    Upon the other side.

Hurrah, hurrah, etc.

But still I cannot take the hand
    That smote my country sore,
Or love the foe that trampled down
    The colors that she wore;
Between my heart and yours there runs
    A deep and crimson tide,
My lover's and my brothers' blood
    Forbids me be your bride.

Hurrah, hurrah, etc.

VI
Between
The
Civil War
And The
First
World War

THE PERIOD BETWEEN the Civil War and the First World War was in some ways analogous to the Jacksonian era, but on a more stupendous scale. At the end of the war, in 1865, America turned with a kind of frenzy to economic expansion. Industrialization, given great impetus by the war, now proceeded with breath-taking speed. By 1900, the United States had forged to the top as the world's greatest power. By almost any standard of economic measurement—steel, coal, and oil production, railroad mileage, number of industrial workers, commercial turnover, and aggregate national income—she was ahead of Great Britain and Germany, her principal competitors.

At the same time, the Westward Movement continued and was brought to a close. In these years, the frontier pushed up the westward slopes of the Mississippi Valley, on to the High Plains. The fabulous Cattle Kingdom, comprising parts of Texas, Oklahoma, Colorado, Kansas, Nebraska, Wyoming, and Montana, developed because of the demand for meat to feed America's teeming industrial population. The age of the cowboy came and went. Hard on the heels of the cattle men came farm settlers with plough and barbed wire, tearing up the grasslands and putting tens of thousands of acres under wheat. By 1917, the frontier disappeared. Steam tractors crawled over the vast expanses where once the buffalo had roamed, where Sioux and Apache had hunted, and where the buckaroos had rounded up their herds.

The era of the cowboy and of open grazing had come to a close by 1890, adding its own never-fading aura to the legend of pioneering romance. But there was little romance in the lives of the factory workers of the East or middle-West. American industry was open shop. Long hours, cruel exploitation, dangerous conditions, and searing poverty were the order of the day. Nor was the average farmer, especially in newly settled areas, much better off. Though American farming in this period became enormously productive as new power machinery was introduced, large numbers of farmers failed to secure any noticeable advantage. The hardest lot of all was reserved for the new immigrants, flooding in by the million from Southern and Eastern Europe to man the mines, mills, and factories, and, as aliens, to toil in grime to create wealth they would not live to share. All these people in the ranks of the dispossessed, farmers, workers, immigrants, watched with angry eyes the pyramiding fortunes of industrial millionaires and the rise of gingerbread palaces of ostentatious splendor.

Some of the songs that arose from the experiences and struggles of workers and farmers and the moods that these express receive attention in the first part of the following chapter. Much of this music-making followed a tradition with which we are now familiar: Traditional melodies and literary forms were used to create new songs expressive of new situations. Many cowboy songs, for example, were set to readily identifiable English or Irish tunes brought to the High Plains from homes in the South or East. What changed were the things about which cowboys sang and the trotting rhythms to which the words were set.

But with the immigrants in this period it was rather different. Millions of people coming into this country after the Civil War from Southern and Eastern Europe brought with them their own heritage of language, song, music, and dance; these were seen now on American soil for the first time in all their wonderful variety. *All of this is part of the American heritage simply because it is here.* American culture, one may predict, will not become truly unique, truly national, until it has learned to absorb and utilize the gifts that these immigrants brought with them. For they are as surely part of the

American bone, fiber, and spirit as the British and Irish heritage that began to root itself in the colonies nearly 300 years before. The existence of the vast but relatively unknown immigrant heritage constitutes an "underground stream" in American culture, a stream private to the groups that preserve and cherish it, but not yet common to all of us.

To make this point concretely and to illuminate the nature and beauty of the "undiscovered" heritage, the second part of this chapter is devoted to immigrant songs. We focus first of all upon the songs of the Jewish people who, between the years 1880 and 1917, came to our Eastern cities from Russia, Poland, Austria-Hungary, and the Ukraine. We may regard the singing of these people to be representative of the mood and fate of many other immigrants who came from the same area during the same period. These songs reveal a new kind of American music that was then coming into being: Jewish immigrants utilized their own musical and literary heritage to express the meaning of the new American experience which they were called upon to undergo.

In these same years, French-speaking immigrants from Canada began to filter down in large numbers into New England to work in the lumber woods, take up farms, and find jobs in the textile factories.* They brought with them elements of the French-Canadian song heritage which, in its own way, rivals that of the British in extent and importance. We have chosen two songs from the great French tributary of the "underground stream" to illustrate, again as concretely as possible, what we mean by this phrase.

The main barrier to our appreciation and use of the immigrant element of national song is a barrier of language; their mood and meaning has to be recreated in the English idiom. This fact underscores the existence of one of the cultural frontiers of our own time.

For the Negro people, the period from 1863 to 1868 represented a climax in the struggle to win freedom and full equality as American citizens. In 1867, Congress framed the Fourteenth Amendment, conferring American citizenship on ex-slaves and their descendants, and guaranteeing them broad political rights under the Constitution. In the years 1867 and 1868, all the Southern states redrafted their own constitutions

*French Canadians [Acadians] would have migrated to the British seaboard colonies during the eighteenth century, but the path was blocked at that time by imperial policy; and so these people entered the United States at the other extremity, via New Orleans.

to bring them into line with the new Federal requirements. For the first time, Negro citizens sat side by side with whites in the state legislatures and in the national Congress.

The bright hopes raised by these years faded rapidly before the harsh counterattack of the unreconstructed Southerners. Over the years, Negroes, with the complicity of the Republican Party, the Congress, and the Courts, were again forced back into the status of helots—hewers of wood and drawers of water for whites, aliens in their own land. In the late 1890's, a cast-iron system of segregation was imposed throughout the South by law; by the turn of the century, the region once again exhibited the most odious features of racism and human exploitation that had flourished during slavery days.

Abandoned and forgotten, the Negro people lived on. Negro prisoners toiled like slaves on the roads and railroads, in the river bottoms, on the levees, in the prison farms and camps. Negro croppers worked day after day like slaves from sunup to sundown, chopping and picking cotton in fields that were not theirs. The tragic destiny and the despair of an oppressed people found expression in profound and beautiful songs: chain-gang songs, prison songs, spirituals, bad-man ballads, shouts, field hollers, and blues. These will receive as much attention as space permits in the third section of the following chapter.

Farmers and Workers

The High Plains had always been the home of wandering bands of Indians: Blackfoot, Cheyenne, Crow, Arapaho, Osage, Nez Perce, Apache, Mandan, Arikara, Pawnee, and many more. These people lived by hunting the buffalo or antelope, gathering berries and roots, and planting corn and squash. Their homes were earth lodges and tepees. Their tools, until the coming of white men, were of bone and stone, their weapons, the bow and arrow and the club.

At the end of the Civil War, the age of steel moved swiftly westward into this prehistoric land. By 1869, the Union Pacific railroad had spanned the central plains through Nebraska and Wyoming, utilizing an army 10,000 strong of track-laying, bridge-building Irish. By 1872, the Atchison, Topeka, and Santa Fé and the Kansas Pacific, had been driven clear across Kansas.

These lines produced a revolution in the life of the High Plains. The buffalo were exterminated; the Indians were broken and their remnants swept into reservations. Stockyards were established at the railheads in Abilene, Newton, Dodge City, Ogalalla, and Ellis, so that Western beef could be hauled to Chicago and the hungry markets of the East. Drovers from the South Texan borderlands began to drive their herds of longhorn cattle up to the railhead cattle towns, over the long trails that led clear through Texas and Indian Territory, or up the Pecos River through New Mexico and Colorado. Between 1866 and 1890, the age of the cowboy and the long trails came and went; during this time 6 million head of Texan longhorns, at the very least, were driven northward either to provide meat for the markets and the Indian reservations or stock the grasslands of Montana, Wyoming, the Dakotas, New Mexico, and Colorado.

During these years the cattle kingdom of the open grasslands came and went in a flash, leaving its own ineffaceable imprint on the national memory. This was an epic of frontier life, and the cowboy was its hero. It was a hardy, dangerous, and challenging existence which kindled, as did the sea years before, a passion in the hearts of adventurous youth; and it was a way of life which only the toughest and most skilful could survive. The trails along which the huge herds had to be driven covered many hundreds of miles of open territory. Rivers had

257

to be forded, sometimes in flood; stampedes had to be met and checked; cattle thieves and Indians had to be fought and driven off. The cowboy was in the saddle day after day for many hours; his moments of rest were few.

From the life of the range and the open ranch arose the cowboy's songs. Like the sailor and lumberjack before him, he had songs both for work and for relaxation. His saddle songs, as might be expected, grew out of the familiar heritage of Irish and English singing which immigrant families brought with them into the West, and which he had learned at his mother's knee. Naturally, modifications occurred; rhythms were molded by the tempo of a horse's stride, and new lyrics were created to express the special joys and fears, the special impact of a horseman's life. Cowboys, too, had songs for the bunkhouse and the camp fire; here, the singing of old ballads, traditional songs, and sentimental ditties was interspersed with endless tales and yarns. The favorite cowboys' ballads told of bold, adventurous men, pioneers and outlaws, like, for example "Sioux Indians" (page 179), or "Brennan on the Moor" (page 264). "The Jam on Gerry's Rock" (page 175) was especially well liked, for the tale it told of death by drowning was only too familiar to men obliged to ford endless swirling streams on their long drives.

The cowboy was a romantic figure from the age of rural America that, by the end of the nineteenth century, was vanishing forever. The swift advance of industrialization and the rise of giant business corporations had a dramatic impact on the American social structure. At the opening of the Civil War, the majority of Americans had still been country dwellers, living upon the land; but in 1917 this was no longer so. The census of 1920 revealed that one-half the population lived in urban communities, that they were dependent for their livelihood on daily labor in mines, offices, and factories, and on the railroads, and that most of them lived in grimy industrial towns.

The huge working class that had thus arisen—by 1917 the industrial army numbered well over 15 million workers—was composed partly of European immigrants and partly of farm people who had fled to the cities. The working class was a very heterogeneous group: not more than one worker in five was a member of the trade union movement. Organization had been slowed by the fierce competition of huge numbers of poor, ignorant immigrants arriving each year, by the avariciousness of employers and their savagely anti-union policies, and by the indifference of conservative trade-union leaders to the plight of the downtrodden and exploited masses.

This period, by and large, was one of terrible suffering for working people, and often of brutal strife between them and their employers. Numerous ballads were created to express the experiences which American workers and their families suffered; they told of the calamities and the tragedies of the worker's life: factory fires and accidents, coal mine disasters, railroad smash-ups, unemployment, hunger, and hard times, strike battles, the murder of union organizers, the destructiveness of floods. The songs were topical and usually set to traditional tunes, including gospel songs, hymns, and spirituals. A few of the best of these are included in the section that follows.

I Ride an Old Paint

This song was originally published in Carl Sandburg's *American Songbag* and comes from Margaret Larkin of New Mexico. It was a favorite of Woody Guthrie's and is perhaps one of the most entrancing of all cowboy songs.

snuf - fy   Are   rar - in'   to   go.

Old Bill Jones had two daughters and a song,
One went to Denver and the other went wrong.
His wife she died in a poolroom fight,
Still he sings from morning till night.

Chorus

Oh, when I die, take my saddle from the wall,
Put it on my pony, and lead him from his stall.
Tie my bones to his back, turn our faces to the West,
And we'll ride the prairie that we love the best.

Chorus

The Colorado Trail

This love song, perhaps one of the finest that we have, was also published in Carl Sandburg's *American Songbag*. It was learned by Dr. T. L. Chapman from a cowboy patient in a Duluth, Minnesota hospital.

Eyes like the morn-ing star, Cheeks like a rose,

Ann-ie was a pret-ty girl, God Al-might-y knows;

Weep all you lit-tle rains, Wail, winds, wail,

All a-long, a-long, a-long, the Col-o-rad-o Trail.

Goodbye, Old Paint

This famous saddle song and dance song was first collected by John A. Lomax before the first World War, and is transcribed here from Lomax's recording of a Montana cowboy. It's a good song for improvising and goes jogging on forever.

Good - bye, old Paint, I'm a-

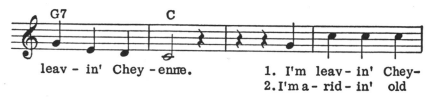

leav - in' Chey - enne, Good - bye, old Paint, I'm a-

leav - in' Chey - enne. 1. I'm leav - in' Chey-
2. I'm a - rid - in' old

enne, I'm off to Mon - tan' Good -
Paint, I'm lead - 'in' 'old Dan,

bye, old Paint, I'm a - leav - in' Chey - enne.

Goodbye, old Paint, I'm a-leavin' Cheyenne,
Goodbye, old Paint, I'm a-leavin' Cheyenne.
I'm off to Montan' to throw the houlihan,
Goodbye, old Paint, I'm a-leavin' Cheyenne.

Goodbye, old Paint, I'm a-leavin' Cheyenne,
Goodbye, old Paint, I'm a-leavin' Cheyenne.
They feed in the coulees, they water in the draw,
Goodbye, old Paint, I'm a-leavin' Cheyenne.

263

Brennan on the Moor

This is one of the best-known Irish "bad man" ballads. It tells of a hero dear to the hearts of his countrymen because he roamed the wild hills rather than submit to British tyranny. It was popular among cowboys both as a bunkhouse and saddle song.

It's a - bout a bold high - way - man my
sto - ry I will tell, His
name was Will - ie Bren - nan, and in
Ire - land he did dwell; 'Twas up -
on the Kil - wart Moun - tains he be -
gan his wild ca - reer, And
man - y a rich gen - tle - man be -

fore him shook with fear, It was

CHORUS

Bren - nan on the moor,

Bren-nan on the moor, Bold,___

gay, and un - daunt - ed stood young

Bren - nan on the moor.

One day upon the highway young Brennan he went down,
He met the mayor of Cashel five miles outside the town;
Now the mayor he knew Willie, "And I think," says he,
Your name is Willie Brennan, you must come along
    with me,

Chorus

Now Willie got his blunderbuss, my story I'll unfold,
He caused the mayor to tremble and deliver up his gold,
Five thousand pounds was offered for his apprehension
    there,
But he with horse and saddle to the mountains did repair,

Chorus

Now Willie is an outlaw all on some mountain high,
With infantry and cavalry to take him they did try,
But he laughed at them and scorned them, until,
     as it was said,
By a false-hearted woman he was cruelly betrayed,

Chorus

Now Willie hung at Clonmel, in chains he swung and
     died,
But still they say that in the night, some do see him ride;
They see him with his blunderbuss, and on the midnight
     chill,
Along the Clonmel highway rides Willie Brennan still,

Chorus

The Farmer Is the Man

The period from the early 1870's to the middle 1890's was one of great unrest among Western and Southern farmers, but primarily among pioneer farmers on the wheat-producing frontier, in the vast new prairie states of the Dakotas, Kansas, Nebraska, Minnesota, Wyoming, and Montana. Declining prices for wheat and cotton on the world market coupled with the extortionate practices of railroads, speculators, and middlemen, combined to produce a series of political explosions among the farmers that culminated in the Populist movement of 1890–1896. Many songs were produced by the farmers who were both musical and militant. Among the best known is "The Farmer Is the Man," an anonymously composed ditty that reflects Jeffersonian sentiments about the primary importance and worth of the farmer in society. The song expresses, in musical form, the famous phrase uttered by William Jennings Bryan in his 1896 "Cross of Gold" speech:

... The great cities rest upon our broad and fertile prairies. Burn down your cities and leave our farms, and your cities will spring up again as if by magic; but destroy our farms and the grass will grow in the streets of every city in the country.

When the farm-er comes to town With his
wag-on bro-ken down, Oh, the
farm-er is the man who feeds them all. If you'll
on-ly look and see, I____

think you will a - gree, That the

A   B7   E CHORUS

farm - er is the man who feeds them all. The

G#m   B7

farm - er is the man, _____ The

E   B7   E

farm - er is the man, Lives on cred - it till the

Bm   E

fall; Then they take him by the hand, And they

lead him from the land, And the

A   B7   E

mid - dle-man's the one who gets it all.

When the lawyer hangs around,
While the butcher cuts a pound,
    Oh, the farmer is the man who feeds them all.
When the preacher and the cook
Go strolling by the brook
    Oh, the farmer is the man who feeds them all.

Chorus

When the banker says he's broke
And the merchant's up in smoke,
They forget that it's the farmer feeds them all.
It would put them to the test
If the farmer took a rest;
      Then they'd know that it's the farmer feeds them all.

Chorus: The farmer is the man,
               The farmer is the man,
               Lives on credit til the fall;
               With the interest rate so high,
               It's a wonder he don't die,
               For the mortgage man's the one who gets it all.

Peter Emberley

Peter Emberley was born in 1863 at Alberton, Prince Edward Island. The ruined homestead on this beautiful coast may still be seen. In 1880, when he was 17, Peter left home and found work as a lumberman in the New Brunswick woods in the valley of the Southwest Miramichi. In the winter of that year, he was fatally injured at Parker's Ridge while loading logs and was taken to Boiestown to die.

John Calhoun, a Boiestown farmer and songwriter, composed this ballad which soon achieved a wide popularity among the people of the Miramichi. That it has served for nearly a century to keep fresh the memory of this youth among the people of New Brunswick and Maine attests to its power. In recent years, the simple wooden cross in the Boiestown Catholic Cemetery was replaced by a stone memorial; the red earth of Prince Edward Island was brought there and scattered upon the grave.

The melody to which the lyric is here set is a variant of "The Bonny Boy" and "The Jam on Gerry's Rock" (pages 18 and 175). All three songs lament the death of a young man in the prime of life; but unlike the other two "Peter Emberley" has had little currency outside of Maine and the Maritime Provinces of Canada.*

*Stewart Holbrook [*The American Lumberjack* (New York: Collier Books, 1962) page 129] calls this ballad the "ultimate in bathos." But he only reproduces one verse of the lyric, and that in a corrupted form. He would have found a Maine version, very close to Calhoun's original, in Phillips Barry, *The Maine Woods Songster* (Cambridge, Mass.: Powell Printing Co., 1939). 68-69.

stand; I was born on Prince Ed - ward's
Is - land, Close by the o - cean
strand; In eight - een hun - dred and
eight - y When the flow - ers bore a bril - liant
hue, I left my na - tive
coun - te - ree, My for - tune to pur - sue.

I landed in New Brunswick,
    That lumbering counteree,
I hired for to work in the lumber woods
    On the Sou'west Miramashee;
I hired for to work in the lumber woods
    Where they cut the tall spruce down,
It was loading two sleds from a yard
    I received my deathly wound.

There is danger on the ocean
    Where the seas roll mountain high,
There is danger on the battlefield
    Where the angry bullets fly,

271

There is danger in the lumber woods,
  And death lurks solemn there,
And I have fallen victim
  Unto its monstrous snare.

Here's adieu unto my father,
  It was him that drove me here.
I thought it very cruel of him,
  His treatment was severe;
For it is not right to impress a boy,
  Or try to keep him down,
For it oft times drives him from his home
  When he is far too young.

Here's adieu unto my greatest friend,
  I mean my mother dear,
Who reared a son that fell as quick
  As he left her tender care;
It's little she thought not long ago,
  When she sang a lullaby,
What country I might travel in,
  Or what death I might die.

Here's adieu unto a younger friend,
  My Island girl so true;
Long may she live to grace the soil
  Where my first breath I drew;
The world will roll on just the same
  As before I passed away:
What signifies a mortal man
  When he lies in the clay?

Here's adieu unto Prince Edward's Isle,
  That garden in the seas;
No more I'll roam its flowery banks
  Or enjoy a summer's breeze;
No more I'll watch those gallant brigs
  As they go sailing by,
With streamers floating in the wind
  Far above their canvas high.

But now before I pass away
    There is one more thing I pray,
I hope some holy father
    Will bless my silent grave;
Near by the city of Boiestown
    Where my mouldering bones do lie,
Awaiting for my Savior's call
    On that great rising day.

Transcribed from the singing of Marie Hare of Strathadam, New Brunswick, at the Seventh Annual Miramichi Folksong Festival, Newcastle, New Brunswick, August 19, 1964.

Hard Times in the Mill

This song arose out of the open shop conditions of textile mills in the South around the turn of the century, when the 12 hour day, starvation wages, and child labor were still the rule.

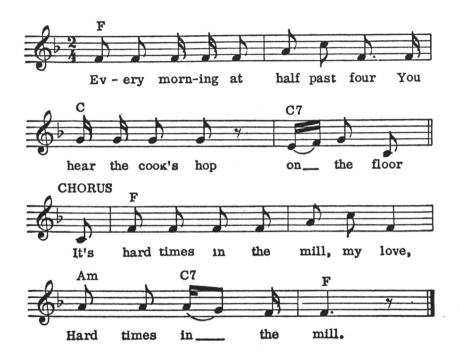

Ev - ery morn-ing at half past four You hear the cook's hop on__ the floor

CHORUS

It's hard times in the mill, my love, Hard times in__ the mill.

2. Every morning just at five
   You gotta get up, dead or alive.
Chorus

3. Every morning at six o'clock
   Two cold biscuits, hard as a rock
Chorus

4. Every morning at half-past nine
   The bosses are cussin' and the spinners are cryin'.
Chorus

5. They docked me a nickel, they docked me a dime,
   They sent me to the office to get my time.
Chorus

6. Cotton mill boys don't make enough,
   To buy them tobacco and a box of snuff.
Chorus

7. Every night when I get home,
   A piece of corn bread and an old jawbone.
Chorus

8. Ain't it enough to break your heart?
   Hafta work all day until it's dark.
Chorus

The Shoofly

The mines in the anthracite coal region of Pennsylvania were opened up before the Civil War by Welsh immigrant miners. Civil War times and the burgeoning demand for fuel for the blast furnaces brought about an immigration of German and Irish workers into the area; and at the end of the conflict, large numbers of Slavic immigrants arrived. The many nationalities involved and the plentiful supply of workers made it easy for the coal corporations to break unions, drive down wages, and convert the anthracite region into a center of poverty, bitterness, and despair. The United Mine Workers did not win a permanent footing in Eastern Pennsylvania until after World War I.

Many songs from this period tell of the hazards and hardships of a miner's life and of the sorrows that his women and children had to endure. Songs and ballads were spread far and wide through the mine regions by itinerant singers (often blinded or crippled miners) and through broadsides. "The Shoofly" dates from the hard times of the 1870's. George Korson, who collected this song tells us: "It was made by a village schoolmaster, Felix O'Hare, who put into it the anxiety and despair that followed the closing of the small mine at Valley Furnace in the Schuylkill Valley in 1871."

The Shoofly was a neighboring colliery, also closed down.

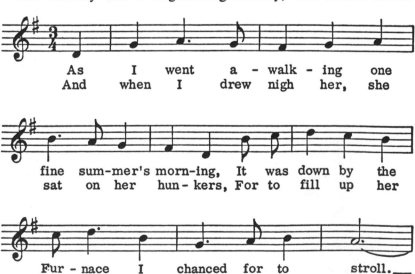

As I went a-walk-ing one fine sum-mer's morn-ing, It was down by the Fur-nace I chanced for to stroll.____

And when I drew nigh her, she sat on her hun-kers, For to fill up her scut-tle she had just be-gun,____

I es - pied an old la - dy, I'll
And to her - self she was

swear she was eight - y, At the foot of the
sing - ing a dit - ty, And these are the

dirt banks a - root - ing for coal;
words the old la - dy did sing:

CHORUS

A - cry - ing, "Och - one! sure, I'm

near - ly dis - tract -ed, For it's

down by the Shoo-fly they cut a bad

vein; And since they con - demned the old

slope at the Fur -nace, Sure all me fine

neigh-bors must leave here a - gain."___

2. " 'Twas only last evenin' that I asked McGinley
    To tell me the reason the Furnace gave o'er.
He told me the company had spent eighty thousand,
    And finding no prospects they would spend no more.
He said that the Diamond it was rather bony,
    Besides too much dirt in the seven foot vein;
And as for the Mammoth, there's no length of gangway,
    Unless they buy land from old Abel and Swayne."

Chorus

3. "And as for Michael Rooney, I owe him some money,
    Likewise Patrick Kearns, I owe him some more;
And as for old John Eagen, I ne'er see his wagon,
    But I think of the debt that I owe in the store.
I owe butcher and baker, likewise the shoemaker,
    And for plowin' me garden I owe Pat McQuail;
Likewise his old mother, for one thing and another,
    And to drive away bother, an odd quart of ale."

Chorus

4. "But if God spare me children until the next summer,
    Instead of a burden, they will be a gain;
And out of their earnin's I'll save an odd dollar,
    And build a snug home at the 'Foot of the Plane.'
Then rolling in riches, in silks, and in satin,
    I ne'er shall forget the days I was poor,
And likewise the neighbors that stood by me children,
    Kept want and starvation away from me door."

Chorus

Reprinted by permission of The Johns Hopkins University Press from *Pennsylvania Songs and Legends,* edited by George Korson (Baltimore: The Johns Hopkins University Press, 1949). © Copyright by George Korson.

The Ludlow Massacre

The Ludlow massacre of April, 1914 epitomizes the era of the open shop when employers exercised an absolute and despotic rule over their industrial serfs; obliged the workers to live in vile company shacks and buy their food in company stores at company prices; and surrounded their people with spies and thugs who watched their movements and intimidated them.

In the coal fields of Las Animas and Huerfano counties, Colorado, John D. Rockefeller and his Colorado Iron and Fuel Co. ruled the lives of thousands of Americans of Greek, Italian, Slav, and Mexican descent. In September, 1913, these workers marched out of the company shacks and took shelter in tent colonies. They were striking in protest against a total denial of personal rights and the violation by the operators of state laws regulating conditions of work in the mines, and for the recognition of their chosen union, the United Mineworkers of America.

All winter long the strike continued, and the workers held out in their tents. In April 1914, Company B of the state militia, recruited mainly from company strongarm men, moved into the Ludlow colony with machine guns and coal oil. When the flaming slaughter was over, 21 people were dead; 13 were children, 2 were women. Louis Tikxas, a mineworkers' leader, and three miners were taken prisoner and murdered by the militiamen in cold blood. The massacre precipitated a general rebellion of Colorado miners which was only put down with the aid of Federal troops.

Woody Guthrie, who wrote the ballad that we reproduce here, was born in Oklahoma in 1912 and grew up in the open shop era that lasted into the early '30's. In the twentieth century, the American labor movement has produced no balladeer whose genius compares to his.

It was ear - ly spring - time when the strike was on, __ They drove us min - ers

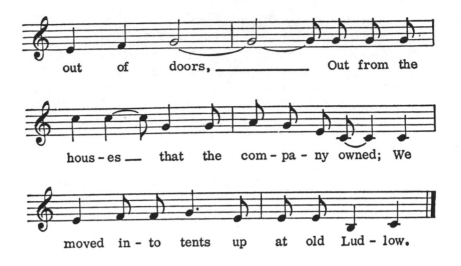

out   of   doors, _____   Out from the

hous - es __   that   the   com - pa - ny owned; We

moved in - to   tents   up   at   old Lud - low.

I was worried bad about my children,
Soldiers guarding the railroad bridge;
Every once in a while the bullets would fly,
Kick up gravel under my feet.

We were so afraid you would kill our children,
We dug us a cave that was seven foot deep,
Carried our young ones and a pregnant woman
Down inside the cave to sleep.

That very night you soldiers waited,
Until us miners was asleep;
You snuck around our little tent town,
Soaked our tents with your kerosene.

You struck a match and the blaze it started;
You pulled the triggers of your gatling guns;
I made a run for the children but the fire wall stopped me,
Thirteen children died from your guns.

I carried my blanket to a wire fence corner,
Watched the fire till the blaze died down;
I helped some people grab their belongings,
While your bullets killed us all around.

I never will forget the look on the face,
Of the men and women that awful day,
When we stood around to preach their funerals
And lay the corpses of the dead away.

We told the Colorado governor to phone the President,
Tell him to call off his National Guard;
But the National Guard belonged to the Governor,
So he didn't try so very hard.

Our women from Trinidad they hauled some potatoes
Up to Walsenburg in a little cart;
They sold their potatoes and brought some guns back
And they put a gun in every hand.

The state soldiers jumped us in the wire fence corner;
They did not know that we had these guns.
And the red-neck miners mowed down these troopers,
You should have seen those poor boys run.

We took some cement and walled the cave up
Where you killed these thirteen children inside;
I said "God bless the mine workers' union,"
And then I hung my head and cried.

Solidarity Forever

The Industrial Workers of the World was organized in 1905 by radical and labor groups intent upon organizing the masses of unskilled and semiskilled workers into a single industrial union regardless of race, creed, or color. Its songster, *IWW Songs,* first appeared in 1906 and over the years was expanded to include lyrics by Ralph Chaplin, Joe Hill, James Connell, and others. Undoubtedly the best of these songs is "Solidarity Forever." Written by Chaplin in 1915, and sung to the tune of "John Brown's Body," it continues to be reproduced until the present time in the *AFL-CIO Songbook,* an official publication of the American labor movement.

1. When the union's inspiration through the worker's blood
        shall run,
    There can be no power greater anywhere beneath the sun.
    Yet what force on earth is weaker than the feeble strength
        of one?
    But the union makes us strong.
Chorus: Solidarity forever!
            Solidarity forever!
            Solidarity forever!
            For the union makes us strong.

2. They have taken untold millions that they never toiled to
        earn,
    But without our brain and muscle not a single wheel could
        turn.
    We can break their haughty power, earn our freedom when
        we learn
    That the union makes us strong.
Chorus

3. It is we who ploughed the prairie, built the cities where
        they trade,
    Dug the mines and built the workshops, endless miles of
        railroad laid,
    Now we stand outcast and starving midst the wonders we
        have made,
    But the union makes us strong.
Chorus

4. In our hands is placed a power greater than their hoarded
   gold,
   Greater than the might of armies magnified a thousand
   fold
   We can bring to birth a new world from the ashes of the
   old,
   For the union makes us strong.

Chorus

Immigrants

Between 1890 and 1914, a total of 15 million people immigrated to the United States. The immigrants—Italians, Poles, Russians, Ukrainians, Czechs, Greeks, Hungarians, and Rumanians—came primarily from Eastern and Southern Europe. One and one-half million of them, or roughly 10 per cent, were Jews.

The last and greatest wave of Jewish migration to America began in 1881. The Jewish people came here principally from the Polish provinces which Russia had acquired as the result of the partition of Poland in 1772. Since that time, the Tsars had established and maintained in Poland a pale of Jewish settlement beyond which Jews were forbidden to go; and they had hounded these people with a bitterly repressive policy which included the direct instigation of pogroms, or massacres, of the helpless minority. In 1881, the assassination of Alexander II touched off a new wave of violence against the Jews and produced the passage of laws imposing new and ferocious restrictions upon them. Large scale migration to America set in and continued without letup until the outbreak of World War I.

The everyday language of the Polish and Russian Jews was Yiddish, a dialect originating with the Jewish settlements in medieval Germany, which the Jews retained as they were driven eastward. The songs of these Yiddish-speaking people were born of the bitterness of poverty and oppression; they drew upon both the Jewish literary and musical heritage as well as Slavic melody to express a many-sided picture of Jewish life. These songs—love songs, lullabies, street songs, ballads—came to the New World with the immigrants. Virtually erased by Hitler and Himmler's nearly total massacre of the Jewish population of Europe, these Yiddish songs constitute a precious part of the American heritage that is preserved in its fullness only here.

In Poland, many of the Jews had been village or small town handicraftsmen; in the United States, they found work at first principally in the clothing industry. Their first experience of America was in the sweatshops and tenements of New York City's lower East Side. Here they were crammed into slums that gave the City's Jewish quarter the dubious fame of having the densest population per square mile in the world. They lived and toiled amid what one observer described as "the endless panorama of the tenements, rows upon rows, between stony streets, stretching to the north, to the south, to the west, as far as the eye reaches."* Here, in dingy, crowded, airless rooms, men, women, and children worked for endless hours, sewing and cutting garments for a pittance.

The first Jewish immigrants found themselves at the mercy of the "sweater," the middleman who gave out the work, set the wages, and took the profit from selling the product of their labor to finishers. The sweater's power lay in the mass of ignorant immigrants arriving daily on these shores with the immediate, pressing need for shelter and bread. As Jacob Riis wrote in 1890:

> As long as the ignorant crowds continue to come and to herd in these tenements, his grip can never be shaken off. And the fresh supply across the seas is apparently inexhaustible. Every fresh persecution of the Russian or Polish Jew on his native soil starts greater hordes hitherward to confound economic problems, and to recruit the sweater's phalanx. The curse of bigotry and ignorance reaches half way across the world, to sow its bitter seed in fertile soil in the East Side tenements.**

"Ot Azoy" and "Mein Yingele" deal directly with the immigrant's experience. The first tells of the weary lot of the Jewish handicraftsman and of the inevitable struggle to set a limit to his toil which resulted in the first victories of unionization in the Jewish garment unions. "Mein Yingele," was written by an immigrant, Morris Rosenfeld, in 1887. It tells its own story of the hardship that long hours of labor in the garment factories inflicted upon working people by denying them the simplest rights and pleasures of life. This song, in the course of time, found its way back to Yiddish-speaking people in Europe and achieved an international renown. "Schlof Mayn Kind," with lyrics by Sholom Aleichem, tells the familiar tale of the woman with little children, waiting anxiously for a letter from America. When will papa write? Is he still living? When will the family be reunited? "Papir Iz Doch Vays" is among many exquisite love songs which the immigrants brought with them to the New World.

*Jacob Riis, *How the Other Half Lives* (New York: Sagamore Press, 1957), 87.
**Ibid, 90.

Ot Azoy Neyt A Shnayder
(Weary Days Are a Tailor's)

CHORUS

Wea - ry days are — a tai - lor's,
Wea - ry days are — his. Wea - ry days
are — a tai - lor's, Wea - ry days — are — his.

From dawn til dusk he sews a - way, A
cent and a song are all his pay.

Chorus

From dawn till dusk he sits and sews,
Hunger and pain are all he knows.

Chorus

From dawn till dusk we work away,
Time was, we worked a twelve-hour day.

> The union broke the twelve-hour day,
> Brought us shorter hours and better pay.

*   *   *

Chorus

> Ot azoy neyt a shnayder,
> Ot azoy neyt er doch!

> Er neyt un neyt a gantse voch,
> Fardint a gildn mit a loch!

Chorus

> A shnayder neyt un neyt un neyt,
> Un hot kadoches, nit kayn brot!

Chorus

> Farayorn, nit haynt-gedacht!
> Hob mir gehorevet fun acht bis acht!

Chorus

> Ober die struksie hot ongemacht,
> Mir arbetn shoyn mer nit fun acht biz acht!

Schlof Mayn Kind
(Sleep, My Child)

Sleep, my child, my   sweet, my pret-ty one,

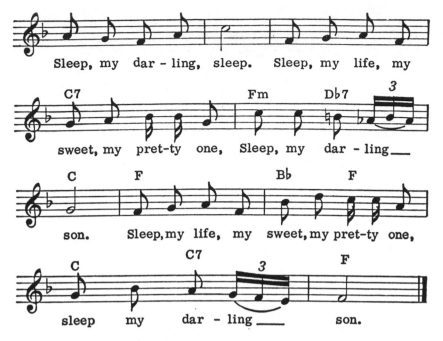

Sleep, my dar - ling, sleep. Sleep, my life, my

C7   Fm   Db7   3

sweet, my pret-ty one, Sleep, my dar - ling___

C   F   Bb   F

son.   Sleep, my life, my sweet, my pret-ty one,

C   C7   3   F

sleep   my   dar - ling___   son.

By your cradle sits your mama,
    Sings a song and weeps.
One day you will understand.
    Why your mama weeps.

Daddy's gone to America,
    Daddy's gone far away.
He has left us here a-waiting!
    Sleep, my darling babe.

In that far-off land, they say,
    Everyone is blest.
In that promised land, they say,
    Weary folk find rest.

Daddy will send us twenty dollars,
    And his picture too.
If he's living, sure he'll fetch us,
    We'll start life anew.

He will hug us, he will kiss us,
    He will leap for joy!
I will stand there, stand there quietly.
    Tears will stream down.

While we wait his happy message,
    Sleep, my darling, do.
Sleep, my darling, since you're little,
    And I watch over you.

*   *   *

Schlof mayn kind, mayn treyst mayn sheyner,
    Schlof-zhe zunenyu.
Schlof mayn lebn, mayn kadish eyner,
    Schlof-zhe, lyu-lyu-lyu.

Bay dayn vigl zitst dayn mame
    Zingt a lid un veynt.
Du vest amol farshteyn mistame,
    Vos zi hot gemeynt.

In Amerike ist der tate,
    Dayner, zunenyu,
Du bizt noch a kind les-ate,
    Schlof-zhe, lyu-lyu-lyu.

In Amerike iz far yedn
    Zogt men, gor a glik.
Un far yedn, a gan-eydn,
    Gor epes antik.

Er vet shikn tsvantsig doler,
    Zayn portret dertsu,
Un vet nemen, lebn zol er!
    Undz ahintsutsu.

Er vet chapn undz un kushn,
    Tantsn azh far freyd!
Ich vel kvaln trern gisn,
    Veynen shtilerheyt.

Biz es kumt dos gute kvitl,
    Schlof-zhe zunenyu.
Schlofn iz a tayer mitl,
    Schlof-zhe, lyu-lyu-lyu.

Mayn Yingele
(My Little Son)

I have a lit - tle son,___ A lit - tle boy so fine, And when I look at him I think, The whole wide world is mine. Rare- ly do I set eyes on him While he's play-ing in broad day-light; I watch him on-ly while he sleeps, I see him on-ly at night.

At dawn my work drives me away,
And keeps me long from home;
My flesh and blood is strange to me,
My son's a joy unknown.

I stumble home in black despair
Through all my empty days
To hear my weary wife describe
How sweetly my child plays.

290

I stand and watch my sleeping son,
My heart is still and sad;
I listen to his murmuring lips
That ask: "Where is my Dad?"

I stand and watch my sleeping son,
And my soul is torn with pain:
One day, my child, you will awake,
But I'll not come again.

*　　*　　*

Ich hob a kleynem yingele,
A zunele gor fayn.
Ven ich derze im, dacht sich mir,
Di gantse velt is mayn!

Nor zeltn, zeltn, ze ich im,
Mayn sheynem, ven er vacht.
Ich tref im imer schlofndig,
Ich ze im nor baynacht.

Di arbet traybt mich fri aroys,
Un lozt mich sper tsurik.
O, fremd is mir mayn eygn layb,
Mayn eygn kind's a blik.

Ich kum tsuklemterheyd aheym,
In finsternish gehilt,
Mayn bleche froy dertseylt mir bald
Vi fayn dos kind zich shpilt.

Ich shtey bay zayn gelegerl,
Un her un ze un sha . . .
A troym bavegt di lipelech:
O, vu iz, vu iz Pa?

Ich blayb tsuveytogt un tsuklemt
Farbitert un ich kler:
Ven du ervachst amol, mayn kind,
Gefinstu mich nit mer.

Papir Iz Doch Vays
(Silver Is the Daylight)

Sil - ver is the day - light, and

blue is the sea, Bright is the

new love, you have brought to me; Let me

stay near you al - ways,

Let our fin - gers twine, Let me kiss your

rose-red lips; let me call you mine.

Last night I went to a wedding, I danced through the night.
A thousand thousand pretty girls danced in my sight;
A thousand thousand pretty girls, but none like you so fair,
With your black and dancing eyes and your black
and dancing hair.

I find you everywhere, in earth, sea and sky.
My love torments me as the world goes by;
My love torments me always, as I stand alone and gaze,
At the black and sparkling vault, where I sing my song
    of praise.

Oh God in Heaven, grant me my cherished dream!
Not pearls nor rubies that vain and falsely gleam,
Grant me a hut for my palace, where my love and
    I may be,
In the green and peaceful meadow, where the silver
    streams flow free.

*   *   *   *

Papir iz doch vays un tint iz doch shvarts,
Tsu dir mayn zis lebn, tsit doch mayn harts.
Ich volt shtendig gezesn draw teg nochanand
Tsu kushn dayn sheyn ponim un tsu halt dayn hant.

Nechtn baynacht bin ich oyf a chasene geven,
Fil sheyne meydelech hob ich dort gezen.
Fil sheyne meydelech—tsu dirkumt nisht gor—
Mit dayne shvartse eygelech un dayne shvartse hor.

Dayn talye, dayn mine, dayn eydeler tason,
In hartsn brent a fayer, men set es not on.
Nito aza mentsh, vos zol filn vi es brent,
Der toyt un dos lebn iz bay Got in di hent.

Ach du liber Got, her oys mayn farlang,
Dem oysher gistu kovid, mit asheynem gang—
Oy, mir, gib a shtibele oyf dem groz dem grinem
Az ich mit mayn zis-lebn zoln voynen derinen.

Son Petit Jupon
Isabeau S'y Promène

The ancestors of the French Canadians came from France's coastal provinces of Normandy and Brittany; in the New World, they settled on shores and islands washed by the waters of the St. Lawrence and the Atlantic. Thus, it is not surprising that many of these people's loveliest songs involve the sea.

Both in Canada and Louisiana, many songs of French origin have survived, and in addition a new, specifically French-American body of song has been created. The two songs reproduced here may both be considered of Canadian origin, though both, in one form or another, are still sung in France. Both are ballads that survive in the singing of French-Americans in the United States. "Son Petit Jupon" tells its charming story with delicacy and humor; the melody is sung on the five-note pentatonic scale, and is evidently very old; it is only one of numerous variants to which the lyric has been set. "Isabeau S'y Promène" tells a tragic story with a lightness of touch and subtlety of expression that effectively accents its sadness. It may be considered a masterpiece of ballad form. The melody is in the Dorian mode (D to D on the white keys of the piano); its original harmonic "feel" will be destroyed if it is accompanied with chords whose notes lie outside the scale as here used. I learned this version of the song from the singing of Mrs. Leo Mitchell of Newcastle, New Brunswick; it was one of her favorites from a childhood spent on the Magdalen Islands, off the New Brunswick coast.

Son Petit Jupon
(The Little Dress of Gray)

Mon père n'av - ait fil -
My fa - ther had no

le que moi, Mon père n'av -
daugh - ter but me, My fa - ther

ait fil - le que moi, Or donc, sur
had no daugh-ter but me, And once he

REFRAIN

la mer il m'en - voie, Ma - rie Ma - de -
sent me out to sea, Mar - y Ma - de -

leine, son p'tit jup - on de
leine, In her lit - tle dress of

laine, Ma - rie, Ma - rie Ma - de -
gray, Mar - y, Mar - y Ma - de -

lon, son tout pet - it jup - on.
lon, Is she going to come my way?

Or, donc, sur la mer il m'envoie
Or, donc, sur la mer il m'envoie,
Le marinier qui m'y menoit,
Refrain

Le marinier qui m'y menoit,   (*bis*)
Il devint amoureux de moi,
Refrain

Il devint amoureux de moi,   (*bis*)
Souvent de moi il s'approchoit,
Refrain

Souvent de moi il s'approchoit,   (*bis*)
Il dit: "Ma mie, embrassez-moi,"
Refrain

Il dit: "Ma mie, embrassez-moi,"   (*bis*)
"Non, non, monsieur, je n'oserois,"

295

Refrain

Non, non, monsieur, je n'oserois,"   (*bis*)
Car si mon papa il savoit,"
Refrain

Car si mon papa il savoit,   (*bis*)
Fille battue ce serait moi,"
Refrain

"Fille battue ce serait moi,   (*bis*)
Mais, ma'moiselle, qui lui diroit?"
Refrain

          *   *   *

And when he sent me out to sea, (*twice*)
The sailor who was with me,
Refrain

The sailor who was with me, (*twice*)
With his affections was too free,
Refrain

With his affections was too free, (*twice*)
He often came and stood by me,
Refrain

And when he was as close as this, (*twice*)
He said, "My fair, give me a kiss,"
Refrain

"Give me a kiss, you are so fair," (*twice*)
"No, no, my friend, I would not dare,"
Refrain

"No, no, my friend, I would not dare, (*twice*)
For if my papa were to hear,"
Refrain

"For if my papa were to hear, (*twice*)
He would chastise me, I do fear,"
Refrain

"He would chastise you, you do fear, (*twice*)
But, ma'moiselle, he is not near!"
Refrain

Isabeau S'y Promène (Isabel)

I - sa - beau s'y pro - mè - ne
I - sa - bel was a - walk - ing

Le long de son jar - din,___ Le long de
Down in the gar - den green,___ Down in the

son jar - din Sur le bord de l'île,___
gar - den green At the is - land's edge,___

Le long de son jar - din Sur le bord de
Down in the gar - den green By the wa - ter -

l'eau, Sur le bord du vais - seau.___
side Where the tall___ ships ride.___

2. Elle fit un rencontre
   De trente matelots,
   De trente matelots
      Sur le bord de l'île,
   De trente matelots
      Sur le bord de l'eau,
      Sur le bord du vaisseau.

3. Le plus jeune des trente
   Il se mit a chanter,
   Il se mit a chanter
      Sur le bord de l'île,

Il se mit a chanter
     Sur le bord de l'eau,
     Sur le bord du vaisseau.

4. "La chanson que tu chantes,
    Je voudrais la savoir,
    Je voudrais la savoir
        Sur le bord de l'île,
    Je voudrais la savoir
        Sur le bord de l'eau
        Sur le bord du vaisseau."

5. "Embarque dans ma barque,
    Je te la chanterai,
    Je te la chanterai
        Sur le bord de l'île,
    Je te la chanterai
        Sur le bord de l'eau,
        Sur le bord du vaisseau."

6. Quand ell' fut dans la barque,
    Ell' se mit a pleurer.

7. "Qu'avez-vous donc la belle,
    Qu'a'-vous a tant pleurer?"

8. "Je pleur' mon anneau d'or,
    Dans l'eau-z-il est tombé."

9. "Ne pleurez point la belle,
    Je vous le plongerai."

10. De la première plonge,
    Il n'a rien ramené.

11. De la seconde plonge
    L'anneau-z-a voltigé.

12. De la troisième plonge
    Le galant s'est noyé.

*   *   *

2. She met a band of sailors
   While she was walking there.
   While she was walking there
       At the island's edge,
   While she was walking there
       By the waterside
       Where the tall ships ride.

3. The youngest of the sailors
   He sang a song of love.
   He sang a song of love
       At the island's edge,
   He sang a song of love
       By the waterside
       Where the tall ships ride.

4. "Your song is such a sweet one,
   I'd like to sing it too.
   I'd like to sing it too
       At the island's edge,
   I'd like to sing it too
       By the waterside
       Where the tall ships ride."

5. "Come with me to my tall ship
   And I'll sing you my song.
   And I'll sing you my song
       At the island's edge,
   And I'll sing you my song
       By the waterside
       Where the tall ships ride."

6. She went on board that tall ship,
   But soon began to cry.
   But soon began to cry
       At the island's edge,
   But soon began to cry
       By the waterside
       Where the tall ships ride.

7. "What's wrong, my pretty lady,
   That makes you so lament?
   That makes you so lament
       At the island's edge,

That makes you so lament
        By the waterside
        Where the tall ships ride?"

8. "I'm weeping for my gold ring
That in the water fell.
That in the water fell
        At the island's edge,
That in the water fell
        By the waterside
        Where the tall ships ride."

9. "Oh, do not cry my lady,
I'll fetch it back for you.
I'll fetch it back for you
        At the island's edge,
I'll fetch it back for you
        By the waterside
        Where the tall ships ride."

10. He dived into the ocean,
But came up with no ring.
But came up with no ring
        At the island's edge,
But came up with no ring
        By the waterside
        Where the tall ships ride.

11. The next time that he dived there
The golden ring did gleam.
The golden ring did gleam
        At the island's edge,
The golden ring did gleam
        By the waterside
        Where the tall ships ride.

12. The third time that he dived there,
The youth no more was seen.
The youth no more was seen
        At the island's edge,
The youth no more was seen
        By the waterside
        Where the tall ships ride.

Son Petit Jupon and *Isabeau S'y Promène* translated from the French by John Anthony Scott.

The Negro People

The Civil War destroyed slavery, but it did not bring to the Negro the freedom for which he had given his blood. In the years that followed the conflict, the Federal Government made many promises to the Negro of full rights, citizenship, land, education, human dignity, and freedom. By the end of the nineteenth century, these promises had been repudiated. A relatively small number of Southern whites continued, as before the Civil War, to control the economic resources of the South and, above all, the land. This fact alone doomed the Negro to a role of continued subordination and inferiority in the Southern system. Between the end of Reconstruction (usually dated from the disputed Hayes-Tilden election of 1876–1877) and the end of the century the Negro fell, or was pushed, back into a voteless, nameless, landless, rightless, poverty-stricken obscurity. Negro men, women, and children lived on in the draughty shacks of slavery days, picking cotton in the fields from sunup to sundown for a bare existence.

Segregation was so fundamental a feature of slave life that it endured long after the institution of slavery itself had been abolished. At the end of the nineteenth century, the Southern states enacted segregation codes that gave the explicit sanction of law to traditional Southern practices. Desperately afraid that the Negro might break out of the isolation imposed upon him and play a new and creative role in the political life of the section, Southern legislators passed laws that openly forbade the Negro to soil the white man's world. A Negro could not drink at the same fountain, sit in the same school, eat at the same table, or ride in the same car, as a white person; and he could not marry a white woman.

Retribution for the Negro who "got out of line" was swift. After the Civil War, the practice of leasing out convicts to private companies for forced labor became widespread. The most trifling offense might spell a sentence of months of work on the roads and the railroads, in the mines or on the levees.* Utilization of convicts in this way not only enriched the private operator but also reduced taxation. The leasing system encouraged wild irresponsibility and horrifying brutality in the use and abuse of human beings; even when it fell into

*Convicts were sometimes used as strikebreakers, e.g., by the Knoxville, Tennessee, Iron Company, 1877–1892. It is instructive that the free miners not only fought the use of scabs, but also protested the barbaric cruelty with which, as they asserted, the convicts were treated.

disuse, Southern states continued to operate their penal institutions on a strict commercial basis and to subject prisoners to the cruelty of a system of forced labor that differed little in substance from the regime of slavery itself. Negro prisoners, in the long years between the Civil War and the First World War, had no rights that a guard need respect. Negro life was cheap; no one cared whether a Negro lived or died, so long as he worked.

Creatively and spiritually, in these years, the Negro people rose far above their tormentors. They created a music unrivaled in the wide spectrum of American singing for its expressiveness, poignancy, humanity, and beauty. This was a music of work songs, spirituals, and blues.

The work songs included chain gang and prison songs, which fulfilled, collectively, a function central to traditional song: to enable people to face and overcome the intolerable ordeals of life, summon inspiration from the depths of the soul, survive, and endure. The singing was, of necessity, unaccompanied except for the rhythms or stresses that might be beaten out by hammer, pick, ax, or shuffling feet. With the blues it was different; they constituted a profoundly personal expression of the misery and humiliations which men and women had to endure daily, a personal statement of human feelings about life and its manifold injustices. The blues were leisure time songs, and therefore accompaniment was both possible and natural. Here, the guitar, which had made its first appearance on American soil before the Civil War, was called into service. To the Negro people goes the honor of making it a native American instrument. Southern blues singers worked out accompaniments in which the guitar not only was used with extraordinary sophistication, but also assumed the role of a second voice. The first, and perhaps the greatest, of the blues singers were country people, often blind or crippled, who wandered from place to place and sang for their living. In the course of time, the blues, like jazz, went to town undergoing as it did so, a gradual change. Spirituals, too, continued to be sung, as in the days before the Civil War, and to perform much the same many-sided function: part devotional music, part work song, part lament.

In the pages that follow, we have tried to select a few of the songs that convey most perfectly the mood and meaning of these years.

Pick a Bale o' Cotton

"Pick a Bale o' Cotton" was a favorite of Huddie Leadbetter ("Leadbelly"), the great Southern singer. Its lively rhythm was well calculated to lighten the monotonous, daylong labor of chopping or picking. For children, it was a natural for dancing and skipping. Recently, American folksingers have taken it to the Soviet Union, where it has proved enormously popular.

2. A me an' my wife can
   Pick a bale o' cotton,
   A me an' my wife can
   Pick a bale a day.
Chorus

3. A me an' my girl can
    Pick a bale o' cotton,
    A me an' my girl can
    Pick a bale a day.
Chorus

4. A me an' my friend can
    Pick a bale o' cotton,
    A me an' my friend can
    Pick a bale a day.
Chorus

5. A me an' my pappa can
    Pick a bale o' cotton,
    A me an' my pappa can
    Pick a bale a day.
Chorus

6. You got to jump down turn around
    Pick a bale o' cotton,
    You got to jump down turn around
    Pick a bale a day.
Chorus

No More Cane on This Brazos

"No More Cane on This Brazos" is a cane-cutting song from the Texan sugar lands and is believed by some to rank with the most sublime songs ever created or sung in the United States. Few songs express more clearly the meaning of human bondage on the Texas and Mississippi plantations *after* the Civil War, when prisoners were leased out to private landowners and driven until they were blind, mad, or dead.

2. Now cap'n, doncha do me like you done poor Shine,
   Oh—
   You done drive that bully till he went stone blind,
   Oh—.

3. Oughta come on the river in 1904.
   Oh—
   You could find a dead man on every turn row,
   Oh—.

4. Oughta come on the river in 1910,
   Oh—
   They was drivin' the women jes' like the men,
   Oh—.

5. Now, wake up, dead man, help me drive my row,
   Oh—
   Wake up, dead man, help me drive my row,
   Oh—.

6. Wake up, lifer, hold up yo' head,
   Oh—
   You may get a pardon, and you may drop dead,
   Oh—.

7. Go down, ole Hannah, doncha rise no mo',
   Oh—
   If you come back, bring the Judgment Day,
   Oh—.

8. There ain't no more cane on this Brazos,
   Oh—
   They done grind it all in molasses,
   Oh—.

9. Some in the prison and some on the farm,
   Oh—
   Some in the fields and some goin home,
   Oh—.

Another Man Done Gone

"Another Man Done Gone" is a simple, haunting, and incomparably beautiful melody transcribed from the singing of Vera Hall of Livingston, Alabama, as recorded by John A. and Alan Lomax for the Library of Congress Archive of American Folk Song.

An-oth-er man done__ gone,____ An-
oth - er man__ done gone____ From the
coun -ty farm, An - oth - er man done gone.

2. I didn't know his name,
   I didn't know his name,
   I didn't know his name,
   I didn't know his name.

3. He had a long chain on,
   He had a long chain on,
   He had a long chain on,
   He had a long chain on.

4. He killed another man,
   He killed another man,
   He killed another man,
   He killed another man.

5. I don' know where he's gone,
   I don' know where he's gone,
   I don' know where he's gone,
   I don' know where he's gone.

6. I'm gonna walk your road,
   I'm gonna walk your road,
   I'm gonna walk your road,
   I'm gonna walk your road.

7. Another man done gone,
   Another man done gone
   From the county farm,
   Another man done gone.

From a 78 r.p.m. recording in the Archive of Folk Song, Library of Congress.

Godamighty Drag

"Godamighty Drag" was learned by Alan Lomax from the singing of Augustus (Track Horse) Haggerty in the Huntsville, Texas Penitentiary. Lomax writes of song and singer:

Track Horse was a powerful, stocky Negro with a wonderful smile, a beautiful voice, and the gift of leadership. When he took the lead in a work song, his buddies sang like demons, and the chips spun through the air like flecks of brown foam. This was his favorite work song— I suspect his own composition. . . . Songs like this helped to clear the live-oaks off the rich river bottom land of Texas, and thus to create the cotton plantations that enriched the state.*

*"Texas Folk Songs," sung by Alan Lomax. Tradition 1029.

2. Done tole me they'd pardon me
    O lawdy,
Done tole me they'd pardon me
    O o my Lord.
By next July sir,
    O lawdy,
By next July sir,
    O o my Lord.

3. July and August
    O lawdy,
July and August,
    O o my Lord.
Done come and gone sir,
    O lawdy,
Done come and gone sir,
    O o my Lord.

4. Left me here rolling
    O lawdy,
Left me here rolling
    O o my Lord.
On this ole farm sir,
    O lawdy,
On this ole farm sir,
    O o my Lord.

5. Gonna write to the Governor
    O lawdy,
Gonna write to the Governor
    O o my Lord.
See if he'll help me
    O lawdy,
See if he'll help me
    O o my Lord.

6. Mamma and pappa
    O lawdy,
Mamma and pappa,
    God amighty God knows!
Done tole me a lie, sir,
    O lawdy,
Done tole me a lie, sir,
    O o my Lord.

7. Done tole me they'd pardon me
      O lawdy,
   Done tole me they'd pardon me,
      O o my Lord.
   Fore next July, sir,
      O Lawdy,
   Fore next July sir
      O o my Lord.

No More, My Lord

"No More, My Lord" is transcribed from a recording made by Alan Lomax in 1947 at the Mississippi State Penitentiary at Parchman. It is a good example of a spiritual that is also a work song; one in which the stroke of the ax on the downbeat is an integral part of the melody. "No More, My Lord" has a deceptive simplicity that conceals an extraordinary musical sophistication. The melody, tranquil and serene, ranks among the finest in our heritage. Compare it to "Sold Off to Georgy," page 206 above. There is similarity, and also development.

have ___ made   me ___ glad.
me ___ where   He's ___ gone?
you may find,   find Him there.

1. I found in Him
   A resting place
   And he have made me glad.

2. Jesus the man
   I am looking for,
   Can you tell me
   Where He's gone?

3. Go down, go down
   Among floweryard
   And perhaps you may find,
   Find Him there.

"No More My Lawd" ("No More, My Lord"). Collected, adapted and arranged by Alan Lomax. TRO - © Copyright 1966 Ludlow Music, Inc., New York, N.Y. Transcribed by John Anthony Scott from *Negro Prison Songs*, Tradition Records 1020. Used by permission.

Settin' Side That Road

This piece is transcribed from the singing of Godar Chalvin of Abbeville, Louisiana; with three lines to the stanza, it is written in the classic blues form. The song is included here as an example of "rural blues" that directly and obviously illustrates the connection between the man's predicament and his musical complaint.

That judge give me six months because I didn't wanna
work;
That judge give me six months because I didn't wanna
work;
That judge give me six months because I didn't wanna
work;

I'm settin' side that road, etc.

Transcribed by John Anthony Scott from *A Sampler of Louisiana Folksongs*, a publication of the Louisiana Folklore Society, collected and edited by Dr. Harry Oster, Louisiana State University. Used by permission of Dr. Ethelyn G. Orso, Editor, *Louisiana Folklore Miscellany*.

The Ballad of the Boll Weevil

At the beginning of the twentieth century the plight of Southern cotton farmers was aggravated by the spread of the boll weevil, an insect blight that entered Texas from Mexico in 1892; between 1900 and 1922, it took a tremendous annual toll of the United States cotton crop. This misfortune fell with a special impact on the poor Negro tenants and croppers of Mississippi, Alabama, Louisiana, Georgia, and South Carolina. Many of them were ruined and after 1909 began to move northward in large numbers to seek jobs. From this time dates the rapid growth of the ghettoes of Chicago and New York.

"The Ballad of the Boll Weevil" has been found in dozens of variants throughout the South, wherever the cotton farmer suffered from the weevil's depredations. We reproduce two of these variants: the first, a commonly sung version of the ballad, and the second a slow, haunting melody transcribed from the singing of Vera Hall of Livingston, Alabama, as recorded by John A. Lomax in the 1930's for the Library of Congress.

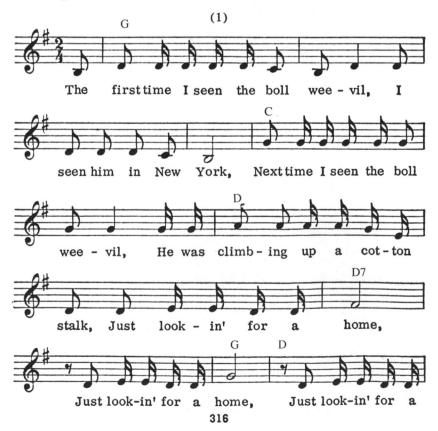

home,   Just look-in' for a   home._____

The first time I seen the boll weevil,
He was settin' on the square,
The next time I seen the boll weevil,
He had all his family there,
    Just lookin' for a home, etc.

The farmer took the boll weevil
And buried him in the sand,
Boll weevil said to the farmer,
"I'll stand it like a man,
    It'll be my home," etc.

Then the farmer took the boll weevil,
And left him on the ice,
Boll weevil say to the farmer,
"This is mighty cool and nice,
    It'll be my home," etc.

Farmer said to the boll weevil
"I see you at my door,"
"Yessir," said the boll weevil,
"I been here before,
    I'm gonna get your home," etc.

Boll weevil say to the farmer,
"You can ride in your Ford machine,
When I get through with yo' cotton,
Can't buy no gasoline,
    Won't have no home," etc.

The farmer say to the merchant,
"I want some meat and meal,"
"Get away from here you son of a gun,
Got weevils in yo' field,
    Gonna get yo' home," etc.

If anyone should ask you
Who it was that wrote this song,
Tell him 'twas a dark-skinned farmer
With a pair of blue duckin's on,

Lookin' for a home,
Just lookin' for a home, etc.

(2)

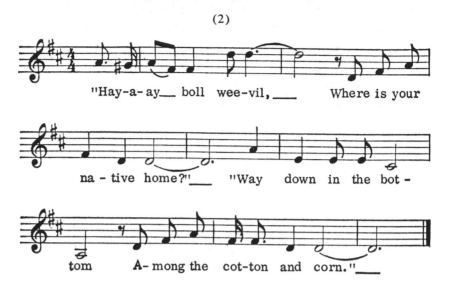

"Hay-a-ay__ boll wee-vil, ___ Where is your na-tive home?"___ "Way down in the bot- tom A-mong the cot-ton and corn."___

First time I seen the boll weevil,
He's settin' on the square;
Next time I seen him,
He had his family there.

Boll weevil here,
Boll weevil everywhere;
They done ate up all the cotton and corn,
All but that new ground square.

Well, the farmer asked the merchant
Uh—for some meat and meal.
"T'ain't nothing doin', old man;
Boll weevil's in your field."

"Hay-a-ay boll weevil,
Where is your native home?"
"Way down in the bottom
Among the cotton and corn."

The Ballad of the Boll Weevil (1) and (2) from Record AFS L51
in the Archive of Folk Song, Library of Congress.

Ragged and Dirty Blues

This is a blues of migrant workers shaken loose from their little holdings, going from job to job in the lumbering camps, on the levees, moving north toward the cities. It evidently had a wide circulation. Blind Lemon Jefferson brought the song from Texas to Chicago and recorded it there for Paramount in the 1920's under the title "Broke and Hungry." William Brown of Clarksdale, Mississippi recorded another version for the Library of Congress Archive of American Folksong in 1942. The version given here is transcribed from the singing of John W. Scott in 1964.

2. Well I'm motherless, I'm fatherless, I'm sisterless, I'm
   brotherless too;
   I'm motherless, I'm fatherless, I'm sisterless, I'm
   brotherless too.
   That's why I tried so hard (mmm) to make this, this trip
   with you.

3. Well they tell me that graveyard is a long ole lonesome
   place.
   That graveyard, well, it's a long ole lonesome place;
   They put you six foot under, (mmm) then they throw
   clay in your face.

4. Well I'm tired of living, honey, I don't know what to do;
   I'm tired of living, honey, I don't know what to do.
   Your tired of me (mmm) and I'm—I'm tired of you.

5. Well I'm goin' to leave you, honey, even if I have to
   ride that line;
   I'm goin' to leave you, honey, and I'll have to ride that line.
   You can just remember one thing, babe (mmm) I don't,
   no I don't mind the dyin'.

6. Well down that road somewhere, honey, down that road
   somewhere;
   Down that road somewhere, well down that road
   somewhere,
   I'll find me a good woman (mmm), I won't have to
   roam, roam no more.

Yonder Come Day

Along the coast of South Carolina and Georgia stretches a chain of islands—St. Helena, Sapelo, St. Simons, Cumberland, and many more—famous before the Civil War for the production of "sea island cotton," from which long-staple cloth of the finest quality was woven. Over the years, the plantations of this area fell upon evil days; but economic decay and natural isolation encouraged the continuation of the traditional singing of the Negro people, slaves and the descendants of slaves, who lived there. In the 1930's Lydia Parrish, a Northern woman, came to live on St. Simons, organized a group known as the Sea Island Singers, and transcribed and eventually published their music. Here, therefore, we can study a singing tradition that has continued uninterrupted since slavery days.

"Yonder Come Day" is a Sea Island spiritual that probably came into use in the years following the Civil War. Traditionally, it is sung by the people, who are Baptists, at the end of a night-long service. The melody is on four notes only, and a conventional harmonic accompaniment is impossible; the best instrument to use would be a flute or recorder.

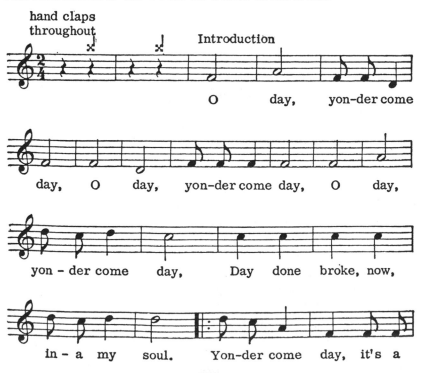

judg - ment day, Yon-der come day, it's a

judg - ment day, Yon-der come day, it's a

judg - ment day, Yon - der come day,

day done broke, now, in - a my soul.

Yonder come day, I heard him say,
Yonder come day, I heard him say,
Yonder come day, I heard him say,
    Yonder come day, day done broke, now, in-a my soul.

Yonder come day, it's a dying day,
Yonder come day, it's a dying day,
Yonder come day, it's a dying day,
    Yonder come day, day done broke, now, in-a my soul.

Yonder come day, it's a burying day,
Yonder come day, it's a burying day,
Yonder come day, it's a burying day,
    Yonder come day, day done broke, now, in-a my soul.

Yonder come day, I was on my knees,
Yonder come day, I was on my knees,
Yonder come day, I was on my knees,
    Yonder come day, day done broke, now, in-a my soul.

Yonder come day, I heard him say,
Yonder come day, I heard him say,
Yonder come day, I heard him say,
    Yonder come day, day done broke, now, in-a my soul.

Yonder come day, that's a New Year's day,
Yonder come day, that's a New Year's day,
Yonder come day, that's a New Year's day,
    Yonder come day, day done broke, now, in-a my soul.

Yonder come day, woncha come on, child,
Yonder come day, woncha come on, child,
Yonder come day, woncha come on, child,
    Yonder come day, day done broke, now, in-a my soul.

Yonder come day, I was on my knees,
Yonder come day, I was on my knees,
Yonder come day, I was on my knees,
    Yonder come day, day done broke, now, in-a my soul.

Yonder come day, I heard him say, *etc.*

VII
BETWEEN
TWO
WORLD
WARS

THE WAR OF 1914–1918 came upon the world about a century after the War of 1812. Both conflicts had their origin in the life-and-death struggles of the European powers, and both drew the United States into their orbit despite an official governmental commitment to a policy of neutrality or, at the very least, avoidance of direct military involvement. There, however, the similarities end. The War of 1812 accelerated the rise of American nationalism, the development of American industry, and the triumphant westward sweep of immigrants and pioneers; and all of this notwithstanding the fact that none of the nation's war aims was even mentioned in the terms of peace. The war of 1914–1918, by contrast, ended with the ignominious collapse of the German enemy and a total military victory that was spelled out starkly in the terms of peace imposed on the vanquished. Yet this victory ushered in a period of national doubt, frustration, bitterness, and confusion rarely equaled in the annals of a civilized people and surpassed only by the mood of black despair that prevailed in Germany itself.

Stranger still, a brief period of hectic prosperity culminated in the most frightful economic catastrophe in American history, the crash of 1929, and the ensuing Great Depression. There had, of course, been previous crashes and previous depressions. This one capped them all in length of duration, numbers of unemployed, the stubbornness with which it resisted treatment, and the sheer mass of human misery and wastage which it imposed.

In 1932, Franklin D. Roosevelt was elected President by a landslide vote; he received a mandate from the American people to effect economic recovery through emergency measures, by utilizing the full powers of the Federal Government. Thus was ushered in the New Deal and, more generally, the Roosevelt era. Roosevelt's tenure of office, from 1933–1945, covered a whole epoch in the life and experience of the nation. It witnessed the rebirth of hope and of a will to struggle against economic and social calamity. This new mood was generated in no small part by the dynamic quality of Roosevelt's leadership and by the bold experimental federal program which he unfolded.

American life in these years moved forward in the ominous shadow of Adolf Hitler. Aflame with Napoleonic ambition, Hitler achieved supreme power in Germany in 1933, established the Third Reich, and immediately set out to tear up the iniquitous Versailles Treaty, conquer Europe, and dominate the world. The regime that he created committed in the 12 short years of its existence acts of barbaric cruelty that characterize it as the most abominable tyranny ever inflicted upon man. By the same token, it was a monument to the bankrupt statesmanship of the Western Powers who had within the space of two decades from the imposition of the Versailles peace permitted the resurrection of the imperialist monster whose earlier annihilation had cost 10 million lives.

In the 1930's the presence of Hitler dominated the world; one cannot understand American life and experience at this time without constant reference to that fact. Similarly, it is not possible to understand American development in the early national period (1783–1815) without reference to the Franco-British struggle in general, and Napoleon in particular. After 1933, as after 1914, the United States gradually emerged from its posture of isolation from European military conflicts and shifted its weight to the weaker side (the Western Allies) in order to prevent the destruction of the international balance of power. The conflict became both total and global in 1942 when the Fascist Powers (Germany, Italy, Japan) found themselves aligned against the Allied nations coalition led by the United States, the Soviet Union, Great Britain, and China. It then became America's destiny to play a part in preventing the engulfment of the globe by Hitler and his allies. For the victory of Fascism over the Allied nations would most certainly have obliterated for an indefinite period of time the very possibility of human progress.

The songs of this stormy period between the beginning of World War I and the end of World War II mirror not only the despair and confusion, but also the hopes and struggles of millions of Americans. We reproduce in the following pages a few of the most expressive from the rich treasury of these years.*

---

*The development of the blues in this period as a form of folk song would require a book in itself. See Chapter VI, above, and Paul Oliver, *The Meaning of the Blues* (New York: Collier Books, 1963).

When Johnny Comes Marching Home
Johnny, I Hardly Knew You

On April 2, 1917 President Woodrow Wilson went before
Congress to ask for a declaration of war against Germany.
The reason given was the violation of the rights of neutrality
and freedom of the seas; since February of that year the Germans had waged unrestricted submarine warfare in an effort
to achieve the effective blockade of British and French coasts.
Vessels approaching British, French, or Irish ports were liable
to be sunk at sight.

In point of fact, the United States had leaned openly toward
the Franco-British side from the very start of the conflict in
1914 and had provided, during the first three years of the war,
massive material and financial aid to the Western belligerents.
American leadership saw in Germany the most menacing
threat to the United States as a world power and was determined to reduce it. To Wilson, a more compelling reason for
entry into the war than the submarine issue was the imminent
collapse of the Russian front. This, coupled with German preparations for an all-out offensive to break the deadlock in the
West and growing signs of Allied military exhaustion, was no
doubt decisive in bringing about direct American intervention.

Wilson stated his war objective in purely altruistic terms.
"We fight," said he, "for the ultimate peace of the world and
for the liberation of its peoples, the German people included;
for the rights of nations great and small and the privilege of
men everywhere to choose their way of life and of obedience.
The world must be made safe for democracy."

The American Army landed in France in 1918 more than
half a million strong; and it was a singing Army. Traditional
marching songs were pressed into service; music hall hits won
popularity with the soldiers, including of course contributions
from the British and the French. *When Johnny Comes Marching Home* falls into the first of these categories; it first made
its appearance during the Civil War and won increasing popularity as the years went by. It is attributed to an Irish-American
bandmaster, Patrick S. Gilmore. An Irish version, *Johnny, I
Hardly Knew You,* was probably inspired by the American
song. *Johnny,* in other words, began life as a war song and
then turned into a protest against war; it is the latter version
that finds most popularity with folk song audiences today. *Mrs.
McGrath* (see p. 121 above) is another example of a tradi-

tional song used during World War I, but in this case the process was reversed. It started life as a protest against war, but Irish troops pressed it into service as a marching song, speeded up the slow tempo, and sung it with rollicking abandon.

When Johnny Comes Marching Home

The old church bell will peal with joy,
    Hurrah, hurrah!
To welcome home our darling boy,
    Hurrah, hurrah!
The village lads and lasses say
    With roses they will strew the way,
And we'll all feel gay when Johnny comes marching
      home.

Get ready for the Jubilee,
    Hurrah, hurrah!
We'll give the hero three times three,
    Hurrah, hurrah!
The laurel wreath is ready now
    To place upon his loyal brow,
And we'll all feel gay when Johnny comes marching
      home.

Johnny, I Hardly Knew You
(to the same tune: slow tempo)

Refrain: With your guns and drums and drums and guns,
          Haroo, haroo,
      With your guns and drums and drums and guns,
          Haroo, haroo,
      With your guns and drums and drums and guns
          The enemy nearly slew you,
    Oh Johnny dear, you look so queer,
      Johnny, I hardly knew you.

1. Where are your legs with which you run,
      Haroo, haroo,
  Where are your legs with which you run,
      Haroo, haroo,
  Where are your legs with which you run
      When first you went to carry a gun;
  I fear your dancing days are done,
      Johnny, I hardly knew you.
Refrain

2. And where are your eyes that looked so mild
      Haroo, haroo,
  And where are your eyes that looked so mild
      Haroo, haroo,

And where are your eyes that looked so mild
      When you first my innocent heart beguiled—
And why did you run from me and the child?
      Johnny, I hardly knew you.
Refrain

3.   You haven't an arm and you haven't a leg,
      Haroo, haroo,
  You haven't an arm and you haven't a leg,
      Haroo, haroo,
  You haven't an arm and you haven't a leg
      You're an eyeless boneless chickenless egg;
  You'll have to be put with a bowl to beg,
      Johnny, I hardly knew you.
Refrain

4.   'Tis glad I am to see you home,
      Haroo, haroo,
  'Tis glad I am to see you home,
      Haroo, haroo;
  'Tis glad I am to see you home
      Safe from the is!ands of Ceylon,
  So low in the flesh so high in the bone,
      Johnny, I hardly knew you.
Refrain

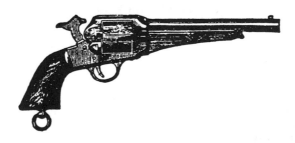

Mademoiselle from Armentières

This World War I vaudeville hit became a great favorite with British and American troops. Over the years, it has exhibited an irrepressible vitality. It proliferated endless (and often unprintable) lyrics during World War I; and it continued to grow during World War II as another generation of G.I.'s in France added yet more (and often unprintable) verses to the list. Even so, the uses of the song were not yet exhausted. When World War I was over *Mademoiselle* immigrated to the United States with the returning soldiers; in the labor struggles of the twenties and thirties, she made her appearance on the picket lines with verses such as these:

> The bosses are taking it on the chin, parlez-vous,
> The bosses are taking it on the chin, parlez-vous,
> The bosses are taking it on the chin
> Because the strikers won't give in,
> Inky dinky parlez-vous.

In the versions reproduced here World War I lyrics are followed by World War II additions.

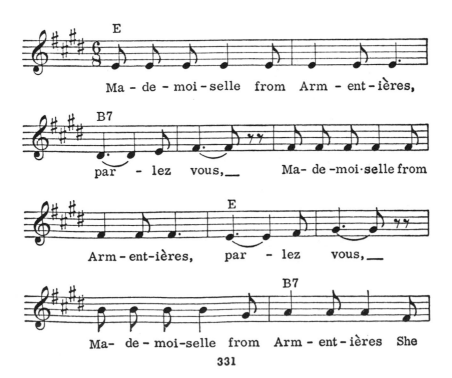

has-n't been kissed for for-ty years,

In-ky din-ky par-lez vous.____

World War I:

Oh farmer, have you a daughter fair, parlez-vous (*twice*)
    Oh farmer have you a daughter fair
    Who can wash a soldier's underwear,
Inky dinky parlez-vous.

The officers get all the steak, parlez-vous (*twice*)
    The officers get all the steak
    And all we get is the belly-ache
Inky dinky parlez-vous.

The M.P.'s say they won the war, parlez-vous (*twice*)
    The M.P.'s say they won the war
    Standing on guard at the cafe door,
Inky dinky parlez-vous.

You might forget the gas and the shell, parlez-vous (*twice*)
    You might forget the gas and shell,
    You'll never forget the mademoiselle,
Inky dinky parlez-vous.

Mademoiselle all dressed in black, parlez-vous (*twice*)
    Mademoiselle all dressed in black
    'Cause her soldier boy he never came back,
Inky dinky parlez-vous.

World War II:

Our top-kick there in Armentières, parlez-vous
Our top-kick there in Armentières, parlez-vous,
    Our top-kick there in Armentières
    Soon broke that spell of forty years,
Inky dinky parlez-vous.

She might have been young for all we knew, parlez-vous
She might have been young for all we knew, parlez-vous
    She might have been young for all we knew
    When Napoleon flopped at Waterloo
Inky dinky parlez-vous.

She got the palms and the Croix de Guerre, parlez-vous *(twice)*
    She got the palms and the Croix de Guerre
    For washing soldiers' underwear,
Inky dinky parlez-vous.

The second lieutenants are at it again, parlez-vous *(twice)*
    The second lieutenants are at it again
    They're winning the war with a fountain pen,
Inky dinky parlez-vous.

The general got the Croix de Guerre, parlez-vous *(twice)*
    The general got the Croix de Guerre,
    The son of a gun wasn't even there,
Inky dinky parlez-vous.

Oh mademoiselle from Gay Paree, parlez-vous *(twice)*
    Oh mademoiselle from Gay Paree
    You certainly played hell with me,
Inky dinky parlez-vous.

Pack Up Your Troubles

This was a popular song among both British and American troops in World War I. But it has retained a permanent appeal among children. Over the years, it has lightened the homeward tramp of many a footsore Cub Scout.

Wandering

The collapse of Germany in 1918 and the return of peace ushered in a period of uneasy transition in American life. Prosperity mingled with poverty, complacency with a sense of rootlessness and drift, law-abiding morality with the lawless gangsterism of the prohibition era. The most exciting singing of these years was that of workers, Negroes, and the poor. Bitter labor struggles led to new picket line and union songs, notably amid the poverty-stricken mining communities of Appalachia. The urbanization of America and the urbanization of the blues proceeded apace.

The precarious prosperity of the twenties vanished in 1929 with the stock market crash of October 24. America spun down into the depths of depression. Factories, banks, schools closed. Thousands lost their homes. The streets were black with homeless men and women. At the depth of the depression, in 1932, some 14 million people were out of work and near starvation. Tens of thousands of these wandered back and forth across the country, living off charity handouts, looking for nonexistent jobs, sleeping in flop-houses or freight cars, or freezing in the cold winter nights.

The same conditions prevailed in the countryside. Hundreds of thousands of farmers were homeless and starving. America's sons and daughters wandered as wastrels in the midst of the abundance which they had themselves created. From this indescribable reality arose new and expressive depression songs, such as *Wandering*. The melody is related to a traditional Irish tune. The lyrics are in part inherited from earlier labor and "hard times" songs.

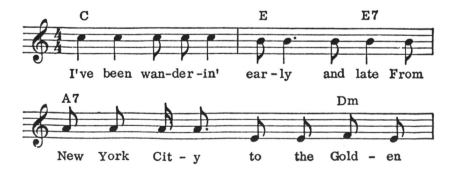

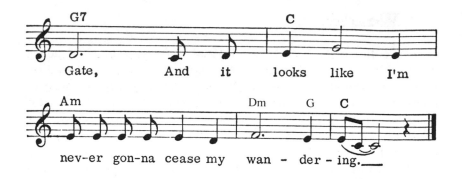

Gate, And it looks like I'm

nev-er gon-na cease my wan - der - ing.___

There's fish in the ocean, there's eels in the sea,
But a red-headed woman made a fool out of me,
And it looks like I'm never going to cease my wandering.

I've been working in the army, I've been working on a farm,
And all I've got to show is the muscle in my arm,
And it looks like I'm never going to cease my wandering.

Ashes to ashes and dust to dust,
If the Republicans don't get you, the Democrats must,
And it looks like I'm never going to cease my wandering.

O, I've been wandering far and wide,
I come with the wind, I drift with the tide,
And it looks like I'm never going to cease my wandering.

Raggedy

In the first years of the depression, the people's only protection from starvation was the charity of their neighbors, family, or friends. In all of the cities of America long lines formed outside of churches and town halls, lines of patient, humble, angry people, waiting for a bowl of soup, a hunk of bread. But whatever pittance local charity could afford was not enough to keep adults from starving nor to quiet children crying from hunger. At Christmas, 1931, a young couple was found starving in a supposedly empty cottage near Anwana Lake in Sullivan County, New York. The *Times* reported that "three days without food, the wife, who is 23 years old, was hardly able to walk." And that same winter, at Youngstown, Ohio, a paper bore the headline FATHER OF TEN DROWNS SELF. Charles Wayne, a steel worker two years without employment, threw himself into the swirling Mahoning River, abandoning forever the destitute family he could no longer help. Reports such as these were frequent at this time; and one of the pioneer achievements for which the New Deal will longest be remembered was the passage of the Social Security Act in 1935, which introduced for the first time the concept of Federal responsibility to cope with the hazards of unemployment and old age.

"Raggedy," a song arising out of the suffering of these years, vividly and bleakly expressed the predicament of a nation.

Rag - gedy, rag - gedy are we, Just as
rag - gedy, rag - gedy can be, Well we
don't get noth- ing for our la - bor, So

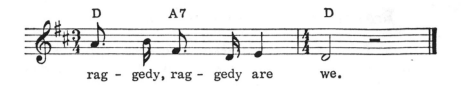

rag - gedy, rag - gedy are we.

Hungry, hungry are we,
Just as hungry, hungry can be,
Well we don't get nothing for our labor,
So hungry, hungry are we.

Homeless, homeless are we,
Just as homeless, homeless can be,
Well we don't get nothing for our labor,
So homeless, homeless are we.

Landless, landless are we,
Just as landless, landless can be,
Well we don't get nothing for our labor,
So landless, landless are we.

Pitiful, so pitiful are we,
Just as pitiful, pitiful can be,
Well we don't get nothing for our labor,
So pitiful, pitiful are we.

Raggedy, raggedy are we,
Just as raggedy, raggedy can be,
Well we don't get nothing for our labor,
So raggedy, raggedy are we.

The Mouse's Courting Song

Everywhere, shantytowns for the homeless sprang up, made of cardboard, newspaper, old boards, orange crates—anything that came to hand. They called them Hoovervilles. Men and women lived in these garbage dumps, and children were born there. Many children didn't go to school at all; some didn't have shoes, and many knew days when there was no food. Some stayed in bed because they had no clothes. But they sang and played and romped, as kids will, in the dingy streets and dusty alleys, around the shacks of Hooverville.

"The Mouse's Courting Song," collected from the singing of neighborhood children in Pittsburgh in the early 1940's, is an American version of "The Frog and the Mouse," which in one form or another has been a favorite with American children for three centuries. In the original British song, which dates from the sixteenth century,

> A frog he would a wooing go,
>   Heigh ho, said Rowley;
> A frog he would a wooing go, whether his mother
>   would let him or no,
> With a rowley powley,
> Gammon and spinnage, heigh ho, said Rowley.

We include this song here, not only as a sample of children's singing during the New Deal period, but also because it beautifully illustrates the process of continuity and development in our song tradition, to the present time.

339

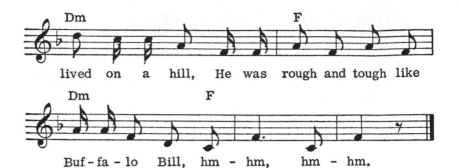

lived on a hill, He was rough and tough like
Buf - fa - lo Bill, hm - hm, hm - hm.

One day he decided to take a ride, hm-hm,
One day he decided to take a ride
With two six-shooters by his side, hm-hm.

Then Mickey rode till he came to a house,
And in this house was Minnie Mouse.

He strutted right up to the kitchen door,
And bowed and scraped his head on the floor.

O Minnie, Minnie, will you marry me?
Away down yonder in the orchard tree!

Without my Uncle Rat's consent,
I would not marry the Pres-eye-dent!

Her Uncle Rat gave his consent,
The Weasel wrote the publishment.

Oh, what you gonna have for the wedding feast?
Black-eyed peas and hogshead cheese.

The first one came was Uncle Rat,
Head as long as a baseball bat.

Second one came was Mr. Snake,
He wrapped himself 'round the marble cake.

The next one came was a little moth,
To spread on the tablecloth.

The next one came was a big black bug,
Carrying 'round a little brown jug.

The next one came was a bumblebee,
With a broken wing and a crooked knee.

The next one came was a nimble flea,
Saying Minnie, Minnie Mouse, will you dance with me?

The next one came was Mr. Cow,
He wanted to dance but he didn't know how.

Last one came was Mr. Cat,
He ruffled and tuffled and ate Uncle Rat.

And that was the end of the wedding feast,
Black-eyed peas and hogshead cheese.

Reprinted by permission of The Johns Hopkins University Press from Jacob A. Evanson, "Folksongs of an Industrial City," in *Pennsylvania Songs and Legends*, edited by George Korson (Baltimore: The Johns Hopkins University Press, 1949). © Copyright by George Korson.

Which Side Are You On?

At the end of 1932, in the very depths of the depression, the American people turned away from Herbert Hoover and the Republican Party. In November, Roosevelt was elected President. Franklin Delano Roosevelt was an experienced politician who had made a comeback into active life from a crippling disease in the early twenties. There was a warmth and directness about the man that won the hearts of the people; and Roosevelt promised action.

One of the achievements for which the New Deal will longest be remembered was the organization of American labor. In 1933, notwithstanding a century of struggle for the right to organize, most American workers still lacked trade unions; conditions of work were hard, bitter, and often dangerous. Under the National Industrial Recovery Act of May, 1933— section 7-A subsequently expanded into the Wagner Act of 1935—workers received the right to bargain collectively with their employers through unions of their own choice.

This law opened the floodgates to the organization of millions of unorganized workers. A new spirit of labor militancy spread across the land; dozens of new songs were born on the picket lines.

"Which Side Are You On?" was written by Florence Reece and set to a traditional ballad tune. It arose out of the struggle of miners in Harlan County, Kentucky to organize a union in 1931, and out of the bloody collisions between miners and gun-toting coal company deputies. In the great organizing movement of the following years, few songs were sung more than this one.

Come all of you good work - ers, Good news to you I'll tell Of how the good old

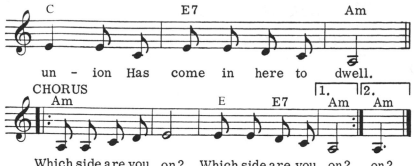

un - ion Has come in here to dwell.

CHORUS

Which side are you on? Which side are you on? on?

My daddy was a miner,
And I'm a miner's son,
And I'll stick with the union
Till every battle's won.
Chorus

They say in Harlan County
There are no neutrals there;
You'll either be a union man,
Or a thug for J. H. Blair.
Chorus

Oh workers, can you stand it?
Oh tell me how you can,
Will you be a lousy scab,
Or will you be a man?
Chorus

Don't scab for the bosses,
Don't listen to their lies,
Us poor folks haven't got a chance
Unless we organize.
Chorus

We Shall Not Be Moved

"We Shall Not Be Moved," another song born of the miners' organizing struggles, this time in West Virginia, and set to an old gospel tune, became during the thirties probably the most widely sung of all labor songs. It may be said literally to have presided over the great organizing movement in which the Congress of Industrial Organizations was born.

The un - ion is be - hind us,

we shall not be moved, The

un - ion is be - hind us,

we shall not be moved, Just like a

tree, that's stand - ing by the

wa - ter, We shall not be moved.

CHORUS

We shall not, we shall not be moved,

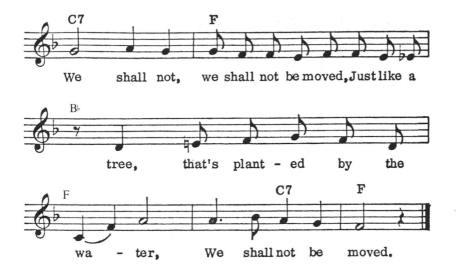

We shall not, we shall not be moved, Just like a
tree, that's plant - ed by the
wa - ter, We shall not be moved.

We're fighting for our freedom, we shall not be moved,
We're fighting for our freedom, we shall not be moved
Just like a tree, that's planted by the water,
We shall not be moved.
Chorus

We're fighting for our children, we shall not be moved,
We're fighting for our children, we shall not be moved
Just like a tree, that's standing by the water,
We shall not be moved.
Chorus

We'll build a mighty Union, we shall not be moved,
We'll build a mighty Union, we shall not be moved
Just like a tree, that's standing by the water,
We shall not be moved.
Chorus

Goin' Down the Road

The early years of the New Deal witnessed the appearance of the Dust Bowl, which converted vast expanses of the High Plains into a wilderness and completed the ruin of tens of thousands of farmers who lived and worked there.

The great dust storms which hit the plains in these years and blotted out the harvests were a result of the ploughing up of the grasslands and the enormous extension of cultivated acreage that resulted from the huge demand for bread and clothing in the first World War. The farmers' problems of mortgaged land, surplus capacity, declining prices, and chronic indebtedness came to a climax in the depression years; the terrible droughts of 1932–1936 and the swirling dust completed the catastrophe. Ruined tenants from the Dust Bowl hit the trail and moved West to California in search of any jobs they could find. "Goin' Down the Road," an old sharecroppers song, expressed both the courage and the despair of people coping with a new calamity. It was taken up, too, by city and farm workers everywhere who were seeking to organize unions to protect them from eviction and to secure fair wages. *I won't be treated this-a way* became almost an official motto of the New Deal and an eloquent expression of the popular mood underlying it.

I'm goin' down the road feel-in' bad,____ I'm__ goin' down the road feel-in' bad,_____ I'm goin' down the road feel-in' bad, Lord, Lord,_And I ain't gonna be

treat-ed this-a way.____

2. I'm goin' where the dust storms never blow,
   I'm goin' where the dust storms never blow,
   I'm goin' where the dust storms never blow, Lord, Lord,
   And I ain't gonna be treated thisaway.

3. I'm lookin' for a job with honest pay,
   I'm lookin' for á job with honest pay,
   I'm lookin' for a job with honest pay, Lord, Lord,
   And I ain't gonna be treated thisaway.

4. Two dollar shoes hurt my feet,
   Two dollar shoes hurt my feet,
   Two dollar shoes hurt my feet, Lord, Lord,
   And I ain't gonna be treated thisaway.

5. But ten dollar shoes fit 'em neat,
   But ten dollar shoes fit 'em neat,
   But ten dollar shoes fit 'em neat, Lord, Lord,
   And I ain't gonna be treated thisaway.

6. I'm goin' where the water tastes like wine,
   I'm goin' where the water tastes like wine,
   I'm goin' where the water tastes like wine, Lord, Lord,
   And I ain't gonna be treated thisaway.

7. Forty cents an hour won't pay my rent,
   Forty cents an hour won't pay my rent,
   Forty cents an hour won't pay my rent, Lord, Lord,
   And I ain't gonna be treated thisaway.

8. I can't live on cornbread and beans,
   I can't live on cornbread and beans,
   I can't live on cornbread and beans, Lord, Lord,
   And I ain't gonna be treated thisaway.

9. I'm goin' down the road feelin' bad,
   I'm goin' down the road feelin' bad,
   I'm goin' down the road feelin' bad, Lord, Lord,
   And I ain't gonna be treated thisaway.

347

Roll On, Columbia

Under the Roosevelt administration, a program of public works construction got under way. Public works, it was thought, might kill several birds with one stone: create jobs, reforest the countryside, check floods and soil erosion, and make abundant electrical power at low cost available to the farmer. The most grandiose of these projects was the building of the Federal dams—the great dams on the Tennessee River, Black Canyon on the Colorado, Grand Coulee on the Columbia River, Bonneville on Cascade Rapids in western Oregon.

"Roll On, Columbia" is one of many songs written by Woody Guthrie when he was in the Northwest and employed by the Bonneville Power Administration. Woody was an "Okie" who led the wandering existence typical of his generation, but what he saw and felt during the Twenties and Thirties he expressed in hundreds of songs, the best of which sum up the mood and meaning of the times. Woody is an American Burns: he immersed himself in the traditional music of his people to produce lyrics of extraordinary intensity, imagination, and tenderness through which throb a boundless love of country and of people.

Green Doug-las firs where the wa-ters break through, Down the wild moun-tains and val-leys she flew, Ca-na-dian North-west to the o-cean so blue, So roll on, Co-lum-bia, roll on.____

CHORUS

Roll on, Co-lum-bia, roll on, Roll on, Co-lum-bia, roll on, Your pow-er is turn-ing our dark-ness to dawn, So roll on, Co-lum-bia, roll on.

Many great rivers add power to you
The Yakima Snake and the Clicketac too,
Sandy Willamette and Hood river too
So roll on, Columbia, roll on
Chorus

At Bonneville now there are ships in the locks
The waters have risen and cleared all the rocks,
Shiploads of plenty will steam past the docks,
So roll on, Columbia, roll on.
Chorus

And on up the river is Grand Coulee dam,
The mightiest thing ever built by a man,
To run the great factories and water the land,
So roll on, Columbia, roll on.
Chorus

These mighty men labored by day and by night,
Matching their strength 'gainst the river's wild flight,
Through rapids and falls they won the hard fight,
So roll on, Columbia, roll on.
Chorus

Words by Woody Guthrie. Music based on "Goodnight Irene" by Huddie Ledbetter and John A. Lomax. TRO - © Copyright 1957 and 1963 Ludlow Music, Inc., New York, N.Y. Used by permission.

Discrimination Blues

The New Deal had its accomplishments, and it had its failures too. It cut unemployment, but did not eliminate it: even at the height of Roosevelt's success, at the beginning of 1937, there were still more than 5 million people out of work. Worst of all, the Negro throughout the nation remained a second-class citizen, first fired last hired, segregated in rat-ridden Jim Crow ghettoes, excluded by white pride and prejudice from the mainstream of American life. In the South, this separation of the races was written into law; it was enforced by courts, police, jails, and most terrible of all, "extralegal" sanctions—beatings, mutilation, and murder.

Big Bill Broonzy, one of the great "country blues" singers and composers, wrote "Discrimination Blues" during World War II. This biting song dramatizes America's unfinished business. The melody is borrowed from the Southern "country blues" tradition: it is similar to that used by Blind Willie Johnson in his gospel song, "Jesus is Coming Soon."

This lit-tle song that I'm sing-ing a-bout__ Peo-ple, you all know it's true,____ If you're black and got-ta work for a liv-ing Now this is what they'll

CHORUS

say__ to you, they'll say: If you're white, you're all right, And if you're brown, stick a-round, But if you're black, O broth-er, Get back, get back, get back.

2. I was in a place las' night,
   They was all havin' fun,
   They was all buyin' beer and wine,
   But they would not sell me none.
Chorus

3. I went to an employment office
   Took a number and got in line,
   They called out everybody's number,
   But they never did call mine.
Chorus

4. Me and a man was working side by side,
   This is what it meant,
   They was payin' him a dollar an hour,
   And they was payin' me fifty cent.
Chorus

We Shall Overcome

Notwithstanding failures, Franklin D. Roosevelt during his first administration had revived hope and faith in the American dream, and he had instilled new life into the country. In 1936, he was re-elected by a landslide: The Republican candidate, Alfred Landon, carried only two states. But in Roosevelt's second administration, the New Deal lost its impetus and went into decline. By 1938, the swift rise of Hitler and the threat of impending war was casting a deep shadow over America; the White House was turning away from the isolationist orientation that had dominated American leadership since the death of Woodrow Wilson and was becoming increasingly preoccupied with problems of international strategy and diplomacy. Soon the demands of an all-out war for survival would absorb all the energies of the American people; the requirements of this war, temporarily at least, would resolve the dire problems of unemployment, excess production, and surplus industrial capacity that had called the New Deal into existence.

The American dream of peace, equality, and prosperity had, despite much hardship and suffering, spurred the hopes and deeds of millions during the New Deal years. At the very opening of the period, the coal miners of West Virginia had given the American people a new song to sing and had set it to the tune of an old spiritual. Better than any other, this song sums up the passionate hopes and aspirations of these years. People who cherish freedom and brotherhood are still singing it today.

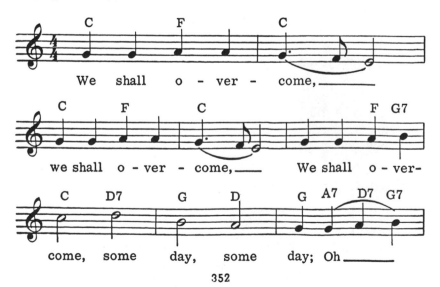

deep in my heart I know that I do believe We shall o-ver-come some day.

We shall organize, we shall organize,
We shall organize some day, some day;
Oh, deep in my heart, I know that I do believe
We shall organize some day.

We shall end Jim Crow, we shall end Jim Crow,
We shall end Jim Crow some day, some day;
Oh, deep in my heart, I know that I do believe
We shall end Jim Crow some day.

We shall walk in peace, we shall walk in peace,
We shall walk in peace some day, some day;
Oh, deep in my heart, I know that I do believe
We shall walk in peace some day.

We shall build a new world, we shall build a new world,
We shall build a new world some day, some day;
Oh, deep in my heart, I know that I do believe
We shall build a new world some day.

We'll walk hand in hand, we'll walk hand in hand,
We'll walk hand in hand some day, some day;
Oh, deep in my heart, I know that I do believe
We'll walk hand in hand some day.

We shall overcome, we shall overcome,
We shall overcome some day, some day;
Oh, deep in my heart, I know that I do believe
We shall overcome some day.

New words and musical arrangement by Zilphia Horton, Frank Hamilton, Guy Carawan and Pete Seeger. TRO - © Copyright 1960 and 1963 Ludlow Music, Inc., New
York, N.Y. Used by permission. Royalties accruing from the use of this song are
assigned to the use of a civil-rights educational institution, the Highlander Folk
School.

Die Moorsoldaten (Peat-Bog Soldiers)

Hitler became Chancellor of Germany in January, 1933, and immediately concentration camps sprang up—"like mushrooms," as William Shirer wrote—where the enemies of the regime were beaten, tortured, and put to death. The thousands of inmates of these first camps were Germans, and this underscores the fact that the first fighters against Hitler and the tyranny of fascism were Germans—Catholics, Jews, Social Democrats, Protestants, and Communists. These people were rounded up and sent off to suffer and die, because they had dared to oppose the National Socialist Party in either word or deed.

"Die Moorsoldaten" was one of the songs which this concentration camp experience produced. The prisoners sang it as they marched to and from their forced labor. When Hitler and Mussolini invaded Spain in 1936, anti-fascist soldiers took up the refrain, and "Die Moorsoldaten" became a marching song and a battle song. Ernst Busch made a famous recording of it in a Madrid studio, while the bombs fell and exploded in the street outside. By 1942, this song was known to millions in Europe; no other created at this time conveys so profoundly and so simply the meaning of the struggle against Hitler.

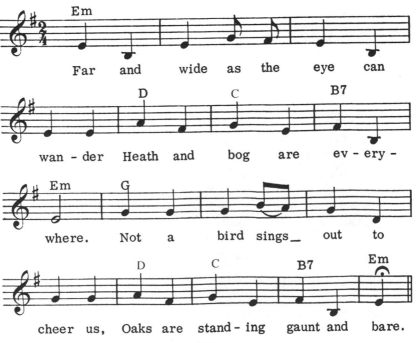

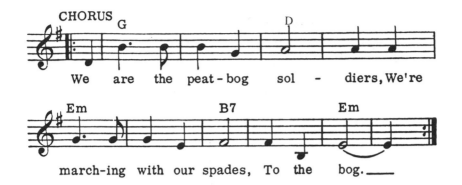

CHORUS

We are the peat-bog sol - diers, We're

march-ing with our spades, To the bog.___

Up and down the guards are pacing,
No one, no one can go through.
Flight would mean a sure death facing;
Guns and barbed wire greet our view.

Chorus
But for us there is no complaining,
Winter will in time be past;
One day we shall cry rejoicing,
Homeland dear, you're mine at last.

Chorus   Then will the peat-bog soldiers
            March no more with their spades
            To the bog.

*   *   *

Wohin auch das Auge blicket
Moor und Heide ringsherum.
Vogelsang uns nicht erquicket,
Eichen stehen kahl und krumm.

Chorus   Wir sind die Moorsoldaten
            Und ziehen mit dem Spaten
            Ins Moor.

Auf und nieder gehen die Posten,
Keiner, keiner, kann hindurch.
Flucht wird nur das Leben kosten,
Fielfach ist umzäunt die Burg.

Chorus
Doch fur uns gibt es kein Klagen,
Ewig kann's nicht Winter sein.
Einmal werden froh wir sagen,
"Heimat, du bist wieder mein."

Chorus   Dann ziehen die Moorsoldaten
            Nicht mehr mit dem Spaten
            Ins Moor.

Ot Kraya i Do Kraya
(From Frontier to Frontier)

World War II broke out when Hitler invaded Poland in September, 1939. So swift was the collapse of organized resistance to his advancing armies that by the summer of 1941 he controlled all of Europe, directly or indirectly, apart from the Soviet Union, the British Isles, and Sweden.

On June 22, 1941, Hitler invaded the Soviet Union, an event which proved to be a turning point in the war. It brought Britain and the Soviets, hitherto distrustful of each other, into direct alliance. When the Japanese attacked the United States at Pearl Harbor on December 7, in fulfillment of their commitments to the Germans, the United States found themselves at war with Germany on the side of the British and the Soviets. Thus, the Allied nations coalition of anti-fascist powers, formally announced on January 1, 1942, came into existence.

Association of the United States with the Union of Soviet Socialist Republics in common conflict with Hitler brought about a thawing out of the somewhat frosty relationship that had prevailed between the two powers since Roosevelt had accorded diplomatic recognition to the Soviets in 1933. Massive industrial and military aid was sent to Russia; Russians visited the United States, made impassioned appeals for the opening of a Second Front in Europe, and were cordially received. Russian songs became popular both on the home front and in the army. "Ot Kraya i Do Kraya" was a Soviet marching song. Americans became familiar with it through a recording of the Red Army Chorus.

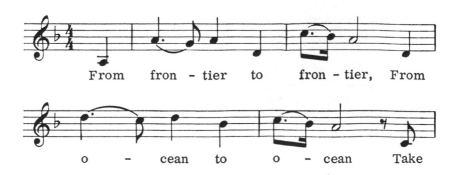

From   fron - tier   to   fron - tier,   From

o - cean   to   o - cean   Take

up your ri-fles to fight for your coun-try, And

to de-fend your soil. Be read-y for

dan-ger, Be read-y for sor-row. Be

1. **Fine**

read-y to fight to the end.   end._____

For country and for freedom,
For a better world to come,
We march again to war, we know the reason why,
We know the reason why:
For country and for freedom,
For a better world to come,
We are ready to fight to the end.

*   *   *

Ot kraya i do kraya,
Ot morya i do morya,
Beret vintovku narod trudovoi,
Narod boevoi.
Gotov'i na gore,
Gotov'i na muki,
Gotov'i na smertn'i boi.

Za zemlyu, za volyu,
Za luchshuyu dolyu,
Idem opyat' no front, no znaya za chto,
M'i znaem za chto.
Za zemlyu, za volyu,
Za luchshuyu dolyu,
Gotov'i na smertn'i boi.

Used by permission of Edward B. Marks Music Corporation. Translated from the Russian by John Anthony Scott.

D-Day Dodgers

In June 1943, the Allies invaded Sicily and in September crossed to Southern Italy. A long and heartbreaking winter campaign ensued as the troops moved slowly up the peninsula. The terrain, rocky and mountainous, was made to order for defensive fighting, and the Germans under Kesselring made the most of it. The attacking forces, advancing in rain, mud, and snow, suffered many casualties before they occupied Rome in June 1944.

At this point, the American-born Lady Astor, a member of Parliament, took it upon herself to criticize the conduct of the Italian campaign, and advised that British troops be pulled out of Italy and used in the invasion of Normandy. In this connection, she used the somewhat tactless phrase "D-Day Dodgers."

Lady Astor's remarks were of course reported in Italy and became the occasion for a crushing retort. The lyric was set to the tune of "Lili Marlene," one of the most widely sung and parodied songs of the war. Originally a German ditty, "Lili Marlene" was "captured" from German P.W.'s and promptly added to the British and American repertoire. "D-Day Dodgers" reproduced here, is more than a soldier's answer to Lady Astor; it is the fighting man's final comment upon the senseless cruelty and heartbreak of war itself.

We're the D - Day Dodg - ers, out in It - a - ly, Al - ways on the vi - no, al - ways on the spree; Eighth Ar - my scroung-ers and their tanks, We live in Rome a -

mong the Yanks, We are the D - Day
Dodg - ers, Way out in It - a - ly.

We landed in Salerno, a holiday with pay,
The Gerries brought out the panzer to greet us on our way,
Showed us the sights and gave us tea,
We all sang songs, the beer was free,

Chorus To welcome D-Day Dodgers
   To sunny Italy.

Naples and Cassino were taken in our stride,
We didn't go to fight there, we went just for the ride,
Anzio and Sangro were just names,
We only went to look for dames,

Chorus The artful D-Day Dodgers,
   Out in Italy.

Dear Lady Astor, you think you're mighty hot,
Standing on the platform talking tommy rot;
You're England's sweetheart and her pride,
We think your mouth's too bleeding wide,

Chorus We are the D-Day Dodgers,
   In sunny Italy.

Look around the mountains, in the mud and rain,
You'll find the scattered crosses, there's some that have
   no name.
Heartbreak and toil and suffering gone,
The boys beneath them slumber on,

Chorus They are the D-Day Dodgers,
   Who stay in Italy.

Partizaner Lid (The Partisan)

World War II was fought by huge regular armies with a massive supporting apparatus of tanks, supplies, heavy artillery, air and naval support. But an indispensable role was also played by irregulars whose contribution was similar to that of the militia and sharpshooters of the American Revolution. These irregulars were called by a variety of names—guerrillas, *maquis,* bushwhackers, partisans. They hid out in the swamps, forests, and hills, keeping watch on German troop movements, ambushing supply trains, blowing up bridges, and demolishing communications. When the Allied invasion of Normandy took place in June, 1944, these people were instrumental in delaying the arrival of *panzer* reinforcements that might otherwise have pushed the British and American troops into the sea before a bridgehead was established. On the Eastern front, these partisans operated in German-occupied Russia and Poland, where Nazi communications were especially vulnerable owing to their extension over hundreds of miles of non-German territory.

Jewish people in Poland took part in this type of warfare. They had good reason to sell their lives dearly; in September, 1939, as soon as German troops were in Warsaw, Himmler's assistant, Reinhard Heydrich, began to plan the extermination of Poland's Jewish population. In June 1940, the infamous extermination center of Oswiecim was set up. Many stirring partisan songs came out of the war. "Partizaner Lid," one of the loveliest of these, is dedicated to Poland's Jewish fighters.

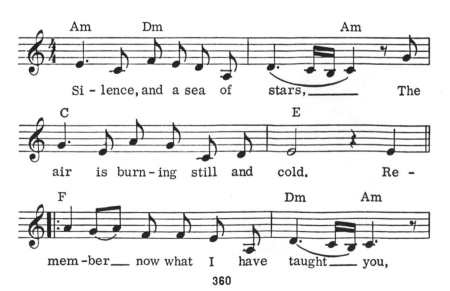

360

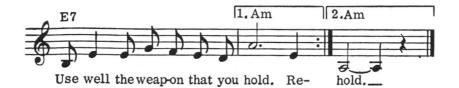

Use well the weap-on that you hold. Re-   hold.

A girl, in winter coat and cap
Firmly grasps her hand grenade;
A girl, with soft and silken face,
Is going on her first raid.

Carefully she aims, and fires,
And her bullet finds its foe.
A carrier, crammed with weapons,
Crashes in the frozen snow.

Dawn, she steals from the forest,
Snow is gleaming in her hair;
She sings of youth and hope and freedom
In a struggle all must share.

         *   *   *

Shtil, die nacht iz oysgeshternt,
Un der frost hot shtark gebrent.
Tsi gedenkstu vi ich hob dich gelernt
Haltn a shpayer in di hent?

A moyd, a peltsl un a beret,
Un halt in hant fest a nagan.
A moyd mit a sametenem ponim,
Hit op dem soyne's karavan.

Getsilt, geshosn un getrofn!
Hot ir kleyninker pistoyl.
An oto, a fulinkn mit vofn
Farhaltn hot zi mit eyn koyl!

Fartog, fun vald aroysgekrochn,
Mit shney girlandn oyf di hor.
Gemutikt fun kleyninkn nitsochn
Far undzer nayem, frayen dor!

Reprinted by permission of Schocken Books Inc. from *A Treasury of Jewish Folk Songs* by Ruth Rubin. Copyright © 1950 by Schocken Books Inc. Copyright renewed © 1977 by Ruth Rubin. Translation from the Yiddish by John Anthony Scott.

VIII
SINCE
THE
WAR

THE YEARS FOLLOWING World War II to the present constitute a new and separate chapter in the history of American folk song. There has been an intense and widespread revival of interest in the traditional song heritage; new songs, some of them rivaling the finest creations of the past, have been born out of the agonies and struggles of our modern age.

Full treatment of the contemporary folk song movement would clearly require a book in itself. The most that can be done here is to give some general impressions as to what is going on, and to indicate the relationship between current song and that of the past.

A great deal of our traditional song had its roots in the life and experience of an America that was predominantly rural. All this has changed. Folk song in twentieth century United States has migrated to the metropolis; it has taken root in the cities. In the period following World War II, it has become emphatically urban. College campus "hoots," North End or Greenwich Village coffee houses, folk festivals, nation-wide TV and jukebox coverage, all testify to this fact. Folk song has become an important feature in the contemporary American scene.

The new outburst of song has been sustained and made possible by the anonymous work of devoted collectors and musicians who, since the closing years of the nineteenth century, have set themselves the task of conserving our national song heritage; thereby, they have ensured that this heritage might ultimately be made available to a potentially enormous audience. Between 1882 and 1898, Francis J. Child published his great collection of *English and Scottish Popular Ballads*. In 1888, there came into being the American Folklore Society, an association of folklore scholars whose purpose was to encourage the collection and preservation of the unwritten and unpublished literary and musical heritage; in the same year, the Society began publication of the *Journal of American Folklore*. In the first years of the new century, state and local folklore societies sprang up to direct, encourage, and finance the collection and conservation of song materials.

In 1910, John Lomax published his path-breaking *Cowboys Songs*. In 1915, the English musician Cecil J. Sharp visited the United States to prepare his *English Folk Songs from the Southern Appalachians,* a pioneer work in awakening American scholars to the incredible extent and variety of the musical resources to be found in the North American countryside. Subsequent years witnessed a rapid accumulation of materials. Elisabeth Greenleaf Bristol and Grace Yarrow Mansfield visited Newfoundland during the twenties to transcribe the words and music of nearly two hundred traditional songs; Dorothy Scarborough published *On the Trail of Negro Folk Songs* in 1925; Frank C. Brown, who had organized the North Carolina Folklore Society in 1913, was instrumental in amassing a vast collection of songs during the next quarter of a century; Phillips Barry, Helen Hartness Flanders, Eloise Hubbard Linscott and W. Roy Mackenzie collected the songs of New England and Nova Scotia; these are but a few of the collectors whose names might be mentioned.

During the thirties, with the development of the phonograph, the collecting and transcription of songs was made more rapid and exact. During the New Deal, an especially important contribution was made by the Archive of American Folk Song which was established at the Library of Congress in 1928 and which became, under the direction of John A. Lomax, Alan Lomax, and Ben Botkin, a national center for the preservation of material recorded on disc and tape.

Then came World War II, and a new generation appeared on the scene. It grew up in the aftermath of war amid the strident persecution of the McCarthy period, in an atmosphere poisoned by hatred, hysteria, and insecurity, in a time when life itself was threatened by the unleashing of nuclear power. Many young people looked at the world with angry eyes; they experienced a sense of passionate alienation from the vapid commercialism of our urban culture, the ugliness and machine-made conformity of urban life. They strove to find roots in the past, a meaning in the present, a sure vision for the future.

This generation has found a part of what it sought in America's songs. Some of these young people, when they were very little, were nurtured on the songs of Woody Guthrie, particularly his *Dust Bowl Ballads* and *Songs to Grow On;* some of them listened to the records of the Almanac Singers, that fabulous band of troubadours who, during the early years of World War II, gathered in Greenwich Village, created the institution of the hootenanny, sang, wrote, and recorded songs; they pored over the *People's Song Book* published in 1947 which made a great many folk songs, particularly songs of labor and of the New Deal, easily and cheaply available; they listened to traditional songs on the records of Burl Ives or studied them in the pages of the *Fireside Book of Folk Songs* (1947). They acquired their taste for blues from the early recordings of Josh White; like the rest of the country, they learned the spirituals from the incomparable singing of Marian Anderson and Paul Robeson.

In the darkest years of the Cold War, wandering balladeers kept this singing tradition alive and patiently educated the tastes of their youthful audience. The tradition of the wandering minstrel is an old one. We need go no further back than to the great blues singers like Blind Lemon Jefferson in the early 1900's, to Carl Sandburg in the 1920's, to Cisco Houston and Woody Guthrie in the 1930's. And in the 1940's Pete Seeger emerged as one of the most gifted of them all. He struggled successfully against McCarthyite persecution and blacklisting that sought to stifle his voice and ruin his career. His message and the force of his example has reached untold numbers of young people. His renown as an American folksinger has become worldwide.

The modern singing movement began to bloom in 1953 with the ending of the Korean War and the partial reduction of acute cold war tension. With the organization of the Weavers (Pete Seeger, Ronnie Gilbert, Lee Hays, and Fred Hellerman) and the famous Carnegie Hall concert of Christmas Eve, 1955, the folk revival was fairly under way. There was a brilliance, an integrity, and an enthusiasm, in the Weavers' singing, which few others could match; a flock of younger performers—the Kingston Trio, Peter, Paul and Mary, the Chad Mitchell Trio, etc.—followed along the path that the Weavers had blazed. By 1960, folk song may have been crudely commercialized. But the market for music, records, and instruments had become enormous. And, in the school systems of New York and New England, another wandering minstrel, Bill Bonyun, singing over the years to hundreds of thousands of children, continued the patient, anonymous work of cultivating the love of song and the integrity of feeling that makes it real.

TV and the juke-box have played a limited but nonetheless significant role in the post-war popularization of the folk song heritage. How significant, may be illustrated by a personal anecdote.

It was 1942, and I was in New York City, just before my departure for overseas duty. I went to a bar in Harlem to listen to the legendary Huddy Leadbetter play his twelve-string guitar. He played all evening, sang in the dim, half-filled room, and finished by singing a lullaby. The beautiful melody came very slowly with an overpowering mood of weariness and sadness. I never forgot this song that I had heard only once, but I never met anyone else who knew it—until it hit the juke-box in 1950. It was a souped-up travesty of Leadbelly's song, but there was no mistaking it: *Good Night Irene*. Since then the list of folk songs that have become national favorites is an impressive one. *Tom Dula, This Land is Your Land, Michael Row the Boat Ashore, The House of the Rising Sun, Scarlet Ribbons, The Battle of New Orleans* are a few of the traditional songs that have been catapulted into fame and even into international prominence thanks to the commercial media.

In the post-war years, Americans have not only rediscovered their song heritage, but have utilized the traditional material for new purposes—to utter a new protest, to shape a new vision. The 1950's witnessed the burgeoning of a fresh lyrical and musical creativity as people began to demonstrate a new militancy in facing and tackling the issues of our time. As we have seen throughout this book, many topical songs have fulfilled, historically, a similar function: to celebrate a victory, to mourn a tragedy, to protest a wrong, to summon inspiration for a struggle or a test.

Songs of this order are being written and sung today. Many of them are freedom songs. The Supreme Court decision of May 17, 1954 declaring segregation unconstitutional was hailed throughout the nation, and most enthusiastically by the youth. They recognized, in the coming struggle to level the barriers of segregation everywhere, the central, most honorable challenge of contemporary American life. The movement that in the following decade hurled itself against the bastions of Jim Crow has been both a youth movement and a singing movement. Young people participating in sit-ins and walk-ins, on picket lines and marches, have faced great ordeals and have gained courage, unity, and inspiration from song. They have sung the traditional freedom songs and spirituals, they have composed new verses and set them to old tunes, and they have composed new songs altogether. Pete Seeger's *If I Had a Hammer* and Bob Dylan's *Blowin' in the Wind*, to cite two instances, have become known and loved by millions; they are examples of new songs born of the freedom movement that have already achieved the stature of folk songs.

Not all of the new songs have been freedom songs. The writers have found inspiration in many and various aspects of the contemporary scene: in the menace of atomic war, poverty and brutality in an affluent society, alienation, the commercialization of sport, capital punishment, and many more. By the early sixties, this modern broadside tradition had begun to make a significant contribution to the literature of social criticism. The writers have found an audience in the coffee houses, at the "hoots," campus sings, and other folk festivals, and through the sale of records. *Broadside* and *Sing Out,* in addition, provide channels of expression and communication.

A number of these new songs have already achieved wide popularity: notably *What Have They Done to the Rain* and *Little Boxes* (Malvina Reynolds); *A Hard Rain's a-Gonna Fall* (Bob Dylan); *Plastic Jesus* (Ernie Marrs); *Where Have All the Flowers Gone?* (Pete Seeger); and *As Long as the Grass Shall Grow* (Peter LaFarge). A few of these post-war freedom songs and broadsides are reproduced below.

Our national song is a body of music of enormous depth and variety. It mirrors the life and soul of our people, gives expression to their inmost feelings and aspirations. In each generation, it summons men and women to cherish the heritage from the past, to become more fully aware of the ties that bind them to each other and to all mankind, to exalt the dignity of human life, to protest cruelty, exploitation, and oppression. Folk song is an instrument of spiritual life and of social struggle. With its help, the prophet's vision of a new Heaven and a new earth will more surely and more speedily unfold.

Plane Wreck at Los Gatos

California fruit and vegetable growers have long used immigrant labor to harvest their crops; in some years since 1900, more than one-fifth of a million such migratory workers have been employed there. Until the depression years of the thirties, Mexican fieldhands, *braceros,* made a special appeal to the California growers. They could be brought in at very low wages and fired or sent back to Mexico when the growing season was over. These noncitizens lived in tent communities, shanty towns, and migrant camps. They have been among the most shamefully exploited and pathetically poor in all the American community. In the nineteen thirties, unemployment was high among U. S. farm workers, and the Mexicans were dispensed with; but World War II and succeeding years witnessed a new manpower shortage and a consequent repetition of the traditional pattern. In January 1948, a group of Mexican deportees died in a plane crash near Coalinga; and Woody Guthrie recorded the tragedy in this broadside. His protest at the inhuman use of human beings is marked by the quiet but angry statement of the lyric and the deep tenderness of the refrain.

The crops are all in and the peach-es are rot-ting,___ The or-ang-es are piled in their cre-o-sote dumps;__ They're fly-ing them back to the

Mex-i-co bor-der___ To pay all their wag-es to Wade back a-gain.___

REFRAIN

Good-bye to my Juan, good-bye Ro-sa-li-ta;___ ___ Ad-i-os muy a-mi-go, Je-sus and Ma-ri-a,___ You won't have a name when you ride the big aer-o-plane,___ And all they will call you will be___ de-port-ees.

My father's own father he waded that river,
They took all the money he made in his life;
My brothers and sisters come working the fruit trees
And they rode the truck till they took down and died.
Refrain

Well, some are illegal and some are not wanted,
Our work contract's out and we have to move on;
Six hundred miles to that Mexico border,
They chase us like outlaws, like rustlers, like thieves.
Refrain

We died on your hills and we died on your deserts,
We died in your valleys and died on your plains;
We died neath your trees and we died in your bushes,
Both sides of that river we died just the same.
Refrain

The sky plane caught fire over Los Gatos Canyon,
Like a fireball of lightning it shook all our hills.
Who are all these friends all scattered like dry leaves?
The radio says they are just deportees.
Refrain

Is this the best way we can grow our big orchards?
Is this the best way we can grow our good fruit?
To fall like dry leaves to rot on my top soil
And be known by no name except deportees?
Refrain

"Deportee" ("Plane Wreck at Los Gatos"). Lyric by Woody Guthrie. Music by Martin Hoffman. TRO - © Copyright 1961 and 1963 Ludlow Music, Inc., New York, N.Y. Used by permission.

In Contempt

The years 1947–1953 witnessed a massive reaction against the personalities and policies of the New Deal. Radicals, artists, intellectuals, liberals, and teachers who had been supporters of Roosevelt or who had taken part in his administration were stigmatized as "agents of a foreign power." Spearheaded by Senator Joseph McCarthy of Wisconsin, a determined effort was made to isolate, discredit, and remove such people from positions of leadership and influence in American life. Congressional committees began to investigate people for their beliefs and associations; many, innocent of any crime, were jailed for contempt of Congress when they refused to submit to this kind of questioning.

Sing Out began publication in May 1950, at the height of the inquisition. In the following years, it would print many new topical songs, and not a few of these would be devoted to the theme of human freedom. The first number of *Sing Out* had upon its cover the words and music of Pete Seeger and Lee Hays' *Hammer Song,* a freedom ballad that has become one of the most widely known and loved songs of our time. *In Contempt* first appeared in the October 1950 issue.

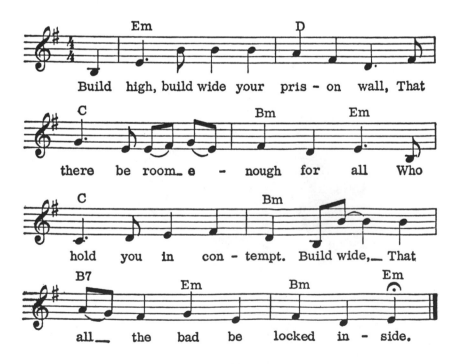

Though you have seized the valiant few
Whose glory casts a shade on you,
How can you now go home with ease,
Jangling your heavy dungeon keys?

The birds who still insist on song,
The sunlit stream still running strong,
The flowers still blazing red and blue,
All, all are in contempt of you.

The parents dreaming still of peace,
The playful children, the wild geese
Who still must fly, the mountains too,
All, all are in contempt of you.

When you have seized both moon and sun
And jailed the poems one by one,
And trapped each trouble-making breeze,
Then you can throw away your keys.

Words by Aaron Kramer; music by Betty Sanders; copyright 1950 by SING OUT! Inc., as printed in *Sing Out!* The National Folksong Magazine; used by permission.

Bull Connor's Jail

In May 1963, the young people of Birmingham, Alabama, staged their famous march in protest against segregation in that city. Not only teenagers but tiny children dressed in their Sunday best were confronted by police dogs and fire hoses, and herded by the hundreds into the filthy city jails. The naked brutality exhibited on this occasion by Bull Connor, Birmingham's tough director of "public security" led immediately to a national protest—the historic March on Washington of August 28. Guy and Candie Carawan were among those jailed. With the help of Ernie Marrs they rewrote *Down in the Valley* to suit the occasion. It was published in *Broadside* #26 (May 1963), and reissued in *Songs for the March on Washington*, August 28.

Down in Al - a - bam - a, In the
land of Jim Crow, There is a place where
Lots of folks go. Bir-ming-ham jail -
house, Bir-ming-ham jail, Wait-ing for
free - dom In Bull Con-nor's jail.

Three thousand prisoners,
 More coming in
Even little children
 Are singing this song.
Chorus

Bull Connor tells us
 "Don't raise a squawk
You need a permit
 Even to walk."
Chorus

Went to the church house
 To sing and pray,
Started downtown and
 They hauled us away.
Chorus

Pushed by policemen,
 Herded like hogs
Some got the fire hose
 And some got the dogs.
Chorus

Crammed in like sardines
 In Bull Connor's can,
Some can lay down,
 But others must stand.
Chorus

Iron bars around me
 Cold walls so strong
They hold my body,
 The world hears my song.
Chorus

Keep On a-Walkin'

This song, to the tune of an old spiritual, was born out of the demonstrations that took place in Albany, Georgia, in July 1962. It has since become one of the most popular of all the modern freedom songs. First published by *Broadside* in August 1962, it was sung by thousands at the March on Washington of August 1963, and was reissued in *Songs for the March on Washington,* August 28, 1963.

Cm

Ain't gonna let no - bod - y, Law - dy,

Fm   Cm

turn me 'round, turn me 'round, turn me 'round,

Ain't gon-na let no - bod - y, Law -dy,

Fm

turn me 'round; Keep on a-walk-in', (yea!)

Fm

Keep on a - talk - in', (yea!)

G7   Cm

March-in' on to Free-dom land.

Ain't gonna let segregation, Lawdy, turn me 'round, turn me
'round, turn me 'round,
Ain't gonna let segregation, Lawdy, turn me 'round,
Keep on a-walkin', (yea!)
Keep on a-talkin', (yea!)
Marchin' on to Freedom land.

Ain't gonna let no jailhouse, Lawdy, turn me 'round, turn me
'round, turn me 'round,
Ain't gonna let no jailhouse, Lawdy, turn me 'round,
Keep on a-walkin', (yea!)
Keep on a-talkin', (yea!)
Marchin' on to Freedom land.

Ain't gonna let no nervous Nelly, Lawdy, turn me 'round,
turn me 'round, turn me 'round,
Ain't gonna let no nervous Nelly, Lawdy, turn me 'round,
Keep on a-walkin', (yea!)
Keep on a-talkin', (yea!)
Marchin' on to Freedom land.

Ain't gonna let Chief Pritchett turn me 'round, turn me 'round,
turn me 'round,
Ain't gonna let Chief Pritchett turn me 'round,
Keep on a-walkin', (yea!)
Keep on a-talkin', (yea!)
Marchin' on to Freedom land.

Ain't gonna let no shotgun turn me 'round, turn me 'round,
turn me 'round,
Ain't gonna let no shotgun turn me 'round,
Keep on a-walkin', (yea!)
Keep on a-talkin', (yea!)
Marchin' on to Freedom land.

Ain't gonna let no Uncle Tom, Lawdy, turn me 'round, turn
me 'round, turn me 'round,
Ain't gonna let no Uncle Tom, Lawdy, turn me 'round,
Keep on a-walkin', (yea!)
Keep on a-talkin', (yea!)
Marchin' on to Freedom land.

Ain't gonna let nobody, etc.

One Man's Hands

This song is the result of a collaboration between Dr. Alex Comfort and Pete Seeger. It has a specific and urgent meaning for our own times and also embodies a permanent human truth.

One man's voice can't shout to make them hear,
Two men's voices can't shout to make them hear,
But if two and two and fifty make a million,
    We'll see that day come 'round,
    We'll see that day come 'round.

One man's feet can't walk around the land,
Two men's feet can't walk around the land
But if two and two and fifty make a million,
    We'll see that day come 'round,
    We'll see that day come 'round.

One man's eyes can't see the way ahead,
Two men's eyes can't see the way ahead,
But if two and two and fifty make a million,
    We'll see that day come 'round,
    We'll see that day come 'round.

One man's strength can't ban the atom bomb,
Two men's strength can't ban the atom bomb,
But if two and two and fifty make a million,
    We'll see that day come 'round,
    We'll see that day come 'round.

One man's strength can't break the color bar,
Two men's strength can't break the color bar,
But if two and two and fifty make a million,
    We'll see that day come 'round,
    We'll see that day come 'round.

One man's strength can't make the Union roll,
Two men's strength can't make the Union roll,
But if two and two and fifty make a million,
    We'll see that day come 'round,
    We'll see that day come 'round.

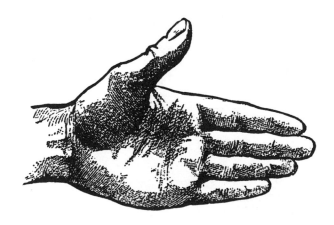

Words by Alex Comfort. Music by Pete Seeger. © Copyright 1962 by Fall River Music Inc. All rights reserved. Used by permission.

Little Boxes

Malvina Reynolds is one of the more prolific contemporary song writers. When *Broadside* made its first appearance in February 1962, she became a regular contributor to its pages. She wrote union songs, ballads about brass hats (*Leave My Van Allen Belt Alone* and *The Little Generals*) and satirical verses about The House Committee on un-American Activities. *Little Boxes* appeared in *Broadside* #20, February 1963. "Much to our surprise," wrote editor Sis Cunningham the following July, "*Little Boxes* is the most popular of all the songs we've printed so far." Another of Malvina Reynolds' songs, *What Have They Done to the Rain?* has become widely known through the singing of Joan Baez.

Lit - tle box - es on the
hill - side, lit - tle box - es made of
tick - y tack - y, Lit - tle box - es on the
hill - side, lit - tle box - es all the same. There's a
green one and a pink one and a
blue one and a yel - low one,__ And they're

378

Little boxes on the hillside, little boxes made of
    ticky tacky,
Little boxes on the hillside, little boxes all the same.
There's a green one and a pink one and a blue one and
    a yellow one,
And they're all made out of ticky tacky and they all
    look just the same.

And the people in the houses all went to the university
Where they were put in boxes and they came out all
    the same;
And there's doctors, and there's lawyers and there's
    business executives
And they're all made out of ticky tacky and they all
    look just the same.

And they all play on the golf course and drink their
    martini dry
And they all have pretty children and the children go
    to school
And the children go to summer camp and then to the
    university
Where they are all put in boxes and they come out
    all the same.

Coda (*retard like a music box running down*)

Sources

GENERAL

Charles Haywood, *A Bibliography of North American Folklore and Folksong* (New York: Dover Publications, 1961), is a guide to published materials and records. Supplement with R. Serge Denisoff, *Songs of Protest, War and Peace: A Bibliography and Discography* (Santa Barbara: ABC Clio Press, 1973), which focuses upon the role of song in antiwar and protest movements from the revolutionary era to the present. The best short introduction to United States historical ballads and song is Russell Ames, *The Story of American Folksong* (New York: Grosset and Dunlap, 1955). Music and lyrics for many songs are provided in a number of works. Highly recommended are: Margaret Boni, *The Fireside Book of Folksongs* (New York: Simon and Schuster, 1947); Joan Baez, *The Joan Baez Songbook* (New York: Ryerson Publishers, 1964); John Langstaff, *Hi! Ho! The Rattlin' Bog and Other Folk Songs for Group Singing* (New York: Harcourt, Brace and World, 1969); Alan Lomax, *Folk Songs of North America* (New York: Doubleday and Co., 1960); and Carl Sandburg, *The American Songbag* (New York: Harcourt, Brace and Co., 1927).

Another good and cheap source for songs is the collection of little songbooks made available by *World Around Us Songs*. The catalogue is obtainable by writing to:

> *World Around Us Songs*
> *Rt 5 Box 398*
> *Burnsville, N.C. 28714*
> *(phone: 704-675-5343)*

Much valuable material is also reproduced in *Sing Out!*, the folk song magazine whose address is 505 8th Avenue, New York, N.Y. 10018. The informative essays which Pete Seeger contributed over many years to *Sing Out!* have been brought together by editor Josephine Schwartz and published in a single volume entitled *The Incompleat Folksinger* (New York: Simon and Schuster, 1972). A complete listing of all songs reproduced in *Sing Out!* since it began publication in the early 1950s is available upon request, as are many back issues of the magazine.

Ruth Crawford Seeger, *American Folk Songs for Children* (New York: Doubleday and Co., 1948) is in a class by itself, not only because it provides wonderful songs for parents and teachers to sing with children, but on account of the introductory essay which explores with grace and profundity the place of music in the spiritual life of young people.

For the study of the national song, records are essential. Here a major resource is the Archive of American Folksong that is housed in the Library of Congress. The list of materials available to the public includes traditional ballads, shanties, spirituals, work songs, blues, miners' songs, cowboy ballads, songs of Native Americans, and many more. The catalogue of recordings may be obtained by writing to the Library of Congress, Recording Laboratory, Washington, D.C. 20540. Information is also available on the nature and extent of the Library of Congress folksong holdings, and on the services provided by the Archive of American Folksong. For this information write to:

Library of Congress
American Folklife Center
Washington, D.C. 20540
(phone: 202-287-6590).

The following are also invaluable sources for folk song records, and their catalogues may be obtained from the addresses given below: Folk-Legacy Records, Inc., Sharon, Conn. 06069; and Folkways Records, 43 West 61st Street, New York, N.Y. 10023. Reference should also be made to state folklore and historical societies for information concerning folk song records made in the separate states.

There is no better introduction to the sound of traditional song than the series of radio broadcasts made by John A. Lomax in 1942 and recorded on five discs under the title *The Ballad Hunter*, issued by the Library of Congress, AAFS L49–53. The series includes field recordings of cowboy songs, blues, railroad and sea songs, spirituals, and the songs of convicts. Special mention may also be made of Burl Ives's general introduction to historical song, *America's Musical Heritage*. This consists of the *Burl Ives Sing-Along Song Book* (New York: Franklin Watts, 1963) and six long playing records on which Ives sings more than 100 of the songs reproduced in the book.

For recordings of folk music made before the era of long play technology see William G. Tyrell, "Musical Recordings for American History," *Social Education*, Vol. 12, no. 5 (May 1948) and no. 7 (November 1948).

THE COLONIAL PERIOD

THE BRITISH HERITAGE   Peter Kennedy, *Folksongs of Britain and Ireland* (New York: Schirmer Books, 1975), is a comprehensive and well-annotated collection of the songs of the British Isles in their endless variety. Francis J. Child's *English and Scottish Popular Ballads*, originally published in five volumes 1884–98, is available in a modern paperbound edition (5 vols.; New York: Dover Publications, 1965). Bertrand Bronson, *The Traditional Tunes of the Child Ballads with their Texts, According to the Extant Records of Great Britain and America*, 4 vols. (Princeton, N.J.: Princeton University Press, 1959–72), brings together the fruits of the researches of dozens of musicians and scholars into the ballads over the past eighty years. Hundreds of the melodies to which these ballads have been sung both in Europe and America are here reproduced. A fine abridgement of this magisterial study is also available, *The Singing Tradition of Child's Popular Ballads* (Princeton, N.J.: Princeton University Press, 1976).

There is a growing body of commentary upon the songs in general and the ballads in particular. David C. Fowler, *A Literary History of the Popular Ballad* (Durham, N.C.: Duke University press, 1969), breaks new ground in tracing the history of the ballad from the fifteenth through the eighteenth centuries, with particular attention to the evolution of ballad style. David Buchan, *The Ballad and the Folk* (London: Routledge, and Kegan Paul, 1972), is a study of the ballad's role in the regional tradition of that most fertile of British ballad areas, northeastern Scotland. James Reed, *The Border Ballads* (London: The Athlone Press, 1975), provides a useful study of regional differences in the genesis and creation of song. A. L. Lloyd, *Folk Song in England* (New York: International Publishers, 1967), provides perspective for the study of the entire British folk song heritage. Bertrand Bronson, *The Ballad as Song* (Berkeley: University of California Press, 1969), is a series of essays on the tunes of the Child ballads.

COLONIAL SONGS AND BALLADS   For the study of this body of music wonderful resources are available in the form of the collections made on a state or regional basis by individual collectors or state folklore societies. For New England see Eloise Hubbard Linscott, *Folk Songs of Old New England* (Hamden, Conn.: The Shoe String Press, 1962), and Helen Hartness Flanders, *Ancient Ballads Traditionally Sung in New England*, 4 vols. (Philadelphia: University of Pennsylvania Press, 1960–65). For Virginia see Arthur Kyle Davis, Jr., *Traditional Ballads of Virginia*, 2 vols. (Chapel Hill, N.C.: University of North Carolina Press, 1929 and 1960); John Jacob Niles, *The Ballad Book* (New York: Bramhall House, 1960); and Mary Boette, *Singa Hipsy Doodle and Other Folk Songs of West Virginia* (Parkersburg, W. Va.: The Junior League, 1971). For North Carolina consult the *Frank C. Brown Collection of North Carolina Folklore*, vols. 2–5 (Durham, N.C.: Duke University

Press, 1952–62); for South Carolina see Charles W. Joyner, *Folk Song in South Carolina* (Columbia: University of South Carolina Press, 1971). John Harrington Cox, *Folk Songs of the South* (Hatboro, Pa.: Folklore Associates, 1963), draws materials from the region as a whole; for Appalachia there is the path-breaking collection of Cecil Sharpe, *English Folk Songs from the Southern Appalachians* (New York: Oxford University Press, 1960). In *Settlers on the Eastern Shore 1607–1750* (New York: Alfred A. Knopf, 1967) John Anthony Scott makes available the lyrics and melodies of nine traditional songs which were sung in colonial America.

There are a number of valuable collections of traditional song from the Canadian Maritimes, notably W. Roy Mackenzie, *Ballads and Sea Songs from Nova Scotia* (1928; reprint ed., Hatboro, Pa.: Folklore Associates, 1963); and Helen Creighton, *Maritime Folk Songs* (Toronto: Ryerson press, 1961), and *Songs and Ballads of Nova Scotia* (1932; reprint ed., New York: Dover Publications, 1966). For the rich song heritage of Newfoundland an outstanding source is Kenneth Peacock, *Songs of the Newfoundland Outports*, 3 vols. (Ottawa: National Museum of Canada, 1965). This comprehensive collection builds upon and supersedes the earlier work of collectors Maud Karpeles and Elisabeth B. Greenleaf.

British field recordings of the ballads are available on *The Child Ballads* (Caedmon Records, 5 discs), collected by Peter Kennedy and Alan Lomax. For American field recordings consult the Archive of American Folksong. The ballads may also be studied from the singing of Ewan MacColl and A. C. Lloyd, *The English and Scottish Popular Ballads*, ed. Kenneth Goldstein (Riverside RLP 12-621 to 628), also *Great British Ballads not Included in the Child Collection* (Riverside RLP 12-629). This series was also published with the same title on "Folk Music of the World" series, Washington label. A pioneer record in which Peggy Seeger and Ewan MacColl sing American and British variants of selected ballads is *Matching Songs of the British Isles and America* (Riverside RLP 12-637). Seeger and MacColl expanded this into a 12-record series entitled *The Long Harvest* (Argo Record Company Ltd., 115 Fulham Road, London, England). This series has been a valuable resource for the study of traditional music and lyrics, especially in the British universities.

Traditional Scots songs and ballads are sung by Ewan MacColl, *Scots Folk Songs* (Washington WLP 733; also issued on the Riverside label, RLP 12-609). An outstanding contribution is made by Jean Redpath, notably on *From My Ain Countrie* (Folk-Legacy FSS 49), and *Skipping Barefoot through the Heather* (Prestige International 13041); and Jeannie Robertson, *Scottish Ballads and Folk*

Songs (Prestige International 13006), and *Scots Tinker Lady* (Riverside RLP 12-633).

Among the many American singers who have recorded traditional songs and ballads we may mention John Langstaff, *Sings American and English Songs and Ballads* (Traditional Records TLP 1009); Andrew Rowan Summers (Folkways Records FA 2348, no title), and *The Unquiet Grave* (Folkways Records FP 64); Richard Dyer-Bennet (Archive of Folk Music FM 103, and Richard Dyer-Bennet Records, no titles); Cynthia Gooding, *The Queen of Hearts* and *Faithful Lovers* (Elektra 131 and 107); John Jacob Niles, *American Folk Songs* (Camden CAL 245); Jean Ritchie, *Ballads in Colonial America* (New Records LP 2005), and Elektra 125 (no title); Jean Ritchie, Oscar Brand, and Tom Paley, *Courtin's a Pleasure and Other Folk Songs of the Southern Appalachians* (Elektra 122); *Maritime Folk Songs from the Collection of Helen Creighton* (Folkways FE 4307). Songs of colonial New England are to be found on Bill Bonyun's *Yankee Legend* (Heirloom HL 500), and Margaret MacArthur, *Folksongs of Vermont* (Folkways FH 5314). See also Bob and Louise De Cormier, *Catskill Mountain Songs* (Stinson SLP 72); Paul Clayton, *Folksongs and Ballads of Virginia* (Folkways FP 47/3); Betty Vaiden Williams, *Folk Songs and Ballads of North Carolina* (Vanguard 9028); and Burl Ives, *America's Musical Heritage*, cited above, record no. 1.

THE AMERICAN REVOLUTION

For this chapter I relied primarily on the Isaiah Thomas Collection of broadside ballads in the keeping of the American Antiquarian Society at Worcester, Massachusetts. Two books by Frank Moore, pioneer collector of historical song, are indispensable for the study of the songs of the revolutionary period: *Diary of the American Revolution 1775–1781* (1860) and *Songs and Ballads of the American Revolution* (1856). For a modern abridgement of the *Diary* which also reproduces words and melodies of revolutionary songs and facsimiles of the broadsides, see John Anthony Scott, ed., *The Diary of the American Revolution 1775–1781 Compiled by Frank Moore* (New York: Washington Square Press, 1967). *Songs and Ballads of the American Revolution* has been reissued by Kennikat Press (Port Washington, N.Y., 1964). Additional material of value is also available in William L. Stone, *Ballads and Poems Relating to the Burgoyne Campaign* (1893; reprint ed., Port Washington, N.Y.: Kennikat Press, 1970), and Timothy Connor, *A Sailor's Songbag: An American Rebel in an English Prison, 1777–1779,* ed. George B. Carey (Amherst, Mass.: University of Massachusetts Press, 1976).

Modern collections of revolutionary song, with useful commentary, include Carolyn Rabson, *Songs of the American Revolution* (Peaks Island, Maine: Neo Press, 1974), and Irwin Silber, *Songs of Independence: The Beginnings, Growth, and Maturing of America's Revolutionary Spirit as Seen Through the Words and Music of Colonial Times* (Harrisburg, Pa.: Stackpole Books, 1973). A number of revolutionary songs with lyrics, melodies, and accompaniments for classical guitar are available in John Anthony Scott, *Trumpet of a Prophecy: Revolutionary America 1763–1783* (New York: Alfred A. Knopf, 1969). The ideological message of the songs is analyzed by the same author, "Ballads and Broadsides of the American Revolution," *Sing Out!* (April–May 1966).

For the British background of the broadside ballad tradition, see Leslie Shepard, *The Broadside Ballad* (London: Herbert Jenkins, 1962). Claude Simpson in a major study, *The British Broadside Ballad and Its Music* (New Brunswick, N.J.: Rutgers University Press, 1966), weds many of the broadsides and the tunes to which they were originally sung. With respect to American eighteenth-century broadsides, much work remains to be done on their publication and annotation. G. Malcolm Laws, Jr., *American Balladry from British Broadsides* has helpful comments (Philadelphia: The American Folklore Society, 1957). John Duffy, ed., *Early Vermont Broadsides* (Hanover, N.H.: University Press of New England, 1975), is a beautifully edited selection of facsimiles.

A pioneer recording on 78 r.p.m. discs, now something of a collector's item, is John and Lucy Allison, *Ballads of the American Revolution and the War of 1812* (RCA Victor VI-P11). Frank Warner sings three revolutionary songs on *Come All You Good People* (Minstrel JD 204). Long-playing records devoted exclusively to songs of the revolutionary period are: Tony Saletan and the Yankee Tinsmiths, *Revolutionary Tea* (Old North Bridge Records, 1776); Bill and Gene Bonyun and John Anthony Scott, *The American Revolution Through Its Songs and Ballads* (Heirloom 502); and Arthur F. Schrader, *American Revolutionary War Songs* (Folkways FH 5279). See also Burl Ives, *America's Musical Heritage*, cited above, record no. 2. For militia marching tunes see *Fife and Drum Music of the American Revolution* (Company of Military Collectors and Historians).

THE EARLY NATIONAL PERIOD

This period of United States history, musically speaking, still awaits its investigators and interpreters. I relied primarily on state and regional collections of the type listed above, supplemented by broadsides and songsters. For the latter, see Irving Loewens' useful *Bibliography of Songsters Printed in America before 1821* (Worcester, Mass.: American Antiquarian Society, 1976). James C. Dick, ed., *The Songs of Robert Burns* (1903; reprint ed., Hatboro, Pa.: Folklore Associates, 1962), remains a major achievement of Burnsian scholarship. Marion Starkey, *Lacecuffs and Leather Aprons: Popular Struggles in the Federalist Era 1783–1800* (New York: Alfred A. Knopf, 1972), and Leonard Falkner, *For Jefferson and Liberty: The United States in War and Peace 1800–1815* (New York: Alfred A. Knopf, 1972), make available twenty songs of the early national period, with melodies and lyrics. For sources on Irish music see under "Sea and Immigration" below.

Records devoted to the folk song of the early national period are scant and of uneven quality. We may mention Ewan MacColl, *Songs of Robert Burns* (Folkways FW 8758); Betty Sanders, *Songs of Robert Burns* (Riverside RLP 12-823); Wallace House, *War of 1812* (Folkways FP 5002); and Burl Ives, *America's Musical Heritage*, cited above, record no. 2. References for outstanding renditions of "The Bonny Bunch of Roses" are given under "Recordings."

JACKSONIAN AMERICA

SEA AND IMMIGRATION   For British shanties see Stan Hugill's excellent study, *Shanties from the Seven Seas* (New York: E. P. Dutton and Co., 1961). American versions of the shanties are provided in: Joanna Colcord, *Songs of American Seamen* (New York: Oak Publications, 1964); Frederick P. Barlow, *Shanteying Aboard American Ships* (Barre, Mass.: Barre Gazette, 1962); and William Doerflinger, *Shantymen and Shantyboys* (New York: Macmillan, 1961). Gale Huntington, *Songs the Whalemen Sang* (Barre, Mass.: Barre Publications, 1964), gives a picture of the whalermen's songs as recorded in journals, logs, and manuscript song collections. *The Story of American Whaling* (New York: American Heritage, 1959) is a first-rate pictorial introduction to the whaling industry. Field recordings of the whale, *Songs of the Humpback Whale*, are available on Capitol Records ST 620.

Irish songs with Gaelic originals, serviceable translations, music, and notes, may be found in Donal O'Sullivan, *Songs of the Irish* (New York: Crown Publishers, 1960). See also Colm O Lochlainn, *Irish Street Ballads* (New York: Corinth Press, 1960), and Patrick Galvin, *Irish Songs of Resistance 1169–1923* (New York: Oak Publications, 1962).

A number of superb recordings of sea songs of this period have been made by modern singers, notably: Ewin MacColl and A. C. Lloyd, *Blow Boys Blow* (Tradition TLP 1026), and *Whaling Ballads* (Washington WLP 724); Bill Bonyun, *Songs of Yankee Whaling* (American Heritage LP 1), and *Roll and Go, The Shantyman's Day Aboard a Yankee Clipper* (Heirloom 504). See also Pete Seeger and Woody Guthrie, *Deep Sea Chanteys* (Commodore FL 30,002); Paul Clayton, *Foc'sle Songs and Shanties* (Folkways FA 2429); Oscar Brand, *Rollicking Sea Shanties* (Audio Fidelity 1966); and Louis Killen, Jeff and Gerret Warner, and Fud Berson, *Steady as She Goes* (Collector Records 1928).

The musical heritage of the Irish immigrants is made available on some fine modern recordings. *The Lark in the Morning* (Tradition TLP 1004) presents field recordings made by Diane Hamilton in Ireland in 1955. Margaret Barry sings *Songs of an Irish Tinker Lady* (Riverside RLP 12-602). Among professional singers of traditional Irish songs special mention must be made of Tom, Liam, and Patrick Clancy, with Tommy Makem, in the following records: *Come Fill Your Glass With Us* (Tradition TLP 1032); *The Rising of the Moon* (Tradition TLP 1006); *Irish Songs of Rebellion* (Everest 2070); *The Boys Won't Leave the Girls Alone* (Columbia CS 8709); and Tradition TLP 1042 (no title). See also the beautiful recordings by Grainne Ni Eigeartaigh, *Irish Folk Songs* (Spoken Arts 206); Mary O'Hara, *Songs of Ireland* (Tradition TLP 1024); Seamus Ennis, *The Bonnie Bunch of Roses* (Tradition TLP 1013); Peg and Bobby Clancy, *Songs from Ireland* (Tradition TLP 1045); and Deirdre O'Callaghan, *Folk Songs from Erin* (Wesminster WF 12025). For a recording by young American singers, see the Fieldston School documentary, *Irish Immigration Through Its Songs and Ballads* (Heirloom Records).

THE WESTWARD MOVEMENT   State and regional collections cited above, under "Colonial Songs and Ballads," were my principal resources, to which should be added: Arnold Byron, *Folksongs of Alabama* (University: University of Alabama Press, 1950); William A. Owens, *Texas Folk Songs* (Dallas: Texas Folklore Society, 1950); Harry B. Peters, *Folksongs Out of Wisconsin* (Madison: State Historical Society, 1977); Theodore C. Blegen and Martin Ruud, *Norwegian Emigrant Songs and Ballads* (Minneapolis: University of Minnesota Press, 1936); Emelyn Elizabeth Gardner and G. J. Chickering, *Ballads and Songs of Southern Michigan* (1939; reprint ed., Hatboro, Pa.: Folklore Associates, 1967); Mary O. Eddy, *Ballads and Songs from Ohio* (Hatboro, Pa.: Folklore Associates, 1964); H. M. Belden, *Ballads and Songs Collected by the Missouri Folklore Society* (Columbia: Missouri Folklore Society, 1955); Charles J. Finger, *Frontier Ballads* (New York: Doubleday, 1972); Edith Fowke, *Lumbering Songs from the Northern Woods*

(Austin: University of Texas Press, 1970); and Phillips Barry, *The Maine Woods Songster* (Cambridge, Mass.: Power Printing Co., 1939).

For New York State there are three outstanding contributions: Harold W. Thompson, ed., *A Pioneer Songster: Texts from the Steven-Douglass Manuscripts of Western New York 1841–1856* (Ithaca: Cornell University Press, 1958); the same author's *Body, Boots, and Britches: Folk Tales, Ballads and Speech from Country New York* (New York: Dover Publications, 1962); and Norman Cazden, *The Abelard Folk Song Book* (New York: Abelard-Schuman, 1957), the fruit of years of collecting and singing in the Catskills.

For the Far West in this era there are two comprehensive sources: Richard E. Lingenfelter and Richard A. Dwyer, *Songs of the American West* and *Songs of the Gold Rush* (Berkeley: University of California Press, 1968 and 1965 respectively). Laurence I. Seidman, *The Fools of '49: The California Gold Rush 1848–1867* (New York: Alfred A. Knopf, 1976), reproduces the words and melodies of twelve Gold Rush songs, many of them with accompaniments for classical guitar. Seven songs of the Mexican War, with melodies and guitar accompaniments, are given in Milton Meltzer's superb study, *Bound for the Rio Grande: The Mexican Struggle 1845–1850* (New York: Alfred A. Knopf, 1974).

For field recordings of woodsmen's songs, see the Archive of American Folk Song, *Songs of the Michigan Lumberjacks* (AAFS L 56); and for the traditional songs of Ontario settlers, *Ontario Ballads and Folksongs* (field recordings by Edith Fowke; Prestige International Int 25014). Frontier songs are sung by Pete Seeger, *Frontier Ballads* (Folkways FP 48-5); by Seeger and Ed McCurdy, *The Expansion of the United States and Frontier Life* in *American History in Ballad and Song* (vol. 1, disc no. 1, Folkways FH 5801); by Paul Clayton, *Timber: Lumberjack Folksongs and Ballads* (riverside RLP 648); Anne Grimes, *Ballads of Ohio* (Folkways 5217); Vivian Richman, *Folk Songs of West Pennsylvania* (Folkways FG 3568); Logan English, *Kentucky Folk Songs and Ballads* (Folkways 2316); and Loman D. Cansler, *Folksongs of Missouri* (Folkways FH 5324). Pat Foster sings Gold Rush songs on *The Fools of '49* (Riverside RLP 12-654). For western songs in general see Burl Ives, *America's Musical Heritage*, cited above, records nos. 3 and 4.

SLAVERY DAYS   Harold Courlander, *Negro Folk Music USA* (New York: Columbia University Press, 1963), is a fine introduction to Afro-American music. Dena J. Epstein, *Sinful Tunes and Spirituals: Black Folk Music to the Civil War* (Urbana: University of Illinois Press, 1977), is a contribution of outstanding importance not only to the history of Afro-American music, but to the history of slavery itself. Sources for songs originating in slavery days are: William Francis Allen, Charles Pickard Ware, and Lucy McKim Garrison, *Slave Songs of the United States* (1867; reprint ed., Gloucester, Mass.: Peter Smith, 1951); Henry Edward Krehbiel, *Afro-American Folk Songs* (1913; reprint ed., New York: Frederick Ungar Publishing Co., 1962); Dorothy Scarborough, *On the Trail of Negro Folk Songs* (Hatboro, Pa.: Folklore Associates, 1963); Lydia Parrish, *Slave Songs of the Georgia Sea Islands* (New York: Creative Age Press, 1942); James Weldon Johnson and J. Rosamond Johnson, *The Book of American Negro Spirituals* (New York: Viking Press, 1929); and Mary Allen Grissom, *The Negro Sings a New Heaven* (1930; reprint ed., New York: Dover Publications, 1969). John Anthony Scott, *Hard Trials on My Way: Slavery and the Struggle Against It 1800–1860* (New York: Alfred A. Knopf, 1974), makes available nine slavery songs with lyrics, melodies, and accompaniments for classical guitar.

White spirituals for the antebellum period in the Southern Appalachians have been brought together by George Pullen Jackson. Among his many works on this subject, the following especially may be mentioned: *White Spirituals in the Southern Uplands: The Story of the Fasola Folk, Their Songs, Singing, and "Buckwheat Notes"* (1933; reprint ed., New York: Dover Publications, 1965); *Spiritual Folk Songs of Early America: 250 Tunes and Texts* (1937; reprint ed., New York: Dover Publications, 1964); and *White and Negro Spirituals: Their Life Span and Kinship* (Locust Valley, N.Y.: J.J. Augustin, n.d.).

What was the sound of slavery? Black singing in the antebellum period was an infinitely varied musical creation, involving field calls, work songs, boat songs, dance songs, harvest songs, love songs, lullabies, laments, and sacred music. One day, no doubt, an attempt will be made to re-create and record the sound of slavery from the manifold clues that survive both in the literature and the singing traditions of the black people. But that time, evidently, is not yet.

THE CIVIL WAR

My main sources here were songsters and other materials in the possession of the American Antiquarian Society (Worcester, Mass.) and the Harris Collection of Brown University (Providence, R.I.). As for Frank Moore, his work in the Civil War field is a source in itself, primarily *The Rebellion Record: A Diary of American Events, with Documents, Narratives, Illustrative Incidents, Poetry etc.*, 10 vols. (New York, 1861–68); *Anecdotes, Poetry and Incidents of the*

War, North and South, 1860–1865 (New York: Collier's, 1867; reissued by the same publisher in 1889 under the title *The Civil War in Song and Story, 1860–1865)*; and the Red, White and Blue Song Series, composed of *Songs of the Soldiers, Lyrics of Loyalty,* and *Personal and Political Ballads* (New York: Putnam, 1864, three titles). Many of the better-known Civil War songs will be found in Irwin Silber, *The Songs of the Civil War* (New York: Columbia University Press, 1960), with piano arrangements and chording by Jerry Silverman. Willard A. Heaps and Porter W. Heaps, *The Singing Sixties: The Spirit of the Civil War Days Drawn from the Music of the Times* (Norman: University of Oklahoma Press, 1960), provide lyrics but little music. James M. McPherson, *Marching Toward Freedom: The Negro in the Civil War 1861–1865* (New York: Alfred A. Knopf, 1967), provides the lyrics and melodies of six black freedom and marching songs.

The outstanding contribution in the field of Civil War song recording is Frank, Jeff, and Gerret Warner, *Songs of the Civil War North and South* (Prestige International 13012), but this disc omits black freedom and marching songs. See also Bill Bonyun et al., *The Civil War Through Its Songs and Ballads* (Heirloom HL 503); and Hermes Nye, *Ballads of the Civil War* (Folkways FP 48-7 and 8). Burl Ives sings a number of Civil War songs on *America's Musical Heritage*, cited above, disc no. 5.

BETWEEN THE CIVIL WAR AND THE FIRST WORLD WAR

FARMERS, WORKERS, AND IMMIGRANTS Labor, railroad, and western songs for this and later periods are abundantly provided in Edith Fowke and Joe Glaser, *Songs of Work and Freedom* (New York: Dolphin Books, 1960); John A. and Alan Lomax, *American Ballads and Folksongs* (New York: Macmillan, 1957); Alan Lomax, *Best Loved American Folk Songs* (New York: Grosset and Dunlap, 1947); the same author's *Folk Songs of North America*, cited above; and John Greenway, *American Folksongs of Protest* (Philadelphia: University of Pennsylvania Press, 1953). Lyrics and melodies for thirty labor, immigrant, and Afro-American songs of this period are given in John Anthony Scott, ed., *Living Documents in American History*, vol. 2 (New York: Washington Square Press, 1968). Labor songs are reproduced abundantly in Philip S. Foner, *American Labor Songs of the Nineteenth Century* (Urbana: University of Illinois Press, 1975), all of them, regrettably, without music. For the coalminers see the work of the pioneer collector of Pennsylvania song, George Korson, notably: *Pennsylvania Songs and Legends* (Baltimore: Johns Hopkins University Press, 1960); *Black Rock: Mining Folklore of the Pennsylvania Dutch* (same press, same date); and

Coal Dust on the Fiddle: Songs and Stories of the Bituminous Industry (1943; reprint ed., Hatboro, Pa.: Folklore Associates, 1965).

For the songs of the Far West in this period, see Lingenfelter and Dwyer, *Songs of the American West*, cited above, and Lester A. Hubbard, *Ballads and Songs from Utah* (Salt Lake City: University of Utah Press, 1961). Many cowboy songs are made available in John A. Lomax's pathbreaking collection, *Cowboy Songs and Other Frontier Ballads* (1910; reprinted with additional melodies and lyrics, New York: Macmillan, 1938). See also Margaret Larkin, *Singing Cowboy: A Book of Western Songs* (1931; reprint ed., New York: Oak Publications, 1963). Additional western material is contained in William A. Owens, *Texas Folk Songs*, cited above, which covers the range of Texan folk song but excludes the Range. Laurence I. Seidman's classic, *Once in the Saddle: The Cowboy's Frontier 1866–1896* (New York: Alfred A. Knopf, 1973), reproduces the words and music of ten cowboy songs with accompaniments for classical guitar.

For Yiddish songs I relied principally on Ruth Rubin, *A Treasury of Jewish Folk Song* (New York: Schocken Books, 1950), and Nathan Ausubel, *A Treasury of Jewish Folklore* (New York: Crown Publishers, 1948). As for French-American singing, an admirable introduction is Edith Fulton Fowke and Richard Johnston, *Chansons de Quebec*, with translations by Edith Fowke (Waterloo, Ont.: Waterloo Music Co., 1957). Additional Canadian songs, both Anglo and French, are provided in the same authors' *Folk Songs of Canada* (same publisher, 1954); and in Edith Fowke, Alan Mills, and Helmut Blume, *Canada's Story in Song* (Toronto: W. J. Gage, n.d.).

Much of the material dealt with in this section may be studied from Library of Congress records in the Archive of American Folksong, supplemented, for the Southern Appalachians, by Alan Lomax's fine field recording, *White Spirituals* (Atlantic 1349). For the songs of the workers see Pete Seeger, *American Industrial Ballads* (Folkways FH 5251), and *The Industrial Era* in *American History in Ballad and Song* (vol. 1, discs nos. 2 and 3, Folkways FH 5801 D and E), and John Greenway, *American Industrial Songs* (Riverside RLP 12-607). For mining songs special mention may be made of the Library of Congress field recording *Songs and Ballads of the Anthracite Miners* (AAFS L16).

Recordings by cowboys are preserved on *Authentic Cowboys and Their Western Folksongs* (RCA Victor LPV 522). Special mention may also be made of Merrick Jarrett's *Songs of the Old West* (Washington WLP 725), which makes available a number of the songs originally published in Lomax's *Cowboy Songs and Other*

Frontier Ballads. See also Burl Ives, *Cowboys, Indians, Badmen and Settlers*, disc no. 6 of *America's Musical Heritage*, (Tradition TLP 1029).

Yiddish songs are recorded by Ruth Rubin (Prestige International 13019 and Washington WLP 726); Morton Freeman, *Jewish Folk Songs* (Tikva T-49); and Theodore Bikel, *Jewish Folk Songs* (Elektra 141). Canadian songs are recorded by Alan Mills, *Canada's Story in Song* (Folkways FW 3000, 2 discs) and *French Canadian Folk Songs* (Folkways FW 6929).

THE NEGRO PEOPLE   For the songs of the Negro people in the postbellum South, the works cited above by John and Alan Lomax, Harold Courlander, and Lydia Parrish are indispensable. Other collections of value are John F. Work, *American Negro Songs and Spirituals: 230 Songs—Spirituals, Blues, Work Songs, Hollers, Jubilee Social Songs* (New York: Bonanza Books, 1940); and Bruce Jackson, *Wake Up Dead Man: Afro-American Worksongs from Texas Prisons* (Cambridge: Harvard University Press, 1972). Frederic Ramsey, *Been Here and Gone* (New Brunswick, N.J.: Rutgers University Press, 1960), is a traveler's commentary that illuminates the roots of Afro-American music. For the history of the blues see Samuel B. Charters, *The Country Blues* (New York: Rinehart, 1959), and Paul Oliver, *The Meaning of the Blues* (New York: Collier's, 1963).

Negro work songs of the postbellum period combined elements of calls, rhythms, and melodies inherited from slavery days. A classic introduction to this type of song is a field recording made by Alan Lomax in the late 1940s, *Negro Prison Songs from the Mississippi State Penitentiary* (Tradition TLP 1020). Lomax has contributed a wealth of further field recording on the themes of black work songs, sacred music, and the blues, including: *Roots of the Blues* (Atlantic 1348); *The Blues Roll On* (Atlantic 1352); *Bad Man Ballads** (Prestige International 25009); *Sounds of the South* (Atlantic 1346); *Negro Church Music* (Atlantic 1351); and *Georgia Sea Islands* (Prestige International 25001 and 2, 2 discs). While these recordings were made after World War II, much of the material included is traditional, dating back to before World War I. The same may be said of the field recordings made in Alabama by Harold Courlander in 1950, a selection of which are available in a six-record series, *Negro Folk Music of Alabama* (Folkways FE 4417–18, FE 4471–74). See also the field recordings made by John A. and Alan Lomax and others in various parts of the South between 1933 and 1942, made available by the Archive of Ameri-

*Includes also recordings of white singers.

393

can Folk Song: *Afro-American Blues and Game Songs* (AFS L4); *Negro Work Songs and Calls* (AAFS L8); and *Negro Blues and Hollers* (AFS L59).

Country blues singers who were born and grew up before World War I, but who brought their art to maturity and recorded their songs after 1918, are legion. We have space to mention just a few of the giants, notably Blind Lemon Jefferson (Riverside RLP 12-125 and 136); Lightnin' Hopkins, *Lightnin' Strikes* (Vee-Jay LP 1044) and *The Roots of Lightning' Hopkins* (Verve Folkways FV/FVS 9000); Pink Anderson, *Carolina Blues Man* (Prestige/Bluesville 1038); Big Bill Broonzy, *Country Blues* (Folkways FA 2326); *Big Bill's Blues* (Columbia WL 111); *Last Session* (Verve V 3001, 2 discs); Mississippi John Hurt (Vanguard VRS 9148, 9220; Piedmont PLP 13157); *Worried Blues* (VSD Vanguard 19/20, 2 discs); Huddie Ledbetter (Leadbelly), who sings Afro-American songs and blues on the Leadbelly Legacy records (Folkways FA 2941, 2942, 2024) and on *Leadbelly* (Archive of Folk Music FM 102); and John Lee Hooker, *I'm John Lee Hooker* (Vee-Jay LP 1007); *How Long Blues* (Battle BLP 6114); *Plays and Sings the Blues* (Chess LP 1454); *The Country Blues* (Riverside LP 12-838); and *Folk Blues* and *That's My Story* (Riverside RLP 12-898 and 321).

BETWEEN TWO WORLD WARS

Songs of the period 1914–45 are scattered throughout many collections. For soldiers' songs see E. A. Dolph, *Sound Off: Soldiers' Songs from the Revolution to World War II* (New York: Farrar and Rinehart, 1942); John Jacob Niles, *Singing Soldiers* (New York: Scribner's, 1927); and Edgar A. Palmer, *G.I. Songs* (New York: Sheridan House, 1944). Steven Jantzen, *Hooray for Peace, Hurrah for War: The United States During World War I* (New York: Alfred A. Knopf, 1971), provides lyrics and melodies for eleven songs sung both by soldiers and by civilians on the home front.

Woody Guthrie made perhaps the greatest single contribution to the popular singing of this period. See Woody Guthrie, *California to the New York Island* (New York: Guthrie Children's Trust Fund, 1960; distributed by Oak Publications), and *The Woody Guthrie Song Book* (New York: Grosset and Dunlap, 1976). For Woody's life' see Henrietta Yurchenko and Marjorie Guthrie's sketch, *A Mighty Hard Road: The Woody Guthrie Story* (New York: McGraw-Hill, 1970), and Jo Klein, *Woody Guthrie* (New York: Alfred A. Knopf, 1980), a major study.

Songs of World War I are sung by the Four Sergeants, *World War I Songs in Hi-Fi* (ABC Paramount 196). Depression songs are recorded by the New Lost City Ramblers, *Songs from the Depression* (Folkways 2396-99). Railroad songs are available on a field recording, *Songs of the Railroad 1924–1934* (Vetco Records LP 103). Woody Guthrie sings his own songs on *Talking Dust Bowl*, *Bound for Glory*, and the classic *Songs to Grow On* (Folkways FA 2011, 2481, and FC 7005, respectively). Pete Seeger and the Almanac Singers sing both traditional and New Deal labor songs on *Talking Union* (Folkways FP 85-1).

SINCE THE WAR

Recent Songbooks for Political Singers is a bibliography of song-books published since World War II and dealing primarily, but not exclusively, with contemporary song. This is Newsletter no. 1 of Resources for People's Culture, 714 E. Meinecke Street, Milwaukee, Wis. 53212 (Summer 1979). For the background of the earlier folk song collecting, recording, and publishing, out of which the folk song revival grew, see D. K. Wilgus, *Anglo-American Folksong Scholarship* (New Brunswick, N.J.: Rutgers University Press, 1959).

Freedom songs both old and new sung by the civil rights movement have been published in a number of books by Guy and Candie Carawan, notably *We Shall Overcome* (New York: Oak Publications, 1963); *Freedom is a Constant Struggle* (New York: Oak Publications, 1968); and *Voices from the Mountain* (New York: Alfred A. Knopf, 1975). For songs sung during the Vietnam War, primarily by United States civilians and soldiers, see Barbara Dane and Irwin Silber, *Vietnam Song Book* (New York: Guardian Books, 1969; available from *Sing Out!*).

Milton Okun, ed., *Great Songs of the Sixties* (Chicago: Quadrangle Books, 1970), provides 82 songs with piano accompaniments and chording that constitute a superb sampling of the musical achievement of a galaxy of songwriters spanning the generations and including John Denver, Bob Dylan, Bobbie Gentry, Arlo Guthrie, Janis Ian, John Lennon, Paul McCartney, Phil Ochs, Malvina Reynolds, Pete Seeger, Paul Simon, and Tom Paxton. Some of these writer-singers have also made available collections of their own songs, notably Bob Dylan, *The Songs of Bob Dylan* (New York: Alfred A. Knopf, 1976, with piano arrangements and chording by Ronnie Ball and Milton Okun); Phil Ochs, *The Songs of Phil Ochs* (New York: Appleseed Music, 1964) and *The War Is Over* (New York: Macmillan, 1968); Jeff Langley and Holly Near, *The Hang-in There Songbook: Music of Holly Near* (Ukiah, Calif.: Redwood Records, 1975); Peter La Farge, *Ballad of Ira Hayes and Other Folk Songs* (New York: Edward B. Marks, 1964); Tom Paxton, *Ramblin' Boy and Other Songs* (New York: Oak Publications, 1965), and *The Tom Paxton Anthology* (New York: UA Music,

1971); Malvina Reynolds, *The Malvina Reynolds Songbook* (Berkeley: Schroeder Music, 1976); Buffy Sainte-Marie, *The Buffy Sainte-Marie Songbook* (New York: Grosset and Dunlap, 1971); and Carly Simon, *Carly Simon Complete* (New York: Alfred A. Knopf and Warner Bros. Publications Inc., 1975).

For mid-century blues there are two good collections available: Josh White, *The Josh White Songbook* (Chicago: Quadrangle Books, 1963); and Kay Shirley, ed., *The Book of the Blues* (New York: Leeds Music Co. and Crown Publishers, 1963; 100 songs with chords).

As sources for the study of contemporary song *Sing Out!* and *Broadside* are indispensable. *Sing Out!* began publication in 1950 as a monthly magazine, and continues to the present (505 8th Avenue, New York, N.Y. 10018). Its columns contain a wealth of material—book and record reviews, articles on contemporary music, melodies and lyrics of songs both modern and traditional.

Broadside began publication in 1962 under the editorship of Sis Cunningham as a monthly magazine specializing in topical song. It has continued publication until the present, but at irregular intervals. During the sixties *Broadside* published hundreds of newly composed songs, often with both lyrics and melodies, some of them very good, some destined to become famous. The writer-singers whose work appeared here included Bob Dylan, Len Chandler, Ernie Marrs, Malvina Reynolds, Mark Spoelstra, and Pete Seeger. *Blowin' in the Wind*, one of the most famous early songs of Bob Dylan, first saw the light of day in *Broadside* no. 6 (May 1962) without even the formality of a copyright notice. *Broadside* is a rich mine for the following topics: nuclear war, the Vietnam War, the civil rights movement, environmental pollution, Native Americans, governmental repression, the violent deaths of workers, athletes, and activitists.

The discography of this period of American singing is enormous in quantity and awaits its critical recorders and evaluators. We can do no more here than to touch upon the highlights.

The Weavers (Pete Seeger, Ronnie Gilbert, Lee Hays, Fred Hellerman) were the pied pipers of the folk song revival of the middle fifties. They recorded five discs for Vanguard: *The Weavers at Carnegie Hall, The Weavers on Tour, Travelling on with the Weavers, The Weavers at Home*, and *The Weavers' Almanac* (VRS 9010, 9013, 9043, 9024, 9100). A host of imitators followed, but the late fifties saw the emergence of three outstanding new talents in the folk song performing field.

The first of these was Joan Baez who in the years 1959–64 re-created traditional Anglo-American folk song for a new generation eager to listen. As time went on Baez began to introduce contemporary songs into her repertoire; she recorded exclusively for Vanguard (VRS 9078, 9094, 9112, 9113, VSD 79160).

The second of these new talents was Odetta, whose repertoire combined blues, chain gang and prison camp songs, freedom songs, with sea songs, lullabies and other traditional material (for example, *Ballads and Blues* [Tradition TLP 1010], and *Sometimes I Feel Like Cryin'* [RCA Victor LSP 2573]).

The third was Judy Collins, who also sang both traditional and contemporary songs, and recorded exclusively for Elektra (among others, *A Maid of Constant Sorrow* [EKS 7243]; *The Golden Apples of the Sun* [EKS 7222]; EKS 7243, no title; *So Early in the Spring, The First Fifteen Years* [no identifying number]).

Throughout the entire period since World War II into the eighties Pete Seeger continued his career as singer and songwriter, making innumerable records. We may mention: *The Bitter and the Sweet* (Columbia CS 8716, cut from the tape of a concert at the Bitter End in 1962); *We Shall Overcome* (Carnegie Hall concert June 5, 1963, Columbia 2101); *At the Village Gate* (Folkways FA 2450, 2451); *Broadside Ballads* (two discs devoted to songs that had appeared in *Broadside*, Broadside Records 301 and 312, available from Folkways); *God Bless the Grass* (Columbia CS 9232); and *Rainbow Race* (Columbia CS 30739). For other Seeger recordings see R. Serge Denisoff, *Songs of Protest, War and Peace: A Bibliography and Discography* (Santa Barbara: ABC Clio Press, 1973), p. 51.

Early in the sixties two major new creative phenomena erupted onto the American musical scene. The first of these was the Beatles, who accelerated in America the process of self-discovery by a generation that sought not only to master its musical heritage but to turn it to fresh contemporary uses. The Beatles recorded exclusively with Capitol Records until they formed their own recording company (2108, 2080, 2222, 2047, 2228, 2309, 2358, 2442, 2553; and *Sgt. Pepper's Lonely Hearts Club Band*, 2653). The second of these new major talents was Bob Dylan whose songs may be heard on various Columbia recordings (including: *The Freewheelin' Bob Dylan* [CL 1986]; *Blonde on Blonde* [CL 2516, two discs]; *Bringing It All Back Home* [CL 2328]; *Nashville Skyline* [KCS 9825]; *New Morning* [KCM 30290]; and *Highway 61 Revisited* [CL 2389]).

Dylan and the Beatles set the stage for one of the most prolific and creative decades in the history of American song. For a discography of a portion of this material see Denisoff, *Songs of Protest, War and Peace* (cited above), pp. 47–52.

The music of the sixties dealt with the meaning of love and freedom, with protest, and with alienation. In this last category in addition to the extraordinary contributions of John Lennon and Bob Dylan, special mention must be made of the music of Paul Simon and Art Garfunkel (*Parsley, Sage, Rosemary and Thyme* [CS 9363]; *Book Ends* [KCS 9529]; *Sounds of Silence* [CS 9269], among others).

Much of the singing of the sixties was done on the streets, not merely in coffee houses and recording studios. Freedom songs both old and new sung by the civil rights movement are available on a number of Folkways records (FH 5594, 5592, 5591). Three discs cut from tapes made primarily by Moses Moon and Guy Carawan have been made available by the Smithsonian Institution under the title of *Voices of the Civil Rights Movement: Black American Freedom Songs 1960–1966*. No printed lyrics are provided with this set, and this is an omission that needs to be remedied if this valuable material is to be used effectively with students. See also Ella Jenkins, Br. John Sellers, and Joseph Brewer, *A Long Time* (Asch Records AHS 850).

Antiwar songs are scattered throughout the repertoire of many singers of the sixties. See, for example, Arlo Guthrie, *Alice's Restaurant* (Reprise 6267); Phil Ochs, *I Ain't Marchin' Any More* (Elektra EKS 7287); Pete Seeger, *Waist Deep in the Big Muddy and Other Love Songs* (Columbia CS 9505); Peter La Farge, *As Long As the Grass Shall Grow* (Folkways FN 2532); Tom Paxton, *Ain't That News* (Elektra EKL 277) and *The Bitter and the Sweet* (CS 8716); Peter, Paul, and Mary (Warner Bros. 1449, no title); *Broadside Ballads*, cited above; and Bill Horwitz, *Lies, Lies, Lies* (ESP 3020). Jacqueline Sharpe sings her own compositions on *No More War* (Cutty Wren CWR 101). For a discography of singles of songs supporting the Vietnam War, see Denisoff, *Songs of Protest, War and Peace* (cited above), pp. 52–54.

After World War II traditional mountain music was evolving in a direction that would make the fortune of Nashville and the music industry during the seventies. Earl Taylor and his Stoney Mountain Boys, *Folk Songs from the Blue Grass*, with jacket notes by Alan Lomax, is a fine introduction to country and western (UAL 3049).

AFTERWORD

Two fundamental sources for the use of folksong in the classroom are: Ruth Crawford Seeger, *American Folk Songs for Children* (New York: Doubleday and Co., 1948), and Ruth Tooze and Beatrice Perham Krone, *Literature and Music as Resources for Social Studies* (Englewood Cliffs, N.J.: Prentice-Hall, 1955). See also John Anthony Scott, *Teaching for a Change* (New York: Bantam Books, 1972), and for English classrooms the excellent work by

Robert Leach and Roy Palmer, *Folk Music in School* (New York: Cambridge University Press, 1978).

The periodical literature includes David Dufty and John Anthony Scott, "How To Use Folk Songs," a pamphlet published by the National Council for the Social Studies (Washington, D.C., 1969); and John Anthony Scott, "Folklore and Folksong in Education," *New York Folklore Quarterly* (Winter 1962), and "Folksong and the Schools," *Teaching and Learning* (1965).

Folksong in the Classroom is a newsletter for teachers, kindergarten through college, that appears four times a year, reproduces traditional songs, provides background material, and suggests ways in which the songs may be used in the classroom. Subscriptions, back issues and other folk song material—including the three articles by Dufty and Scott cited above—may be obtained from the editor, Laurence I. Seidman, 140 Hill Park Avenue, Great Neck, N.Y., 11021.

Recordings of Fieldston students singing many of the songs reproduced in *The Ballad of America* were made during the years 1960–67. A number of these songs were reissued on a long-playing single, *The Best of Fieldston*. This record, too, is available from *Folksong in the Classroom*. For the convenience of teachers we list the songs on this disc here rather than in the discography.

They are:

The American Revolution	Nathan Hale
Early National	Napoleon Bonaparte
Sea	Blood Red Roses
	Greenland Whale Fishery
Immigration	Brennan on the Moor
	Mrs. McGrath
	The Praties They Grow Small
	The Farmer's Cursed Wife
	Silver is the Daylight
	(Papir Iz Doch Vays)
The Negro People	Hushabye
	No More Auction Block
	O Freedom
	Ragged and Dirty Blues
	Discrimination Blues
The Cowboy	Colorado Trail
New Deal	Wandering
	Raggedy
	Which Side Are You On?
	We Shall Overcome

Recordings

Below will be found, under the appropriate chapter heading and song title, a list of available recordings of a number of songs included in this book.

THE COLONIAL PERIOD

The British Heritage

Bawbee Allen (Barbara Ellen)
Ewan MacColl
*The English and Scottish
    Popular Ballads*
Riverside RLP 12-624

Ewan McColl
The Manchester Angel
Tradition TLP 2059 (variant)

Joan Baez 2
Vanguard VRS 9094 (variant)

I Will Give My Love an
Apple
John Langstaff
*American and British
    Folksongs and Ballads*
Tradition TLP 1009

Cynthia Gooding
The Queen of Hearts
Elektra ELP 131

Andrew Rowan Summers
Folkway Records 2348

The Keys of Canterbury
Jean Ritchie and Oscar Brand
Courtin's a Pleasure
Elektra 122

Burl Ives
America's Musical Heritage,
    album 1

The Sycamore Tree	Peter, Paul, and Mary *See What Tomorrow Brings* Warner Bros. Records 1615
	Jean Ritchie *Jean Ritchie* Elektra EKL 125 (variant)
The Trees They Grow So High (The Bonny Boy)	Grainne Ni Eigertaigh *Irish Folk Songs* Spoken Arts 206
	Ewan MacColl *The English and Scottish* *Popular Ballads* (variant) Riverside LP 12-269
	Joan Baez Vanguard VRS 9094 (variant)
	Peg Clancy *Songs from Ireland* Tradition TLP 1045
The Bonny Lass o' Fyvie	Ewan MacColl *Scots Folk Songs* Riverside LP 12-609
	Jean Redpath *Slipping Barefoot through the* *Heather* Prestige International 13041
	Chad Mitchell Trio *Singin' Our Mind* Mercury Records MG 20838 (with added verses)
Sir Patrick Spens	Ewan MacColl *The English and Scottish* *Popular Ballads*, vol. 2 Riverside RLP 623/4

John Langstaff
*English and American
    Folksongs and Ballads*
Tradition TLP 1009

Colonial Songs and Ballads

Siubhail a Gradh

Deirde O'Callaghan
Folk Songs from Erin
Westminster 12025

Irene Saletan
Revolutionary Tea
Old North Bridge Records

Johnny Has Gone for a
    Soldier (Hudson Valley)

Burl Ives
America's Musical Heritage,
album 2 (variant)

Jane Wilson
The Making of a Nation
Life: The Sounds of History,
vol. 2

The Death of General Wolfe

The Best of Ewan MacColl
Prestige 13004

Sweet William

Peggy Seeger
*Matching Songs of the British
    Isles and America*
Riverside LP 12-637 (also on
    this record a fine Scots
    variant sung by Ewan
    MacColl)

The Old Man Who Lived in
    the Woods

Bill Bonyun
Yankee Legend
Heirloom 500

Springfield Mountain

Frank Warner
Come All You Good People
Minstrel JD 204

The Young Man Who
  Couldn't Hoe Corn (The
  Lazy Man)

Bill Bonyun
Yankee Legend
Heirloom 500

Jean Ritchie, Oscar Brand,
and Tom Paley
Courtin's a Pleasure
Elektra ELP 122

Jenny Jenkins

Bill Bonyun
Yankee Legend
Heirloom 500

Margaret MacArthur
Folk Songs of Vermont
Folkways Records 5314
(variant)

Frank Profitt
Sings Folk Songs
Folkways FA 2360

THE AMERICAN REVOLUTION

Young Ladies in Town

Gene Bonyun
*The American Revolution
  Through Its Songs and
  Ballads*
Heirloom 502

The Rich Lady over the Sea

Bill Bonyun
*The American Revolution
  Through Its Songs and
  Ballads*
Heirloom 502

Tony Saletan
Revolutionary Tea
Old North Bridge Records

The Folks on t'Other Side the
  Wave

Bill Bonyun
*The American Revolution
  Through Its Songs and
  Ballads*
Heirloom 502

Sir Peter Parker	John Anthony Scott same
	Burl Ives *America's Musical Heritage*, album 2

Nathan Hale	Bill Bonyun
	The American Revolution
	    Through Its Songs and
	    Ballads
	Heirloom 502

	Ira Resnick *The Best of Fieldston* *The Ballad of America*
The Dying Redcoat	Frank Warner *Come All You Good People* Minstrel JD 204

	John Anthony Scott
	The American Revolution
	    Through Its Songs and
	    Ballads
	Heirloom 502

The Battle of Trenton	Tony Saletan *Revolutionary Tea* Old North Bridge Records (variant)

The Battle of the Kegs	Bill Bonyun
	The American Revolution
	    Through Its Songs and
	    Ballads
	Heirloom 502

Paul Jones's Victory (Poor
    Richard and the Serapis and
    Alliance)
	Frank Warner
	Come All You Good People
	Minstrel JD 204

The Ballad of Major André   Gene Bonyun
                                   The American Revolution
                                      Through Its Songs and
                                      Ballads
                                   Heirloom 502

Lord Cornwallis's Surrender   Bill Bonyun
                                   same

THE EARLY NATIONAL PERIOD

Caitilín Ní Ullacháin   Joseph Ransohoff
   (Cathaleen Ni Houlihan)   *Irish Immigration Through Its*
                                    Songs and Ballads
                                 Heirloom Ed. 2

Green Grow the Rushes O   Ewan MacColl
                                 The Songs of Robert Burns
                                 Folkways FW 8758

                                 Betty Sanders
                                 The Songs of Robert Burns
                                 Riverside RLP 12-823

Jefferson and Liberty   Ed McCurdy
                                 American History in Ballad
                                    and Song
                                 Folkways FH 5801

                                 Wallace House
                                 The War of 1812
                                 Folkways FP 5002

Napoleon Bonaparte   Hilary Baum, Linda Schryer,
                                    and Lindsay Stamm
                                 New England Whaling
                                    Through Its Songs and
                                    Ballads
                                 Heirloom Ed. 4; also on *The*
                                    Best of Fieldston, The
                                    Ballad of America

The Bonny Bunch of Roses O   Bobby Clancy
                                 Songs from Ireland
                                 Tradition TLP 1045

	Ewan MacColl *Scots Street Songs* Riverside RLP 12-612
	Seamus Ennis *The Bonny Bunch of Roses* Tradition TLP 1013
The Constitution and the Guerrière	Wallace House *The War of 1812* Folkways FP 5002
The Hunters of Kentucky	same
John Anderson My Jo, John (Johnny Bull, My Jo, John)	Betty Sanders *The Songs of Robert Burns* Riverside RLP-1283
Mrs. McGrath	Suzanne Karfiol, Edward Needle *Irish Immigration Through Its Songs and Ballads* Heirloom Ed. 2

JACKSONIAN AMERICA

Sea and Immigration

Haul on the Bowline	Paul Clayton *Fo'c'sle Songs and Shanties* Folkways Record FA 2429
	John Binnington *Roll and Go* Heirloom 504
	Ewan MacColl *Blow Boys Blow* Tradition TLP 1026
Blood-red Roses	A. C. Lloyd and Ewan MacColl *Whaling Ballads* Washington 724

Peter Kinoy
*New England Whaling
Through Its Songs and
Ballads*
Heirloom Ed. 4; also on *The
Best of Fieldston, The
Ballad of America*

Leave Her, Johnny, Leave Her   Paul Clayton
Fo'c'sle Songs and Shanties
Folkways FA 2429

The Golden Vanity   Pete Seeger and Woody
Guthrie
*Deep Sea Chanteys and
Whaling Ballads*
Commodore Records CR-11
(variant)

Ewan MacColl and Peggy
Seeger
*Matching Songs of the British
Isles and America*
Riverside RLP 12-637

Off to Sea Once More   Ewan MacColl and A. C.
Lloyd
Whaling Ballads
Washington 724

Bill Bonyun
Songs of Yankee Whaling
American Heritage

John W. Scott
*New England Whaling
Through Its Songs and
Ballads*
Heirloom Ed 4

The Greenland Whale Fishery   Bill Bonyun
Songs of Yankee Whaling
American Heritage

	The Weavers
	Travelling On
	Vanguard VRS 9043
The Banks of Newfoundland	Ewan MacColl
	Blow Boys Blow
	Tradition TLP 1026
The Praties They Grow Small	*Irish Immigration Through Its Songs and Ballads*
	Heirloom Ed. 2
The Farmer's Curst Wife (The Devil and the Farmer)	Paul Clayton
	Unholy Matrimony
	Elektra 147 (variant)
	Seamus Ennis
	The Bonny Bunch of Roses
	Tradition TLP 1013
	Richard Dyer-Bennett
	Archive of American Folk Music
	FM 103
	Richard Sinaiko
	Irish Immigration Through Its Songs and Ballads
	Heirloom Ed. 2
The Castle of Dromore (Caislean Droim an Óir)	Paul Robeson
	Robeson
	Verve MGV 4044
	Liam Clancy
	Tradition TLP 1024
	Deirdre O'Callaghan
	Folk Songs from Erin (Gaelic)
	Westminster 12025
The Pesky Sarpent	Lynn Gold
	The New World
	Life: The Sounds of History, vol. 1

Hush, Little Baby	Burl Ives *America's Musical Heritage*, album 4
	The Weavers at Carnegie Hall Vanguard VRS 9010
Let's Go a-Huntin'	Alan Lomax *Texas Folksongs* Tradition TLP 1029
	Bill Bonyun *Let's Go a-Huntin'* Heirloom EP 501
When I Was Single	Paul Clayton *Unholy Matrimony* Elektra 147
The Single Girl	Jean Ritchie *The Sweep Westward* Life: The Sounds of History, vol. 4

The Lumberman's Alphabet	Gus Schaffer
	*Songs of the Michigan
	  Lumberjacks*
	Library of Congress, Music
	  Division, AAFS L56

The Jam on Gerry's Rock	Bill McBride same
Sioux Indians	Alec Moore *The Ballad Hunter*, part 1 Library of Congress, Music Division, AAFS L49
	Burl Ives *America's Musical Heritage*, album 6

	Pete Seeger
	American History in Ballad and Song
	Folkways FH 5801
The Fools of Forty-Nine	Pat Foster
	Gold Rush Songs
	Riverside LP 12-654
Santy Anno	Odetta
	Ballads and Blues
	Tradition TLP 1010
	The Weavers at Home
	Vanguard VRS 9024
The Dying Californian	Pat Foster
	Gold Rush Songs
	Riverside RLP 12-654

Slavery Days

Roll, Jordan, Roll	Carol Brice
	The Union Sundered
	Life: The Sounds of History, vol. 5
Hushabye (All the Pretty Little Horses)	Alan Lomax
	Texas Folk Songs
	Tradition TLP 1029
	Alan Lomax
	Collector's Choice
	Tradition 2057
	Joan Socolow
	The Negro People Through Their Songs and Ballads
	Heirloom Ed. 3
	Peter, Paul, and Mary
	See What Tomorrow Brings
	Warner Bros. 1615

Hangman, Slack on the Line	Almeda Riddle *Bad Man Ballads* Prestige International 25009
The Rose of Alabama	Frank Warner *Songs of the Civil War* Prestige International 13012

THE CIVIL WAR

Song of the Southern Volunteers	LaVonne Beebe *The Civil War Through Its Songs and Ballads* Heirloom 503
Flag of the Free	Ed Wilson same
Eibhleen a Ruin (Treasure of My Heart)	Jean Redpath *From My Ain Country* Folk-Legacy Records FSS 49
	Deirdre O'Callaghan *Folk Songs from Erin* Westminster WF 12025
The Homespun Dress	Jean Ritchie *The Union Sundered* Life: The Sounds of History, vol. 5
On to Richmond!	Frank Warner *The Civil War Through Its Songs and Ballads* Heirloom 503
General Lee's Wooing	Ed Wilson same
	Freedom Songs
Many Thousand Gone (No More Auction Block)	*The Best of Fieldston* *The Ballad of America*

Oh, Freedom	*Odetta* *Ballads and Blues* Tradition TLP 1010
	Pete Seeger *We Shall Overcome* (Carnegie Hall, June 5, 1963) Columbia CW 2101
Roll, Alabama, Roll	Frank Warner *The Civil War Through Its* *Songs and Ballads* Heirloom 503
	Hermes Nye *American History in Ballad* *and Song*, part 5 Folkways FH 5801
Sherman's March to the Sea	Bill Bonyun *The Civil War Through Its* *Songs and Ballads* Heirloom 503
The Southern Girl's Reply	Frank Warner *Songs and Ballads of* *America's Wars* Elektra EKL 12

BETWEEN THE CIVIL WAR AND THE FIRST WORLD WAR

Farmers and Workers

I Ride an Old Paint	Burl Ives *America's Musical Heritage*, album 6
	Woody Guthrie *Sod Buster Ballads* Commodore FL 30002
The Colorado Trail	Cisco Houston *Cisco Special* Vanguard

	Sue Pomeranze and Ellin Kardiner *The Best of Fieldston* *The Ballad of America*
Goodbye, Old Paint	*The Ballad Hunter*, part 1 Library of Congress, Music Division, AAFS L49
Brennan on the Moor	same
	Jeannie Robertson *Songs of a Scots Tinker Lady* Riverside RLP 12-633
	The Clancy Brothers and Tommy Makem Tradition TLP 1042
The Farmer Is the Man	Pete Seeger *American Industrial Ballads* Folkways FH 5251
Peter Emberley	Marie Hare Folk-Legacy Records FSC-9
Hard Times in the Mill	John Greenway *American Industrial Folksongs* Riverside RLP 12-607
	Pete Seeger *American Industrial Ballads* Folkways FH 5251
The Shoofly	Daniel Walsh *Songs and Ballads of the Anthracite Miners* Library of Congress, Music Division, AAFS L16
Solidarity Forever	Pete Seeger *Talking Union* Folkways FP 85-1

Ot Azoy Neyt a Shnayder
  (Weary Days Are a Tailor's)

Ruth Rubin
Yiddish Folk Songs
Prestige International 13019

Mayn Yingele (My Little Son)

Ruth Rubin
same

Papir Iz Doch Vays (Silver Is
  the Daylight)

Ruth Rubin
Yiddish Love Songs
Washington 726

Morton Freeman
Tikva Records 49

Bill Horwitz
The Best of Fieldston
The Ballad of America

Isabeau S'y Promène (Isabel)

Pete Seeger
Champlain Valley Songs
Folkways FH 5210

The Negro People

Pick a Bale o' Cotton

Huddie Ledbetter
Take This Hammer
Folkways FP 4

No More Cane on This Brazos

Alan Lomax
Texas Folk Songs
Tradition TLP 1029

Another Man Done Gone

Vera Hall
Blues and Hollers
Library of Congress, Music
  Division, AAFS L49

Odetta
Ballads and Blues
Tradition LP 1010

	Pete Seeger *At the Village Gate* Folkways FA 2451
	Ella Jenkins *A Long Time* Asch Records AHS 850
Godamighty Drag	Alan Lomax *Texas Folk Songs* Tradition LP 1029
No More, My Lord	*The Ballad Hunter* Library of Congress, Music Division, AAFS L51
	Negro Prison Songs: Mis- sissippi State Penitentiary Tradition TLP 1020
Settin' Side That Road	*A Sampler of Louisiana Folk Songs* Louisiana Folklore Society A-1
The Ballad of the Boll Weevil	Vera Hall *Sounds of the South* Atlantic 1346
	The Weavers on Tour Vanguard VRS 9013
	Boll Weevil Library of Congress, Music Division, AAFS L51
Ragged and Dirty Blues	Blind Lemon Jefferson Riverside Jazz Archives 12-136
	John W. Scott *The Negro People Through Their Songs and Ballads* Heirloom Ed. 3

Yonder Come Day   Bessie Jones and Group
                                   Georgia Sea Islands
                                   Prestige International 25002

BETWEEN TWO WORLD WARS

Johnny, I Hardly Knew You   Cynthia Gooding
                                   Languages of Love
                                   riverside RLP 12-827

Pack Up Your Troubles   The Four Sergeants
                                   World War I Songs
                                   ABC Paramount ABC 196

Raggedy   Pete Seeger
                                   American Industrial Ballads
                                   Folkways FH 5251

Which Side Are You On?   *Weavers' Alamac*
                                   Vanguard RS 9100

Goin' Down the Road   Burl Ives
                                   America's Musical Heritage,
                                       album 6

                                   Elizabeth Cotton
                                   Negro Folk Songs and Tunes
                                   Folkways FG 3526

                                   Big Bill Broonzy
                                   Last Session, 1
                                   Verve V3001 (title: *I Ain't
                                       Gon' Be Treated This-a
                                       Way*)

Discrimination Blues   Bill Bill Broonzy
                                   Big Bill Broonzy Memorial
                                   Mercury MG 20822

                                   Dennis Berger
                                   *The Negro People Through
                                       Their Songs and Ballads*
                                   Heirloom Ed. 3

We Shall Overcome	Pete Seeger *We Shall Overcome* Columbia CL 2101
	Voices of the Civil Rights Movement Smithsonian Institution R 023 F
Die Moorsoldaten (Peat-Bog Soldiers)	Ernst Busch and Chorus *Songs of the Spanish Civil War* Folkways FH 5436; or *Songs of the Lincoln Brigade* Stinson LP 52
D-Day Dodgers	Ewan MacColl *British Army Songs* Washington 711
Partizaner Lid (The Partisan)	Ruth Rubin *Yiddish Love Songs* Washington 726
	Morton Freeman *Jewish Folk Songs* Tikva Records T49

SINCE THE WAR

Plane Wreck at Los Gatos	Cisco Houston *Songs of Woody Guthrie* Vanguard 9089
	July Collins 3 Elektra EKL 243
Keep On a-Walkin'	Freedom Singers *Broadside Ballads* 1 Broadside Records 301

	SNCC Freedom Singers *Voices of the Civil Rights Movement* Smithsonian Institution R 023 D
One Man's Hands	Jackie Washington *Newport Folk Festival* 1963, vol. 2 Vanguard 9149
Little Boxes	Pete Seeger *We Shall Overcome* Columbia CL 2101; or *Broadside* BR 203

Afterword

The Ballad of America was first published in 1966 in the midst of stirring events. The year before, the civil rights movement in the South had reached its climax with the march from Selma to Montgomery in the spring of 1965. By that time a primarily Southern movement was spreading to the North and the West as well. Uprisings had taken place in Harlem in 1964 and in Watts in 1965. These ghetto riots were sparked by immediate burning grievances, in particular police brutality; they also produced manifestoes for social justice which all the world had to read in the light of the burning buildings.

In 1966, too, intervention in Vietnam reached its height with the presence in that country of half a million American troops. The United States found itself in the morass of the longest, bloodiest, and most costly colonial war in which it had ever engaged.

These events were accompanied by a transformation in the mood of American youth. The early fifties had been a time of youthful passivity. The silent generation, as it was called, accepted with little protest the conclusion that conformity to established norms was the wisest course if you wished to hold a job or to achieve advancement in a professional or business career. Young women absorbed the message beamed to them through the slick magazines, movies, and television. The purpose of a woman's life, it seemed, was to raise kids, polish floors, and, in general, devote her hours to creating the home beautiful.

1955 to 1965 was the period during which this transformation in the mood of youth occurred. The Supreme Court decision of May 17, 1954, was interpreted by black Southerners—primarily young ones—as a decree wiping out all discriminatory barriers separating the races, putting the ax to segregation as a badge of slavery. These young people took to the streets both to demonstrate support for the Supreme Court's position and in order to enforce it personally, with their own hands. The first of these great street actions, the Montgomery bus boycott of 1955–56, ended with the overthrow of the city's discriminatory bus ordinance and a clear-cut victory for equal rights over municipal bigotry.

During the following years there took place hundreds of street actions against compulsory segregation in all its forms. Many of these demonstrations were interracial. White youth as well as black now began to see that the struggle against racism was the most honorable of causes, the advancement of American democracy itself. This new goal was not merely the possession of the avant garde: the entire younger generation was affected. Indeed, there was more than a little of old-time revivalist spirit in the speed with which the passion for equality spread among the young. Sometimes all that it took to spark the flame was a single speech. Students in small towns and backwoods colleges were swept off their feet, flocked to the civil rights banners, and joined the marching ranks.

After 1965 the Southern movement flagged, lost its inspiration, its direction, its sense of purpose. But other groups in other parts of the country took up not only the civil rights cause but other social causes as well. Poverty, unemployment, environmental pollution, urban decay and crime, inflation, the plight of the aged, the misery of lonely and alienated human beings, the Vietnam War and the threat of nuclear holocaust, all these problems were subjected to scrutiny, exploration, and debate.

The generation of the sixties was, by 1966, both angry and articulate; above all it expressed itself lucidly and passionately in its music. It sang of love and freedom, of the evils of modern life, of the abuse of power, of the injustices of the social order. This singing was a bright illumination of contemporary American experience, and it was also a gift to the future. Historians of the time-to-come who study the song lyrics of the postwar era will find them of incomparable value in grasping the mood, the thought, and the experience of the embattled defenders of American democracy in this turbulent time.

When, after 1955, young people began to find their voices, they did not at first sing songs of their own creation. They began by going back to the roots of their musical heritage, looking for and rediscovering the folk songs of the American past. These were, for the most part, the cherished traditional songs of a rural culture—ballads, blues, lullabies, work songs, sea songs, gospel songs, spirituals, love songs, dirges, laments, and many more.

By the late fifties this revival of interest in traditional song was well under way. Young people were gathering on college campuses, in coffee houses, in music centers, in the streets and parks, in the corridors of the schools, and at folk festivals in order to exchange songs, to learn them, and to sing. They thronged by the thousands to sit at the feet of professional balladeers who traveled the college circuit. The manufacture of guitars became a mass industry; stringed instruments began to outnumber bicycles on the campuses.

In 1966 when *The Ballad of America* was published this folk revival had already passed its height and was on the wane. This is not the same as saying that young people were then singing less—on the contrary. But by 1966 the singing of traditional song was rapidly giving way to a fresh lyrical creativity. Here young people were following a pattern long established in the American community where for hundreds of years the absorption of a cultural tradition and its use for the purpose of creating something new had been merely two sides of the same coin.

The generation that came to maturity in the late fifties and the early sixties was an urban generation. It had not been raised in the rural environment from which so many of the traditional songs came. But it had at its disposal nonetheless abundant musical material with which to educate itself in what was essentially a rural singing tradition. Since the beginning of the twentieth century, folk song scholars, in a remarkable but unpublicized effort, had begun to seek out, to record, and to transcribe the musical heritage of rural America. As late as the forties and the fifties a number of the old rural singers were still around—like Mississippi John Hurt, Big Bill Broonzy, Josh White, and Huddie Ledbetter. So too were balladeers like Woody Guthrie, Cynthia Gooding, Bill Bonyun, Pete Seeger, and Burl Ives, singing scholars like Alan Lomax, Carl Sandburg, and John Jacob Niles, interpreters of the black tradition like Marian Anderson and Paul Robeson. All these and others made the riches of the folk song heritage available to the young generation with the help of the new long-playing record technology that made its appearance in the late forties. This technology also made possible the dissemination of some of the wonderful old field recordings in the possession of the Archive of American Folksong at the Library of Congress.

With the help of resources such as these the new generation began to find its voice in the middle fifties. In going back to these cultural roots the young people went back to school, seeking to master the melodies, the literary styles, the human meaning of the singing past. The folk song revival, then, may be seen as the sign of an educational process. Inevitably and in its own time the new generation began to innovate, to create new songs that explored the meaning of human experience in the contemporary world. This upsurge of creative song changed the role and the context of the folk revival. Like a scaffolding that has outlived its usefulness the old songs were discarded when the time was ripe; but of course the old remained embodied in the new. The songs of the sixties utilized traditional melodies, imagery, literary styles; as reworkings of the ancient ballads and songs they were new wine in old skins.

One might give many instances of this process of lyrical innovation; one excellent example, taken from the time when the new creative process was in its early phase, is Richard Farina's "Birmingham Sunday." Farina's ballad tells the story of four little black girls killed in the bombing of a Birmingham, Alabama, church on September 15, 1963. Farina took the melody and the literary form of an old Scottish love-lament, "I Once Loved a Lass." The theme of the Scottish song deals with a maiden who goes to church to be married while a jilted lover looks on with an aching heart; in Farina's version the little girls go to church not to celebrate marriage but to encounter death. The singer's heart still aches; he has lost something that he loves. "Birmingham Sunday" expresses an ancient pain and also a sorrow that is entirely fresh. The whispered protest with which the song ends is, in its own way, as terrible as the thunder of cannon:

> This Sunday has come, this Sunday has gone,
> And I can't do much more than to sing you a song,
> I'll sing it so softly it'll do no one wrong,
> And the choir kept singing of freedom.

Now, as we move into the 1980s, a new problem presents itself in the musical education of the American young.

Each new generation needs, just as the young people in the fifties and sixties did, to master its heritage before it moves forward to fresh and independent creative life. But, as noted, the musical heritage has been primarily a rural one, at least until the onset of massive industrialization in the second half of the nineteenth century. It will not be easy to transmit this under the conditions of the late twentieth century urban environment. You cannot learn songs from people's lips in the raucous streets or amid the metallic commotion of the average workplace. Nor are the commercial media, television movies and radio, of much help, with significant exceptions. Media presentation of the American past has been on the whole musically barren. The cowboy saga is a good example of this. The media over the years have literally worked this theme to death, yet millions of viewers still remain totally ignorant of the dozens of great songs through which the cowboy expressed his life and his soul and which, infinitely more than barroom brawls and pistol duels, constitute his enduring contribution to the people's hertiage.

To be sure, during the folk song revival great recordings of traditional song were made not only by the old-timers but by younger singers as well. But with the passage of time and notwithstanding a limited number of reissues, these records are lost, scattered, and used up; they become collector's items, available only in a limited number of music libraries. Some of the new singers of the sixties wrote down their songs and accompaniments and published them in their own songbooks. These too, as time passes, vanish into oblivion or take their place in history with the rest of the musical Americana that line the scholar's shelves. Even if some of this material does survive in readily usable and accessible form, this only puts the problem one step further back. Young people in the future will need to penetrate beyond the barrier of the fifties and sixties, and engage in a fresh search for roots among the enduring traditional sources.

Where and how, then, is the musical heritage to be preserved and made accessible? How is it to be given back to each new generation to which it rightfully belongs?

Folk song has for many years found a home in summer camps and schools. Kindergarten and elementary school teachers, in particular, have long been teaching folk songs to their pupils. This practice, no doubt, owes much to John Dewey's educational principles which have been applied in progressive schools since 1900. To this day the music manuals used by teachers in hundreds of public schools contain folk melodies embalmed amidst much additional and miscellaneous musical material.

Ruth Crawford Seeger, musicologist and music editor, was a noted pioneer in the movement to bring American folk song into the classroom. Her *American Folk Songs for Children*, first published in 1948, is a landmark in twentieth-century educational folk song literature.[1]

During the early forties Ruth Crawford Seeger was a parent-teacher at the Silver Spring Cooperative Nursery School in Maryland. She decided to launch an experimental year at the school during which American folk songs would be used with the children. For this purpose she selected songs from the field recordings which she had played at home, and some of which had become favorites with her own children; she culled material from folklore journals, songbooks, and the Library of Congress Folk Song Archive. Where necessary she made transcriptions of these songs, provided simple piano arrangements, and took them into the classroom.

The result was an educational experiment of extraordinary significance. Mrs. Seeger communicated to the children traditional sounds and traditional songs. This sparked creativity as her pupils not only listened and sang, but began to improvise. Mrs. Seeger, along with the teachers and parents who worked with her, strove, as she tells us "to maintain a balance between two of the outstanding values which music like this possesses for the child—the vigorous beauty of the traditional text, and an inherent fluidity and creative aliveness which invites improvisation as a natural development in the life of the song."[2]

The songs which Mrs. Seeger sang with her tiny pupils were not "childish" songs; they covered the gamut of American folk music—ballads, blues, work songs, prison songs, spirituals, western songs, slave songs, lullabies, sea songs. In the introduction to her

[1] New York: Doubleday and Co., 1948.
[2] *American Folk Songs for Children*, p. 20.

book she posed the fundamental question, Why folk songs for our children? The answer that she gave is perhaps as valid today as it was in 1948; it still provides the central reason why the schools need to be involved with folk music, and why the classroom is the proper place for this to happen.

Folk music, Mrs. Seeger wrote, has been bound up with life in this country, and with the making of America, from the very beginning. *Our children*, she said, *have a right to be brought up with it.*[3] Such songs as these are never "finished," in the sense that their capacity to grow, to yield new meanings with the passage of time, is exhausted. Thus the songs that become a person's property when he is a child will belong to him as an adult. These songs are cultural possessions and the companions of life. They link living with dead, old with young, adult with child, man with woman, individual atom with the nation itself.

Yet another compelling reason for the use of folk song in the classroom was added by Ruth Tooze and Beatrice Perham Krone when they published *Literature and Music as Resources for Social Studies* (Englewood Cliffs, N.J.: Prentice-Hall) in 1955. Folk music, they wrote, along with folklore and art, is a key to the understanding of a people's way of life, a "sort of distilled essence of their values and experiences."[4] If this is so, then two conclusions need to be drawn. Folk song is, first, a key to the American past, American values, and the American experience. But second, folk song is a key to the understanding of other peoples as well. This means that folk song may be a central instrumentality for the creation in the American child of an awareness of, and a compassion for, the world community. Tooze and Krone, be it noted, penned their words in the early fifties when the McCarthyite hysteria was at its height. They raised their voices in a plea for the use of folk song as a classroom approach to other peoples, not excluding those of the Third and Socialist worlds. "If this era is to be constructive," they wrote, "*all peoples must receive consideration; or, it may be, there will be none to receive it.*"[5] "People must learn to respect each other, to realize their likenesses, to enjoy their differences, to appreciate their varying expressions of beauty."[6]

In their book Tooze and Krone offered abundant suggestions for ways in which the classroom teacher might seek to accomplish the goal of creating in young people a sympathy and respect for human life at all times and in all places. They stressed the varied appeal of song to children at all ages; they urged teachers to use music not

[3]Ibid.
[4]*Literature and Music as Resources for Social Studies*, p. 3.
[5]Ibid., p. 449, emphasis added.
[6]Ibid., p. 454.

merely as a weekly specialty but as the bedrock of a humane education.[7]

These three teachers, Seeger, Tooze, and Krone, were all concerned with folk song as it might be used with kindergarten and elementary school children. But the teaching of the folk-song heritage belongs at the high school and college levels as well. There are compelling reasons for this.

Folk songs, in the first place, are historical documents, primary sources that provide firsthand information about human experience at any given historical moment. Virtually every aspect of human life is dealt with in these songs. They are, in effect, the story behind the headlines, the true history of humanity that is screened from the student's view by the textbook's dull recitation of battles, elections, treaties, constitutional enactments, and territorial acquisitions.

One may say the same thing in a different way by stressing the fact that folk songs provide weapons with which to counter the dehumanization of the past, to rescue the classroom from the tyranny of abstraction, and to breathe new life and reality into the educational process. Folk songs help students to set aside stereotypes and to discover real people, who, though long dead, literally speak to the present generation from their graves. The unveiling of this human reality in the past stimulates wonder and curiosity. It motivates the student to learn more.

Folk songs do more than add color and human interest to the study of the past, important though that is; often they provide factual information just as other primary sources do. They accomplish this in a way palatable for beginners because they draw upon the resources of art—verse, rhythm, imagery, repetition, and melody—to convey their message. Historical song thus provides the student with an instant reply of the past, an instant awareness of it transcending space and time.

One fine example of the song's role as primary source for important historical evidence is "General Lee's Wooing" (see p. 233). These verses, an elegy on the struggle at Antietam Creek in September 1862, provide indispensable information about it. The dramatic illumination which the song affords of a supremely important historical event enables the student to grasp the significance of the

---

[7]The message was summarized in a German round which the authors included in their book.

All things shall perish under the sky:
   Music alone shall live,
   Music alone shall live,
   Music alone shall live,
Never to die.

[Ibid., p. 251]

Emancipation Proclamation which Lincoln issued on September 27, 1862, one week after Lee's defeat. Songs such as this, of course, have their place at the elementary level; they belong in high school and college history classes as well.

The fact that we argue for the use of the *same* song at *different* educational levels reveals another important aspect of the use of song in the classroom. Many songs have a depth and complexity which enables them to grow with the child and to provide fresh insights into the past at different stages of his growth. Here the slave lullaby "Hushabye" (pp. 204–5) is another fine example of the role of song as primary historical source.

At the nursery and elementary school levels "Hushabye" may be sung and enjoyed simply as a lullabye with a beautiful melody, rich imagery, and tranquil mood. When used with older children it enables the teacher to raise interesting questions. The singer of "Hushabye" is a black woman cradling a white child; her song both soothes the babe in her arms and laments the fate of black children who lie uncared for in the meadow. Who exactly, in the antebellum South, cared for these black children—did the babies of slaves really lie out unprotected in the fields while their parents worked, or were there day care centers? Exactly how well were men and women who toiled from sunup to sundown able to care for their families? An awareness of questions like these makes it possible for a young person singing "Hushabye" to see it as a lament for black children under slavery and, to that extent, a judgment upon slavery itself.

Beyond this, as the child grows older, "Hushabye" has other messages to convey. The artistry of the song tells a great deal about the black people who were able to create something so powerful and so beautiful with which to express the deepest of feelings. Such music has a dimension that makes it comprehensible to people everywhere. In its own way it celebrates and affirms the unity of humankind.

Documents, primary sources, that show this profundity both factual and human must surely be worth the historian's careful attention. They are indeed for children, but not for children alone.

Folk songs are documents of a special type precisely because they possess literary qualities that enable them to be considered not only as historical evidence but as genuine literature. This literary quality of the songs is inseparable from their quality as music and as primary source material. Yet it demands special attention. Songs are models of literary style that have not yet been exploited nearly as fully as they should be by students and teachers of literature at both high school and college levels.

A striking feature of many of our traditional songs is simplicity of language and economy in the use of words. Yet there is nothing simplistic about the lyrics; they address themselves to the fundamentals of the human condition. Facts are communicated swiftly and with brutal directness; the message delivered with these facts cuts to the bone. The reader will find many good examples of this in *The Ballad of America*; as among the finest of examples we might cite "The Bonnie Lass o' Fyvie" (p. 20), "The Rich Lady over the Sea" (p. 59), "The Greenland Whale Fishery" (p. 143), and "The Ballad of the Boll Weevil" (p. 316).

Simplicity of language, too, does not necessarily imply poverty of image. On the contrary, powerful images are evoked by even the simplest of songs. These images not only compel the listener's attention, but even invite him to participate actively in the reception of the message—to visualize it, even to help create it. Take for example the following from "Hushabye":

> When you wake, you shall have
> All the pretty little horses;
> Blacks and bays,
> Dapples and grays,
> Coach-a six-a little horses.

Are there two people in the whole world who will visualize this succession of images in exactly the same way? The clues provided are simple, but they open up for the receiving mind visions of incredible color and movement. It is worth noting, too, that with the exception of four words of two syllables the entire picture is painted with monosyllables.

The songs, too, provide many lessons in the use of dialogue, humor, and satire which will repay study by high school and college students. "The Battle of the Kegs" (pp. 78–80) provides a superlative example of all three literary and dramatic techniques. Since Hopkinson's song is more invention than historical fact, some might question the contention that songs such as this, while being excellent literature, have anything to do with history. Nonetheless the song carries a message that was historically true and that was indeed intended to cut to the bone for the contemporary American audience. "Do not fear the British," the song said. "They appear to be strong but in reality they are weak. It is they who are afraid of us, and it is we who will prevail." Literary and artistic techniques are here shown as weapons to be deployed for the advancement of a revolutionary struggle. The song is simultaneously both a first-rate historical source and a literary invention of extraordinary quality.

A word must be said, finally, about the melodies with which the traditional songs are wedded. Such melodies have been evolving in the Western world for many centuries; they are in themselves works of art. As such they constitute an almost infinite resource for songwriters and composers who seek inspiration in the use of authentic American themes. These musical resources of the nation, great as they are, will be further enriched as ethnic folk song in all its variety becomes assimilated into the American culture.

A general objection to the use of folk song in the classroom remains to be considered. There are dangers when literature and art are taken into the classroom. Are they not liable to get mangled in the process? Is there no danger that pedagogy with its texts, assignments, recitations, tests, and the rest will destroy and deaden the student's interest in folk song, rather than awaken it? Will not the heavy-handed approach of the schoolroom style rob singing of the joy, freshness, and spontaneity that are its very essence?

No one can dismiss such dangers lightly, for they do exist. But two points may be made which are relevant to a discussion of this problem.

Folk songs, in the first place, are of value because they help to transform the students, to enable them to grow in an imaginative, emotional, and human way. But the transformative quality of the songs may also affect the teachers; they are weapons against dehumanization in adults as well as in children. As teachers learn to shed bureaucratic attitudes toward the young, power complexes, petty pedantry, and the rest, they will discover a new community of learning with their charges. People who share songs together may more easily and more informally share the entire learning process.

The Ballad of America itself, in the second place, is, to use the jargon, a field-tested package. All the songs reproduced in this book have not only been sung by students in the classroom, they have been sung by informal groups squatting in the school corridors and by larger numbers of students presenting them on the school stage. The songs in this book have in fact been selected by the students themselves—it is they who by their own choice have helped to create this musical history of the American people. This they did in the years 1960–65 when the folk revival was at its height. This is only a single example of the use of folk song in the high school classroom, but we will rest our case with it.[8]

[8]For a fuller account of the role of Fieldston students in the creation of *The Ballad of America* see John A. Scott, *Teaching for a Change* (New York: Bantam Books, 1972), chap. 8, "Social Studies and the Stage"; and Beth Bryant, "History Hootenanny," *Folk Music* (August 1964), pp. 16–19.

Index of Titles and First Lines

NOTE: Titles of songs are in *italics*. When a song title and first line are exactly the same, only the title is given. Titles followed by an asterisk have no accompaniment.

General Index

John Anthony Scott is a graduate of Oxford University and has a doctorate in history from Columbia University. He teaches the history of law at Rutgers University (Newark, New Jersey). For many years he has drawn upon folk song as a resource of primary significance in helping students to become aware of the past and to communicate with it. In preparing *The Ballad of America* Scott collected songs all the way from Nova Scotia to the Georgia Sea Islands: the book that resulted is, in the most literal sense, the product of classroom life and experience. Co-editor of *Folksong in the Classroom*, a magazine for teachers, Scott is the author of numerous articles on folk song and its educational uses.

ST

AFGHAN
TALES

⚊ AFGHAN ⚊
TALES

Stories from Russia's Vietnam

OLEG YERMAKOV

TRANSLATED BY MARC ROMANO

WILLIAM MORROW AND COMPANY, INC.

New York

Library of Congress Cataloging-in-Publication Data

Yermakov, Oleg.
   [Short stories. English. Selections]
   Afghan tales / Oleg Yermakov ; translated by Marc Romano.
     p. cm.
   ISBN 0–688–12394–5
   1. Afghanistan—History—Soviet occupation, 1979–1989—Fiction.
I. Title.
   PG3489.8.E687A27   1993
   891.73′44—dc20
                                                           92–46348
                                                                CIP

Printed in the United States of America

First Edition

1 2 3 4 5 6 7 8 9 10

BOOK DESIGN BY PATRICE FODERO

✦ CONTENTS ✦

 BAPTISM

THE RECON COMPANY LEFT THE CAMP AT NIGHT. HEAD-lights out, its BMPs rolled northward. The lights of the camp quickly disappeared, and the infinite warm spring night engulfed the column.

The soldiers riding on top of the caterpillar-tracked machines were looking at the heavy trails of constellations above them. Kostomygin was staring up at the shining trails too, and thinking that the rumble of their engines could probably be heard in the remotest *kishlak* on the farthest end of the steppe, assuming, of course, that it had an end. . . .

A half hour later a dull moon appeared low over the steppe. The moon slowly rose, the night brightened, and the outline of scrubby hills began to show against an expanse of black and white.

Straight ahead, white walls and towers were becoming distinct. The column was slowly drawing nearer to a *kishlak*.

"Okay, wake up!" the captain said into the radio microphone he was holding to his throat. The commander of each BMP heard the message, and one after the other reported in: number so-and-so, I read you. The BMP guns wheeled left and right, and the soldiers reached for their assault rifles and began to stir.

The column tore through the *kishlak* without slowing down, but nothing happened.

Kostomygin managed to spot dark slits on the towers, houses with flat roofs, lush gardens behind *duvals*, the large-eared sil-houette of a donkey next to a barn.

Beyond the *kishlak*, the road—it was now easy to make out—

9

led down an incline and crossed a shimmering river. Still at the same speed, the machines forged through the wide, shallow waters and pressed onward.

Kostomygin had gulped down the fragrant air of the *kishlak*'s flowery gardens, and now there was a sweetness in his mouth. He bared his face to the warm wind, sensed the weight of his ammo pouch against his side, felt the tightness of his short laced boots, the lightness and freedom of his camouflage gear, and all of it pleased him: this moon, this terrible steppe, the flowery sweetness in his mouth, his comfortable uniform, the weapon across his chest, the speed of these powerful machines through the endless black-and-white plains under bright and alien constellations.

The column came to a halt on a ridge between two low hills. The soldiers clambered down from the machines and stretched their legs.

They drew up in pairs and began to march along the road. The drivers and mechanics stayed with their machines.

The company moved through the hills. Everyone was silent, sullenly looking around at the surrounding hilltops, which were clearly outlined against a backdrop of stars. The moon had sailed across to the western edge of the sky, turned the color of bronze, and was already shining less brightly than before.

A few steps behind him Kostomygin heard Oparin, like him a green kid, jangling his belt buckle while trying to pull the stopper from his canteen. Then there was the sound of a dull thud and Oparin hurtled forward into him. Kostomygin spun around to face him. Hastily replacing his canteen on his belt, his head hunched into his shoulders, Oparin resumed the march. Directly behind him, striding briskly, was Shvarev, a tall, long-legged sergeant.

Have to watch out, Kostomygin thought to himself, turning away.

The sparrows—the guys who'd served more than six months—

often warned the kids to keep on their toes and do everything they were told. Any mistake a kid made during an operation, they said, would be "investigated" by the veterans once they returned to camp. A recon company wasn't an artillery unit or a labor or infantry battalion; everyone had to be on the ball, everyone had to be at least as good as any "beret."

After a month's service, Kostomygin had seen enough old-timers' hearings for his tastes, and under no circumstances did he want to be among the accused at the next one. And here was Oparin already on the blacklist. He'd have to stay alert.

The moon vanished, the steppe became dark once more, and the stars began to shine more brilliantly. The company was marching rhythmically along the hills.

The night had cooled off. A bird whistled from the steppe.

Footfalls could be heard directly ahead.

"Hurry!" Shvarev ordered in a loud whisper, and Kostomygin broke into a run. We're too late, he thought to himself.

They ran for a long time, sweating, swallowing dust.

Kostomygin was clutching his assault rifle in one hand and his canteen in the other, but his magazine-filled ammo pouch was pounding him brutally in the ribs, so he let go of his rifle and grabbed the pouch instead. But the rifle striking against his chest was even more painful, and he grabbed for it again.

They ran so hard and for so long that Kostomygin's breath started to come out in rasps, and he swore that he would never again, not in a million years, touch a cigarette.

Finally they reached the very last hill and spotted the silhouettes of towers, houses, and *duvals* in the steppe below. The wind was blowing from the *kishlak*, and Kostomygin caught the same gentle aroma of flowers. The wind picked up strength, and a powerful flowery wave cascaded over the panting, dust-covered men in their soggy and acrid-smelling clothes.

At the base of the next hill there was a fork. One road, the road they had been running along, led to the *kishlak*; the other wound down to the steppe. Two platoons, under the command of the captain and a lieutenant, moved off toward the *kishlak*; the rest of the company lay low on the hill, taking cover behind boulders and training their light machine guns and assault rifles on the fork.

Kostomygin carefully lowered himself against the rocks, feeling their dampness, how pleasantly they cooled his stomach and chest. He spat dusty, viscous saliva and wondered: Well, can we drink from our canteens now or what? He glanced around, gingerly loosened his belt, raised the canteen to his chest without taking it off the belt, removed the stopper, bent his head, extended his lips to the canteen's neck, and sucked in a mouthful of water. He swirled it around his mouth and swallowed, thinking it a pity to spit it out. He sucked on the canteen once more, then replaced the stopper, tightened his belt, and thought: Maybe a smoke now.

Only one star, Venus, remained in the sky. The road became light, the *kishlak* seemingly nearer. The road was deserted. Everyone was watching it, Kostomygin included. He was thinking that all of this was senseless: no one would show up, there wouldn't be any shooting—the sun would simply rise and they would return to camp. It was his first operation, and he didn't believe it would turn out like the ones in the company veterans' vivid stories.

He grew bored staring at the road along which no one would come, yawned, and closed his eyes to rest them for a while. He fell asleep for no more than a few minutes and awoke with a start. No weakness, he told himself, and once more he began to watch the road assiduously.

It became lighter; nightingales began to chirp in the *kishlak*'s gardens, and a cock crowed several times in succession, drowning out their trilling with its guttural craw.

When the sky and the steppe began to turn red in the east, a harsh, incantatory wail arose from the *kishlak*. Kostomygin's sleepiness vanished in an instant; he reached for his rifle and, stretching his neck, peered over the rocks. The wail arose again, and Kostomygin's heart sank: This is it, battle. But the soldiers lying down near him remained calm. He glanced around at them, deflated, and resolved to cautiously ask the sparrow Medvedev what was going on. Medvedev grunted and told him in a whisper that it was just the keening of one of their priests.

The sun came up. The steppe extended, greenish, to the horizon, and in the *kishlak* cocks were shrieking, cows lowing, and a donkey braying. The sky was turning a full, radiant blue. To hell with this war, Kostomygin thought.

The captain reappeared, shook himself off, and said: "You can smoke."

The soldiers roused themselves, yawned broadly, began talking to one another, struck matches, inhaled cigarette smoke, shielded their eyes with their hands.

The captain was gloomily watching the *kishlak*.

"Sanych," he said to the radioman, "pull the men back from the *kishlak* and tell the drivers to get their carts here now."

"Comrade captain," said Shvarev, "maybe the caravan has passed through already?"

The captain shook his head.

"No. The estimate was that it would take them all night to get here from the mountains. They couldn't have set out before night. So they left late in the evening yesterday and shouldn't have reached here before early morning."

"Unless what?"

"Well, unless they had rocket-powered camels," the captain answered grudgingly.

The radioman contacted the platoons in their positions around the *kishlak*, then the BMP drivers and mechanics.

The captain sat down on a rock, took off his cap, pulled out a comb, and unhurriedly began to run it through his hair. Shvarev lingered by him, kicking at pebbles and now and then whistling wistfully.

"What's with you, Shvarev?" the captain asked at last.

"Comrade captain, maybe they managed to slip into the *kishlak* somehow?"

"So then the boys were there all night for nothing? Unless, of course, they got some sleep out of it."

"Maybe, comrade captain, we could just go in and shake the place down a little. Maybe it's packed with guns and *doukh*s."

The captain thoughtfully blew the comb clear, then deftly slipped it into its sheath and put it away. Shvarev looked at him expectantly.

"How many notches do you have, Shvarev?" the captain asked wearily.

"What notches?"

"On the butt of your gun, Shvarev, the butt of your gun. You think I don't know where you put them? I know everything, Shvarev, and one of these days I'll write you up for malicious destruction of weapons."

"Oh, not destruction—we do it very lightly. A little scratch, that's all," the gray-eyed, well-built Salikhov said with a smile.

"And why do you put notches on the butt of your gun?"

Salikhov reddened and shrugged his shoulders: "Where else to put them?"

"You? On your boots and fists."

Everyone burst out laughing.

Everybody else's face is brown, but his is the color of milk, Kostomygin suddenly thought, looking at Salikhov's long, delicate features. What does he have, a special dispensation from the sun?

Salikhov was the most popular man in the company. He had a good singing voice and played the guitar beautifully. He never swore at anyone, never put the kids through the mill, never even shouted at them. He spent all his free time on the playing fields with friends from home who were serving in an infantry company—even their practice sessions would attract spectators. If the weather was bad he would lie in bed with a book. In his village back home a wide-eyed, raven-haired girl with a face as milk-white as his was waiting for him; a large photograph of her rested on his bedside stand, and the woman-hungry men in the company would sometimes pick it up and stare at it with voluptuous long-ing. Salikhov's girlfriend often sent him thick, fat envelopes, and everyone envied him. Around his neck hung a leather pendant with a lock of her hair in it. Everyone envied Salikhov.

Kostomygin wanted to become friends with him. He poured his heart out in letters to his brother, but what was a letter? Good conversation with an intelligent person was something else en-tirely. He thought that Salikhov was probably pining for a kindred soul, but Kostomygin was too shy to go up to him and start talking about serious books and stuff like that. He wished that Salikhov would somehow get a conversation going with him, but Salikhov didn't talk to kids and in fact hardly seemed to notice them at all.

"So how many scratches do you have on the butt of your gun, Shvarev?" the captain asked. He was watching the platoons return from the *kishlak*.

"Six."

"Isn't that enough for you?"

"No."

"You're a real Dracula, Shvarev."

Everyone laughed.

"What are you laughing for?" the captain asked with a smile. "Any of you know who Dracula was?"

"No," someone answered.

"So what the hell are you laughing for?"

"Who was Dracula, comrade captain?" the sparrow Medvedev asked obsequiously. "Did he put notches on his gun too?"

"No," the captain answered. "He was a ruler who smashed helmets in the fifteenth century."

"Into heads?" Medvedev ventured. The captain nodded, and everyone laughed as though it were the funniest thing in the world.

"Well, I haven't gone that far yet," said Shvarev with a self-contented grin, "so I couldn't be Dracula."

"Yes," the captain agreed. "There is a difference. He was a prince, not a sergeant."

15

* * *

The BMPs arrived. The soldiers split up into sections, got out their dry rations—canned pork, canned cheese, sugar, bread—and, squatting on the ground among the machines, settled in to breakfast.

Shvarev polished off his can of meat in a flash, rolling his eyes with pleasure, then ate his soft yellow cheese, gulped down all of his sugar, and drained half his canteen. He paused as though listening for something before sighing: "That barely made a dent."

"Yeah," the driver Mamedov broke in, "and you've g-got such a b-big dent!" He pointed his finger at Shvarev's lean stomach and began to laugh. "You stuff yourself and don't get any f-fatter. No g-girl will ever love you. They only like f-fat men."

"W-well," Shvarev said, squaring his shoulders, "w-well, Mamed, where you come from, ladies are maybe happy with stomachs, but our women—they need something more substantial." He glanced over at Oparin and shouted: "What the hell you grinning at? Suck it down. In the field you do everything fast, you eat, you . . ."

Oparin stopped grinning, stuck his spoon into the pinkish meat, and interrupted: "Comrade sergeant, do you want it? I'd rather just have the cheese."

Kostomygin looked at Oparin, then turned his head away.

Some kind of swine, that Oparin. He did his best to get along with the old-timers, hoping that they'd take a liking to him and stop breaking his balls all the time. He was the only kid who washed their leggings and clothes for them. The others had flatly refused and taken a beating for it, but after that no one bothered them. Oparin still did every old-timer's washing.

"Whoever buckles in buckles under," his older brother had warned him, and after a while Kostomygin had come to see that it was true, although now he would add to what his brother had said: sure, but always keep a sense of proportion in mind. Krylov, for instance, hadn't been aware of that; he would refuse to do anything for the old-timers, even the pettiest and least objectionable thing, and in return they had made him live "by the rules." No one in the army lives by the rules: to fulfil every regulation day and night would be too much for anyone, any common soldier, any general, any marshal—his first day of living "by the rules" would leave even the most gung-ho firebrand in tears. So Krylov hadn't been able to take it, and he'd written a gloomy letter home telling the whole story. His relatives had forwarded the letter to the Ministry of Defense, and soon afterward a commission had hauled into camp and an inquiry was launched. Krylov had urged the other kids to tell the truth, but nobody really wanted to. The kids figured, pragmatically enough, that they wouldn't drag every last old-timer into a disciplinary battalion, that maybe a couple would be punished but the rest of them would still have to be put up with—and so Krylov found himself utterly alone. Over the course of the proceedings it became clear that Krylov had been treated fairly, or at least by the rules. The matter was closed and Krylov was assigned to an auxiliary unit—in the pigsties. Kostomygin often saw him tooling around among the mess tents, covered with dirt, unshaven, carrying pails of slop that he would have to pour out, splashing the swill all over his hands and boots, into a steel barrel mounted on a cart— they called it the "cabriolet"—that was pulled along by a captured white donkey named Doukh.

No, you have to maintain a sense of proportion. Krylov didn't, and neither did Oparin—even if he really didn't want the meat, he should have offered it to someone of his own rank, to Kostomygin himself, for example. So they were the two poles, Oparin and Krylov, that you had to avoid. Should I write my brother, see what he thinks? Kostomygin thought to himself.

"Listen!" Shvarev said sharply. "If it was winter, and I was really cold, you'd give me your coat too? You know what the winters are like here?"

"Yeah, b-but b-by this winter you'll b-be stuffing yourself on your mama's b-blinis," Mamedov reminded him.

Shvarev brushed him off. "Drop it, Mamed. Well, Oparin, would you?"

Oparin cast him a cowed glance.

17

"Answer me."

"If it was absolutely necessary..." Oparin mumbled, then fell silent.

"And if your girlfriend was here, you'd let me have her?"

"You're joking, comrade sergeant," Oparin said, smiling shyly.

"Let's just suppose. Answer me."

Oparin was flustered, and his eye twitched.

"Answer, you little s-slug," hissed Mamedov, his eyes gleaming.

Oparin flinched and said in a barely audible voice, "It's too..."

"What?" yelled Shvarev.

Oparin finished the sentence: "To suppose that, it's too much."

"You're a shit, a maggot! How did you get to be in recon? You should be drummed out, like Krylov. Eat your own damn meat. I don't want it. On an operation you choke it down if that's what it takes."

"You b-bolt it, you b-beat 'em," added Mamedov.

"That clear?" said Shvarev. "Your second mistake so far. You remember the first?"

"Yes," Oparin answered limply, digging into the meat.

Shvarev lit a cigarette and distractedly looked over at Kostomygin.

"Hey, Kosty, what are you looking away for? Proud, are you?"

"I'm just watching the *kishlak*," Kostomygin replied.

"No," said Mamedov, "not just that. He h-hates Oparin."

"You hate Oparin?" Shvarev asked.

"No," Kostomygin lied.

"Just watch it, or you'll be in the same boat."

"I think the k-kids are g-getting a b-bit uppity," Mamedov noted. He took a swig from his canteen. "Just yesterday I asked for a civilian cigarette and K-Kosty wouldn't b-bring me one."

"Seriously?" Shvarev narrowed his eyes and looked at Kostomygin.

"Yeah. We g-gotta k-keep a close eye on 'em all. We b-break Opie's balls but we forget the rest."

"Fine," said Shvarev. "When we get back to camp, Kosty, Mamedov and I want to see a pack of Javas. Opie here will count to a hundred and we'll see a pack of Javas. Got it?"

"Yes," answered Kostomygin.

"What?"

Kostomygin corrected himself. "Understood."

Mamedov shook his head. "They're g-getting uppity."

After breakfast the men climbed aboard the machines and the column set off for home.

Outside the *kishlak*, on the bank of the river that had shimmered so prettily the night before, the column overtook an ancient open yellow Toyota truck filled with armed men in multicolored turbans and loose-fitting clothes. Next to the driver sat a thin, mustachioed man wearing the uniform of a militia officer. He got out of the truck and, smiling, made his way over to the captain's BMP.

He greeted the captain: "*Mondana bashi khub yesti!*"

The captain climbed down from his machine and shook the man's tawny hand.

"How are things, Akhbar?"

"*Khub*, commander," answered the militia officer, his eyes searching for someone among the soldiers on the BMPs. He spotted Kuchechkarov, a Tadzhikistani, and waved to him: "Akhat!"

The small, dark-haired soldier came down to join them. After clasping the Afghan officer's hand and kissing him three times on his stubbled cheeks, Akhat began to translate. It turned out that the men were on their way to the camp with news that a large caravan laden with arms had made it into Padzhak, a nearby *kishlak*. Unconvinced, the captain asked how they were so sure that the caravan was carrying arms—maybe it was just loaded with cloth or food or whatever, maybe it was just an ordinary caravan of itinerant traders. The militia officer was affronted and answered that he had people in Padzhak, people with sharp eyes and honest tongues. The captain asked him when the caravan had appeared. At dawn, the officer said. Well then, they've probably left already, the captain suggested, while you were on your way to tell us they simply left again. A rabid jackal would have to have bitten them if they left in the daytime, the officer Akhbar retorted.

"Who are they?" Kostomygin asked Shvarev.

"Oh, guys from Spinda-Ulya. There's a militia detachment stationed there," Shvarev said lightly. "The least little thing and they rush off to us for help. But they're some hosts. Mamed, you remember that shashlik?"

Mamedov nodded and clicked his tongue in delight.

"Well, looks like something's up," continued Shvarev, his eyes sparkling. "Hey, Kosty, Opie! It'll be your baptism! I have a feeling they weren't headed to the camp for nothing."

The mustache was losing patience, gesticulating angrily to the captain that his information was true, and the captain was already beginning to suspect that maybe it was—the caravan they had been waiting for had veered off into Padzhak, and that was that—but nevertheless he continued to question Akhbar about every little detail: how many camels, how many men, had anyone out of the ordinary shown up recently, and so on. Only after all that did he radio back to camp and try to get in touch with the unit CP. The CP answered about ten minutes later.

After talking with the CP, the captain waved to Akhbar, swung his machine around, and headed off down the road that led back along the river. The whole column followed, the Afghans in their battered Toyota bringing up the rear.

"It'll be your baptism, sonny boys!" shouted Shvarev, slapping Kostomygin on the back. Oparin's face assumed an expression of joy, and he began to wave his assault rifle around in a warlike manner.

* * *

The column was flying along the sparkling little river amid swirling clouds of sunlit dust. The column was roaring, spewing palls of black exhaust, gravel crunching loudly under its treads, and Kostomygin, hypnotized by the deafening noise and the speed of their movement through the sunlight, the dust, and the rich absinthe smell of the steppes, was thinking that he would write his brother a crazy letter, crazy! That night, the aroma of flowery gardens, that moon, these hills under the stars, the nightingales, the ambush they'd laid, the muezzin's cry at dawn, their disappointment, and then this meeting, the sun, the dust, the clattering, the soot, and now expectation, uncertainty: What would happen in Padzhak? What would Padzhak look like? How would they take the caravan? How many rebels would they find? What would they look like—savage, bearded? Who would die—didn't someone have to die? If Oparin, for instance, was killed . . . He was sitting here now, and in an hour he'd be dead. Or even Kostomygin himself—he'd have time for his whole life to flash before his eyes, then he'd die in the dust, scorched by the sun, they'd send his body home, his family and friends would cry and cry. . . .

But he was sure that this time it would all be real, he'd write to his brother about his first real operation, and he would write to him because he wouldn't die, he would in fact never die—well, of course, sometime he probably would, but God knew when, years and years from now, a century . . .

Padzhak turned out to be a smallish *kishlak* not much different from any of the ones Kostomygin had seen already: gray *duvals*, some high, some low, gray towers, some round, some polygonal, gray houses, square or rectangular, all of them looking like narrow-windowed little boxes, and very rich, very lush gardens. Padzhak stood on a river, and the steppes that surrounded it were already brown and sparse, but its gardens were green and flourishing. The column had barely made it to the *kishlak* when Kostomygin smelled its fragrant aroma, and once again that sweetness was in his mouth.

For fear of snipers the soldiers slipped on their helmets and flak jackets and took cover behind the machines. But the *kishlak* seemed utterly peaceful: roosters were strutting along the *duvals*, an old man was leading a hump-backed cow down a street, and inquisitive children were scampering around, sticking their necks out for a peek at the kafirs and their dust-covered machines.

"Yes, we've got our little doves now," said Shvarev, dragging on a cigarette.

"What are we waiting for?" asked Kostomygin.

"Impatient, eh?" Shvarev smiled. "Uncle Vitya knows what he's doing." ("Uncle Vitya" was what the old-timers called the captain among themselves.) "Don't worry, he knows his stuff." But a half hour later even Shvarev was beginning to fidget and cast worried glances toward the captain's machine.

"Mamed," he called out to the BMP driver, "why do you think he's dragging his feet?"

Mamedov shrugged. "G-God knows. Maybe the CP is s-sending us some infantry."

Shvarev frowned. "How many could there be in that caravan, anyway? Ten, maybe? What, twenty at the outside?"

"B-but what if the whole *kishlak* rises up?"

"If we wait for infantry the *doukh*s will bury all the guns and we'll never be able to prove it's the same caravan we've been waiting for all night." Shvarev spat into the dust.

"No, it's b-better to wait," countered Mamedov. "More fun with the infantry here t-too."

"Comrade sergeant, can I drink now?" Oparin asked.

"You 'can' go take a flying fuck," Shvarev yelled back.

Oparin corrected himself. "Permission to drink?"

"On an operation you have to conserve water," Shvarev answered.

Oparin sighed and stole a glance at the shimmering river.

"What are you looking at the river for? Only donkeys and natives drink river water, and the slime doesn't affect them. Im-mu-ni-ty. You'd catch yellow fever, or typhus, or some sort of syphilis."

"Got it," said Oparin, and he ran his dry tongue over the black crust on his lips.

Shvarev heard something and froze.

"What is it?" Mamedov asked.

"Looks like they're here."

Then they all heard the distant rumble, turned their heads, and began to scan the road. Soon they could make out clouds of dust on the steppe.

Kostomygin groped for the safety catch on his assault rifle and flicked it to full automatic.

An infantry company and four tanks were heading toward the *kishlak*. Less than ten minutes later the operation began.

Akhat Kuchechkarov raised the megaphone to his mouth and shouted a few short phrases into the *kishlak*, then paused for a few moments and did it again.

Telling them to surrender, Kostomygin figured.

A few minutes passed, but no one appeared or came out. Kostomygin stared at the *kishlak*, astonished, unable to understand how its inhabitants had managed to clear the streets of all the chickens and donkeys and children—the place was deserted and silent.

Akhat looked over inquiringly to the captain, who said, "That's enough." Akhat dropped the megaphone into the hatch.

A few BTRs and BMPs slowly advanced into the *kishlak*, followed by helmeted and flak-jacketed soldiers with their rifles at the ready. They entered from only one direction—to avoid shooting one another, Kostomygin supposed—and fanned out into the alleys.

The *kishlak* was silent.

Someone pounded on a door with the butt of his gun, and Kostomygin flinched when he heard the harsh sound of the blows against wood.

"Over here," Shvarev said, swinging toward a house that was entirely surrounded by a low *duval*. He kicked at the heavy gate. It opened a few moments later and out into the street came a bony old man, leaning on a cane, with a wrinkled face, yellowish hands covered by translucent skin, and a look of indifference in his eyes.

"*Nis, nis dushman,*" he croaked.

Shvarev swept past him, saying nothing, and went into the courtyard.

"Medved! The gateway!" he shouted, then ran into the house. Oparin, Kostomygin, Salikhov, and a few men from the infantry company rushed in after him.

They searched the whole two-story building but found no one except a little group of women in chadors and children crowded into a small room in the remotest part of the house, nor anything other than rags, crockery, and food.

One of the infantrymen suggested stripping the chadors off the women—who knew if they really were women? But Salikhov rejected the idea out of hand, and since everyone in the regiment knew who he was and at one time or another had seen what he was capable of on the playing field, even among friends, no one dared to cross him now.

They went out into the courtyard.

"We'll check the barn," Shvarev said, and they were just about to do so when there was a crackle of gunfire and the wooden gates creaked. The soldiers hurried to the entryway.

Medvedev was leaning against the gates, gasping for breath.

Gunfire erupted all over the *kishlak.* The soldiers started shooting back through windows and at the gardens and rooftops. A machine gun was hammering and a grenade exploded.

One of the BMPs lumbered up, and they dragged Medvedev toward it. Kostomygin stared dumbly while they hauled the wounded man onto it and dropped him into the hatch. Through his legs Kostomygin felt a sort of trembling in the earth, and when he looked down he was flabbergasted by what he saw. Little plumes of dust were rising up from the ground all around him. He hurled himself backward against the *duval.*

"Over here!" bellowed Shvarev. Kostomygin came back to

24

his senses and ran into the entryway, but splinters were flying off the wooden gate and he threw his hands up to protect his face. His head started to shake uncontrollably.

"What is it, what is it?" Shvarev yelled, pulling Kostomygin's hands apart. "What is it?" Shvarev bent down to examine him. "Ah! Nothing! Splinters!"

Kostomygin rubbed his eyes, blinked a few times, and looked around.

"What should I do?" he asked Shvarev.

"Shoot at that house!" Shvarev pointed at the house next door, then fired a volley into one of its windows.

And Kostomygin, taking cover behind the *duval*, began to unleash long bursts of fire into the house.

"Shithead!" yelled Shvarev. "Don't waste ammo!"

It was hot, dust was gritting in his teeth, and more than anything he wanted to take off this hot, heavy helmet and this cumbersome flak jacket. Kostomygin would fire off a short burst, pause for a moment, once more pop up from behind the *duval* and rattle off a few bullets through a window into the tall, vast house, but he couldn't manage to hit the machine gunner, who shot from one window, ducked, then moved to another and shot from there.

Gunfire was raging all over the *kishlak*. Now and then a grenade exploded. There was dust in the air and a strong smell of gunpowder. The rapid-fire cannons of the BMPs were roaring, machine guns firing loudly and heavily. The stench of powder mixed with the odor of trees in bloom made Kostomygin feel sick. He was becoming desperately tired of raising himself halfway up, shooting, crouching down again, then getting back up, pulling the trigger, and yet again ducking back down behind the *duval*. It was so hot, the powder and the flowers were reeking so much, Kostomygin's ears were ringing, his throat was parched, the machine gunner kept hammering and hammering, and none of this would ever end, Medvedev no doubt whimpering, tortured, in the stifling interior of the BMP, none of it would ever end....

Which window would the machine gunner shoot from next? And where was Oparin?

Kostomygin turned his head and to his left saw a damp red face with bulging eyes. His feeling of nausea grew worse. He wanted to force Oparin to shoot, to stop just standing there next to the *duval*, paralyzed, head bowed, assault rifle hanging limply from his arms, but all of a sudden he realized that the machine gunner wasn't firing anymore. He cautiously peered out and stole a glance at the dark empty windows. He stuck his head out farther and saw that coming from the house into the courtyard was a broad-shouldered man with his hands in the air, behind him was a hunched-over young boy, and then, behind them both, Salikhov and one of the infantrymen.

"They got them!" Kostomygin cried out, shocked, to Shvarev.

Shvarev, already on the run, called out, "Opie! Kosty!" Kostomygin and Oparin ran after him.

They ran into the street, reached the gates of the neighboring house, and entered the courtyard through a narrow little door.

Without saying a word, Shvarev ran up to the lean, broad-shouldered, hook-nosed man, dressed in a long, tattered blue shirt and struck him in the chin with the butt of his gun. The man's head jerked back, but he remained on his feet. The wide-eyed boy standing just behind him reeled and cried out as though it was he who had just been hit. The man straightened up, blood streaming from his mouth.

"Which one of these shits got Medvedev?" Shvarev yelled.

The man looked at him sullenly, his jaw muscles flexing under the black stubble that covered his cheeks. The boy pulled off his grubby turban and buried his face in it.

"Now what?" asked Salikhov.

"They shot Medvedev," Shvarev said, looking around.

Salikhov nodded.

"So." Shvarev wiped the sweat off his face with his sleeve. "That's it. *Murd*, guys, *murd*. That's it, *khana*," he said to the prisoners. The boy's shoulders began to tremble, and the man's eyes narrowed.

"So," Shvarev muttered. "So . . ." He looked around again, his eyes met Oparin's, and he repeated again, "So."

"Then let's do it quickly," the infantryman said in a low voice, "before an officer sees them." He moved closer to the boy and raised the barrel of his assault rifle to the turban that was still shrouding his face.

Shvarev stopped him. "Wait." He looked around once more, then glanced at Kostomygin and Oparin. "Wait. Kosty! You take the man. Opie! You finish off the other one."

"Let the youngsters do it? Sure, why not?" the infantryman said approvingly, then stepped aside.

Kostomygin felt as though the back of his neck had turned to ice. It was horrifying, in this heat, for anything to feel so cold. His teeth began to chatter. He clamped down on them and looked at Shvarev, and wondered what he was saying, and to whom.

"Come on!" Shvarev yelled.

The sun hung low; the steppe beneath it and the swathe of sky above it were glowing crimson, and the bitter, scorching air was slowly cooling off.

The long column was snaking its way over the twilit steppe, banners of gray dust fluttering over it. The column was returning to camp. The soldiers, shoulders slumped with exhaustion, were sitting on top of their machines. The prisoners rode inside, hands bound.

Dust was caking their eyes and catching in their throats, but the soldiers would not ride in the interior of the BMPs; anyone inside would be mashed against its metal walls if one of the machines hit a mine, but if you were sitting on top you'd just be thrown to the ground. It was a simple truth known to everyone who fought in Afghanistan. The prisoners taken with the caravan knew it too; they would sweat and quiver whenever the machine they were in ran over a pothole or struck a boulder with its undercarriage, and pray to Allah that He remove all mines from their path. Or maybe they were praying for Him to send everyone—the detested kafirs and them themselves—to hell with one mighty explosion. The truth was, if a BMP ran over a mine very few would live to tell the tale: the ten-ton machine would flip onto its back like an empty tin can, and anyone sitting on top would be flattened into a pancake.

The column was bringing eleven prisoners and a mass of war trophies back to camp: Italian-made land mines, heavy-caliber machine guns, rocket launchers, crates of ammunition and grenades, and a whole shipment of American and West German medical supplies.

The infantry officers were pleased with the operation and knew that the CP would be too. The commander of the recon company was gloomy and sour: Medvedev had died on the road home— the bullet had torn through his intestines—and the leader of the first platoon, a lieutenant, had taken a serious head wound. They hadn't managed to work cleanly this time . . .

Kostomygin, the only person in the whole unit to ride inside a BMP, was lying back on a crate of shells. He was chain-smoking and didn't give a damn if the machine ran over a mine or not. All the same to me, he thought angrily.

It was true—whether or not the machine blew up made absolutely no difference to him. He was thinking about Oparin and Salikhov and the hook-nosed man with bloodstained lips. He didn't want to think about any of it, he just wanted to fall asleep any way he could, to sleep such a sleep that he wouldn't wake up for a thousand years, nor remember anything afterward. But it was impossible not to think, not to remember. He thought, he remembered.

He remembered everything precisely, even though during the battle itself he had felt as though he was someone else, and the events had been ghostly and confusing. But now everything was crystal-clear, like a film in slow motion.

He remembered it all vividly, every sound, every voice, every movement. He remembered how the ground under his feet had trembled, how the wooden gates had splintered and slivers of wood had flown into his face, how they had run through the dimly lit rooms in that house, how one of the infantrymen had suggested checking the women under those veils to see if they had mustaches. And he remembered how he had grown tired of firing into the windows of the house next door, and after that the hook-nosed man coming out into the courtyard, his hands in the air, and then the boy, then Salikhov and the infantryman. . . . But still, wasn't it interesting, the way they had pulled the thing off? Interesting, shit—what difference did that make now? He couldn't care less.

He had fired a short burst into the broad chest of the hook-nosed man, and the man had fallen down, twisted in the dirt, blown scarlet bubbles from his nose, then stopped moving.

. . . But Medvedev had died on the way back. Was he really dead? It meant nothing. . . .

And Oparin? Who would have believed it? Who in hell would have believed it?

Kostomygin thought about Oparin. He hated Oparin. He remembered how he had turned around and seen Oparin's sweaty red face, a coward's face with bulging eyes, and he groaned with hatred and loathing.

He didn't do it, because he's a coward. A coward, a coward, Kostomygin repeated to himself, but it didn't make him feel any better.

Oparin had not fired. Shvarev had threatened him and screamed at him, but Oparin had not fired. What would it have cost him to pull the trigger? What the hell would it have cost him? He had burst into tears and begged them to let him go. Let him go? Where? Home to Mama? He had fallen apart completely, bawling his eyes out, begging them to let him go. God, what they'd do to him back at camp!

Why should I care what they do to that shit? To hell with him. He's a coward, he'll always be a coward, he's not even worth thinking about. That Salikhov, though . . . Kostomygin pulled on a cigarette. He had already smoked himself to the point of nausea, he was barely able to keep himself from being sick, but he reached into the pack for another and lit it off the preceding one. That Salikhov, Kostomygin wondered, frowning. He hadn't really been there, had he?

But Salikhov had been in that narrow little courtyard too. He and the infantryman who'd helped him capture the rebel machine gunners.

Yes, Salikhov had been there too, and once it had dawned on him that Oparin wouldn't shoot, that Oparin would rather have shot himself instead, once that had dawned on Salikhov, he had walked up to the boy, who still had his face buried in the dirty, tattered turban, and he had killed him with a backhand blow. He had killed him barehanded, and no one had felt any surprise. He did it so quickly that you could have thought the boy had just died—his heart had stopped all of a sudden and he had just fallen down dead.

Kostomygin, buffeted around on top of the shell-filled crates, took another drag from his cigarette, and he didn't want to die after a long, long time, after a thousand years. He wanted his heart to stop right then. But it didn't happen.

UNIT N CARRIED OUT

EXERCISES

DAY AND NIGHT THE BATTALIONS HAD BEEN STORMING THE Iskapol Mountains in the province of Gazin. Howitzer and rocket batteries, airplanes, and fast, narrow, speckled helicopters poured tons of steel onto the hills. The cold autumn air smelled of gunpowder, and dust clouded the sun and stars. During the day helicopters came for the dead and wounded. At night, moonless and starry, a transport plane circled high above the hills and dropped flare bombs that burst into handfuls of orange suns. The fluttering spheres would slowly sink down, lighting the ravines, cliffs, and heights, as well as the steppe extending around the hills, where the regiment's field camp lay. The infantry would climb up accompanied by the thudding of heavy machine guns, explosions, the clatter of rapid-firing grenade launchers. When the orange suns died out the infantry would dive to the ground. After a short lull the artillery officers would cry out from the steppe below and the preliminary barrage would begin.

The rebels, firmly entrenched in caves and rock outcroppings, had a large base in these mountains and were well stocked with water, food, medical supplies, and ammunition. They were fighting with insulting effectiveness.

When the howitzers and rocket installations fell silent one could make out, under the stars, the mournful, indistinct drone of the transport plane's engines. The infantrymen lay prone against the rocks, wiping their sweat-damp and dirt-encrusted faces and raising canteens to blistered lips, waiting for the hiss of flare bombs up above.

Silence, darkness.

The men caught their breath, drank their water, and began to feel the cold—it was autumn, and though the sun warmed during the day, at night the air was icy and dried the soldiers' sweat within moments after an attack.

They waited.

Something was holding up the transport plane; the infantrymen were starting to become used to the quiet.

A few more minutes passed, and then there was a hiss and a crackle above them—the flare bombs lighting up. The captain shouted, "Company, forward!" The men got up and started to climb. A machine gun hammered overhead and tracer bullets began to skitter against the rocks, ricocheting into the air in every direction. The infantrymen leaped from outcropping to outcropping, firing off short bursts, their faces burning, their stomachs freezing cold. One of the red-hot streams of bullets cut into a soldier running up the hill; he collapsed—it was the captain—and spat blood, then didn't move anymore. He was dead. A lieutenant took over and the attack was resumed.

The lieutenant led the company toward the summit, where the rebels had dug themselves in on a crest. The rebels were on the verge of losing the heights; their heavy machine gun had stopped firing and they were shooting with pistols and assault rifles. Battle was raging everywhere on the summit and shells were exploding on the next hill over. The company closed in, lobbed grenades onto the crest, and the assault rifles and pistols fell silent. After a pause, motioning for the others to follow, the lieutenant was the first to fling himself over the top.

Beyond some boulders was a flat little plateau on which the heavy machine gun stood, and scattered around it lay empty metal shell casings and four bodies torn to pieces by shrapnel. A fifth man was dragging himself downhill. The lieutenant caught him, kicked him, and the rebel rolled over onto his back and raised his shattered hands. After ordering the soldiers to drag him back to the little plateau, the lieutenant radioed the battalion commander a report on the winning of the crest and the casualties they had taken. The commander ordered him to leave a few machine gunners behind on the captured hill and to strike the neighboring hill from the north. Four men stayed while the rest of the company climbed back down.

The soldiers left behind on the hill drank and smoked.

The wounded man whimpered; his hands were in tatters and he had been shot in the leg. The four bodies, blood still seeping from them, lay motionless. The machine gunners, glad to be staying here, inhaled their acrid smoke. Maybe it was all over for the time being and they wouldn't have to go through that hell again: in the morning the whole regiment would head home, laden with war trophies, to its tent city, where there were baths, clean sheets, meals three times a day, letters, movies every night, pay chits— and, in the commissary, filtered cigarettes, orange jam, biscuits, condensed milk, Indian coffee, grape juice. Not to mention Tanya in the library, who never glanced twice at the soldiers, though they certainly looked at her; she had red lips, somewhat heavy legs with little tendrils of black hair on them, large, prominent buttocks; she sweated and her shirt was always damp under her arms and along the crook of her back, but you could go to the library anytime to look at Tanya and smell her aroma of perfume and sweat. And now the captain would miss all that forever. Dead? Nothing had ever touched him before, not bullets, not yellow fever, not typhus. One time he and a soldier had been coming down a *kiariz*, flashlights in hand, following an underground corridor. The corridor suddenly made a sharp turn and on the other side they ran into some rebels, so the two opened fire and threw themselves backward. The first one they pulled out of the *kiariz* was the soldier, who had been shot in the calf. The captain was alive and completely unharmed. And now he was dead.

Cigarettes are great; only idiots quit smoking. Or drinking— teetotalers are fools. After an operation you'd give a year of your life for a bottle of vodka. You wash yourself clean in the baths, then you pour yourself, in your standard-issue cup, some pure, bitter-tasting vodka. They ship it from home in tanker trucks and it costs thirty chits, expensive, but what the hell. You pour yourself some. The amount in your cup is worth roughly seven chits, nearly the monthly pay of a common soldier. But who cares: for half an hour you feel like a human being, no boredom, no fear, your brain sparkles, and two years—it's nothing.

The shooting died down on the other crest: a lull.

"On your toes, men," said the sergeant in command of the group.

The machine gunners already were.

Up above, the transport plane was droning. Not bad, being a pilot. It wasn't the artillerymen who were gods, but the pilots, in their black leather helmets and blue flight suits. But of course they got it, too—the rebels loved going after aircraft, and especially capturing the crews of downed planes and helicopters. There was nothing worse than being taken prisoner by the rebels. They knew how to kill slowly, dealing out death by degrees. The company had once found the body of the NCO Vorobyev, who'd been through two days of it: a swollen bluish-gray carcass with gray hair that only the captain could identify as him. Not for anything in the world to be taken prisoner. No, the gods of the war weren't the artillerymen or the pilots but the staff officers. But even they died—although rarely enough—since after all they were in the war too, not above it. The gods were elsewhere, above it.

"The artillery's about to hit them," one of the machine gunners said in a hoarse voice. "If they don't get us instead. They're dumb enough to."

"The lieutenant spoke to them on the radio," the sergeant responded.

The prisoner moaned, and everyone glanced at him. He had wrapped his hands in the long folds of his shirt, but blood was seeping through the cloth.

"They killed . . . the captain," the sergeant said.

No one answered him.

* * *

The captive's broken hands were itching and burning. It felt like they were being devoured by clouds of hairy insects whose jagged pincers were ripping into his skin, his flesh, into his veins and cartilage, their sheer number and weight pulling his arms downward. The prisoner lay on the ground, his back against a boulder, and clutched his hands to his chest.

They killed the captain, thought the sergeant. Again he glanced over at the prisoner.

A spasm hit the wounded man.

His hands should be bandaged, thought Grashchenkov, a machine gunner who had been shot in the thigh in his first few days of service.

Under the stars came the mournful engine sound of the invisible transport plane.

Soon the rocket installations and the 122-millimeter howitzers would open up, everything would burst into flames, start to rock, shudder—soon . . .

In the silence the hoarse-voiced soldier said, "Something's flying past over there."

The soldiers scanned the sky and made out a glimmering speck—far away, high above the steppe, an aircraft on the horizon. It seemed to be a passenger jet; it was flying from north to south, sailing noiselessly through the sky, navigation lights blinking on its wings and undercarriage, making its way toward India or Pakistan. The soldiers watched its pulsing lights.

The captain hunched over, drew a pack of cigarettes from his breast pocket, lit one. The others, smelling the smoke, lit up too, cupping their cigarettes in their hands. Silence—was it over, maybe? The rebels had surrendered, the all-clear signal would come soon, and in the morning the battalions would return to camp.

The prisoner whimpered more loudly, and they all stared at him. Grashchenkov took his pack off his shoulders, undid it, and pulled out his personal kit. The others figured that he'd decided to eat something, and since they were hungry too they unslung their packs, took out their biscuits, tin cans, and sugar, prizing the cans open with their bayonets. The smell of sausage meat wafted up. Grashchenkov tore open his packet; bandages and gauze glimmered white in his hands. The sergeant stopped eating and looked at him.

"What are you doing?" he asked.

"I'm going to bandage his wounds."

"Put those away."

"Why?"

"We can't waste them," the sergeant said.

"Speak for yourself. I can waste mine."

The others were eating their meat, crunching their biscuits, looking around at the darkened hilltops, silently casting glances at the sergeant and the soldier with the bandages.

"You hear what I said, Grashchenkov?" the sergeant asked.

The prisoner was lying back, eyes closed, hearing nothing. Houris in translucent gowns were dancing around him, lifting him by the arms toward the top of a green mountain where, in the shade of the pale rose Lotus, true believers were lying around, chalices in their hands, drinking tea and looking with smiling eyes at the visitor; perfume emanated from the Lotus, fountains with arching streams of iridescent water surrounded it, and above the Lotus white doves flittered back and forth. . . .

There was no preliminary artillery barrage; the transport plane dropped flare bombs.

"No—I'm going to dress his wounds," said Grashchenkov. He stood up and headed toward the captive, but a burst of machine-gun fire got there first. Grashchenkov looked at the orange-colored face, its mouth torn, an eyeball dangling, its nose twisted off to the side.

"A bit more time would have been nice," the hoarse-voiced

soldier commented, stashing the rest of his meat, sugar, and biscuits back in his pack. The second soldier turned aside and quickly polished off his own can, threw it away, licked his spoon clean, popped his lump of sugar into his mouth, and took a swig from his canteen.

Meanwhile the battle on the crest had started up again. While waiting for the green flares, the machine gunners trained their sights on the neighboring summit, which the whole company was now stealing up on from the north. The sky was orange, the hills were orange, and the shadows and crags had turned deep black. Muzzle flashes leaped up and down the slope, red streams of gunfire intersected each other, grenades exploded. Their minds blank, the machine gunners lay on the rocks, which were becoming colder and colder, stared at the neighboring summit, at the intertwining bursts of tracer bullets, and waited.

"The company got lost," the hoarse-voice soldier ventured. "They got scattered all to hell." But just then, as though anxious to prove him wrong, a brilliant flash hit the summit and a bright ball of green light stretched down the side of the hill.

"Fire!" the sergeant ordered heatedly.

The machine gunners opened up on the summit, the company climbing the hill began to shoot, a second company started up from the southern slope, and assault rifles hit the rebels from the west.

"They're in for it now," the hoarse-voiced soldier said.

But the rebels held on, and bullets began to whiz over the heads of the machine gunners.

"They're still in for it," the hoarse-voiced soldier repeated, loosing long bursts into the neighboring summit. Suddenly he moaned, stood up, arched his back, his desperate fingers trying to pry a fire out of his spine, then fell.

The sergeant glanced back and saw dark figures in the middle of the slope to their rear. He fired a burst at them and cried out when a sharp invisible claw ripped open his shoulder. Grash-chenkov and the second soldier turned around, and, balancing the machine gun in his arms, Grashchenkov began to spray the slope with bullets.

"Behind the rocks!" the sergeant shouted, throwing himself over a boulder. The second soldier leaped over and hurled himself to the ground.

"Grashchenkov!" shouted the sergeant.

Grashchenkov stepped backward, dropped the machine gun, raised his hands to his chest, slumped down into a squat, and began to cough wetly. The second machine gunner crawled toward him, grabbed him by his flak jacket, pulled him down, and dragged him behind a boulder. He took out his first-aid kit, tore it open, and reached for the bandages and gauze. Grashchenkov was lying on his back, not saying anything, wiping his bloody lips over and over again. He looked at the orange sky, not saying anything. He felt no pain. He felt clouded and languid, as though he'd just drunk a whole bottle of vodka by himself. Bullets were skittering off the rocks. The soldier applied a wad of gauze to his lips, and the little white cushion immediately filled up and darkened. The soldier quickly removed Grashchenkov's flak jacket and fatigues. Grashchenkov groaned and coughed, beginning to feel the pain at last, and the dark wad of gauze fell from his lips. The soldier picked it up again and wiped Grashchenkov's cheeks and chin with it.

"Christ, get some bandages on him," the sergeant said, but the soldier just kept wiping away the blood Grashchenkov spat up each time he coughed.

"You keep shooting—I'll take over!" the sergeant shouted, crawling to Grashchenkov and pushing the stupefied soldier aside. The soldier picked up the machine gun and began firing. The sergeant took out his kit, pulled bandages and gauze from it, found the wounds gurgling on Grashchenkov's chest, and, wincing from the pain in his shoulder, began to bandage him. He finally managed to do it, more or less, but Grashchenkov stopped twitching, his limbs stretched out, and he quickly grew stiff.

"That's it," the sergeant said, gingerly touching his own hot, wet shoulder.

"We have to get out before we're surrounded!" the soldier shouted, dropping the machine gun and picking up his assault rifle. "The magazines are all empty!"

"Grashchenkov's got more!"

But Grashchenkov's pack was resting on the section of the crest where most of the gunfire was crackling.

"Let's get out of here! Back down the hill!" shouted the soldier, crawling back to the rear. Wheezing with pain, the sergeant followed him.

They reached the middle of the slope, stood up, and broke into a crouched run, but red tracers ricocheted all around them and they dropped back down. The shooting came from everywhere: above, below, the path they were trying to retreat along. The sergeant and the soldier began to return fire.

Moments later the sergeant's gun misfired and fell silent, quickly followed by the soldier's.

"What now, Jenya?"

The sergeant said nothing.

"Jenya, you alive?" the soldier cried out.

"Grenades . . . you have any?" the sergeant asked.

"No."

"Then here."

"What's this for?"

"Take it." The sergeant dropped a grenade into the soldier's hand and pulled the pin from another. He pressed the pale metal plate of the detonator to the grenade's ribbed body with his fist, then thrust his hand under his body.

"What are . . . No, wait," the soldier said, crawling off in the other direction. "You don't have to . . ."

The sergeant lay on his stomach and didn't say anything. Up above them figures appeared in silhouette—men were creeping stealthily down the slope. The detonator clicked, and there was a hollow-sounding explosion; the sergeant rocked, then was

41

thrown up and onto his side. The rebels opened fire. The last machine gunner threw his grenade to the ground, tore his handkerchief from his pocket, waved it over his head, and yelled:

"*Doust*! I give up! No, don't shoot! *Mondana bashi...khub yesti*!"

MARS AND THE SOLDIER

1

THE ROOM WAS BRIGHT—THERE HAD BEEN A SNOWFALL IN the night. The first snow had always elated and invigorated him, but today the old man was not well. He had woken up and seen Moscow covered in white, and it had suddenly struck him that this first snow would be his last. The old man drove away the thought, the dark thought of white snow, tried to think of other things instead, and he did, but something inside him pined, aching and burning with grief. And then the pains in his old body faded away; his heart began to beat evenly, his head became clear, but his mood remained somber. The old man yawned sadly and furrowed his thick black brows.

After breakfast, dressed in a dark blue two-piece wool suit, the old man sat in his armchair, laid his fleshy white hands on his large soft belly, and through watery eyes looked at Moscow, his vast white Moscow. . . .

2

Sorokoputov warmed up a little by rolling around in the narrow, narrow cave; he contorted himself, pulled his knees into his chest, and remained like that, rigid. His arms, tied behind his back with rope, felt heavy and half-dead. From time to time he wriggled his fingers, but his blood was flowing too slowly through

45

the constricted veins anyway and his hands were freezing, growing more and more numb. Sorokoputov didn't know how long he had been in this rocky crevice—maybe a day, maybe a day and a night. He needed water and cigarettes.

It was cold. Sorokoputov was lying on his side, rolled up in a ball, listening to the muffled sounds of battle that had started up again a short time before. Shells were landing dully in the surrounding mountains. That inspired hope. No—hope had never abandoned him, not for an instant: From the very first he had known that all of this was nonsense and foolishness, that in a few moments he would hear shouts of "Hurrah!" and the heavy slab of stone would move aside and deft, helpful hands would pull him out of this crypt, cut the rope, raise a lighted match to his cigarette. "Hey, Sorokoputov, how the hell did you make it through?" "God only knows, guys, somehow it just happened. Like in a dream." "Sure, Sorokoput, now you'll have something to tell the ladies."

He knew that everything would end up precisely that way. It was a feeling, a feeling of good fortune that nothing could undermine. Everything would be all right; all he had to do was be patient and wait.

Sorokoputov lay on the stones, listening for explosions, waiting.

3

How does the poet have it? Here the snow like cherry blossoms, here cherry trees blooming as though covered with snow . . . thought the old man in the blue two-piece suit. He was looking out his large window at the snowbound city. Soon it will be spring . . . if I live till then. He picked up a slender volume, his favorite. In moments of sorrow he loved to read these poems, even though they made him sadder still. A fleeting idea: Their mouths would all be agape. He imagined them all, mouths gaping, staring with round sheeplike eyes at the slender volume of poems in their sovereign's hands. Him and that poet—scandalizer, rake, womanizer, suicide. Yes! I love . . . the old man said to them all in his mind, then smiled bitterly.

He put on his gold-rimmed spectacles, opened the little book, and slowly leafed through a few pages until he found something about snow and a cherry tree: "The cherry tree is shedding snow . . ."

4

Everything would be all right. The most important thing was not to lose that presentiment of good fortune. Most important . . . yes, most . . . what is the most important thing? Well, it's . . .

Sorokoputov was hanging from a branch over a distant rushing river. His arms were tied and he was gripping the branch in his teeth. They were being torn out of his gums with a cracking sound; he couldn't spit them out, so he would have to swallow them. Soon he would fall, crash into the river, die. He fell headlong toward the water but landed smoothly; he strained his arms, the rope broke, and then he was swimming. The sun was shining, the water was warm, and the riverbanks were covered with large red flowers on a background of green. Clumsy birds of some sort were flying low over the water, gentle, downy birds with feminine eyes that grazed him with their wings. He was laughing. . . .

Sorokoputov woke up, thinking that he had once had the same dream before. Or no, it had actually happened. Yes, it had—he and a friend had been fishing in the Dnieper at the end of May; it was hot, they had gone swimming, and in the sky gulls were fluttering, storks and herons soaring. After swimming they had lain down on a sandbar, a hot, yellow sandbar. They had sat next to it in the evening, listening to pikes splashing in the water. It had rained during the night, and in the morning wild roses had blossomed all around their tent.

The sounds of battle approached. Somewhere nearby, very close, grenades were exploding and a heavy-caliber machine gun was pounding relentlessly.

What was it? Day, night?

Hurrah, they're shouting hurrah! Mow the *doukhs* down with machine guns and get me out of here. Well, where are you, you cowards?

Sorokoputov waited.

The most important thing was not to lose faith. In time anyone who doesn't believe in his own fate is killed. But he believed—he knew that sunlight would soon scatter into the cave. The ones who don't make it are the ones who don't really believe, the ones who don't understand life or know what happiness is. But he understood, he knew—it was rain at night and in the morning the blossoming of wild roses.

Sorokoputov flinched when he heard a grinding of stone. The slab was moved aside and a harsh light, like the rays of dozens of projectors, burst into the cave. The noise of explosions and machine-gun fire poured in, and Sorokoputov was deafened, blinded. Someone's hands grabbed his legs and he was dragged out of the stone crevice.

He squinted, saw nothing, then made out the bright sun and white mountaintops. Standing over him were men in long, flowing shirts, fur-lined vests, woolen cloaks, turbans, and astrakhan caps. The light brought tears to his eyes, and the drops trickled down his dirt-encrusted cheeks. Over the heads of the men with dark, thin faces hung mountaintops covered with the year's first snow. The gelid air was shaking with explosions and machine-gun bursts.

One of the rebels, a broad-shouldered man with a gray beard, made a sign with his hand—get up. Sorokoputov rose quickly to his feet. He stood on his cramped, trembling legs, his teeth chattering, and looked into the graybeard's eyes. They were exhausted, dark, moist. Sorokoputov looked into them with hope.

The graybeard nodded his head, and machine guns opened up from the left and the right. A searing wind struck Sorokoputov in the chest; he fell on his back, turned over onto his side, hunched himself up. Sorokoputov's legs twisted in the new-fallen snow, and he moaned, breathing scarlet bubbles from his nose.

5

The old man was reading poems in his armchair by the window. He read about a she-dog and her whelps, about a cow and her calfs, about the leaves falling from a maple tree, about an izba with blue shutters, about vanished youth, cherry trees and apple trees in bloom. He sighed and moved his black, youthful-looking brows.

The old man turned to another page with his thick white fingers. He buried himself in a new poem, and his heavy, porous face began to quiver:

We are dying,
We leave in grief and silence
But I know
That . . .

The old man tightened his lips and frowned. He read on:

But I know
That Russia won't forget us.

The old man's protruding lower lip started to tremble, then his lower jaw, then his head, and a heavy salted tear rolled down the page.

WINTER IN
AFGHANISTAN

In the farthest corner of the long, high tent a kerosene lamp was burning on a bedside table where the veterans were playing cards. The lamp cast a purple shadow over the stool on which the cards were dealt, over the faces of the players, over streams of cigarette smoke, and over the soldier who was standing motionless in the aisle between rows of bunk beds.

In the middle of the tent a round iron stove was roaring, and the few young soldiers sitting on stools next to it were brandishing leggings that belonged to the old-timers. Toreadors on wooden horses—although it's hard to imagine a toreador willing to wash someone else's leggings.

Some of the men were dozing, sprawled on their beds, while others were talking idly among themselves; two soldiers had found a place near the cardplayers and were sewing little strips of white material into the collars of cotton field jackets. A pudgy soldier, his booted feet resting on his bed frame and his hands thrust under his head, was lying back, staring up at the netting of the bunk above him, singing songs. Everything he sang was to the same tune, and he sang every song in the same quiet, uninflected voice— he sang mechanically, thinking of other things.

The tent was hot and muggy and smelled of lighting fluid, tobacco, dirty clothes. The soldiers had eaten not long before and now, full and satisfied, were waiting for the nightly roll call.

The pudgy soldier was singing, "No fence, no yard, no familiar face. . . . There's no vodka, no women, won't ever be any. . . ."

The toreadors were furiously fanning the stove with their rags, and on one side it was beginning to glow an angry red.

A couple of men were already snoring.

Cards flicked against the little table. The veterans were playing "joker," smoking, making wisecracks, not paying any attention at all to the soldier standing nearby.

"Looks like I'll stand," said a broad-shouldered young red-head in a tattered field jacket. He had a large, hairy chest, a small head, long arms. They called him Udmurt of Phnom-Penh. He was a Russian from the Udmurt Republic whom the old-timers from the tour before his had nicknamed Udmurt, and for some reason "from Phnom-Penh" too. Even now he was still called that behind his back.

"And I'll fold this time," a small, swarthy, fine-featured soldier said angrily—Sanko, a Belorussian whose last name really was Sanko. He threw his last card, a ten of clubs, onto the stool.

"Ah," said Ostapenkov. "I'll take that."

"You'll take that," muttered Udmurt from Phnom-Penh, "and so these come out." He quickly put down two cards.

The lithe, skinny, big-eared Tatar Ivanov fixed his clear round eyes on the cards, bit his narrow lips between his sharp white teeth, and covered Udmurt's two cards with the six of clubs and the queen of hearts.

Udmurt glanced at the wide-eyed queen with flowing hair and announced, "She reminds me of someone."

"Valechka," said Ostapenkov.

"Valechka's hair is darker," Sanko retorted.

"But she has the same eyes, like a lamb's," Ostapenkov said.

Ivanov was left with the jokers. He picked up the deck of cards and began to shuffle them fluidly with his long, strong, dry fingers. Ostapenkov rooted through his pockets, found his cigarettes, lit one off the lamp, inhaled, and tried to blow a smoke ring. On the second attempt he succeeded.

"Charlie Chaplin," he began, "left a million to whoever could make twelve smoke rings, blow a stream of smoke through them, then have that stream turn into a smoke ring too. He was one hell of a smoker."

"Crazy," said Udmurt. "Twelve."

"Sure, but what if you practiced?" Sanko picked up a cigarette, lit it, and started to blow out thick batches of smoke without managing to produce a single ring.

"You might be okay at it once you've spent the million on smokes," said Ostapenkov, grinning.

"Still, a million . . ." Udmurt from Phnom-Penh said in a soft voice.

"Yeah, a million," Ostapenkov repeated. He paused, glanced quickly at the soldier in the aisle, and in a different voice demanded, "You have something to tell us, Dulya?"

The soldier in the aisle—his last name, Stodolya, had been changed into Dulya—looked at the lamp and said nothing. He was a young man, docile, into whom a simple truth had been beaten, since his very first days of service with the company, the way it had been beaten into every other kid, with fists: if you spit at the group it will wipe itself off, but if the group spits at you you'll drown.

The group was divided into three castes: the sparrows, the spooners, and the old-timers. The first had six months under their belts, the second a year, the third a year and a half. Kids and demobs didn't belong to any caste: the first were beneath the group, under its heels, and the second were somewhere off to the side, on the periphery. By long-standing convention the demobs could order a cigarette or a cup of water brought to their beds in the middle of the night, but they didn't abuse the custom; in general they acted with a certain degree of reserve, and more often than not they tried to keep their voices down—they were living out their last weeks in the barracks, whose masters, as everyone clearly knew, were the old-timers, who still had six more months to serve, who could suddenly turn angry, recall old grievances, and, rallying the whole group to their side, avenge themselves with their fists against the demobs. It had happened before in the camp.

The group lived by its own special rules, whenever or by whomever they had been thought up. At their root lay one dialectical formula: everything is in flux, everything changes, and those who were at first nobodies became old-timers—it was as inevitable as the collapse of imperialism. It was difficult to raise an argument against it, and certainly nobody did. That wasn't allowed. Which was also one of the rules: keep quiet unless someone asks you something. The right to ask questions was reserved to members of the higher castes. And if you were asked something you had to answer. That was another rule, and it was now being broken by the big-nosed, big-eyed soldier nicknamed Dulya.

He was standing in the aisle, looking at the lamp, silent.

"You still have..." Ostapenkov glanced at his watch; forty minutes to go until lights out. "...half an hour."

"We know, we know!" said Sanko. "Another hand?"

Sanko put a card down on the stool.

Ivanov covered it. "I know..." He fell silent for a moment, casting a sidelong look at Dulya. "I know certain facts. *Facts*," he repeated.

"Really?" Ostapenkov asked.

"Yes." Ivanov drummed his fingernails on the stool. "But later, later."

"Don't hold back, tell us," Sanko said impatiently.

Ivanov shook his head.

"Let's hear the story he's got for us."

The pudgy soldier who had been singing to himself dropped his feet to the wood-planked floor with a crash, threw on his oilskin, and left the tent. After a few minutes he came back, his oilskin dripping with rain. He took it off in the doorway and shook it dry. He went over to his bunk, hung it on the bed frame, and reassumed his former position, only this time with his wet, clay-crusted boots on the floor instead of up on the bar. He lay down, not saying anything, and then started another song: "No more running, no more jumping, no more singing, no more loving; my drunken youth has swirled away into the mist...."

The soldier nicknamed Dulya stood in front of the cardplayers, his shoulders slumped and his legs crossing now this way, now that. He was looking at the lamp, whose light seemed hot to him, and though his eyes were aching he would not take them off the flame behind its cloudy glass. It was easier to keep quiet when he stared at it. For some time he felt that way, or at least it felt like some time.

"Water," said Udmurt, his eyes on his cards.

Dulya gladly went off to get it—dinner had consisted of over-salted pearled barley and stringy, oversalted pork, and he was dying of thirst. The metal tank of drinking water stood on a table near the tent's entrance. He turned the tap, got the water, gulped a cupful, and wanted to drink some more but Udmurt shouted out, "What's keeping you over there, you giving birth?" Dulya poured out some more water, returned, and handed the cup to Udmurt, who swallowed it greedily.

Dulya went back to standing motionless in the aisle. Again the yellow light of the lamp began to stream into his eyes.

She's nothing anyway, he thought, and was suddenly struck with shame. He felt ashamed for thinking it, ashamed for imagining that she was here, in this long, shadowy tent, that she was standing somewhere nearby and, understanding nothing, staring at him.

"Twenty minutes to go," Ostapenkov said.

Dulya fixed his eyes on him.

"What are you looking at?"

"Hit him in the head, he'll tell you," said Udmurt.

"There's still time for that," Ostapenkov answered. He wanted to add that things weren't so simple, but he didn't say anything—it would be too much of a compliment to the kid Dulya. He'd already been paid enough attention as it was. Since they'd read the letter no one had so much as lifted a finger against Dulya, even though he'd flagrantly violated one of the rules—he hadn't answered his elders' questions. If it hadn't been for Ostapenkov the others would of course have thrashed him long before. But Ostapenkov wouldn't let them. For the time being he had begun to take an interest in the matter—there was something significant, something frightening behind all this. They always grilled the new men, punished them, bled them dry, so to speak, to find out everything: what their lives had been like back home, what their work had been, how many girls they'd had, the hair color, the eye color of their sisters, relatives, cousins, how many liters they'd drunk before they were inducted into the army. From the married men they would extract the secrets of their first married night. Could anything be more intimate, more terrifying, than one's first night of marriage? But now Ostapenkov sensed that yes, there could be, and the thought astonished him.

"Hey, Dulya, just watch out," Ostapenkov said, shuffling the cards. He'd lost this time.

"Should we let him sit down?" Ivanov asked. "You're tired, aren't you? Want to sit down?"

Dulya nodded his head uncertainly.

Ivanov sighed. "Well, keep standing then."

When they heard the joke, Udmurt, Sanko, and the other soldiers burst out laughing. Ostapenkov didn't. The kid's stubbornness was beginning to annoy him.

The game continued.

The stove sang its endless hymns of fire. Rain was beating on the tent. Outside it was winter, snowless, muddy, wet, with cold fogs in the morning and icy midday winds.

It was quiet, the war in wintertime. The regiment rarely went out on operations. Tanks got bogged down on the steppes, not to speak of wheeled vehicles. Even the rebels preferred to rest— the paths and passes through the high mountains were choked with snow.

Winter was almost peaceful, although sometimes some tireless officer or other would throw his detachment out on road patrol somewhere in the green zone, whose vast stretches of vineyards were white and impassable for the whole season. Or a mine would explode under some wheeled vehicle bringing flour or canned food to the regiment from Kabul. Which didn't compare at all to the war during the summer, when the regiment conducted one operation after another. In the summer, over every sort of terrain, in ravines, on heights that stretched into the clouds, in the desert sands, in ancient green earthen towns, in secluded *kishlaks*—everywhere was gunfire, everywhere explosions of mines and grenades, glittering bursts of tracer bullets at night, columns raising billows of dust, houses collapsing, fields of grain being trampled to the ground. The summer was hot, reeked of absinthe, and on the sides of the road lay black hulks of recently destroyed vehicles and fly-matted, swollen, foul-smelling camels with whitened eyes. The summer was hot.

But for now it was winter and the soldiers busied themselves with peaceful chores, grew fatter, ruddier, paler.

Ten minutes remained until lights out. Dulya had to say yes or no, but he remained silent. He was afraid to confess—he knew that until his very last day they would not let him have a moment's peace. He was well aware of what happens when the attention of the whole group falls on one man alone. There were a few perpetual kids in the regiment: one had tried to shoot himself, another had drunk the urine of a yellow-fever victim in order to get himself a few months in the hospital, a third had broken down, sobbing, on his first operation. They were laughingstocks, and not only to their immediate neighbors: the entirety of the group had noticed them, knew who they were. Any fledgling sparrow could accost a perpetual kid, call him names, pull his ears, kick him, or force him to sweep the barracks or clean out the latrines. Perpetual kids were always mud-caked and riddled with lice, yet they got used to their particular position, even came to see it as natural—probably had to, if they were to keep on living.

But his tongue couldn't even manage to form itself around the word "no." And if I don't say anything it will mean yes, he thought, horrified.

And then that letter. He hadn't managed to destroy it in time and Ivanov had taken it from him. She had had a bad dream and then written him that letter, which was like a prayer, with the word "God" in every sentence. The old-timers had fallen on Dulya with questions, but he remained silent.

Sometimes a comforting thought came to him: I didn't write that letter; *she* did.

The longer he stayed quiet the harder it would be to remain so, and the more horrifying it would be to say anything. It would be best not to think of anything or anyone, to remember nothing. But...

In the heavy sunlit air, flecks of down were soaring over pass-ersby, newspaper stands, cars; the down flew obliquely between houses, brushing their hot, rough stone walls with its fluffy cheeks, snagging on the jagged edges of windowsills, floating effortlessly inside through every open pane. He wanted to close the window, but she said no, leave it be, and the window stayed open, and the down flew through it into the house.

While she was making coffee in the kitchen he wandered along the bookshelves that took up two whole walls in the room; it was the library of her father, who worked as a baker at a breadmaking plant. The numerous books were all old, dog-eared, heavy, sober-looking. His eyes were caught by one with a black rose on its spine, and when he opened it he discovered that it was a collection of Chinese poetry from the Tan dynasty. He found the titles of the poems funny: "I Picture What I See from My Grass-Roofed Hut"; "I Will Arise Early"; "A Poem in Five Hundred Words About What Was in My Soul as I Traveled from the Capital to Fin-sian"; "On a Spring Night I Rejoice for the Rain." They were like the poplar-flecks that clung trustingly to the gray walls of the houses, like a little girl running off from her mother to greet strangers passing by, like a man walking down a crowded street who thinks of something funny, cannot control his lips, his eyes, his cheeks, and breaks into a smile. The poets had names that rustled, rang, and whispered: Yan Tsun, Wan Wei, Liu Yan-tsin. One was like a gentle wind or the breathing of someone asleep: Du Fu.

They read them aloud. At first they took turns, but when he did it the results were poor.

With the wine of Szechuan
I would dispel my sad thoughts—
Only I don't have a farthing
And no one will lend me one.

He read that, but it came out as flat and banal as a teenager complaining to a friend that his parents wouldn't buy him a pair of jeans or a cassette player. He felt the truth of the image and refused to read any more. Then she read, and the poems became exactly what they were meant to be: sighs, tears, spring rains, lamentations, grass, birds, mountains, towers, trees, waterfalls, snowflakes the size of mats. She began to read a poem by Du Fu, "The New Bride's Farewell":

In spring the morning glory's shoots
Are utterly fragile.
And so it is with me:
When a soldier is married in the village
It's too soon to rejoice. . . .

She suddenly fell silent, hung her head, and closed the book, which started to shake in her hands. He kissed her pale fingers, which were clutching the book's cover, and she burst into tears.

It was only July then, he still had two and a half months ahead of him, he was planning on enrolling in the institute, he wasn't really thinking about the army at all, much less the war, but she was crying and going on about how it was all so terrible, terrible. But why, why, he asked, and she answered: I don't know, stop pestering me, go away, you're keeping me from studying.

It was only July, the beginning of July; he was passing his days with his textbooks, getting ready for the entrance exams, and he saw the future clearly. They would spend five years in the auditoriums and libraries of the institute, then they'd go off to some faraway village, amid pine needles and blue-gray hills. They would have their house and garden, the garden blossoming white in the spring, and on fall mornings they would gather apples—that was it. It was true that she didn't want to live in the country, but he was determined on it. While only in his second year of high school he had read *The Life of the Archpriest Avvakum*, and from then on he had been consumed by a desire to dedicate his life to something. Just how to go about doing that he wasn't sure, and he was tormented by the thought that he would never find it, that his life would be tedious and wasted. But in his heart smoldered the sermons of that indomitable man:

> In my sadness I pondered what to do—preach the word of God or run away somewhere? Because my wife and children had bound me.
>
> And seeing my grief, my wife approached me cautiously and asked me, My lord, what is making you grieve?
>
> I told her: Wife, what should I do? There is a winter of heresy abroad—should I speak or remain silent? You have bound me!
>
> And she said: Lord have mercy! What are you saying, Petrovich? I myself have heard you read the Apostle's words: Art thou bound unto a wife? seek not to be loosed. Art thou loosed from a wife? seek not a wife. The children and I give you our blessing: dare...

And only toward the end of his school days, when he read about the Populists who had gone off to teach in the country, did he find that something.

They were still preparing for their entrance exams, but they discussed the future as if they were getting their degrees the next day or the day after. She proposed a compromise: they would work for only three years in the country, the minimum time the regulations demanded, and then come back. But the inflexible

Petrovich was whispering something else in his ear, arguing that he would have to go forever, until the grave, and live in the boondocks to educate—electrification plus television notwithstanding—the benighted people. It was for that very reason, when he thought about his future life in the country, that he fell in love with the white garden and the wooden house with its wide windows and its big stove solid as a medieval keystone.

The white specks of fluff were sailing through the windows, tumbling over one another, and ahead of him were five years of study at the institute, then a long life in the house surrounded by its white garden—but she had shut the book and was crying.

He wasn't accepted into the institute.

He flinched when he heard the sharp sound of Ostapenkov dropping his cards onto the stool.

"What then, you've swallowed your tongue?" Ostapenkov asked him through clenched teeth.

"Christ, even a goat would understand," said Sanko. "Why won't he talk? And his old lady's letter with 'God' for every other word, Christ. We should tell the zampolit and the captain."

Ostapenkov cut him off. "No, we can take care of this ourselves. He won't stay silent. We'll loosen his tongue somehow or I'll be damned."

"But even a goat would understand," Sanko retorted.

"We're not goats," answered Ostapenkov, tightening his muscles.

"Well then, that's it," the Tatar Ivanov pronounced softly and resolutely. He raised his bright round eyes and fixed them on Dulya. "We once had a Baptist on our logging team," he added. "Or maybe he was a Seventh-Day Adventist."

Udmurt started to laugh.

"In short, a true believer," Ivanov continued. "I know the kind, I've studied them. For example, you're drunk and you say to him the first thing that pops into your head, and, like a virgin before her first abortion, he—"

"Then she isn't a virgin," noted Udmurt.

"—before her first abortion, he goes pale and starts to tremble. He answers: 'Why did you say that, what makes you act this way?'"

"And then you nail him," Udmurt said.

Ivanov shrugged his shoulders in disgust. "Bah. Just get your hands dirty."

"You said facts," Ostapenkov said impatiently. "What facts?"

"Facts you shall have. Alyokha!" Ivanov shouted. "Get over here!"

One of the toreadors jumped up from his stool—a round, swarthy runt of a boy. He came up, stopped, sniffed through his snub nose, looked around with moist eyes at the old-timers, and loudly said, "Here!"

"Look at them," Ivanov prompted.

Everyone took a look at the two kids.

"So, Alyokha, how's things? How's life treating you?"

Alyokha glanced at him inquiringly and, having read something or another in his eyes, answered in an almost offhand voice:

"They fuck us, but we're becoming men!"

Everyone burst out laughing.

"All right, Alyokha, you can go," Ivanov said with a good-natured smile. "You see?" he asked his comrades.

"Sure we saw, but so what?" Sanko said.

Ivanov looked at him with a fatherly reproach.

"Long ago I noticed—I noticed from the very first—that this Dulya, this Dulyette, wasn't like the others. All the kids are like kids, but... Well, here's your first fact," he said ominously. "Who has heard Dulya swear? Who"—he raised his voice—"who remembers Dulya cursing at anyone?"

Everyone in the tent fell silent; the inquisitive were all straining toward the site of the trial. The old-timers were coming up and settling themselves, grinning, on beds and stools; even the spooners were moving in closer. The kids and sparrows were listening from a little way off, craning their necks and timidly catching one another's eyes.

"There," said Ivanov. "That was the first fact. The second. Whenever someone is hit, taught to have some brains, Dulya's eyes are like a virgin's before her first abortion—"

The door to the tent opened slightly and the orderly's head appeared. "The captain!" the wide-eyed head shouted hoarsely before disappearing again.

The toreadors picked themselves up from their stools and started rushing around the tent, using leggings to disperse the tobacco smoke. The spooners and old-timers—who by the rules could sit or lie down on their bunks fully dressed—stood up, straightened their beds, and sidled off into the corners.

"Give those back!" shouted Udmurt in a desperate whisper, and the kids raced to return the leggings, which were warm and almost dry.

The door opened and, stooping over to avoid hitting his head on the lintel, into the tent stepped the company commander, a senior lieutenant.

"Compan-ee!" the duty sergeant wildly cried out. "Attenn—"

"At ease," the senior lieutenant said, straightening up and walking into the middle of the tent. He was tall, well-built but narrow-shouldered, with dark sardonic eyes, hard thin lips, a cleft chin, a small but full mustache, and a scar running from his left ear to his Adam's apple.

He looked around, turned to the roaring stove, and shook his head.

"Damp it," he said casually. A spooner twisted shut the valve to the fuel tank.

"You've been warned already," said the commander.

A week before, the regiment had been informed that a platoon from a unit stationed near Kandahar had been burned to a crisp in its tent—the orderlies and guards had fallen asleep and burning fuel had leaked out of the stove and spread across their tent's wood-planked floor.

His eyes still on the scarlet side of the stove, the senior lieutenant asked the soldier standing behind him, "Vorontsov, what's that in your hand?"

"Nothing, comrade senior lieutenant," the soldier answered innocently. Vorontsov was Alyokha's last name.

The commander sighed. "Nothing now—but what was it before?"

"Nothing."

"Ostapenkov, come over here," the commander said in a dull voice.

Ostapenkov walked to the middle of the tent and the commander turned to face him.

"Come on, say it: 'Comrade senior lieutenant, Private First Class Ost-a-penkov at your orders.' We're not on the kolkhoz anymore, are we?"

"Comrade senior lieutenant..." Ostapenkov started to say with an abashed smile.

The commander interrupted him. "What did Vorontsov hand off to you?"

"Nothing. To me, nothing."

"To whom, then? You, Udmurt?"

"Absolutely not, sir!" Udmurt bellowed.

"Vorontsov," said the commander. "Let's just suppose I'm walking down the street in your village. Let's say I run into you, Vorontsov. You're with a girl, you're wearing a tie—"

Vorontsov grimaced. "I don't wear herrings. Christ."

"Keep your mouth shut unless you're asked something," Ivanov whispered loudly.

"So let's suppose I run into you. With a girl. No herring— you're in a denim suit. Have you saved up enough chits to get a denim suit yet?"

"No."

"How come? Everyone else has. What have you done with it all? They took it from you, hmm?"

"No, I spent it on shit," Vorontsov muttered quickly.

"Christ, shit," repeated the senior lieutenant, frowning.

"Baa... at the bakery, on jam, on, er..."

"Stop saying 'baa'—you're not in a stable," Ivanov said in another loud whisper.

"Fine. So I run into you, take off my shoes, peel off my tattered socks that haven't been washed in a year, hand them to you, and say, 'Quick, wash these and wring them dry or I'll piss on you and wring you dry.'"

Everyone burst into laughter.

"How would you answer me then? You'd pop me one between the eyes and that would be that. Right?"

"Him against you, no way," said one of the old-timers.

"So he might whistle to his little friends or pick up a sledge-hammer. Right?"

His eyes filled with devotion, Vorontsov looked at the commander and answered, "No."

The commander smiled. "Well, maybe not me—someone else. What's the difference? Maybe Stodolya, for instance. How would you answer him?"

Vorontsov glanced at Stodolya. "Him? He-he-he."

"Exactly. The same with all these other shits. Why don't you tell them all to go to hell? Whose leggings were you washing?" the commander said severely. "Tell me or you're off to the cooler."

"For what?" Vorontsov cried desperately.

"For your own good. And why does it reek of smoke in here? You, Stodolya, were you smoking or what?"

Everyone burst into laughter again—Stodolya was the one nonsmoker in the company.

"Were you?"

Stodolya shook his head.

"Not you—then who? Come on, answer me!"

Stodolya looked at him without saying anything.

"Why won't you speak?"

Everything became deathly quiet.

"I don't know. I didn't see," Stodolya answered at last in a metallic voice.

"Of course—how would you know? Your head is filled with any old nonsense, anything but duty, you don't take any notice at all of daily realities, so to speak. You're asleep on your feet.

What do I have to do, talk to each one of you in the corner? So that no one else sees, no one else hears? Is that it? Or are you going to start sending me notes? Is that the new routine? No one knows anything, no one hears anything, people are set up, no one says anything, their noses are broken, they're given black eyes, and *them*: I fell, I was walking along, I slipped, and when I woke up—a black eye! Well, one day I'll cite you all! Don't grin, Ostapenkov, you're the first one into the disciplinary battalion!" The commander fell silent and glanced at his watch. "Regimental roll call is canceled," he said.

The soldiers broke into a joyous buzz.

"The rain. And New Year's coming up. So . . . Well, is everyone more or less here? Who's on duty tonight? Topady—Topady, who will be your orderlies?"

Sergeant Topady called out three names.

"All of them new guys again. It won't do. Let's try it once more. Udmurt will go on duty, and Ivanov and Zharov. Questions?" The commander looked at his watch once more and headed toward the exit. "Lights out in half an hour. I'll come back to check, and if I find any one of you in a vertical position I'll whip him—you'll only have yourself to blame. To work, orderlies, and no more nonsense. That'll be all."

"I'm not going on guard duty," said Zharov—the pudgy soldier who sang to himself all night. He was a demob, the last of the Mohicans—all of his friends had returned to Russia a month earlier, but he had been forced to stay behind because he had had a fight with a staff officer.

The staff officer had taken to sitting in the officers' latrine at night in order to catch, through a crack in the door, glimpses of a curly-haired head that appeared fleetingly over the top of gossamer curtains in a lighted window opposite the latrine. Valya, a typist in the headquarters pool, had a rich assortment of prospects in the regiment, and the staff officer—not handsome, undersized, the worse for wear—didn't exactly shine among them. So at night he would sit in the latrine across from her window. One fateful evening the staff officer fell into a state of great excitement after he caught sight, through the gossamer curtains, of her white breasts and a bit of her stomach. He woke up in the middle of the night, tossing and turning, and couldn't manage to fall back asleep. He was tormented by those breasts with their dark nipples, that bit of white stomach. The staff officer got up, dressed, and, not knowing exactly why, went out to stand underneath Valechka's window, which as it turned out was slightly open. He opened the shutters and climbed halfway into the room, and the first thing he saw, glowing white in the darkness, was a pair of panting bodies. One of the bodies leaped up, and the staff officer fell from the windowsill, blood pouring from his nose onto his uniform. Without a word, he got up, again climbed halfway into the window, then tumbled back out along with the half-dressed soldier. They rolled around on the ground, wheezing and throwing punches. Valechka closed her window and watched them, biting her lips, and groaned in exasperation. The commander of a tank battalion, out to answer a call of nature, spotted them, and, figuring that the enemy had infiltrated the camp, raced off to the officers' quarters to sound the alarm. During the investigation, which was conducted by the chief of staff himself, the staff officer lied. He said he had seen someone trying to open the window and had caught the burglar, and so the fight had broken out. Valechka repeated over and over that she didn't know anything, that this was the first time she had laid eyes on either the soldier or the staff officer—she had been asleep, she had heard noises, shouts, gunshots. Zharov talked all manner of nonsense to save Valechka's reputation, which long before had been irretrievably lost. In the end the chief of staff put an end to the matter, brought the inquest to a close, and severely reprimanded Valechka and the staff officer. But he demoted Sergeant Zharov, threw him in the cooler for ten days, and promised him that he'd be seeing the new year in with the regiment and not back home.

"Don't be a goat, Zharov," the commander said softly. "You know I would have let you go a long time ago, but... If it was up to me you could loaf around for days on end. But high command wants to know if you're pulling your weight or just kicking pears off a tree. Judge for yourself—I can't very well lie."

"I'm not going on guard duty," the ex-sergeant repeated in an indifferent voice. He took off his belt. "Write a memo to the head of the disciplinary tribunal."

"It's not too warm in the cooler right now."

"Write it," Zharov said sullenly.

"You're beginning to annoy me."

"Write it."

"You think I won't?"

"Write it."

The commander grunted. "Fine. You still have plenty of time left to rot in the cooler," he said. "It'll weigh on my conscience." He sighed, then said, "Aminzhonov, you'll be the third. And no fooling around!" he said loudly to everyone else.

The soldiers answered him with a delighted roar, and the senior lieutenant went back out into the rain knowing that the men loved him more than ever.

The cardplayers returned to their places, struck matches, and started to smoke. Zharov undressed, lay down, and covered himself with his flannel blanket, even though lights out wasn't for another half an hour. Alyokha Vorontsov filled three battered green pots with water and placed them on the stove, which had fallen silent but was now starting to clatter again—the valve had been given a spirited twist counterclockwise.

Ivanov and Udmurt were furious; they weren't at all pleased about being assigned guard duty. Ostapenkov walked over to Alyokha Vorontsov, who was sitting next to the stove with a cellophane packet of captured tea. Sensing the worst, Alyokha stood up, a sorry grimace on his face. He prepared himself to carry out the order "Heart to arms!" This strange command never sounded strange to anyone who received it: to obey it all one had to do was stick out one's chest and take a punch on the second button down from the top of one's shirt. In the baths it was immediately obvious which kids and sparrows were the stupidest and slowest: in the middle of their chests, all black-and-blue, they bore the "Order of Fools"—bruises. Vorontsov readied himself for a blow to the heart, since after all he had blundered three times—he hadn't managed to give back the old-timers' leggings in time, he had spouted nonsense without being asked, and he had said "baa" as though he was in a stable.

But Ostapenkov put his hand on Vorontsov's shoulder and said, "Sit down, brew us some strong tea."

"Yes, sir!"

Ostapenkov fell silent, then suddenly asked him, "Listen, would you give Dulya a couple of punches?"

"Dulya?"

"Uh-huh."

"Why?"

"Because. If we really, really asked you to. An experiment."

Vorontsov blinked confusedly and muttered, "But why? There has to be a reason."

"We'll find one."

"Really? I don't know . . . If it's absolutely necessary . . ."

"It is. We'll come for you later, then," said Ostapenkov. "Make the tea and then get into bed. We'll wake you when it's time."

Ostapenkov walked back to his spot, where Ivanov, Udmurt, Sanko, a few other old-timers, and two spooners, both friends with the old-timers, were waiting.

"So where is that guy?" Ostapenkov asked.

"Not here. No doubt he ran off to drop a load," said one of the spooners.

"And who authorized him?" Ostapenkov asked. He called to the duty sergeant, who said that Boiko and Sarakyesyan had asked permission to go, but not Dulya. Ostapenkov's face contorted— what Dulya had done was in itself already unheard-of, since every kid and sparrow was required to say where and for how long he was going to be away on personal errands, which as a rule meant a trip to the latrines and nothing else. True, sparrows were allowed to visit friends from home in other units or to go to the library, but kids were free to do neither. Although a trip to the library was permitted under one condition—that the kid could recite the regulations of the guard by heart. It goes without saying that no one passed the test.

"Come on, drop it," Ivanov said. "He's no squealer. I've studied his kind, and that much is clear."

"So he'll just walk back in and not mention it," Sanko said quietly, trying to recall if he'd ever hit Dulya or merely only sworn at him.

"Let him try," Udmurt said, scratching his hairy chest.

"He just forgets that he's only a kid," Ivanov said.

Ostapenkov lit a cigarette, inhaled the smoke, and pensively twisted the spent match in his fingers.

"And if he doesn't mention it, then what?" Sanko asked.

"Drop it, guys," said the second spooner.

"He's sitting in the toilet," an old-timer proposed.

They became silent.

"How long until lights out?" asked Sanko.

Ostapenkov looked at him sullenly. "We'll tear him apart first."

Ten minutes passed, twenty, and Boiko and Sarakyesyan returned from the latrines. They hadn't seen Dulya.

"Get the shrimps and sparrows into bed," Ostapenkov said. "We'll see this thing through. Call lights out, Topady."

The Moldavian duty sergeant looked at his watch and barked, "Lights out!"

The company began to get ready for bed: the sparrows hastily, the spooners slowly, the kids with lightning speed—a thunder of boots, clanking belt buckles, and creaking mattress springs.

The old-timers and the two spooners drank their black tea, sweating and breathing noisily. With the tea they had biscuits and sugar. The biscuits smelled like mold, as did everything else in winter: tea, dried noodles, soup, powdered potatoes, bread. If you had a connection in the commissary you didn't eat bread but brought biscuits back to your mess. The bread was baked in the camp, and the loaves were dense, flat, coarse, coffee-colored, reeking of bleach, and very sour. They left everyone in an agony of heartburn that sometimes led to vomiting. The officers ate another kind of bread—wheat bread, fully risen, soft, light-colored: officers' bread. Decent flour and strong yeast rarely made it to the camp. War is war.

"No. It wouldn't do him any good," Ivanov said. "The big shots wouldn't look at him twice—a squealer and a believer at that."

"My brother was telling me," the first spooner recalled, "that someone like that turned up on his ship—my brother was in the navy—and they got him transferred to shore duty."

"That's it?"

"That's it. Believers serve—it's usually the Baptists who refuse. Easier to go to prison than carry a gun . . . the goats. Just means this guy isn't a Baptist, that's all."

"But what did we ever do to him that was so bad?" asked Sanko. "Christ, I never even touched him. Yelled at him a bit, like at the others, but what the hell, are we supposed to treat him like a lord or what? Everyone has to go through the same thing. They're lucky they never ran across Khan. Did we ever crush cigarette butts out on his heels or smash in his teeth? Do you remember when Khan tied up that gypsy and had everyone spit in his face?"

"Nearly drowned him. That gypsy's probably hitting our columns now, the son of a bitch. We have to get him," said one of the old-timers.

"Khan's also hitting now—a piss pot somewhere around Vorkuta."

"We should catch that damn gypsy."

"Most likely he's swilling whiskey in Chicago."

Sanko stood up, yawned loudly, and said, "Well then."

Ostapenkov cut him off. "Where you off to?"

"Bed. I haven't been sleeping too well," Sanko answered, sitting down on his bunk.

"You can catch up in the train on the way to see Khan in Vorkuta. You'll sleep soundly enough," Udmurt laughed.

"Let's go find him," said Ostapenkov.

"This rain," the second spooner muttered dejectedly.

Ostapenkov turned to face him. "I didn't quite catch what business you had here."

"We're, uh . . ." The spooner smiled weakly.

"Let's get to bed, Seryoga," the first spooner said to him. Both of them moved off, smiling wanly.

"I don't think he ran off specifically to spill the beans, either," said Ostapenkov.

"Which means . . ."

"One of two things. He's with some friend from home, or he's skulking around the regimental CP."

"I'm going to tear that sneak in half, I'm—" Udmurt stopped cold. "Did you hear that?"

There was the sound of another explosion, followed moments later by yet another. The soldiers went out into the street, into the rain and darkness.

"Mortars," a guard said. "They're hitting the first battery."

At the edge of the camp flames were blazing in the pitch black and dull thumps were reverberating—the battery responding with howitzers.

"Let's just hope there's no alert," said Sanko.

More shells burst, and a chorus of howitzers answered them: Boom! Boom! B-B-Boom! Strings of tracer bullets rose red at the edge of the camp, intersecting before fading away into the darkness. The rattle of automatic rifles could barely be distinguished from the incessant spatter of rain on the roof of the mushroom tent. Shells started bursting more rapidly, and then the heavy machine guns and rapid-firing grenade launchers opened up. The rain was pounding, the howitzers hammering "Boom! Boom!" The night exploded with a meaty crackle, scattering flames in every direction.

The old-timers went back into the tent and stood around the stove, smoking, silent. The probability of an alert weighed on them. They didn't want to fight in a winter rain at night, they just wanted to lie down under their blankets, to hell with everything, and plunge themselves into dreams of home.

"Shit," Sanko said in a strange thin voice.

"What?" Ostapenkov asked him sharply.

"What, what! Fuck him, let him cart an icon around on his gut if he wants to!"

"Oh yeah?" Ostapenkov's eyes narrowed. "And what if we have to fight with him tomorrow? And attack? Hmm?"

"That's right," agreed Ivanov.

"He'll run away for sure," Ostapenkov continued. "He'll throw down his gun, turn tail, and they'll jam a barrel rod through your eye while he snivels and saves his own ass. These Baptists and Adventists . . . they should all be sent to the North Pole so we don't have to breathe their stinking incense. Motherfuckers! Motherfuckers!"

"I know his kind. And I've been keeping my eye on that pisser for a long time," said Ivanov. "The way he looked at that prisoner . . ."

"He wants to stay clean! But no way!" Ostapenkov clenched his fist. "No way—better he hang himself right now. Either he's a hundred percent recon or he gets the hell out. In a recon company there's no place for angels."

"Ostap." All of a sudden a sarcastic voice was heard off to one side. "Hey, Ostap."

Ostapenkov whirled around, startled. The ex-sergeant Zharov was looking at him from between the bars of his bunk bed. He was lying under the covers, his hands clasped behind his head.

"Don't be scared, it's only me."

"Me, scared? What, of you?" With an effort of will Ostapenkov tried to relax the muscles in his face, but the smile came out strained—cheeks twitching, lips quivering, eyebrows in motion—and his face hardened again almost instantly.

"Maybe right now you're not scared of me," Zharov said in a conciliatory voice.

"I've never been afraid of you."

"That's how it seems to you now. You're fooling yourself. From time to time I used to fool myself that I wasn't afraid of Khan. But I was scared of him, even though we were called up at the same time." Zharov picked up a pack of cigarettes from a stool, drew one, lit it. "I watched you there, taking that kid apart, and . . . Ostap, you mind if I tell you something?"

"No."

"You'll be sorry. Later."

"Me?" Ostapenkov laughed.

The door creaked. Everyone turned to look and saw, in the entrance, a man with a darkened face. He stood in the doorway, dripping water, and behind him was the rustling, pounding, churning night. The guard shoved him in the back and closed the door from the outside. Stodolya said nothing. Everyone was looking at him, at his soaked and drooping trench coat, at his old, long since worn-out cap with its scorched earflaps, at his huge, tattered, mud-stained leather boots, at his dark blue lips, his sharp wet nose, his sunken eyes.

"Get over there by the stove," said Udmurt.

Ostapenkov glanced at Udmurt, then again fixed his eyes on Stodolya. "Ah," he said in a hoarse voice, "an apparition. . . ."

Stodolya remained silent.

"Where have you been?" Ostapenkov asked him.

Stodolya raised his eyes, moved his lips.

"What? I couldn't hear you!"

"I believe in God," Stodolya repeated.

 THE BELLES

THEY BROUGHT US TO THE STEPPES; WE SAW TENTS, GRAY expanses, mountains on the horizon, and we came to live here: eating, sleeping, marching, falling ill with hepatitis and typhus, cleaning gun barrels, obeying officers, feeding fleas. We became tanned, thin, we made friends, we stopped waking up at night when the forward posts opened fire on positions. We learned to smoke hash, to look doomed prisoners calmly in the eye, to not think of the future, to write dispassionate letters home.

There was a first day and a second, a twentieth, a sixtieth. The sun would float in the sky, the sky bright, the sun burning hot. We hated the sun: on operations, when the battery remained among the red sand dunes for days on end, the men from Vologda and Archangel got bloody noses.

It seemed that there was no time, only eternity. But when someone was carried to a helicopter under a sheet we would convince ourselves that time still existed for us, that eternity was that stretcher sailing off forever. And we would think: allow us to return for one moment to our villages and cities, and then let it happen—let them send us to eternity then, if it's so necessary. But most would leave straight from here, from these steppes, mountains, and deserts, and they would leave blackened, their shirts in tatters, barefoot.

Time passed, but slowly.

It was the hundredth day. In the sky steel lizards were flying around with metallic fruit in their claws. The sun was sucking the last drop of sweat from every pore, there was no water in the canteens, the water truck had slipped into a ravine, dust lay in the riverbeds. A parched, parched land. Then the speckled lizards would appear, the ripe fruit start to burst and slice to pieces the hides of pack camels, donkeys, and men: donkeys, men, and pack camels would bellow and the parched land would be irrigated, flooded. But the sun drank it all up immediately, and only rusty husks remained.

This is why, toward evening, that great yellow star grew heavy, sticky, troubled, and brown.

Time passed. It was the three hundredth day; there still remained days and days, nights and nights, and sometimes I could see a little hill with a row of spruce trees, a church, gardens, peasant huts—I could see The Belles.

The Belles, not The Bells. On the steppes I savored the melodiousness of this mistake, which is precisely what the peasants called and still call the village.

In The Belles there is a church with a tall steeple; there are neither icons nor windows in the church, birches and maples grow in the cupola, and the bell tower has no bell.

Up in the loft, poring over my books, I could cast my eyes out the dormer window and see the church, missing its cross but with its thin small spruces and its maple tree. People had knocked down the crosses, smashed every piece of glass, torn out its window frames and doors, and would have taken the bricks too, had even chiseled away at its walls, but they had given up—church masonry is solid. But trees don't give up, weeds and trees do their work, they scratch away at the cupola and the walls, day and night they grow and, working their fingers, make the cracks and chinks larger, and in winter every fissure and wrinkle is filled with ice and covered with snow: spring comes, and during the day the ice melts but at night it freezes—nature labors tirelessly, building itself and beginning to destroy every work of human hands as soon as men stop working.

In autumn the little trees on the church were yellow, the maple crimson. From the loft window, before which stood a table with books, ashtrays, and a jar of kavas, I watched the church being devoured by nature, and it was easy for me to imagine it as a sort of Angkor Wat abandoned by the people because a flood had turned all the surrounding fields into a swamp and famine had broken out—like that royal city of the medieval Cambodian empire and its squares, temples, marketplaces, palaces, and colonnades punished by nature's right hand. Into the city stole the first wild shoots, loosening, gnawing at everything, and then the jungles rushed in, and engulfed Angkor Wat, the glory of Indochina.

I come to the little hill with its spruces and gardens and I drink water from the well, and no one sees me because everyone thinks I'm in the East, and they write letters to me there.

I meet the old man on the little hill and say: I'm back now, let's go home and have some tea. But he doesn't hear me.

The old man is a great lover of tea; he had developed a taste for it at the front, although people in Russian villages don't think much of the drink and instead make do with milk and kissel, which is more nourishing, more filling.

The old man made the tea expertly, and we sat over it for a long time, and I helped steer him toward his favorite theme, and he told me the usual mystic, eerie tale. How he went into the yard to do his business at the most dangerous and unpleasant hour, at midnight, how he went out and saw the straw roof of the cowshed moving, splitting open, and a pair of legs appearing. . . .

I tell him: Grandfather, it's me, I've come back, let's go into the house, you'll play and sing. He doesn't hear; he's looking elsewhere.

It's true that the old man doesn't really know how to play, but there's an accordion in the house and, spurred on by wine, he picks it up, draws strange melodies from it, and sings old convict songs: "And across the mute mysterious taiga, the far Siberian lands, the tramp escaped from Sakhalin, along a narrow animal path . . ."

*   *   *

And then I slowly soar into the house, alone, and for fear of seeing them all at once I climb up to the loft, where there is a chest, old-fashioned, girded in iron around its corners. In it are all sorts of things: old, empty purses, glass beads, crumbling magazines about beekeeping, some handkerchiefs and rags, a few heavy church books. Before the war these books hadn't interested me much, for some reason. . . .

The loft was my office, where I could read in peace or write long letters to friends, or to a hermit philosopher in the Baikal. The old man had written to me in the army to say that he had built me a studio out of logs near the bathhouse, and it made me sad to think that I wouldn't have to climb up to the loft for solitude anymore, although it was possible to sit there only in the autumn or on rainy summer days—if the summer was hot the loft turned into an oven, a desert, like the copper bull in which, according to Gogol, in old days the Poles used to put refractory Cossacks.

I could see a lot from the loft: churches, the street—long ago it was the same Old Smolensk Road that the French had followed, pillaging villages on the way, to Moscow, with bands coming out of the forests to spear them with pitchforks and hack at them with axes. I could also see the spruces near the school—seven or eight spruces, tall and dark, over which the autumn sky was often incredibly brilliant, and looking at their tops against the brilliant sky I would vividly recall the Baikal, where I had met a woman from The Belles. I had managed to see a few things before the war, and it was easier for me than for those who hadn't.

I could see all that and the birch forest too. The view from the window was limited and blocked by bushes. But from the studio next to the bathhouse I could barely see any of it. Just the garden.

But that was beautiful too.

I remember the garden glowing under the autumn moon.

All day long under the yellow lime trees—and above them, in the bluest of skies, the falling sun was burning and blazing—the old man and I had been splitting birch wood. There were also pieces of aspen branches that the old man was cracking with a sharp hatchet while I shattered birch logs with a heavy maul—the birch was dense and knotted. We finished toward evening and went into the house, where our labors were rewarded with drink. And the old man picked up his accordion to sing: "And across the mute mysterious taiga..." But I went outside to smoke.

I walked by the still-flowering cosmos and phloxes; from the autumn flowers wafted a faint draft, a thin, barely perceptible aroma. I circled around the house and saw the whole garden under the moonlight. I saw the asparagus bush speckled with the quicksilver of roses; I saw innumerable dully glowing apples throwing off a greenish light in the dark foliage.

I cast a glance at the lime trees beyond the fence, where a little pile of birch wood was burning silently and weakly. And over the bathhouse roof, with its severe black chimney, hung the Big Dipper.

I remember the garden in spring.

I got up before dawn; brewing tea, I rattled a spoon, dropped a saucer, and woke up the woman, who came out of our room, frowning angrily, and said that I was going to rouse the whole house because of my idiotic fishing; I offered her tea but she refused and, yawning, left. I drank my tea, grabbed my cigarettes and a piece of bread, slipped out into the hallway, found a fishing pole and a jar of worms, quietly opened the door, and carefully descended the front steps, which didn't creak at all. In the garden I saw the mist, and, in the mist apple, and cherry trees in bloom. The branches and tree trunks were dark, the mist gray, the flowers white. The soft, tilled earth in the vegetable garden was black; the seeds had already taken and little green shoots were coming up here and there.

I stood in the middle of the hazy early-spring garden with my fishing pole, and all of a sudden it struck me as, yes, idiotic.... I put the pole down on the grass, went up to the window behind which the woman was sleeping on a couch, and drummed my fingers on the windowpane. The house was divided into three rooms by thin plywood partitions, and I was afraid that everyone would hear me and, deciding that some pilgrim had appeared—there are still pilgrims wandering around Old Russia, and more than one tattered old man or wrinkled old woman had been by the house at The Belles before, with no family, no roots, no identity card, to spend the night and in the morning get some bread and treacle for the road—they would think that one of these visitors had knocked, and they would all come out to greet him. But the curtains parted and I saw the pale smear of a face framed in tousled hair and the woman's slightly startled eyes. I raised a finger to my mouth and with a nod of my head indicated that she should come outside. She nodded her head to say: Why? With a movement of my head I answered: Because. She shook her head and mouthed: No. The curtains drew closed and I leaned back against the wall of the house, lit a cigarette, and began to wait.

In the village the first roosters crowed hesitantly.

The cigarette went out and I tried to strike a match so that the woman—if she was still on the couch—would hear and would know that I was waiting. The match cracked perfectly; the woman must have heard it.

The soil under the apple trees near the bathhouse hadn't been turned, and it had been left unplanted so that there would be grass to feed the rabbits near at hand. Right there. And I was wearing a thick new down coat.

I reached for a second cigarette.

Under the apple trees by the bathhouse. In the mist.

The roosters sensed that dawn was breaking in the east and started calling out. The mist grew thicker. Someone passed by in the street; at first I only heard the footsteps, then I made out a dark figure, though of a man or a woman I couldn't tell. Probably a woman, a milkmaid.

I let the figure walk by—there was so much mist in the garden that no one could see a thing.

But then the mist suddenly took on colors and started thinning, dissipating; birds burst into song, dogs began to bark, buckets clanged at the well, a tractor started up somewhere nearby, and rays of sunlight fell on the village and hung in the garden among the dark and flower-dappled trees. The door creaked, the front steps creaked. I was getting cold. I peered from behind a corner of the house, and saw, yawning, scratching himself, unshaven, heavy, the old man in his undershirt and wide blue shorts.

Winters are terrible in the hot, dusty East. When I went into the army I thought I would be living in perpetual warmth. Sure, of course there would be changes of seasons: scorching summer, hot autumn, and a soft winter of warm rains. And the first winter there wasn't much snow, it all melted during the day, and on the European new year it teemed with rain, not a warm rain, true, and cold mists rose on the steppes from morning until midday. But the second winter was harsh: snow, bitter cold, wind—it was best not to climb up onto the freezing metal of a self-propelled gun without gloves. On operations we were issued felt-lined boots with rubber soles, down-filled pants, and a few trench coats per team that we would use to cover ourselves with at night in the self-propelled gun in the icy desert or in the pale mountains under the stars. Our faces were blackened by the winter mountain sun and the freezing desert winds.

Our weatherproof tent was heated by two little stoves. It was warm when the stoves were running on heating fuel, but after a platoon in another regiment was burned to death in its tent we were forbidden to use liquid fuel anymore. They brought us coal, but not much, and for coal kindling wood was needed. Empty ammo boxes would do the trick, but then first one stool disappeared, then another, and soon the only things you could sit on in the tent were bunks. The officers chewed us out, but not harshly. The stoves didn't work well and in the morning our clothes and hair would have turned gray with frost. And when I was drying my leggings by the stove at night or lying under my two damp blankets and listening to the whistle of the wind off the steppes, I would start to think about the winters at The Belles.

In winter the house at The Belles would become the House.

The garden was bare and black and choked with snowdrifts, snowdrifts everywhere, and the fields glistened in the sunlight, and the only way one could make it to the birch forest was on skis, and the river flowed soundlessly under solid ice and snow—as though there had never been a river there, as though its swimming holes and their yellow and white water lilies, multicolored dragonflies, and singing frogs had been nothing more than a dream. Wolves would howl in the fields at night.

The first to get up was the old man's wife. She would light the large burner in the stove and use the stove fork to put cast-iron pots of potatoes and beetroots on the flame; then she would go into the big room to light the firewood that had been drying overnight in the smaller, unpainted, ceramic-covered stove. If the temperature hadn't risen above thirty below during the night, the house would get cold: you crossed the naked floorboards barefoot and even the sweetest drowsiness vanished as if by magic. And there, in the stove's smaller chamber, the logs of birch and aspen started blazing and collapsing with a groan. All that could be seen from the couch was the stove's reflection in the enormous mirror over the brown cupboard; waking up, I watched the glowing, burning-hot rays crossing each other in the cold depth of the mirror. And in the darkness I saw the cheap icon with its kerchief and paper flowers, and the sleeping woman beside me.

Smoke was wafting gently from the stove, and with the smoke came heat as well, and soon the air in the house became acrid, hot, and damp, and one had to throw off one's bedcovers.

The copper pendulum of the heavy wooden clock on the wall was swaying back and forth. It was morning, but outside it was still pitch-black: the stars were shining, the plaster on the house was cracking, and occasional straining sounds reached up from the river—the ice was splitting in the cold.

But to leave the odorous house for the nocturnal morning, to wash one's overheated face in the icy darkness, was a joy. And afterward to wait the whole incandescent day for the return to the house, with its stoves, soft felt boots, the anticipation of evening tea and long conversations with the old man. Comfortable, lazy winters.

And the voluptuousness of spring. And the June storms, the abundant roses of July, the blue of August. And the time of autumn labors and feasts, when the forest turns yellower and yellower with every passing day, the little maple on the church cupola is drowned in ocher, the rye and wheat are being harvested in the fields, the peasant women are bundling sheafs of flax, the days are very hot, the nights already cold, and luminaries tumble, raising dust, from the vault of the heavens. . . .

Standing on stepladders and stools, the woman, the old man, and the old man's wife are picking apples from the branches, and I am lugging full willow baskets into the hall, carefully tipping them on their sides, and with a thud the apples spill out onto old tablecloths. We have taken care of the apples in one day, the apple trees are empty and light, all but for the antonovkas, whose time has not yet come.

Preserves and jam are being made, golden juice is slowly streaming from the wooden press, and I am already sick of apples, and the woman is sick too. But she, it seems, not from the apples.

So, finished. For his labors the old man demands wine. I demand it too, but without speaking. The old man's wife fetches a clay jug from the cellar.

Now we break our backs for the potatoes. We go to the field armed with pitchforks. The old man and I dig them up; the women squat down and pick the lumpy tubers from the earth. Here a day is not enough. In the evening we will load the dry potatoes into sacks, carry them down into the basement, and empty them out. At dinner I sit like a wooden statue. The women reward us with potatoes and creamed mushrooms and pancakes.

But then we have emptied the very last sack, and a little while later we have burned the leafy tops—throughout the whole countryside, the whole land from the Baltics to the Urals, little wisps of aromatic smoke are rising.

The days are becoming shorter, the sun colder, the skies clearer. And the radio is threatening rain. The kitchen garden should be turned for winter before the bad weather sets in. The old man says that we'll make it, but we don't, and under low drizzling gray clouds we are bent over, our clothes soaked with sweat and moisture, our faces warm and cold at the same time. The earth fills with weight and sticks to our shovels, and soon enough a real rain is beating against our oilskins and old felt caps.

But that's it. The house is ready for the siege: its belly is packed with potatoes, the larder has been stuffed with barrels of pickled cabbage, mushrooms, and cucumbers in brine, and the barrels reek of garlic, dill, and currant leaf; the shelves are crowded with jars of preserved fruit and jams; there are stacks of firewood under the lime trees, and on the wall behind the stove are bunches of dark red and golden onions; the storm windows have been put up, and between the panes are wadding and glossy scarlet pods of native pepper—looking at them makes one long for Christmas. The hay loft is piled to overflowing.

"Well then," the old man says, rubbing his callused hands. "Eh?"

His wife is content and without any extra talk she puts a jug on the table, then another. My woman hardly eats anything; her face is pale and her eyes sickly. The old man asks me:

"Have you been baptized?"

I answer no.

"That's bad," the old man says. "You should be baptized, going off to the army. Soon there will be—" The old man pauses. "There will be someone else." He looks at my woman. "You and the newcomer"—my woman blushes—"will be baptized together. All right?"

In the evening I sit in the loft with a lamp in front of the black window, smoking Grodno cigarettes and writing long letters to friends and to the hermit philosopher who lives among pine trees and rock outcroppings on the shores of Lake Baikal. Rain against the roof.

It rains and rains.

I walk up the softened path, a new willow basket on my back, through the garden. I pass through the gate, cross the potato field, open the barn door, fill the basket with hay, throw the cord across my shoulder, wind the end around my hand, haul the hay-filled basket toward the house, and look at my tracks—black smudges against white. Snow has fallen during the night.

I don't go in to the cow—she doesn't like me, menaces me with her horns, looks darkly at me. I call the old man, who pours the hay into her manger. The cow breathes and ruminates; she has long eyelashes and is called Marta; she is red.

The woman is a redhead too, and her breasts are heavy and her belly enormous. Time passes, and one day a nursling appears, who screams, dribbles, burps milk, sleeps, wakes up, and suckles and suckles. There are diapers everywhere, rose-colored diapers strung up across the wintry garden too. The woman lubricates her swollen nipples with grease so they won't chap. The nursling suckles and suckles, dozes and suckles, and flies into a rage if a rubber pacifier is slipped into his mouth instead of live, soft, warm flesh.

A young man, bearded, fresh, overserious, arrives on a white crisp sunny Sunday. From his briefcase he pulls a vial of holy water, a brush, a cross, a book, a taper, and a cassock. The nursling listens attentively to Father Alexander, looks at the flame on the taper, and shoves his hand into his mouth.

After having read the appropriate prayers and sprinkled me and the baby with holy water, Father Alexander smiles shyly and puts the cross on the baby, and then on me.

The baptism ends with a meal. The old man insists: a little vodka, Father Alexander, a little vodka; Father Alexander says no, no, but the old man presses him and Father Alexander takes a little sip. On the other hand he eats well and gladly accepts the old man's tea....

*   *   *

I dream of the old man and Father Alexander, and I dream of the red-colored Marta chasing the chubby naked nursling around the garden, she catches him, rolls over on her side and exposes her udder like a dog, closes her eyes. . . . In the weatherproof tent, in a self-propelled gun amid pale icy mountains, in the shadow of reddish rocks, I dreamed of a low hill and a row of spruces. The days went by, it was the seven hundredth day, and more and more days, and finally I dreamed my last dream of The Belles.

Speckled helicopters were flying around in the sky, the tank treads were crunching, and from time to time a spurt of smoke, sand, metal, and shreds of leather, clothing, and rubber would rise up into the air; a helicopter would land and soldiers would run toward it dragging a tarpaulin. We were creeping into a mountain range that stretched toward Pakistan, and over and over again we would come to a halt and dig trenches. The earth would drum under our pickaxes and shovels, with the sun scorching, flies clouding, taut red blisters bursting in our palms. Once the guns were in place we would open fire into the mountains and inhale dust and gunpowder. Before morning came we would break everything down and move somewhere else. Helicopters were continually evacuating soldiers with torn pants and wet, sticky shirts. Two years of life on the steppes and in the mountains lay behind us. We seemed to have been forgotten; we wandered through the ravines and plateaus gouging out trenches, drinking raw water from canals and streams, sluicing the rocks with our diarrhea.

We were sitting around smoking and watching a turtle. The sergeant was tapping it with a hammer. He was hitting it harder and harder. Suddenly the battalion commander ran up and shouted: Pack it up, battery! Back to camp! And the sergeant swung, struck, and the turtle's armor burst and spattered our boots.

Darkness fell. We were ready, the second battery was ready, as were the infantry battalion, the tank crews, and the mortar batteries—everyone was ready, everyone was waiting. Plump stars hung over the mountain peaks, and then the start commands rang out, and engines roared to life, the column shook, creaked, and ground stones under its treads.

No one slept. The column was running with its lights out. The peaks stood black and massive, and the column slowly wound its way through rocky pads, under granite faces, the length of long, tense tails.

For two or three hours the column headed toward the mountains.

Day broke.

I was sitting behind the heavy machine gun, leaning against the top of a hatch, staring at the now-colorless stars, at the grayish crags and peaks, staring in a daze, eyes wide, shaking my head, mouth open, and the stars were bursting like blisters, a crowbar struck the armor of a gigantic turtle, the blisters burst, and suddenly a breach lit up. I squeezed through with difficulty, getting myself dirty, and the old man saw me on the white road and ran, barefoot through the snow, past the lime trees, past the well, along the spruces, and vanished into the church; he ran into the church, and in its empty windows a copper light flared up, and a pealing of bells illuminated the peasant huts and my muddy face; I trembled, stooped over, sank down, and fell to my knees in the snowy earth.

THE SNOW-COVERED HOUSE

It WAS AUTUMN, AND MISTS ENVELOPED THE GARDEN IN THE morning, it rained, the birds were silent. People, the trees, the dogs, and the mute birds were waiting—the first snow was due to fall any day. And a woman was waiting for a man.

The woman lived in an orange-roofed wooden house surrounded by a bare, gnarled, fluttering garden. The house with the orange roof stood among other wooden and brick one-story houses on the outskirts of a city of steel and concrete. From a window in the house one could see the onion dome of the old Church of St. John Chrysostom, which, framed by the black branches of the lime tree, was a pleasant sight. But she only rarely and by chance looked out through this window; more often, and more purposefully, she would sit by the opposite window, the southeast window. From this window one could watch the street down which the man would be coming home from the war in the East.

The house had two rooms, wallpapered green, a kitchen, and a white stove. On a wall in the hallway hung a reproduction of Van Gogh's *Red Grapevines in Arles*—women were picking grapes amid crimson shrubs, a man was walking down a road as translucent as a river, and behind him the sun was burning low over the earth. The painting—those terrible crimson smears and that black silhouette on the road—frightened the woman. The woman would try not to look at the painting, but the painting compelled her to look at it, and when she did her arms and legs turned into cotton wool. She would have been happy to take it down and

95

hide it away somewhere, but it was the man's favorite painting and for some reason she was afraid to remove it. Nor for two years had she washed the shirt the man used to wear before the war. All in all she had become superstitious in these two years. She would think to herself that she was superstitious, a silly fool, and smile wryly, but she prayed anyway. At school she led the children in discussions about atheism, but at home, staring off to the east, she would whisper a prayer she had made up herself: "God-God-God, beloved and dear, gentle and tender, I love you and I implore you, God-God-God." She couldn't imagine what would happen if a student or a fellow teacher overheard her prayer. When she thought about it she went pale and broke out into scarlet spots. She knew that there is no God, that there are all sorts of chemical processes, evolutions, and a few strange things that science hasn't explained yet, although eventually it would. And she was sure that no one, no benevolent God, heard her prayer, that her prayer wouldn't save her man at war in the East—while she was whispering by the southeast window the telegram would have already arrived at the war registry, they would already have sent her a notice to come to the war registry so they could solemnly inform her: "Your husband . . ." They would already have loaded the metallic box into an airplane, and the airplane would already be droning in the skies over Russia. She understood everything clearly. But one time she had woken up and whispered through her tears: "God-God-God, I love you and implore you." And from then on it had become a habit.

A short note had come. The man had written that this would be his last letter—soon a helicopter would fly into camp and take them away, though just now the weather was too bad for flying, but soon.

It was late in the autumn and the icy mists smelled of snow.

The woman would awaken very early, and get up to do her hair. After her bath and breakfast she would sit down in front of her mirror, her tubes, little boxes, combs, and perfume bottles laid out on her little table, and start to primp and arrange her light-colored and neither very thick nor long hair. The scruffy gray cat would stretch, come over to her, arch its tail, and purr deeply while rubbing itself against her legs, and its fur against her legs would raise goosebumps.

She usually gathered her hair in a bun at the back and fastened it with a rubber band, but recently she had been going off to school with intricate crowns and waves on her head, and the male teachers were saying about her—aha—and taking a second look, and they realized that she was very young, that her cheeks were white, her lips the color of roses, that she had beautiful calves and arms, and when she walked . . . it was best not to look at her too long from behind when she walked. And they remembered that her husband was serving in the army somewhere.

She had been an ordinary young woman, like hundreds and thousands of others, but when her man was about due to come home she suddenly changed—and the bald Boris Savelyevich, the Russian teacher, stared after her in astonishment, his mouth went dry, and wild thoughts rushed by in his head like heavy freight trains. And the athletics instructor, a man of deeds and not dreams, flirted with her during recess and asked if he couldn't come split her wood for her. And yes, the boys of course goggled their eyes at her, mechanically tugging on their sparse little mustaches, picking at the pimples on their foreheads, and drawing in their imaginations pictures no less wild than the fantasies of Boris Savelyevich.

The women at the school were shocked and mortified. The athletics instructor, the Russian teacher, the groundskeeper, the drill instructor—all had stopped paying attention to them and, as though in the grip of some powerful elixir, were now casting voluptuous looks at that woman and making half-pleasant, half-ribald double entendres to her. But what had happened? Nothing at all. Nothing new in her clothes, no lipstick, no shadow on her eyelashes—everything the way it had been before. Only the hairstyle was different.

For her part, the headmistress had immediately formulated an explanation for the change that had occurred: a graphic expression of sexuality. That was bad—it was a pernicious influence on the moral atmosphere. Some measures had to be taken—but which measures? The graphic expression of sexuality was not prohibited by a single paragraph in the regulations. The headmistress examined her subordinate carefully but found a violation nowhere: skirt sufficiently chaste, blouse opaque, no excessive makeup. Hairstyle? The headmistress had the same one, crowns and waves too, everyone had crowns and waves and curls, so that it was in fact her former hairstyle, a simple ponytail, that had been provocative, while this one had simply joined the general chorus of hairstyles. Absolutely nothing extraordinary here...but good Lord, the way she flashed her eyes around like that—sexual, dangerously explosive!

The woman waiting for her man to come home from the East did not notice the cold scorn of the ladies at school, or the rapture of the pimpled adolescents, or the attentions of the scholastic knights—the muscled athletics instructor, the dry, wrinkled drill instructor, the bald, dreamy Boris Savelyevich, the fat, gray-haired groundskeeper with the false left eye. She was waiting.

When she came home from school she lit the stove, heated two pails of water and used one to wash the floors, wiped the furniture down with a damp cloth, and continued cleaning and scrubbing things even though the house had been sparkling for a long time now. The cat wandered after her from room to room, watching all these preparations with an air of sarcasm. In fact he looked at everything skeptically—he had intelligent eyes, his bushy light pelt bristled on his jowls like muttonchops, and he was content, sluggish, fluffy.

The woman tried not to raise her eyes to *Red Vineyards*, and she succeeded for some time, but in the end her eyes were pulled to the painting. She stared at it fixedly and told herself: What of it, then? Autumn, red leaves on the vines, women collecting grape clusters into baskets, the sun hanging in the distance, and a common tramp is marching down the road that flows like a river, he's a vagrant—the people are laboring and he's walking along, his hands thrust in his pockets, whistling, no doubt, and it's obvious that he has neither a home nor a family, and he has no idea where the road is leading—that's all. And, to be honest, it was unfathomable what the man saw in this crap. A crazy artist had put—no, thrown—paint on a canvas, and now everyone says, "Oh! Oh! Oh!" The first thing I'll do when he comes back is say I don't like this piece of crap, oh God, I'll tell him . . . God-God-God, beloved and great, good, gentle, I love you and pray to you . . .

But no, not at first, at first I didn't hate this stupid painting at all, before I had been indifferent to it, but then one autumn he wrote a letter in which he mentioned crimson grape leaves behind a shattered, shell-pocked *duval*, and—so. . . . And that tramp isn't a tramp but a messenger, and he knows where he's going. . . . What nonsense!

Later she took the second pail off the stove, fastened the door on its hook, drew the blinds, and took a bath in a large basin. After her bath she dried herself off with a long, thick, soft towel and moved from the kitchen into the bedroom, where she stopped in front of the big mirror in the corner. She looked at herself from every side, slapped her taut, still-childless stomach, and tried to see herself through the eyes of the man, who was no longer fighting the war in the East but sitting and waiting for the weather to clear so he could fly home in an airplane. He was sitting there in the East, in some weatherproofed tent with a makeshift stove, sitting there with all his suntanned, broad-shouldered, dour friends, smoking a cigarette, not saying anything, or maybe talking in his deep, slow voice . . . telling them that he had a house with an orange roof, a stove, a cat, and a wife. . . .

After eating she would sit in the southeast window correcting workbooks and preparing for the next day's lessons. She would sit with her head hunched over the table and hear, or rather sense, someone walking down the street; not moving, holding her breath, she would raise her long eyes with their short pale lashes to the window and look outside. Someone would in fact be walking down the street: a woman carrying bags, the old neighbor in his tattered winter hat, a yoke slung over his shoulder, a little boy, a drunk, a flashily dressed young woman, or just a mutt ranging around on its pressing dog business. The garden was black and bare, and rivulets of rain were coursing down the rough torsos of the apple and plum trees. Rain-rain, splish-splash-plosh-plash-plish—but the ground was already soaked through and couldn't absorb the water from the skies, and there was water in every dip and cranny, flowing in streams toward the river. Rain-rain, splish-splash, plish-plash, plish-plash. . . .

The cat was dozing on the sofa while it rained. Everything was all right with him; he didn't remember the man fighting the war in the East right now, and he wasn't waiting for anyone.

But of course he's not fighting now, no, not fighting, the woman thought, forgetting about the workbooks and tomorrow's classes, no, not fighting but sitting in his tent, and against the tent splish-splash-rain. And thinking of me and of the distant view from the roof, the prominent roof—before the war he had stained it himself in that orange color, the best in the world, the color of good luck. God! If you grant me my wish I promise never again to tell the schoolchildren that you don't exist—I can leave the school so that I'll never tell anyone you don't exist, I can go to church every day to listen to the priests sing, to light candles in front of the icons—just make it so that he comes back, I beg you.

Toward evening her ears were aching with the song of the rain, her eyes loathing the street and the passersby. She fed the cat and let it out into the street, then made a supper of tea and biscuits—she couldn't eat anything more—and after supper she bolted the door, turned out the light, undressed, and climbed into bed. She lay there breathing softly and listening. For a long time she couldn't fall asleep. She lay there and listened intently. It was awful, and her feet were freezing. The house was warm but her feet were freezing. Since the man had left for the East her feet would freeze in bed. And it felt as though the house were in the middle of a forest and someone was roaming around it, rapping his nails against the windows and scratching at the door.

Are there really women who live their whole lives without a man? she asked herself. It's awful to be alone, and your feet feel cold in bed.

The Chinese say . . . What was I thinking about? Oh, yes, yes, she remembered, about the dead boy lying with open eyes in a dark room.

A year before she had left her house in the morning and had seen a person in the ditch near the house next door; it was a fair-haired teenager with thin shoulders, long legs, and his jacket in the mud.

The world was always threatening; as soon as she had begun understanding things she perceived that, and later she knew it. The world was threatening even when the man was around—absolutely. But—he had hard shoulders, strong fists, a peaceful air, and a deep, confident voice. He stood between her and the world. But then they had sent him to the East, and the world had drawn inward and pressed in on her.

But the Chinese . . . the Chinese what? But the Chinese say yin and yang, everything that exists, yin and yang, the feminine principle and the masculine. Yang is everything powerful, bright, solar. Yin is everything weak, dim, lunar. Lord, how true. And to sleep alone, so cold, is really like having moonlight and not blood flowing inside you. . . . God-God! Bring me back my yang!

A week and a half had passed since his last letter. The woman cleaned her nest every day, and every morning decorated her hair with crowns and curls, and the school Don Juans continued to run after her like rats enchanted by the Pied Piper's magic flute. And very soon the snow would begin; the people, the dogs, the trees, and the birds were all waiting for it. And the woman in the house with the orange roof was waiting for her man. She was yin, and at night her feet were as cold as ice.

And at last, on Monday, early in the morning, flakes, shreds, and wisps began to fly, and the earth parted from the black sky and dimly started glowing. Snow.

The woman didn't have classes that day, but she got up early and saw that the sky had become unglued from the earth. She threw on a man's sheepskin coat and went out onto the doorstep. The cat, who had spent the night tooling around somewhere, sang a short hoarse song and darted into the house. The snow was falling in lumps. The lumps were flying and flying down, hanging from the branches of the apple and plum trees, plopping into puddles, sticking to the orange roof, paving the matted, heavy road, rounding off and softening the roofs and chimneys, trees, flowerbeds, stacks of firewood. The woman's heart suddenly stood still, her breathing faltered, and for a moment she sensed a terrible lightness, as though she would break away from the doorstep and soar around in the sky. It immediately passed. Her face burning, the woman went back into the house. She realized that it would be today.

The cat mewed stridently—me! meow! me!—and the woman fed it. She didn't want to eat anything; she drank cold tea and chewed on a sweet. A flame was already rising in the stove and pots of water stood on the burners. The woman turned on all the lights and carefully examined the room. She made the bed and stacked her notepads and books in a pile on the table. She washed the floor. Her face was blazing, her heart beating heavily, painfully, and her head was spinning.

"What's the matter with me?" the woman asked out loud, and thought: What's the matter with me? Not today, perhaps, what am I... tomorrow, perhaps... or in two days, three, four.

But her face was on fire, her heart was thumping as though she'd been running for miles, and from time to time her head froze and turned numb. In the street the snow was falling coarse and white. The flame was fluttering in the stove... fluttering somehow playfully, not like usual, and even the tramp in the Van Gogh painting was walking more joyfully down the liquid, translucent road, and those huge-rumped women were more cheerfully plucking clusters of grapes off the vine and putting them in large baskets. The woman took a bath and scented herself with a green-colored perfume, put on a dress, and did her hair.

It was slowly getting lighter. Too slowly. The woman had no idea what to do now. Everything was ready; the house with the orange roof was waiting for its master from the East—the doorstep was waiting, the stove was waiting, the rooms were waiting, and the French winegrowers were hurrying to gather every cluster before his arrival.

Day broke. The snow was still falling. The earth was white and soft, the roofs were soft and white, as were the apple and plum branches and the rounded hills and tiny little houses and small gardens beyond the river, and the cupola of the Church of St. John Chrysostom, but the fences and walls stuck out a mournful black.

The woman wandered around the house, bent down, absentmindedly petted the cat. She took some book down off the shelf, leafed through it, read a few sentences without understanding them, slammed it shut, and replaced it in the rows of books. The clock showed ten. Snow was still flying outside the windows.

Should she bake some blinis? No, the blinis would get cold, and they weren't as good reheated. Should she put on some lipstick? But he didn't like it when she wore lipstick. But suppose he liked it now? But what if he didn't? The woman put some lipstick on in front of the mirror. She smiled. No, too bright. She rubbed her lips lightly with cotton wool. Now there was almost nothing.

It was snowing outside the windows.

For some reason it seemed to her that he wouldn't come right now. He wouldn't come at eleven, he wouldn't come at twelve. He would come in three hours, or six, but it couldn't be right now—it would be impossible for him to show up that early.

At twelve the snow slackened, and the air gradually lightened and became clear and frosty, although the sky was not blue but in fact had remained gray. The world was fresh and plump. . . .

The woman smiled—she had thought of some work to do. She threw off her dress, put on some woolen trousers, a sweater, and a knitted ski cap, grabbed some gloves, put on her boots, and went out into the street. Squinting from the whiteness, she plowed through the snow to the toolshed, opened the door, and brought out a wooden shovel.

She was clearing the walkway. The snow was light, but a lot of it had fallen and the woman was growing breathless and flushed. She was sweeping the walkway of snow and thinking: There, a white holiday. She was also thinking: It would be nice if he were here this minute, when my cheeks are rosy, I feel fresh, and he will find me all fresh in the middle of this fresh garden. It's just too bad that snow is pasted all over the orange roof.

But neither at that moment nor in the others she spent in the garden with the shovel did he arrive.

After clearing off the whole walkway the woman reluctantly headed into the house. At the doorstep she stopped, turned around, and inspected the garden. A blue-gray bird was sitting in the far apple tree. A few tiny, black, rotten, wrinkled apples were hanging on the far apple tree, and the bird flew up to pick at them. The woman stood motionless. The bird looked like a pigeon, only more graceful. The woman was watching the smoke-colored bird and trying to remember what it was called. The forest visitor twirled its head, stuck out its neck, and pecked at the black fruit, then looked nervously around. Nothing terrible happened, nothing was creeping toward it through the garden, and the bird was already boldly nipping at the apple, and again, and again. Then a second bird silently appeared, perched on the very same tree, and then the first let out a guttural, throaty sound and the woman remembered what the birds were called—turtledoves. And again the woman's head began to spin and her body turned weightless. Today. And perhaps now.

* * *

It was two in the afternoon. The birds had left the garden and the garden was empty. Every now and then people went by in the street: men, women, children, old people—all of them alien and hateful.

When evening set in the woman fried yesterday's potatoes on the electric burner and heated some tea. She couldn't even eat the potatoes—she tasted them and covered the pan with a lid. She drank a cup of tea and ate a bit of buttered white bread. Neither at seven at night, nor ten at night, nor one in the morning did the doorstep creak under the man's weight. The woman turned out the light, undressed, and lay down. She had kept her woolen socks on so that her feet wouldn't freeze, but her feet froze even in the thick woolen socks, her face was freezing, and rare warm drops were sliding down her cold face.

In the morning she woke up and sensed a sort of dry clarity in her soul, and she thought: Not today. And her dreams, such an odd kind of dreams, had also said: Not today. But she did her hair. She ate breakfast and fed the cat.

Then, while she was gathering her notebooks, she saw through the window that the mailwoman, in a sweater and shawl and with a satchel at her side, was walking along the fence. The mailwoman went as far as the gate, thrust newspapers and one envelope into the flat metal box, and walked off unhurriedly down the liquid and muddy road.

The mail just brought the latest newspapers, the woman thought slowly. And in the envelope is just a letter from some girlfriend, she thought, staring, in a daze, out the window at the blue mailbox.

She stood up. She went down the doorstep and walked down the path through a cold mist toward the mailbox that hung on the gate's dark crosses.

Someone simply sent me a letter. That's all. That's all there is to it, she thought drunkenly.

She drew the newspapers and the letter out of the box.

The now-gray flesh on her face broke out into wrinkles, a vein protruded on her temple, dark semicircles spread under her eyes—and with a simian face the woman unsealed the envelope.

A SPRINGTIME WALK

SOFT COUNTRY ROADS WERE CARRYING THEM UP ONTO HILL-tops, leading them down into damp depressions, and the sky was now coming nearer, now casting precipitously upward, a sky of rare clouds and larks beating their wings.

The young man in his threadbare, greasy cloth cap was riding slightly ahead; he was the guide, he'd been riding or walking these roads for several years, he knew their every twist and turn, every tree and hill along the way. He was cranking the pedals and now and again looking over his shoulder at his companion.

The soft roads were bearing them through green hills, green fields, the clouds were standing still in the sky and the sun was shining yellow. He looked at her over his shoulder, stretched his thick lips, and she smiled in response. He was thinking: It's wonderful, of course, that she's coming too, that at last she's seeing these places, it's wonderful, but it would be better if I were alone. He was used to being alone. At first it had been overwhelming, especially at night—some bird would cry out, a branch fall, footsteps rustle—but then his fear had vanished. And one day he became sure that he was better off alone: he had blabbed about the coffee ponds to a classmate, who asked to come along, and everything had turned out awful—the classmate had talked and talked, laughed loudly, greedily hauled carps out of the water, tried to hit a duck with a rock, cut down sapling aspens for no reason, and more than once had said that there was nothing to be afraid of in a forest, a forest is just a bunch of trees . . . and everything was awful, everything was wrong. Of course she wasn't the classmate. But still.

They crossed the train tracks—oil-soaked ties, the crunch of the embankment, the black caps of the railway spikes, and the narrow, shiny tracks running off into the distance—and he thought: Yes, soon. The soft country road picked them up again, and again they were emerging over the brows of hills and going down into damp, fetid defiles.

Yes, soon, he was thinking. In three days. That's all. Then two years of it. Boots, barracks. But that was nonsense—two years wasn't twenty-five years the way it had been in the old days.

And he started wondering if it had been right to bring her with him. What could they see in one day? To go everywhere—to the pines, to the red stream, to Fox Hill, to the ponds, the village—would take more than a day. But because of her they had to be back in the city by nightfall. Her parents knew nothing, they were sure that their daughter had walked to the institute in the morning and that from after lunch until evening she would be taking notes in the reading room at the library. But in her case along with her schoolbooks and notepads she had put sneakers, trousers, a T-shirt, bread, and sausage, and she had come to him, changed, and there she was, riding next to him down the soft road on a bicycle he had borrowed from a friend, laboriously cranking its pedals, not asking to stop, although she wasn't used to it and was already getting tired, smiling whenever he glanced back at her. And her T-shirt was already damp. It was morning, but the sun was hot. May.

The traveled road forked away, but they kept going straight. They rode down an overgrown, deteriorating road that soon led into a swamp.

She dutifully took her sneakers off after he did, rolled her trousers up to her knees, and gingerly sank her white feet into the cold and oily mire.

"Are there snakes here?" she asked, breathing heavily.

He was walking in front. He looked back and said:

"Snakes? I've been coming here for three years . . . and in three years I . . . not once . . ." And he fell silent; he had spotted a brownish-green rubber pretzel off to his left. A small snake was lying motionless on a dry, sunny hummock. One would have thought it was dead, but its eyes were moist and two dots of sunlight were shining in them.

He took his eyes off the hummock and calmly said:

"No. These are blessed places, I swear."

They were steaming hot, bathed in sweat, mosquitoes were attacking them, and they were slapping their faces, twitching their shoulders, and racing to make it across the swamp. The mire bubbled, sucked, and gurgled under their feet. The mud was cold, the air warm, the sun burned the clothes on their backs and shoulders.

Just like that, he was thinking, not one snake in three years, but today, on this last day . . . He turned around, cast a glance at his companion's legs. She looked at him quizzically and put on an expression of cheerfulness. Her face was wet, red, stained with bloody smudges; there was a dark crushed mosquito on her cheek.

"We'll be out of this soon," he said.

He should have come here alone. And now he was afraid that she would be bitten by a snake.

They made it across the swamp, walked for a while over hard ground through thickets of willow, and found themselves in a glade under a hillside. The clearing was yellow with flowering dandelions. Bees and bumblebees were toiling away, glassy wings were flashing everywhere over the flowers, and they could hear a quiet velvet humming. A white clay eye was visible over where the glade met the hillside and started rising smoothly. A spring was pulsating and circles were spreading out on its transparent surface.

"This is it, isn't it? The Bedouin God?" The young woman dropped her bicycle and walked to the spring. She bent down over the roiling water, froze, and glanced back helplessly at him. He came over and looked into the spring. On its slimy white bottom, slowly rotating as though performing a lazy dance, was a dead frog. He rolled up his sleeves, plunged his arm up to the elbow in the water, pulled out the frog, and tossed it into the flowers.

"One time," he said, wiping his hand on his trousers, "I found a gray bird with an eye torn out in this spring. A hawk or harrier must have just missed it."

"The Bloodthirsty God," she answered, staring at the spring in disgust.

He shrugged his shoulders and leaned down over the water. After drinking some he looked, mockingly, at his companion. She pursed her lips and turned away.

"Drink! What's the matter with you?"

"Nothing. You didn't have to tell me about that bird."

"It was a long time ago. Drink."

Her mouth was as hot and dry as the land of those Bedouins with their camels. He'd made that up himself—the God of the Bedouins. She smiled.

"Drink," he repeated.

"Drink, drink," she mimicked, then frowned, bent her head down, and stretched her lips out to the longed-for water. Afterward she looked at her feet, wiggled her muddy toes, and said: "I should wash myself off."

He pulled a small cup out of his backpack, scooped water from the spring, and poured it over her feet. She rubbed her feet and gasped from the cold. Then she quickly put on her socks and shoes and jumped around in place to warm up. Her bangs were hitting her forehead and her breasts were jiggling under her T-shirt.

He took his eyes off her, lay down in the grass, and said: "Let's rest."

She sat down a little way off.

The bumblebees were buzzing.

"But isn't this place called something? The stream is the God of the Bedouins, of course, but the clearing?"

He answered that it wasn't called anything.

"But I would have this clearing christened something. It's so nice."

"What would you have christened it?" he asked reluctantly.

"Anything . . . whatever comes to mind." She wrinkled her brows. "Bumblebee Meadow. Hmm?"

He was looking at the sky through his eyelashes and said nothing.

"Isn't that good?" she asked.

"They're everywhere here."

She didn't understand. "What?"

"Meadows. There are lots of flowery clearings around here."

"Fine, if you want to be that way, be that way," she said, turning away.

She felt hurt. He had to say something, but the sun was burning his flesh through his shirt and his tongue was thick, and his eyelids were heavy, and he didn't want to think about anything, he didn't want anything. He was lying back, silent. She was sitting and watching the striped bumblebees. The bumblebees were settling down on the dandelions gathering nectar, and roving through their stamens as though through a soft yellow forest.

Two sparkling points, brownish-green rubber pretzel, you didn't have to be here today, on this last day, and now I have to worry about you biting the girl. The snake raised its head slightly and smiled a thin smile. He shuddered, opened his eyes, and remembered that the girl was probably feeling hurt. He sat up and said: "Yes, that's it, it's fine, fine."

"What?" she asked in an indifferent voice, her eyes narrowed. She wasn't looking at him, but her eyes were filled with aloofness and disdain.

"Come on. Bumblebee Meadow."

"Ah," she responded. "Thanks for the favor."

He burst out laughing, and the girl looked at him severely. He stopped laughing.

"Sorry, but it's funny," he muttered. "What are we arguing for?"

"I have no intention to argue. As far as I can tell we have nothing to argue about. And anyway I can . . . I know the way back."

She knows that I'm wondering if it was right to bring her along on this last walk. I could have refused to, but I didn't, I wanted her to come, didn't I? So why am I being an idiot?

"Oh, come on, let's not fight. Why are we, really? Are we going to . . . what for? I just haven't had enough sleep, that's all. I feel a bit tired."

"So sleep. I won't disturb you."

"I don't want to anymore. I'm ready for anything. Shall we get going? You rested up? You're not tired, are you?" he asked her solicitously, looking her in the eyes. "Do you want some more water? Shall I bring you some? Let me get you some." He stood up, went to the stream, and brought back a cup of water. "Drink. It's good water. I've never had better. Have you?"

The girl couldn't restrain herself and burst out laughing, snorting into the cup and spraying his face.

They left the hollow and came out onto a knoll blooming with long-stemmed golden flowers. She asked what the flowers were; somehow they were very familiar to her but she couldn't remember. He didn't manage to answer; the young girl spotted something on the meadow and cried out.

Out of the copse onto the meadow—it hadn't been mowed for years and years, it was overgrown; thick wild carrots branching like pine trees, and wormwood bushes, had shot up in it—came a horse. It was stocky, brown, with bulging flanks, a tangled mane, thick legs. The horse bowed its massive head, tore up some grass, and slowly chewed while casting its eyes around. At last it spotted the human beings. The horse stopped chewing and, pricking its ears and flaring its nostrils, stared at the two figures in the midst of the golden flowers. Realizing that they weren't elks, but humans, it snorted, bared its teeth, whinnied angrily, swung around, and trotted quickly back into the birches.

"It ran away," she said softly. "But where did it come from?"

"I don't know. Maybe it escaped," he replied in a whisper, then coughed and added, out loud, "It's from some village. It didn't like something and it ran away. Maybe it didn't like pulling a cart, and ran off."

"You said there wasn't a populated village around here."

"From some far-off village. Wasn't it great?"

"Yes!"

"But there are loads of elk around here. And wild boars. One chased me once."

"A wild boar?"

"Yes. It was with its family. I walked straight into them and it charged me, and there were only bushes around, not a single tree. But apparently it wasn't really angry—it chased me away and then returned to the others."

"I can picture you running."

"I was sprinting. I knew it wasn't chasing me anymore but I kept running anyway. After that I bought a gun. From this dealer."

"So where is it?"

"Bah." He waved his hand, threw his leg over his bicycle, sat on the seat, and looked impatiently away.

The young woman was thinking how safe and nice it would be with a gun and asked him again where it was. He answered that he'd lost it, and she asked him where. He nodded his head off to the side: somewhere, over there somewhere.

They were riding down the brambled road. In the swamp, among the intertwined willow branches, the horse was standing motionless.

A bird was soaring high in the sky. It was an old brown bird of prey with a mottled, light-colored breast. It was describing circles in the thick blue between the clouds. Far below, gray, yellow, and golden patches were revolving slowly, puddles flashing out. Air currents were ruffling its feathers and washing over its hook-beaked gray head. Below was the iridescent watery earth where birds and frogs were sibilating, bees and mosquitoes droning, where everything was restless and hot. The old bird was floating in the blue between the clouds, where everything was quiet and cool.

The horse was hiding in the bushes at the edge of the swamp.

Mosquitoes and horseflies were flitting over the warm mountain of thick, sweaty flesh, and, their wings vibrating, were searching for tender spots, plunging their proboscises into the animal's flesh, sucking its blood. Flies swarmed over the suppurating wounds on its rump; the wounds were symmetrical, round, and deep. The horse stood among the bushes, narrowing its big brown eyes off to one side, pricking its ears to the sounds of the stifling spring day, striking at the blood-engorged suckers with its tail, shivering from the memory of the humans among the yellow flowers.

Deep in a swampy thicket, in the warm brown hollows between the hummocks, a herd of elk was sleeping lightly. Badgers and foxes with their whelps were dozing in their burrows on Fox Hill.

They crossed the meadow, made it over a depression that rolled into a field by pushing their bicycles beside them, climbed onto their bicycles again, and soon reached the hill. At the base of the hill they dismounted and clambered up through the grass and flowers.

The flower tips knocked against their ankles. Buzzing angrily, startled bees and bumblebees would rise up from the flowers, hover around their faces, and then reluctantly fly away.

A midday wind picked up.

The leaves on the bushes were fluttering, and the flowers and weeds bent and stood up again. The wind was drying their sweaty faces and cooling off their damp clothes. The girl's short dark hair was whipping and lashing against her forehead and cheeks.

They climbed to the summit of the hill. The girl looked around.

Below them green lagoons were boiling, and winy, violet, and lime dots and smudges glimmering. Larks were darting around in the translucent thickness of the blue sky, islands of willow and birch were floating off toward the horizon, and in the distance hung emerald hills and dark forests of pine.

A wild cherry bush was in bloom on the hill's western slope. A strong wind was blowing, and the aroma of wild cherry was barely perceptible on the summit of Fox Hill.

He took off his cloth cap, held his close-cropped knobby head into the wind, and told her that he sometimes spent the night here. The girl remained silent. He didn't say anything more, and they stood quiet, looking around from the soft, green heights of Fox Hill.

They climbed back down, and he asked where she wanted to go next: to the red stream, to the coffee ponds, or to the village? But only one of them. It was already three o'clock and they'd be getting back late no matter what. At the red stream they'd be able to swim and sunbathe. There were cranes living on the coffee ponds now, and she'd never seen a live crane before. But in the village—he was telling her about the village: oh, the village! It was joy, pure and simple. To the village, she said.

The village stood near an old birch wood. First they spotted the long, thick birches, and after they had climbed a small hill there was the village.

The village was in blossom. The gnarled cherry trees were in bloom, the apple trees, the lilac bushes. Around the izbas and in the vegetable gardens were the dull yellowish coronas of dark henbanes, the fluttering of egg-white dandelions, rosy meadowsweet, golden, pyramidical strands of flax. Purple honeysuckle cups were hanging in the stinging nettle, and their first flowers were extending their pale lips. Spreading hawthorn bushes were in bloom near the mossy, mold-covered well. Starlings and thrushes were chirruping, gray forest birds were trilling, chirping, whistling, flitting from branch to branch and littering the ground with white petals. Green moss covered the beams of the empty-windowed izbas, on whose rotted, collapsing roofs slender aspens, birches, and camomiles were sprouting. Everything smelled of flowers, greenery, rot, and mold.

"And I've fixed up a bathhouse. That's my hut over there." He looked at her expectantly. "Like it?"

"Here?" she asked, dismayed, and looked around. "Yes. Only . . ."

"What?"

"Only that . . . it's just strange. Is that smell coming from the well?"

"Yes. I get water from a stream. There's a stream in the woods."

They walked down the short village street between gray tumbledown izbas, past vegetable patches and gardens with dilapidated fences sticking up here and there from the green undergrowth.

A twisted bough hung above the door of the bathhouse hut.

"That's the Guardian," he said, and then the girl made out a crooked mouth, a few thick hairs, and an empty eye in its forehead.

The door creaked and they entered the hut. Once she was used to the dark she could see a stove, an iron bed with a torn straw-packed mattress, a table, a little glass-paned window, and just below the ceiling a shelf with a pile of candles, some matches, a packet of salt, a kettle, a cup and spoon, a pot. Everything smelled of must and stale smoke.

"It's so odd," she murmured.

"We'll make dinner outside," he said, and took the kettle and pot from the shelf.

He headed off toward the stream. The girl sat down and immediately felt worn out, exhausted. She didn't want to eat, but to lie down and stretch out her heavy, swollen feet. She lay back and fell into a doze.

When she went out he was already building a fire. He struck a match and lit the kindling; the flame licked the dry twigs and a moment later burst up and started to flicker against the bottom of the kettle and the water-filled pot.

"Do you come here in the winter too?" she asked, squatting down in front of the fire.

He nodded.

"It's odd here," she said. "Nice, but odd somehow. How did you find all this?"

"I was riding around looking for mushrooms and came across the ponds. Probably carps there, I thought. . . . I came back with my fishing gear. There were carps, sure enough. And there you are."

"But how did you lose the gun? It doesn't feel right without a gun. Wolves and everything. And people could . . . Some fugitive. Huh? Do people come here often?"

"No, the swamp keeps them away. But sometimes a fisherman might. And in the winter hunters on skis come after rabbits."

"The winter, sure, that must be great. A blizzard, wolves, and you stoking a fire."

The water in the pot came to a boil. He wanted to toss in the groats but the girl asked if she could do it all, and he handed her the salt, the spoon with wire around its handle, the bag of groats, and the can of stewed meat. She poured three handfuls of groats and a pinch of salt into the boiling water and, her face turned away from the hot embers, began to stir the mixture with the wire-handled spoon. He was sitting across from her, looking at the fire and thinking: In three days now, and then for two years. But that's okay, it's not twenty-five years. And there's no war. Two years, it's nothing.

The groats swelled and turned white. The girl shook the stewed meat out of the can into the pot and mixed the rose-colored lumps in with the kasha. She took the pot and the kettle off the crane and poured tea leaves into the kettle. She wiped off her flush moist face and looked at him: I'm doing this pretty well, aren't I?

They ate in the hut, in front of the little window. They ate their smoky-tasting kasha and soft black bread in silence, looking out the little window. Then they drank the tea. The girl was wondering if it was really true that the city existed somewhere, if it was really true that they'd only left it that morning.

A sharp, crisp, angry shriek echoed from the street. The girl choked, started coughing, and shot a frightened glance at the hut's master.

"It's a peregrine. It lives in the wood. A rare bird."

119

The girl nodded. But fright remained in her eyes. After a few moments she said, "But still, the gun... with a gun... how on earth did it happen?"

The single-barreled sixteen-gauge was lying under a thick layer of silt at the bottom of one of the seven coffee ponds. But he answered anyway:

"I lost it."

"Are you lying?"

"No."

"You're lying," she said. "It's so obvious. You're better off never lying. Anyone could tell straight off."

"Why are you so interested in that gun?"

"No reason. Just that it would be better to have it."

"Not better. That I know.... I threw it in the water."

"You did?"

"What are you looking at me like that for? Who cares? It was my gun, I bought it, and shells too, from a dealer, and then I decided to throw it in the water."

"Why?"

"I was tired of it. Even a branch shoots out once a year. A gun much more. Even if you don't want to shoot anyone."

They fell silent. The girl sighed.

"You feel bad about that?" he asked sarcastically.

"Aha," she replied. "In three days you'll be in the army and they won't give you just a gun there, but grenades and a machine gun."

"Oh, so it's about that."

"I'm smart. Aren't I?"

"You sure are. They will, but so what? Three times on a firing range and that's it. Someone I know came back from the army and said that in two years he'd been on a firing range three times, and that was it. Shooting at cardboard men."

"But they could ship you..." The girl hesitated.

"Where?"

"Wherever they want, that's where. They could send you to that war. Couldn't they, Vitya?"

He shrugged his shoulders. He poured tea into his cup and sipped it. He had forgotten about the war. Somehow forgotten completely. The newspapers talked about it hazily, sketchily. It was unclear whether Russians were fighting there or planting trees or building kindergartens.

The old bird cried out again, and immediately afterward a distant, abbreviated sound echoed. A moment later it echoed again.

"A storm?" he asked himself, unsure, and rose from the table to go into the street. The girl smiled, perplexed and happy, and went out too.

The sky over the village and the wood was perfectly clear. A strong wind struck the birch leaves every now and then. The air felt fresh.

The sun was already low in the west. It was shedding a slanting light on the golden fields, the dappled birch trunks, the rotted, collapsing roofs, the black scraps of fence, the white gardens.

"There," he said, pointing at the sky over the trees.

"That's the peregrine?"

A bird with brown plumage and a multicolored breast was circling overhead.

"Can you smell," she asked hoarsely, then cleared her throat, "the smell of the gardens?"

"Because it's going to rain," he answered, not looking at her. "We have to get going . . . the roads will be soaked."

In India . . . the tropical rains . . . for weeks, she thought. She was looking helplessly at the sky over the wood, but the sky was clear.

"Was it okay? Did you like it?" he asked.

She nodded in silence.

"And it wasn't too terrible without the gun?" he asked, smiling.

She shook her head.

"Would you like us to come back in two years?"

"Yes."

"For a long time."

She forced herself to smile. "Yes."

"Let's get going," he said, and went back into the hut. He gathered the spoons and cups, picked up the pot and kettle, and walked to the stream.

She remained exactly where she was and watched him walk toward the birches, walking among the birches. The trunks and leaves would screen him, he would appear again and then vanish. . . . She should have washed the dishes herself, she was thinking, but she didn't move or call out to him. He went farther away until he became a mere outline, ghostly. The sun was shining on the birches. The birch trunks were dotted with sharp black stains, burrs, specks. The ancient bird of prey was circling over the treetops.

The edges of storm clouds were gathering over the wood.

He raced back, rushed into the hut, put the clean dishes on the shelf, came out, and picked his bicycle up by the handlebars.

"Let's go!"

She followed him obediently. She wanted to say, The rain will start soon, let's stay and wait it out, forget about parents, who cares about them . . . I don't want to think about parents. She walked behind him in silence.

They emerged onto the country road, got on their bikes, and rode off.

The rain sprinkled a little and then stopped. It's too bad Russia doesn't have those tropical rains that last for days, weeks, months, she thought.

When they had climbed the hill she looked around.

The storm clouds had blown to the south. Above the village and the wood the sky was blue. The gardens in the village were white. There, no doubt, the soft gray forest birds were once more trilling and chirruping, trilling and chirruping, flitting from branch to branch and littering the ground with petals.

A FEAST ON THE BANK OF A VIOLET RIVER

ALL NIGHT LONG, PENS WERE SCRATCHING AT STAFF HEAD-
quarters, and all night long the soldiers who had completed their
tours were milling around. All discharges had been postponed for
the last three months, and for that whole time the soldiers felt as
though they had been living alien lives. They went out on raids
and sometimes died. Yesterday they had returned from the usual
raid and hadn't immediately believed the orders to present themselves, with their service papers, at headquarters. The night was
sultry and moonless, the stars hung like lanterns in the sky, the
cicadas had gone crazy, dust wafted off the steppes, a smell of
disinfectant rose from the long, wagonlike latrines, and from time
to time the forward guard regiment fired off short bursts of tracers
to ward off sleep. This last night was routine, but to those smoking
and waiting their turn on the headquarters steps it seemed insane.

Morning came, and everyone being transferred to the reserves
formed up on the parade grounds.

They were waiting for the regimental commander. The headquarters doors opened and out onto the steps came some sort of
officer or messenger, but the commander himself was not to be
seen.

But then, accompanied by an escort of majors and lieutenant
colonels, all of them stocky, suntanned, and sullen, the commander came down the steps. The parade ground fell silent. The
commander walked slowly, limping on his left leg and leaning on
a freshly carved cane. On his last operation he had jumped down
clumsily from an armored transport and wrenched a tendon, but

almost no one knew about his unfortunate mishap. The commander shuffled along, wincing slightly. Thinking that he had been shot, everyone looked at his wounded leg and cane with respect.

The commander came to a halt in the middle of the grounds and glanced around at the soldiers.

This severe fellow will now say a few uncharacteristically warm words, everyone thought, and the throats of the more sentimental began to tighten.

After stopping and looking around, the commander pointed his cane in the direction of a lanky red-headed soldier standing in front of him.

"Come here," the commander said.

The soldier, who was wearing a customized uniform that had been crimped and altered to suit his tastes, left the ranks, clicked his heels, raised his hand to the small, trimmed-back visor of his officer's cap, and stated his name and unit. The commander looked him up and down in silence. The soldier shifted from foot to foot and stared guiltily at the white wooden cane.

"What are you, a ballerina?" said the commander, grimacing in disgust.

The commander did not manage to address a farewell speech to his soldiers. While he was yelling at the officers for not keeping an eye on what the soldiers were doing to their dress uniforms, while he was screaming at one soldier, "What are you, a ballerina?" and while he was screaming at all the soldiers, "Are you ballerinas or soldiers, you motherfuckers?" the report came from Kabul that the helicopters had taken off, and an adjutant hurried out onto the parade ground to inform him of the fact. The commander fell silent, waved his hand, and ordered the vehicles brought up.

The MI-6, a heavy, cumbersome helicopter, couldn't land at the camp—it needed solid ground to take off from, and although work on a landing strip had begun, it hadn't been followed through and finished. And so covered trucks under the protection of two armored transports had to drive the demobilized soldiers to the provincial center, where there was a military airfield.

It was no more than ten miles from the camp to the city and the road ran through flat empty steppe, so there was no danger of attack. The only thing was that the commander had forgotten to have the way cleared by a sweeper—a heavily armored vehicle, a little like a tank, that clears a road of mines. His leg was aching and he had too much else to do: in two days the regiment was to set out for Kandahar.

The machines tore down the dusty road, carefully avoiding craters old and new.

Along the road were green fields of potato and grain and long rows of dusty, pyramidical poplars. The column reached the city, and everyone looked at it for the last time: at the earthen houses, towers, *duvals*, at the yellowish irrigation ditches, the muddy sewers and implausible gardens with their streams, flowerbeds, lawns, and arbors, at the domed mosques and the earthen, ornamental, flower-covered fingers of the minarets, at the *dukan* stalls piled up with all kinds of multicolored wares, at the small horses decorated with paper ribbons and harnessed to light carriages, at the ragged, bearded, barefoot beggars resting in the shade of plane trees, at the women in chadors, at the young boys hawking cigarettes and condoms, at donkeys laden with bundles of kindling . . .

On the airfield the staff and regimental officers who had accompanied the demobilized soldiers drew the men up into ranks and began what the soldiers called the "frisk." The officers ordered them to empty their bags, "diplomats," and pockets and lay everything out on the ground. They moved through the ranks briskly, forcing one man to squeeze out his tube of toothpaste, palpating another man's sling or cap. They didn't find any hash on anyone. They did, however, find and confiscate a Koran, a string of rosary beads, a pack of pornographic playing cards, and a Pakistani newspaper containing photos of hunted-looking prisoners surrounded by grinning, mustachioed men in turbans. From Ninidze they took five pairs of German sunglasses, considering that a bit too many. Ninidze grew heated and tried to argue that he wasn't planning on being a speculator, he was just bringing them back for friends. The noise attracted a lieutenant from the special section, a man with a pale sweaty face and thick, wrinkled eyelids rimmed in red.

"What is your name?" he asked Ninidze. He was the only officer in the whole regiment who addressed the soldiers formally. He was gazing placidly at Ninidze, who lost all inclination to argue that he wanted something nice to give to his friends. But Ninidze explained what they were for anyway.

The lieutenant took out his handkerchief, wiped his pale face, and asked, "Where did you get that Japanese thing?"

"Which one?"

"That one, that radio."

"I bought it," answered Ninidze, blanching.

"The receipt."

Ninidze ventured with a smile, "What receipt? I bought it from a *dukan*. They don't give you receipts."

The lieutenant picked up the radio and examined it. To Ninidze it seemed that he was about to sniff the radio with his bony nose.

"You bought it," the officer muttered. "You bought it. But it could be . . . couldn't it?"

"What?"

"Anything."

"No," Ninidze objected. "This thing, I bought it."

The lieutenant smiled a sickly smile.

"Yes? Shall we find out?"

"How?"

"Very simple. For that we must return to camp."

"You're joking," said Ninidze.

"No, I'm not joking at all."

"Comrade first lieutenant," said Romanov, a brown-eyed, high-cheekboned, thickset sergeant.

The lieutenant looked at him.

"Comrade first lieutenant, we've been together, us five, from the beginning to the end," said Romanov, nodding his head toward Ninidze and the men around him.

"I understand," the officer retorted. "You're right—the five of you should return to camp. It will turn up, what needs to be found out. Where are you from? The recon company? Well, boys . . ."

"That's not necessary, comrade lieutenant," said Romanov.

"Not necessary?" The officer slid a glance over the men around Romanov, lingered on the lusterless eyes of the small, runty Reyutov, looked at Romanov again, and asked him:

"Why is he stoned?"

"Who?" Romanov answered in a surprised voice.

"That one there." The officer pointed toward Reyutov with his eyes. "Are you stoned?" he asked Reyutov.

"No," Reyutov replied.

The lieutenant fell silent for half a minute. While he was silent the demobs from the recon company imagined having to drive back to camp again and see its trenches, its depots, its long latrines, the rows of weatherproofed tents; hear how the captain would let out a whistle when he saw them and the zampolit would say: I warned you, I really warned you, that sooner or later every secret would come out.

"Well then," sighed the lieutenant. He fell silent again and shot a glance over the soldiers' heads. And they all heard the rumbling clatter, turned their heads, and saw the black objects in the sky above the gray-blue mountains.

"Yes. It is in fact a lot of sunglasses," Ninidze muttered.

The lieutenant looked at him happily.

"There we go," he said.

"Yes. Exactly," Ninidze added.

"And you?" The officer turned to face Reyutov. "What do you have to say?"

"I don't smoke hash."

The clatter was growing louder; the objects had passed the

mountains, were already moving across the potato and grain fields on the outskirts of the city, and were becoming longer and thicker.

All the demobs who had already been dismissed were talking loudly among themselves, beating dust out of their jackets and service caps, and, keeping their distance, watching the rangers and the regiment's lieutenant.

An infantry major on leave who was accompanying the group as far as Tashkent walked up to him and called out, "Comrade lieutenant."

"We're not really sure what to do: return to camp or fly to the Union," the lieutenant responded.

The major raised his eyebrows.

"Something serious?" he asked, looking up. The helicopters were about to land.

"There's always something serious. Everyone has something serious."

The major looked intently at the lieutenant, then glanced away.

The helicopters landed and started to trundle heavily and clumsily down the airfield. The wind picked up and the soldiers clutched at their caps.

"What now then?" the major shouted, holding on to his cap and turning away from the wind.

"All right," the lieutenant answered with a condescending smile. "But that one there, the stoned one, he could stand a lesson." He menaced Reyutov with a finger. "All right. Fine," he said, and walked off toward the officers standing around a small white stone house on the edge of the airfield.

Romanov couldn't restrain himself and swore. The major didn't catch what he said, although from Romanov's lips he gathered what it was and shook his head. But what he had said was about right, and the infantry major had to smile.

In Kabul the helicopters managed to land just before the whole valley was engulfed in a *samoum*. The soldiers climbed out of the helicopters and immediately looked at the giant winged machine, painted white and blue, with "TU–134" written on its side, that they'd spotted from the air. Then they turned their heads to the east and their eyes went out—moving noiselessly down the valley from the east, shutting off the sky and the mountains and their colorless, glimmering glaciers, carpeting the gardens and hillsides covered in earthen dwellings, was something shaggy and brown. It was still windless on the airfield and the sun was shining in the deep blue sky, but right nearby everything was impenetrable and foreboding, which was why the approaching *samoum* seemed to be something supernatural and filled with doom, like the sounding of the seven trumpets.

When all the soldiers were out of the helicopters the major led them across the airfield to the transit camp. The camp, surrounded by barbed wire, was not far from the airfield, at the foot of mountains that were hot and scorched below and cold, blue-gray, and swathed in snow and ice above.

"Faster!" the major shouted, and everyone, casting glances at the city, hurried behind him.

The city was already half engulfed in the *samoum*; the soldiers could make out the dust clouds, and they saw the whirlwinds driving pieces of paper, leaves, gray scraps, tatters of rag. The major was hurrying, everyone was hurrying, treading sharply across the concrete. They were hurrying along, clutching their caps in their hands. They were hurrying along behind their rapidly striding major, but the yellow shadow of the *samoum* already lay over them. Halfway there the brown blizzard caught them.

They lost their way and only after an hour—lashed by sand and stones, caked with dust, angry, gasping for breath—did they find themselves at the transit station. The camp commander assigned them tents. The tents were filled with dust too, but the sandy wind no longer cut into them and burned their faces, stones no longer struck them in the head, and, most important, they were finally able to smoke.

The *samoum* died down late at night. In the camp everyone but the guards was asleep. The camp was full of soldiers being transferred to the reserves and of new recruits, all of them asleep,

131

all dreaming different dreams, and in their dreams all hoping for different things: the demobs believing that tomorrow they would fly out of here forever, the recruits thinking of benevolent commanders, kindly old-timers, and places where there wouldn't be much shooting.

In the middle of the night the alarm on Ninidze's wristwatch beeped. Ninidze awoke, got up, left the tent, looked around. It was quiet, dark, and above him the stars glimmered blue, green, and red. A few scattered lights were burning in the city. Above it rose the dark mountaintops. Ninidze went back in, drew his radio from his "diplomat," threw his jacket over his bare body, shoved the radio under it against his breast, left the tent, and, glancing around, headed toward the farthest end of the camp.

He was walking toward the edge of the camp, carrying the radio under his jacket, where it was sticking to his sweaty chest, and entreating his Old Man to make sure he didn't run into the duty officer.

He met no one and reached his goal, a long wood-planked building. He walked through the narrow door and froze—he had seen a lighted cigarette in the darkness. He wanted to leap away right then, but he collected himself, went to the rear wall, found a hole, dropped his pants, and sat down. His neighbor was silent, smoking and occasionally spitting. Ninidze sat and waited. Finally his neighbor left, and after waiting for a bit Ninidze drew out his sweat-bathed trophy and dropped it into the hole. The radio fell with a loud plop.

Ninidze returned to his tent, undressed, and lay down on his bare iron frame—for fear of fleas they had stripped all the mattresses from the bunks and stacked them in a corner. He listened tensely for a few minutes, but nothing could be heard except the heavy breathing and snores of his neighbors, so he let himself relax, sighed deeply, entreated his Old Man to make sure they would fly out in the morning, and fell asleep.

* * *

Morning came, sunny.

After breakfast a large party of demobs was taken to the airfield. Those left behind could see, through the barbed wire, when an hour later the party was seated in the aircraft, could see the aircraft go down the runway, pick up speed, break away from the gray concrete and rise up into the air, make a half-turn over the city, and fly away to the north.

Those left behind were sitting in the smoking areas, going through one cigarette after another, and sullenly watching the recruits, who seemed like some sort of mock soldiers to them, flown in here not to fight but to act in a play about war—their faces were so fresh and clear, and they were so unconvincing in their attempts to hide their terror, forcing themselves to laugh and joke, scowling and swearing copiously. But however coarsely and shamelessly they swore, however much they frowned and postured, it was obvious that the recruits were terrified and had no idea how they would endure for two years what these sunburned, mustachioed men in their caps and insignia-covered, bemedaled jackets had endured.

There were no more large aircraft to be seen on the airfield, and the demobs were saying to each other, "A-okay, let's catch some sun."

But at midday a transport plane landed and someone remembered that a friend who had flown out a year before wrote that his group had shipped home in a cargo plane, and everyone came alive and started to argue if it was true or not.

A half hour went by. The infantry major appeared. He gathered his group and led it to the camp gates. Here some captain or other, wearing glasses, read the roll call and the troops in the group cried out: "Present!" "Present!" "Present!"

Another half hour went by. The soldiers stood obediently in front of the gate under the full sunlight. Sweat streamed down their faces. The soldiers stood and humbly watched their major, who was smoking off to one side. But then the captain in the eyeglasses appeared again and the soldiers fixed their eyes on him. The captain nodded to the major, walked to the head of the line, and ordered the guards to open the gate; the guards opened the gate, the officer motioned with his hand, and the soldiers walked out.

The officers in the customs shed, all of them very young, turned out to be pleasant and lenient. They examined things less quickly and efficiently than the regimental searchers had, squeezing out only one of the many tubes of toothpaste and cutting open a couple of bars of soap. In one of the bars was an Afghan banknote. The officers laughed: What do you need this for in the Union? As a memento, the soldier answered. The officers gave it back. They didn't find hash on anyone. Nor, in fact, did they go out of their way to look for it. They paid no attention at all to sunglasses, jeans, Pakistani cigarettes, and so on, even though it had been said at the transit station that they were beasts in customs at Kabul, nothing like the searchers at one's own regiment—you could kiss goodbye to anything that didn't come from a Soviet store.

Ninidze was gloomy when they went out the customs-shed door and headed toward the cargo plane.

"What's with you, Murman?" asked Romanov.

Ninidze remained silent.

"Murman," Romanov called out again. "Hey, Murman, come on, you'll drink some hooch today."

Ninidze smiled sadly.

"No, probably not today," corrected Shingarev.

"But he'll taste some nice Tashkent wine," said Romanov. "Today."

"Sasha and I only drink vodka," said the hefty, broad-shouldered Spivakov in his deep voice. "Right, Sasha?"

The small Reyukov smiled but said nothing.

"We'll drink everything," said Romanov. "But the wine has to be red. It's the wine of victory. Isn't that so, Shingarev-Holmes?"

"Yes." Shingarev, the lapsed student, nodded his head. The nickname had been bestowed on him by the captain: when he had been wounded in the buttocks by bullet fragments at Kandahar and had begun to moan, the captain had comforted him by saying that Sherlock had been wounded at Kandahar too.

"We'll drink everything, wine and vodka," Romanov repeated.

"And beer," someone said.

"And women too!" someone else in the group exclaimed.

"Hey, is tail expensive in Tashkent?"

"Forty, if the client doesn't have a face like a brick wall."

"And if he does?"

"Fifty."

"The opportunists! Back in Tokmak they'd give themselves for a chocolate bar!"

They came to a halt, laughing, in front of the cargo plane. The major on leave walked toward the pilots standing in the shade of the wings. After talking with them for a few moments he came back and said that the plane hadn't been unloaded yet and that they would, once more, have to do their bit for the army.

"So we have to wait for a truck now?" they asked him cheerlessly.

"No, we'll set it all right on the ground."

"We're sick of loading and unloading. This is brutal. We're free men, for Christ's sake," someone said.

"You shut up, free man," the others broke in. "We'll unload it, comrade major, no problem."

"Why don't you all just unload it," the "free man" was heard to say.

The major broke into a stream of obscenities and asked if any of them wanted to go home, and, stripping to their waists, they all went off to unload the plane.

They lugged out and set down to the side of the aircraft cases, sacks, boxes, and bluish, foul-smelling sheep carcasses. They scurried up and down the gangway, lugging out cases, boxes, sacks, and carcasses. The sun was scorching their bare heads and their backs were shining with sweat.

After they unloaded the aircraft they wiped themselves off with their handkerchiefs and put their shirts and jackets back on.

Then they climbed into the hot aircraft and scattered to sit along the fuselage; there weren't enough seats, and the slower ones ended up having to settle on their bags and "diplomats" or on newspapers. Reyutov managed to find a place next to a window, but just then a round-faced artilleryman came up to him and simply said:

"Let me sit there."

Reyutov stared at him with his dull eyes.

"Just try sitting there," said Spivakov.

The artilleryman glanced at Spivakov and silently moved away.

"Pansy artilleryman," Spivakov muttered with a smirk.

A little while later the pilots in their clean and beautiful pale blue suits entered the cabin, and after a few minutes the gangway in the tail section rose smoothly and the dim ceiling lights overhead lit up.

The aircraft lurched and started to roll gently down the runway.

Breathing was difficult. Their faces shone in the stifling semi-darkness and looked almost black. The place stank of sweat and sheep meat.

The aircraft began to shudder, and they tensed as though it was they who had to gather their strength, break into a sprint, and leap into the air. The aircraft hurtled down the runway, rose, filling up with gravity, and suddenly started gliding smoothly, and everyone knew that it had taken off, that they were flying away forever.

Tashkent, the city of women, was illuminated by the rays of the evening sun. Its west-facing windows were shining; in its shady and, especially at this hour, verdant gardens innumerable fountains were gurgling coolly. Tashkent was noisy, vast, elevated;

136

well-dressed people with well-fed faces, untroubled, unclouded, were walking along its streets. It was a city of feminine eyes, hair, lips. Women were everywhere the demobs looked: in shop windows, on buses, in cars, in house windows, doorways, stalls— they saw women everywhere, women young, middle-aged, old, girls, women full-figured, ugly, narrow-hipped, Rubenesque, almond-eyed, wide-eyed, dark-haired, red-haired, women with beauty marks on their cheeks, bare-shouldered, in skirts, in transparent gowns. In short, it was an amazing city and in its streets the demobs felt, more than anything, just like the recruits at the transit station in Kabul.

They were going crazy and didn't know where to go or what to do next. They had been to the airport and the train station and learned that tickets to where they had to go were all sold out for nearly the next whole coming week, and now they plodded down the streets, stopping at yellow barrels to gulp down kvas, arguing and debating what to do. Spivakov suggested saying to hell with it all, buying vodka, and finding some secluded corner where they could have a good party. Shingarev objected: what if a patrol caught them? The idea of sitting in a Tashkent cooler didn't please anyone, and everyone except Spivakov hesitated: to drink or not to drink.

They were walking through the streets, arguing and debating, falling silent whenever they came across a girl or woman and staring her up and down from head to toe.

Ninidze proposed buying their tickets and living in a hotel for a week. They rejected this fantastic notion out of hand—what hotel? Spivakov was saying over and over that the best thing to do would be to buy some vodka, find some secluded place, get drunk, and only in the morning try to figure out what was what. Shingarev proposed bribing a conductor and riding in between the train cars, if need be, to Orenburg—from there it had to be easier to fly out or catch a train to Tblisi, Moscow, Kuibyshev, Rostov-on-the-Don, and Minsk, and they could have their party on the train without fear of any patrol. This satisfied everyone.

Ninidze instantly painted a picture of the woman conductor with whom they'd be negotiating: youngish, plump, with pink ears and cheeks and no prejudice at all.

They returned to the station.

On the way to the station they went into a shop and bought canned fish, fishcakes, bread, cucumbers, wine, and vodka. "*Bon appetit*, boys," the woman behind the counter, a redhead with thick lips, said to them.

"Mmm, what shameless eyes," Ninidze groaned when they were back on the street.

They loitered around on the platforms until dark, talking to conductors and promising them at first fifty rubles, then seventy-five, a hundred—but they were turned down.

It got completely dark, and Spivakov was saying that he'd done enough begging when the arrival of another train was announced and they decided to try their luck once more.

The train arrived, its brakes squealed, it came to a halt, and a noisy throng of people rushed to the cars, but the demobs hurried toward the last one—for some reason it seemed to them that it was more fitting for outlaws to ride in the last car. They hurried to the last car, and Ninidze entreated his Old Man: "Please, make it that . . ."

People were stretching tickets out to a graying, corpulent conductor. In the side of his mouth the conductor was holding a cheap cigarette. He would puff on the cigarette, take a ticket, palm it, stick his palm in the light coming in through the door, hand the ticket back, and nod his head: pass.

The crowd around him thinned out, and Shingarev said to the conductor confidentially:

"We have this problem . . ."

The conductor took all the soldiers in with a quick glance and growled:

"Well?"

"This is the thing."

"What?"

"The thing is, we'll pay you—" Shingarev began.

"Oh no, oh no," the conductor interrupted him.

"—a hundred rubles . . ."

"No." The conductor looked at his watch. "That's it, the matter's closed."

He turned around and strode onto the walkway between the cars.

"Were you ever in the service, Grandpa? You must have been in the service sometime. Listen, this problem . . ."

From the walkway the conductor glanced over their heads to the platform, in case some straggler was rushing to make it aboard, and without answering Shingarev he began to close the heavy door. The door was nearly shut when at the last moment Romanov stuck his leg in the crack.

"Hey!" The conductor let out an astonished yell and flung the door open.

"Will you answer me like a human being?" Romanov said.

With a kick the conductor knocked Romanov's leg off the threshold and slammed the door. Romanov started hitting the thick dusty glass with his fists. The conductor stood on the other side of the door and looked at them. He took out his pack of cigarettes, drew one out, blew into the cardboard mouthpiece, lit up, and again stared at the soldiers. The train pulled out shortly afterward, and Romanov spit on the dirty window.

When the train had moved some way off the conductor opened the door and screamed:

"Shitbags!"

After roaming for a while in the vicinity of the station they came across a park. There was a river there, narrow and straight. The river gave off a faint reek, but they decided it was nothing and settled themselves down by the water. From time to time people passed through the park, but the soldiers were screened from their eyes by the bushes running along the river. Along the opposite bank extended the blind walls of some squat brick edifice over which lampposts towered, casting a violet light on the dark roof, the river, and the soldiers. They were glad to discover how light and yet secluded it was here. They were even happier once they had spread newspapers on the grass and on them laid out bread, the canned food, the cucumbers—and once they looked at the colonnade of bottles sparkling so brightly.

"Not a bad little restaurant," Spivakov said.

Everyone was quick to agree that the little restaurant was just great.

"Then let's get to it," Spivakov said. He had set out little paper cups and was reaching for a bottle of vodka when Shingarev stopped him.

"The port first."

"I don't want to mix, I just want vodka," Spivakov answered.

"No, we have to drink the port first."

"No one tells me I have to do anything anymore."

"It was agreed. We agreed to drink red wine, it's the wine of victory," Shingarev insisted.

Romanov and Ninidze backed up Shingarev, and Spivakov conceded. Shingarev poured the port out into cups. They raised their cups, brimming over with dark wine, carefully toasted with them, and drained them. On the next round Shingarev choked and started coughing. He put his empty cup down and raised his hands to his chest.

"I've spilled on myself, shit," he managed to force out, and again started coughing.

"It's nothing, *bidzho*," replied Ninidze, leaning toward him and examining his shirt.

"Feels pretty sticky," Shingarev retorted.

Romanov lit a cigarette and raised the burning match to Shingarev's chest, and everyone saw the big dark stain on his shirt.

"Wash it out," Ninidze advised.

"Then he'll have to wash the whole shirt," Romanov said.

"It'll get wrinkled, and where can I iron it? Christ..."

"Nonsense, just brush it down," said Spivakov.

Romanov threw out an idea.

"Maybe if your tie was on."

Shingarev drew his tie from the pocket of his jacket, which was lying off to the side on his "diplomat," and put it on.

"Well, how's that?"

"Give us some light."

Romanov lit a match.

"You can barely see it. If you keep your jacket on, no one will even notice it, probably," said Romanov.

"Just forget about the damn clothes. I say to hell with them. Me and Sasha say to hell with them, right, Sasha?" Spivakov asked.

Sasha Reyutov's narrow violet face wrinkled—as always, he smiled without a sound. Spivakov poured some vodka for himself and Reyutov and asked if he should pour some for the others. Ninidze and Romanov nodded, but Shingarev declined. They drank the vodka and, puffing loudly, set into the food. Shingarev drank port.

"All the same to me," Spivakov continued his train of thought. "Me and Sasha will ride in our underpants as long as it's homeward, huh, Sasha?"

It was the middle of the night. People had stopped passing through the park. The violet river stood still in its banks. The sounds of the railroad could be heard easily: the bored voice on the loudspeaker, whistles, the crack of coupling cars, wheels clicking, diesels rumbling.

Ninidze, who had suddenly forgotten how to speak proper Russian, was cursing the lieutenant from the special section, cursing the staff officer who had confiscated the sunglasses, cursing whatever authorities for not allowing them a normal return home; he flew into a rage and started screaming in Georgian. But no one was listening. Spivakov was still regretting that he had been too scared to bring a couple of slabs of hash in his shoulder pouch or soles—he claimed that vodka didn't do anything for him, he said he was so used to hash that vodka seemed like water; he too was cursing the lieutenant who had slandered Sasha Reyutov—Sasha, who never in his life had tasted the sweet herb of hash. Romanov was chain-smoking, showering himself with ashes, and looking warmly at his comrades. From time to time he would tilt his head back and stare at the poplar trees illuminated by the blue-violet light of the lampposts—he stared for ages, smiling, at the poplars. The only one still sober was Shingarev, who was straining his ears and peering around.

It was the middle of the night. The poplars and the motionless violet river had fallen silent. From somewhere beyond the sleeping houses came the sounds of the railroad.

"Murman," said Romanov, lighting another cigarette. "Hey, come on, stop cursing. Such a day . . . a night. And you, Shingarev-Holmes, I swear I don't even want to look at you. Drink some vodka and get rid of that paint."

"Someone has to stay sober," Shingarev replied.

"Here? What, here, on a night like this?" Romanov leaned his head back and fell silent, staring at the sky.

"Get drunk, Shingarev-Holmes," said Spivakov. "It's not doing anything for me. I'm sober as a saint."

Romanov roused himself. "Should we sing? Something soulful. 'We're not diplomats by afoca . . .' Fo . . . How does it go? You're not diplomats by afoca . . . Fo, fo! Ha-ha! Afocation! Ha ha!"

"No, right now that won't do for music," Spivakov said. "But hey, Murman, get out your made-in-Japan."

Murman-Ninidze said gloomily:

"The radio ain't, someone stole it."

"What? How, who?"

"At the transit shtation, zip, zap, gone!"

"Why didn't you say something?" Romanov yelled.

"What, what. What could've I said?"

"What, what do you mean, what? We would have beaten the daylights out of them all! All those dogs! What do you mean, what? All of them . . . those scum, the bast . . . All my life, that conductor . . . his face, in a hundred years . . . I'll rip the damn thing off!" Romanov yelled.

"The foolishness begins," said Spivakov, frowning.

"Don't shout," Shingarev said to Romanov. "And why all this about the conductor?"

"What? Why are you always afraid of everything? Let them come over to us. Just let them." Romanov hit his palm with his fist. "A patrol, the cops. They want to start something with recon? Well, let them!" Romanov hit his palm with his fist harder and faster.

"Strange," muttered Spivakov. "How could it have happened? Murman, you were sleeping on your 'diplomat' and you didn't go anywhere at night, did you? Then how did they pull it off?"

"Some sort of deviltry," Ninidze answered, lifting his hands.

He felt someone looking at him, glanced to the side, and saw a narrow face lit up in the violet light: dark wrinkles, long bony nose, thin dark lips, a dark patch of eyes. "If Reyutov knows something, make it so he stays quiet," Ninidze entreated his Old Man. It had become a habit—to entreat someone, someone he imagined as gray-haired, intelligent, powerful, generous, someone he called Old Man—since his first raid: he had been in an extremely tight situation and somehow without thinking about it he said, "Old Man, make it so that . . ." And he had made it out of that scrape without a single scratch.

Reyutov said nothing. He was even staring off to the side somewhere. How could Reyutov know anything? Ninidze relaxed.

"It went the way it came," Shingarev said all of a sudden.

"Whaddaya mean?"

"It went the way it came," Shingarev repeated coldly.

"How'd it come?"

"You know how."

"Whatya trying to say?"

"He needs a drink, quick." Romanov pointed his finger at Shingarev.

"I understand," Spivakov said. "I see right through these sissies."

"Guys!" Romanov waved his hands. "Don't! Let's drink instead."

"Nah, talk," demanded Ninidze.

"Drop it, drop it," Shingarev muttered.

"No, talk, tell everything, Shingarev!"

"I know what it is," said Spivakov. "He's been wanting to say it for a long time, I've seen it. He's been a sissy from the very start. This is what he's been wanting to say, he's been wanting to say that we're bringing trophies home and he isn't. That's it, isn't it? I don't care. Those things we got in the war, I couldn't care less about them, understand?"

"There we go!" Ninidze exclaimed. "That's it! That's what he's leadin' at. That what you leadin' at? You're too good, eh?"

Shingarev's mouth was already open to agree, yes, yes, that's what I've been wanting to say, but he happened to glance at Reyutov, he was struck by some thought about Reyutov, and he announced softly:

"I didn't want to say anything like that."

"Kids. Guys." Romanov picked up a bottle. "Such a day . . . a night." He became pensive.

"What, you asleep? Pour it," Spivakov growled, sticking out his cup.

"Wait . . . it was . . . I was thinking . . . the thing I wanted to say . . ."

"Pour, will you?"

"No, but . . ." Romanov shook his head. "No, I forgot." He poured vodka into the cups, more or less. "Come on, let's just drink, that's it, no more about all this. To hell with it! Liberty, that's the thing. And that's all . . . these tricks and turns . . . these scores, to hell with them. But liberty—yes! But! That wasn't what I was thinking. It's gone, vanished."

Romanov was sitting, his cup in his hands, frowning, his eyes rooted to the center of the "table," his lips moving; the vodka overflowed the edge of his cup and ran down his hand.

"Drink, don't spill it."

Romanov glanced absently at Spivakov, drank down his vodka without a wince, and burst out:

"Hey! I remember! I have this feeling—" He looked around. "This feeling . . . that someone's missing."

"Of course someone's missing," Spivakov mumbled.

"No, no, it's not that, not them."

"Okay, lie down, go to sleep."

"No, you have to understand."

"Look, just lie down, lie down, sleep, the ground's warm."

"You don't understand. I'm saying that someone isn't among us—he was, but now he isn't." Romanov looked at those sitting around the "table."

"Lie down," said Spivakov. "We're all here."

Romanov looked around at his comrades, finally noticed Reyutov, and froze. He was looking at Reyutov with wide-open eyes, saying nothing. He remained silent for a long time. Everyone was quiet, watching him and Reyutov.

"Ah!" Romanov shouted. "Ah, Reyutov! Sashka! Ha ha! Well! Ha ha ha!"

"Just as I said—foolishness," growled Spivakov.

Romanov stopped laughing.

"Everyone," he said, "everyone gathered, and the feast . . . it . . . continues. They're feasting . . . these . . . ex-recons." Romanov took a deep breath and started to sing: "We were marching so far a-away, where almost no one's ever gone! We were waiting in ambush for years . . ." He fell silent. His eyes found Reyutov and fixed on him.

Reyutov's narrow violet face covered with furrows—he was smiling.

"It's me," he said to Romanov. "Don't worry."

"Sasha," Romanov uttered in a raw voice. "Sasha . . . an amazing thing . . . you understand." He fell silent. "I just remembered . . . how we were flown in to the regiment."

145

"And what?" asked Spivakov.

"What?" Romanov pulled himself together. "Nothing! Just amazing. Amazing...it was...it. And everyone...we were waiting in a-ambush for years, despite the snow and the rain!"

"Yes, that's exactly what I was thinking about too," Shingarev said to himself. "I was thinking, I was thinking. I'm drunk anyway. Have to concentrate and remember how we were flown in to the regiment." He concentrated and remembered how they had been flown in to the regiment after three months of training in a camp in the mountains of Turkmenistan; out of the crowd of recruits the commander of the recon company had chosen the enormous Spivakov first, and Spivakov had said that the five of them were sticking together, and he asked the commander to take the others. The commander gladly agreed to take the wiry, lithe Ninidze, the strong, broad-shouldered Romanov, and him, Shingarev, but Reyutov he flatly refused. Well, Spivakov said to Reyutov, do something Rostov-on-the-Donish. Reyutov started to say no, Spivakov pressed him, and finally the captain became interested in whatever it was this puny boy could "do." Seeing curiosity on the captain's face, everyone prodded Reyutov, and Reyutov, blushing, sang a Kazakhstani chastushka. The captain's heavy face broke into a smile and he asked what else Reyutov could do. Reyutov innocently answered that he could play the accordion and knew a million chastushkas. The captain raised his eyebrows—a million?—and enlisted Reyutov in the recon company.

"So, still think you're too good?" asked Ninidze, moving toward Shingarev.

"Shut up," said Romanov.

"I'll calm them down right now, I'll brain them right now." Spivakov tried to stand but couldn't. He looked at his legs, puzzled, and called to them: "Legs!"

Romanov burst out laughing. Even Ninidze smiled. Spivakov attempted it again, rose, stood for a moment, wobbling, and sat back down heavily.

"My legs." He threw up his hands. Everyone started laughing, and Reyutov's narrow face soundlessly wrinkled.

"And ya said vodka did nothin' for ya."

"Traitors," Spivakov said to his legs.

"Quiet!" Romanov shouted. "Quiet! Umm..." He hit himself on the forehead. "Shit, shit! I forgot... what a toast, and I've lost it."

"Fine, let's just drink." Spivakov grabbed the bottle, held it up to his cup, and dropped it. "Agh! This is really foolishness! And my right hand—the same thing! A traitor."

"Quiet!" Romanov shouted again. "The toast, here it is. Let's drink to... that is, to, that is, that... that our hands and legs may betray us, but never our friends!"

Spivakov approved. "What a toast!"

"And now give him your hand," Romanov demanded of Shingarev. "Your hand to Murman."

"We weren't fighting," Shingarev answered.

"Is it so hard to give him your hand?"

Shingarev remained silent.

"Agh, idiots." Romanov turned toward the river. Suddenly he started to take off his shirt. "Who'll go swimming with me?" he asked in a businesslike voice.

"I won't let you," Spivakov said.

"We'll see about that. We've yet to see, as they say. The old recon man will go bathing. He will bathe. That's it. I'm sick of you all. Do your butting without me, my rams. But I will swim," said Romanov.

"Where to?" Spivakov asked sarcastically.

"Far away, that's all. Oh, you'll butt away here and you'll be gored by a ram. Or a mosquito. Or a bull. A big bull with a muzzle like this: mooo!"

Shingarev was the last to fall asleep.

By early morning everyone was sleeping, but Shingarev held out, rubbing his eyes, shaking his head, smoking, pacing. But then even he fell asleep.

They were sleeping around the ravaged "table." Ninidze was

lying, covered by his jacket, with his head on his "diplomat." Romanov, naked to the waist, lay on his back with his arms sprawled out; he was shivering and grinding his teeth. Reyutov was lying nestled against the large, hot, hoarse-breathing Spivakov. Shingarev slept sitting up, his head on his knees.

At dawn the poplars, silent all night, started to rustle. Ripples appeared on the river.

A warm rain descended on the city.

The rain tapped against bottles, empty cans of food, matchboxes, against the black crust of an uneaten loaf of bread, "diplomats," cap visors; the newspapers disintegrated and the cigarette butts strewn among them turned black and swelled.

Without waking up, Ninidze pulled his jacket over his head. Reyutov pressed himself into Spivakov's side. No one else moved.

SAFE RETURN

THE GIANT GENERAL GRINNED AND SAID THAT ORSHEV WAS going to be in the regiment forever now; Orshev would try to sneak away but the general always caught him, and Orshev decided to kill the general—he would steal up to him, now in the form of a snake, now in the form of an old man, a child, a woman, a tank; but the general would always recognize him and hide behind an iron door: Orshev was hallucinating under his damp sheets. He was hunting some general; feasting with black, swollen, foul-smelling corpses on a white mountaintop; becoming light as a wood shaving, terrified of the wind, then suddenly heavy as a granite monument and sinking up to his knees into the earth; sometimes he could see his lungs, transparent sacks tightly packed with worms; he'd run into his house and throw a grenade into a cake lying on a festive table, and leap out through the door, then lean his weight against it, and his friends, parents, and children would scream and pound on the door, but he wouldn't let them out, and the grenade would explode; or he'd race around a garden, naked, after a nimble old woman, someone else would help him catch her, and both of them, snarling and biting at each other, would fall on her. . . .

Orshev was hallucinating in the stuffy, overcrowded ward of a medical unit, and at the same time the last group of soldiers bound for the reserves was flying to Kabul. The men he had been living beside for two years had flown away forever. They had wanted to return to Russia together. For two years the return home had been their favorite topic: they would imagine out loud,

151

with relish, either on night-guard duty or after a battle or around a fire behind the bathhouses—where in the evening they usually cooked up some potatoes, drank tea, and smoked hash—they would spend hours imagining how they would walk down the gangway in Tashkent, jingling their medals, buy cognac, sit down in the train and start drinking, laughing, and remembering, and terrified women would huddle in the corners, their mouths open, listening and watching while they—wiry, tanned, daring—drank, laughed, and remembered the war.

But this is how it turned out.

On the last operation—for three weeks the battalion, along with government troops, had been besieging the Urgan gorge—the soldiers went swimming after their umpteenth sortie into the mountains. The river was fast, clear, and cold; the muddy, sweaty soldiers had plunged into the torrent, lain back, and let it pull them under, then they jumped out of the river and sprawled out on the hot white sand; their cooled bodies grown hot again, the soldiers would once more go into the water. Orshev stayed in the river longer than anyone else—his stupid idea had been to soak up enough cold and liquid to last until night without his feeling either heat or thirst. He found a submerged boulder in the middle of the river, grabbed hold of it, stretched himself out, and let the water rock him up and down and move him from side to side. The sun was small and bright in the sky; high up on the hunchback ridge a few rare cedars were growing. A swath of soft sand extended along the river's left bank; the sand was white, the bodies lying on it dark and muscled. The soldiers were talking, joking, smoking, not thinking about the fact that tomorrow they would have to climb into the mountains once more. It felt good. But toward evening Orshev started to have sharp pains. It was an inflammation of the lungs, and his temperature shot up to 105.

Orshev's comrades had already been home for a long time before he was discharged from the medical unit. Thin and sallow, Orshev returned to his company. The bunks that had belonged to him and his friends, the prestigious bunks on the lower tier, were occupied by the old-timers who were now bosses in the company. Orshev headed to the officers' quarters and found the company commander. The captain talked frankly with him, allowed him to smoke right there in the office, poured him tea, and got out some white bread and sugar. The captain said that helicopters would be coming any day to bring more recruits and that Orshev could fly back to Kabul when they arrived. But what did "any day" mean? It could be tomorrow or the day after, in a week, in a fortnight. But then again, tomorrow morning a column would be heading to Kabul for supplies. "Of course, driving to Kabul in a truck is risky business, you know that yourself, Orshev. But on the other hand, it's tomorrow morning for sure. Which means that you'd be in Kabul by evening, and the next day, if you manage to catch a plane, in the Union. I'm not recommending anything—you have to decide on your own." Orshev agreed to go. With a smile the captain handed him his papers. "So then, congratulations, your fighting's over."

Orshev wandered through the little tent city flooded in steely sunlight, and stood for a bit at the edge of the camp, smoking and looking at the steppe, empty, silent, infinite. He should go to the baths. But it was hot, and in any case his illness had softened his firm body and he felt lazy, weak, and flaccid. But he should go anyway. Orshev plucked up his courage and headed for the battalion baths.

The plump attendant was sitting with a book on the front steps of the bathhouse. Orshev greeted him and asked if there was any water. "For you we'll find some," the attendant answered. Orshev sat down wearily beside him and admitted that he wasn't especially eager for a bath. "Your eyes don't look too healthy. It's obvious they discharged you too soon," the attendant said, slamming his book shut. "When do you fly out?" Orshev answered that he'd be leaving with a column tomorrow. The attendant frowned in displeasure. "I wouldn't go; it would be better to wait a month for a helicopter. Stay here and wait it out. You can sleep at my place, and tomorrow I'll be getting a ton of shit we can smoke. What do you say?" Orshev shook his head: he was tired, he was tired of hash, tired of everything.

He washed himself halfheartedly in tepid water, then dried himself off. Before getting dressed he carefully examined the seams of his fresh T-shirt and shorts—brand-new things from the storehouse were often already infested with fleas. While Orshev was busy in the baths the attendant brought a pot of water to boil on the fire behind the bathhouse and brewed some tea.

They sat on the steps, gulping tea, nibbling on biscuits and sugar, looking at the little regimental town. The tents, the wood-planked mushrooms of the sentry posts, the latrines, the dump, the mess tents, headquarters, the storehouses, the officers' quarters, the parade grounds, the depots—everything looked gray with the dust and sun.

Orshev sat until evening with the attendant and could have stayed there—the attendant slept in the bathhouse dressing room—but he wanted to spend his last night in his tent, which after all had been home for two years.

Orshev returned to his tent in the twilight and lay down on his bunk without undressing or turning back the sheets. The company was at nightly roll call and the tent was quiet. Orshev stared at the springs of the bunk above his and mulled over his condition with dissatisfaction. Something wasn't right, he thought; he wasn't really well yet. Or was it just the normal weakness one felt after being sick? Orshev dozed off.

He was woken up by a touch on his shoulder. He opened his eyes and saw an unfamiliar young soldier. The soldier was smiling in confusion. With his eyebrows and a light shake of the head Orshev asked: Well? "I've been sent by the Soviet Army senior Khmyzin," the young soldier muttered. Orshev said nothing. The young soldier continued cautiously, "He asks that you give him his place back." Orshev raised himself to his elbows and looked around: there were no old-timers, there was no Khmyzin in the tent, just youngsters, sparrows, and spooners. "If he's so brave,

why hasn't he come to tell me himself?" Orshev oasked sarcastically. "That's your answer?" the young soldier asked. "Go
away," Orshev said, but without anger. The youngster immediately left. But he returned quickly and said that the senior Khmyzin was warning him: once they finished smoking he had to get
out. Orshev didn't reply. They're smoking, which means that
they're all together, the jackals, he thought. The youngster was
waiting for an answer but didn't dare remind him. Orshev was
lying back with his eyes closed. At last the old-timers came into
the tent. Khmyzin, a stocky, squat, broad-chested young man,
looked around at his comrades, walked determinedly up to Orshev's bunk, and loudly said: "Orshev! Get out of my bunk!"
Orshev opened his eyes and stared at Khmyzin. Khmyzin's comrades started to move. "Stop, you jackals!" Orshev yelled, raising
his hand imperiously. The old-timers froze. "Khmyzin," said
Orshev, "you want to flex your muscles, fine. But are you a man?
Then speak for yourself. I always speak for myself." "That's fair
enough," one of the old-timers said at last. "But he called us
jackals," another ventured uncertainly. No one answered him.
But even if they had grudges against the ex-old-timers—Orshev
and his comrades—in this quarrel they agreed, reluctantly, with
Orshev. First of all, the worst of the ex-old-timers, the ones who
deserved to be taught a lesson, were already long since home, and
why should Orshev have to take a beating for everyone else?
Second, there was nothing unnatural in the fact that they bore
grudges against the ex-old-timers, no—as it was, so it will remain:
yesterday they were abused, today they abuse. Third, beating the
daylights out of a demob, a soldier who had been through hell
and high water, would have set a bad precedent for the younger
soldiers, who were now obeying their seniors as though they were
gods—wise, powerful, bold. And for that matter Orshev had, all
in all, never been that bad—he had busted a few balls and made
others do all sorts of work for him, but he wasn't mean or ran-
corous and he had never come up with refined humiliations for
the youngsters, sparrows, and spooners. And now the jackals had

forgiven him and agreed that it was right: one against one. The old-timers drove everyone from the tent, cleared away all the stools, scattered into the corners, and fixed their eyes on Khmyzin and Orshev. Orshev didn't have a belt on; someone told Khmyzin to take his off, and he did. Everything became silent. And awkward. "Come on, Khmyzin, let him have it!" someone cried out, and Khmyzin moved toward Orshev with his fists clenched and his head tucked in.

They closed in on each other. Khmyzin jerked his left shoulder to distract Orshev and with his right fist swung from the side and struck him in the temple. Orshev staggered and turned pale. Khmyzin swung toward his stomach, but Orshev managed to deflect him. Khmyzin threw another barrelhouse right with a straining grunt, but Orshev parried that blow too. Orshev meanwhile had been on the defensive, coming back to his senses after the blow to his temple. Khmyzin attacked. He was now completely fearless, and his former indecision—how could he be fighting with an ex-old-timer, with someone he had never even dared look in the eye before?—had vanished without a trace. Seeing that Orshev was doing little more than defending himself, Khmyzin flew into a rage and, grunting heatedly, started showering punches on his opponent. In his fervor Khmyzin grew careless and was astonished—everyone was astonished—when he found himself down on the ground. Khmyzin leaped up, shaking his head and spraying dark red drops, and Orshev immediately caught him under the eye with his left elbow and slammed his right fist into his cheek. Khmyzin gasped, bowed his head, shielded it with his hands, and started moving backward. Orshev kept pressing him, landing heavy and accurate punches to his head, back, and liver. Everyone watched in silence. Suddenly Khmyzin stopped, bellowed, straightened up, and hurled himself on Orshev in an attempt to turn the fistfight into a wrestling match, but Orshev deftly stepped out of the way and struck Khmyzin in the nose. Khmyzin's lip was already split, and now blood was flowing from his nose. The crazed Khmyzin again hurled himself on his opponent and this time managed to break through past his fists, clutch Orshev in his arms, and pull him down to the ground. Khmyzin found himself on top, grabbed Orshev by the hair, and started beating the back of his head against the floor. The pain brought tears to Orshev's eyes and he broke loose from Khmyzin, hammering him in the sides with his fists. Everyone watched in silence. At last, covered in Khmyzin's blood, Orshev hit his opponent in the throat, and Khmyzin started wheezing and bit Orshev's hand. Orshev grabbed Khmyzin's ear with his other hand and tried to tear it off. Khmyzin screamed and let go of Orshev's hand, but Orshev kept twisting the ear and Khmyzin was forced to climb off him. Panting, Orshev raised himself on all fours. Khmyzin did too. They stood up slowly without taking their eyes off each other. "You . . . had enough?" Orshev asked, and leaned against the back of the bunk. "No . . . it's you . . . you . . . who's had enough," answered Khmyzin, spitting out blood and wiping his nose on his sleeve. Orshev pushed himself off the back of the bunk, lashed his arm out, and struck Khmyzin in the neck with the edge of his hand. Khmyzin bowed his head again. Orshev stood up and waited. Khmyzin started, it seemed, to settle down. "That's it," Orshev said, but suddenly Khmyzin lunged toward him and smashed his forehead into Orshev's face. Orshev fell back against the bunk and clutched his nose, which was welling with blood; now both their noses were shattered. Stemming the blood with his hand, Orshev steadied himself against the bunk, looking at Khmyzin with dull eyes and holding his right arm at the ready: one more blow and he would go down. But Khmyzin didn't have the strength to attack; he was pouring sweat, wiping off blood, his breathing raspy and broken, and reeling on his unsteady legs.

"Looks like that's it," someone said in a loud voice. Orshev and Khmyzin kept their silence. "Go wash yourselves off," they were advised. They dragged themselves outside the tent, and in the street young soldiers poured pots of water over them.

Orshev was the first to return to the tent. He pulled off his torn, bloodstained clothes and collapsed on the covers of his bunk.

Khmyzin came into the tent. He approached the disputed bed

and said hoarsely: "Orshev, get out of my place." Everything fell silent in the tent. "But it's my bunk," Orshev answered after a moment. "Climb up into the upper row. There's a bunk free there. I won't sleep up top anymore. Enough. A year and a half. Enough," Khmyzin pronounced stubbornly. Orshev sat up. "You're nothing. Climb up onto the second level," Khmyzin muttered. "Go to hell," Orshev said. "Climb," Khmyzin repeated. Orshev stood up and hit Khmyzin, but the blow fell short and landed on his chest. Khmyzin stepped back two paces, stumbled into a table, and caught his foot in it. "Khmyzin!" the others yelled. Khmyzin didn't turn around at the shout; he stood half facing Orshev so he could have more room for a swing and punch, but Orshev didn't wait: gripping the edge of the upper bunk in his hands, he hoisted himself up and kicked Khmyzin. Khmyzin flew backward, landed between the bunks with a crash, and was still. Orshev collapsed onto his reconquered bunk. "Hey, you've killed him," they were saying.

The orderly woke Orshev up at five in the morning—the column was heading out at six. "How's the other one doing?" Orshev asked, yawning. "He's sleeping," the orderly replied. Orshev got up, stiff, grimacing, and went out into the street in his shorts and T-shirt.

It was warm, birds were whistling; the bulbous red sun was lying on the edge of the steppe.

The orderly filled a pot with water from the barrel and poured it over Orshev. Orshev gingerly washed his aching face, nodded to the orderly, and, carefully drying his face with a towel, went back into the tent. His dress uniform was hanging from the frame of the bunk—before he woke Orshev up the orderly had brought it from the storehouse. Orshev dressed, picked up his case and cap, went to the middle of the tent, and looked around. He spotted Khmyzin. He was asleep, his arms stretched out and his mouth wide open; there were dark bruises on his face, blood was caked around his nose, and his lower lip was split in half by a jagged black furrow. A small satisfied smile crossed Orshev's lips; he waved his cap at the sleeping Khmyzin and left the tent.

The commander of the column grinned when he saw Orshev's swollen face: "So, party boy, have a good time?" Orshev answered that he was no party boy, he had just slept a lot at the medical unit. "Yes, of course," the captain retorted. "I'd guess what, little eagle, two, three liters? But anyway, where do you want to ride? A wheeled vehicle? A BTR?...A wheeled vehicle? Well, take your pick."

Orshev walked the length of the column, stopped next to a truck, and asked the driver: "Can you take me?" "Get in," the driver answered. In the cabin Orshev took off his jacket and hung it on a hook. He asked for some water, drank it from the aluminum canteen, leaned his head against the back of the seat, and lit a cigarette.

Ten minutes later the column pulled out. At its head, tail, and middle went armored transports with infantry aboard, the column guard. The column was slowly driving past the regimental CP. When Orshev's truck driver drew up alongside the little stone house, Orshev said to himself, "Amen."

The column picked up speed and started rolling along the steppe road, raising dust, rocking, rumbling. The sun was shining to one side, its rays piercing through the dust that shrouded the machines. Dust filtered into the cabin and stuck to the eyes and lips, tickled the nostrils, covered the hair. The driver was calmly smoking a cigarette in the dust—its moistened end was already dirty. Orshev was bouncing a bit on the springy seat and staring at the blurry outline of the tarp on the truck ahead of them. The driver was the quiet type, thank God, and had only been interested in why Orshev had stayed at the camp so long; he had said that in six months he would be going home too, and that was that. Orshev was content. After two years he was tired of these army conversations: about going home, about girls, about decorations, stripes, about good chow. And anyway he had a splitting headache from the fight, as though he had really been drinking or smoking hash all night long.

Sometimes one of the vehicle's wheels hit a pothole and the

driver and Orshev flew up from their seats. It was twenty kilo-
meters from the camp to the first tarmac; the rebels liked to plant
mines along this stretch, and the road recalled the surface of the
moon. Although vehicles could blow up on the tarmac too. But
at least there was no dust there. It'll be paved road soon, Orshev
was thinking.

The column traveled through clouds of dust on the steppe road
for half an hour before it came to the tarmac and headed south
along a straight gray road. Orshev took the bandage off his nose,
rubbed his face, picked up the canteen, rinsed out his mouth, and
drank. The driver lit a cigarette and said happily: "It's nothing,
just six months and I pull out of here." Orshev thought about
it—six months, which means twenty-four weeks, which means
180 days—and his jaw tightened anxiously.

All around lay the steppes, with small, smoke-colored heights
and peaks rimming their edges. In the lifeless steppes were rare
yellow *kishlaks*. Sometimes the *kishlaks* came right up to the paved
road. They were gloomy collections of tumbledown buildings
surrounded by high walls. Houses, walls, wooden gates—everything was gray and primitive. The people—men in turbans, cloaks,
and loose pantaloons, women in dark shapeless gowns—would
only rarely and timidly animate the sunlit little streets and gloomy
squares. But behind the *duvals* was a mass of lush gardens, fresh,
green, delicate gardens. . . .

The column was moving swiftly. The mountains were coming
closer, massive, reaching to the sky, reddening—the valley was
becoming narrower. And soon the column was driving through
the red-and-brown mountains. The road started to wind and rise
up into the pass.

Orshev tossed a cigarette butt out the window and lit another;
he was carefully watching the cliffs that towered up in either
direction. Leaning forward, his brows knitted, the driver was
turning the steering wheel and whistling, almost inaudibly, a monotonous little air. Orshev glanced sidelong at the sky and said:
"Hand me your assault rifle." The driver shook his head: no way.

160

Orshev smiled crookedly and by way of justifying himself said that not having an assault rifle was like not having an arm, and that he'd never gone anywhere without his. Gripping the wheel firmly in one hand, the driver got out a pouch of grenades and handed it to Orshev. After a moment's hesitation he passed Orshev a second pouch too. Now Orshev had four grenades. He sighed with relief.

The column was climbing up a stone road pitted with craters. The cliffs loomed over the vehicles. The feet of the cliffs were black with scorch marks. To the right yawned a precipice, not very deep, on whose bottom were charred wrecks, wheels, scraps of iron, and shreds of rubber. The forward vehicles were already crawling through the saddle of the pass. Their engines were roaring, a pall of black smoke hung over the road, and the deep blue sky lay above the gray cliffs. Orshev was holding the pouches on his knees with one hand and smoking, and the driver was whistling his simple tune more and more loudly. And suddenly the vehicles ahead of them came to a halt one after the other until Orshev's driver had to stop too. "Some idiot has broken down," the driver ventured, and once more started whistling. Orshev took a sip from the canteen—the water was already warm. The driver was whistling and drumming his fingers on the steering wheel.

A minute passed. The column stayed where it was, its engines idling. The driver was whistling and drumming. Orshev glanced down at the black scraps and debris. It was hot, hard to breathe, and beads of sweat were rolling down their faces. What the hell could have happened up ahead? One of the armored transports must have overheated, common enough at the height of day in summer. Or a truck's motor had died.

"Change the record, chief?" Orshev asked. The driver stopped whistling and drumming, closed his eyes, leaned back against the seat, and started breathing evenly and deeply, feigning sleep. Orshev smiled. I should have waited for a helicopter, he thought. I don't know what came over me to climb into that river. Right now I could be . . . yes, home, a white shirt . . .

The engines roared to life, and Orshev's driver opened his eyes and started whistling again. The column got going. Well, if nothing has happened so far, nothing's going to happen, thought Orshev, but then he corrected himself: In this pass.

The column made it through the pass and climbed downward. The mountains receded a bit from the road. The sun was at its zenith; the slabs of stone on the mountains were glimmering as though made of glass, and the sky burned one's eyes. The driver put on teardrop-shaped sunglasses that made him look like a Sicilian mafioso. The rocky heights were sparkling, the roadside boulders were sparkling, and the truck's hood was burning. Orshev squinted, squinted, and fell asleep.

"They hit one," voices said loudly, and Orshev, startled, looked at the driver, who caught his eye and pointed off to the left with his head. The column was making its way around a few military vehicles with Afghan markings on their sides and a red-and-white passenger bus lying on its side in a ditch, its perforated undercarriage facing the road. Civilians and soldiers were crowding around the bus. There were no dead or wounded to be seen; they had probably been carted away already. A skinny, mustachioed soldier who looked like Don Quixote was pouring out a canteen over his comrade's reddened hands. The civilians' pantaloons and cloaks were torn and stained with fuel and blood. A bony old man was sitting apart from everyone else, his head buried in his knees, rocking back and forth. Also standing off to one side were some women in chadors. Two small barefooted boys who had glanced at the column and lost interest in it were now trying to inspect the undercarriage of the bus—their heads were shoved into one of its gaps—but a gray-haired soldier started screaming at them. The Afghanis stared at the column.

The truck Orshev was riding in dropped down into the ditch, drove parallel to the road for a while, then returned to the tarmac. The driver started whistling. Orshev looked at his watch and asked: "Listen, do you stop for lunch or eat it on the road?"

"We stop. We'll be coming to a river soon. That's where we usually stop for chow."

"Mmm. The thing is, I haven't eaten since yesterday."

"So chow, what's the matter with you? What, you don't have anything to eat?" "I do. But I don't want to eat alone." "Forget it, chow down." "No, not alone. I'll wait for a while."

Orshev was rocked to sleep again. He woke up when the column came to a stop before a bridge. Two engineers and a German shepherd were already roving over the bridge. The other soldiers were smoking, wandering around the vehicles, throwing off their sweat-stiff jackets, and jumping into the river to wash themselves off; Orshev and the driver went too. They returned to the vehicle refreshed, left its doors wide open, and laid out their food: black bread, sugar, two cans of stewed lamb, and two cans of cheese. They ate in silence. First they ate the meat with the sour bread, then the sugar and cheese. They drank some water and lit cigarettes. Far away on the steppe they sighted a caravan—a line of camels, little silhouettes of people walking, white sheep.

"Ah, Pathanis," the driver said lazily, then yawned. "No bullshit for them—war or no war, they just roam around."

"Gypsies," responded Orshev.

"We had a gypsy once." The driver stirred. "But whatever, a gypsy's a gypsy: black, big-eyed, cunning. We went down to Kabul one time. They made us take a bath at the pass. Afterward the gypsy got sick. He was in the medical unit, then in Kabul, and from there to the Union, and we never saw him again."

"What was the matter with him?"

"Something like his liver. Or his stomach. They say he was a tobacco fiend. But what an idea—a gypsy in the army."

"So, what, he wasn't the type?"

"Of course not. A gypsy would be a gypsy even in Africa. Give him a whip, a horse, and the wind. All he gets here is the whip. I like them."

Orshev didn't understand. "Who?"

"Gypsies, of course. They don't care about anything. A horse, a whip, and the wind. And we're the asses." The driver stared ruefully at the steppe, where, at the base of the bare mountains, tiny camels and thin silhouettes of people were moving along amid the soft white fleece of sheep.

Kabul was lit by an evening sun, viscous, hot, swollen, and murky, that was resting on the snow-covered peaks. The city lay in a mountainous valley, a huge city of earth, stone, glass, and pavement; fluffy gardens and tall, pyramidical poplars everywhere; among the gardens, the glittering windows, and the white walls were the blue cupolas of mosques and soaring yellow minarets.

The column halted at a fenced-in lot at the edge of the city. Orshev put on his jacket and cap, picked up his case, and turned to the driver. His heavy hands on the wheel, the driver looked at Orshev. "Well," Orshev said, then paused. "Until we meet in the Union?" He held his hand out to the driver. The driver took his hand limply and answered that it was unlikely they'd meet again; the Union was pretty big. "Six months is nothing," Orshev said, and climbed down from the cabin.

He found the captain and asked him if they'd take him to the transit camp. "Ah, listen, our chauffeur is exhausted, why don't you wait until tomorrow morning?" the captain said merrily. "Where are you racing off to? No more planes are flying, and there are fleas at the camp. Spend the night with us. I'll tell you a bedtime story about the White Ox. What, you don't want me to?" The captain burst out laughing. Orshev was staring sullenly at him, not saying anything, when an airplane started to drone in the sky over Kabul. The captain, the infantrymen, and Orshev looked up. In the sky, soaring, gaining altitude, was a white aircraft with a purple stripe from its nose to its tail. "Oh! Look! Your airplane's gone bye-bye!" the captain exclaimed with a laugh.

"It isn't one of ours," one of the infantrymen objected. "Ours are white-and-blue."

"But a new directive came down that ours have to have a red stripe. What, you didn't hear? Well, brothers, you're out of touch," the captain said. The infantrymen were puzzled. Was it true? "And how. Listen up. Is our flag red? A Pioneer tie? A passport? Service papers? Hmm? So why should our planes be white-and-blue? There they are, flying overseas, with no ideological content, no ideological content at all in their coloring. How could that be? Either an oversight or provocation." The captain looked at Orshev. "Oh! Oh! The demob's going to rip me apart now, ha ha ha!"

"Comrade captain . . ." Orshev began, then shut up.

"But admit it, if I didn't have my stripe—no, my stripes—you'd hit me now, wouldn't you? Ha ha ha! Come on—watch it—honestly now. Wouldn't you?" the captain asked. The infantrymen and the armored transport driver started to mutter peevishly.

"Comrade captain, come on, the guy should really be given a ride."

"You would, oh, but how you would," the captain said. "I can see it in your eyes. I'd guess you did in a pile of *doukhs*, little eagle? But! Okay, okay, I'm joking. Stop pouting, we'll get you there. We'll get you there safe and sound. Corporal, come here!"

Orshev, four infantrymen, and the corporal climbed onto an armored transport and headed off toward the city. Orshev's eyes picked out the quiet driver's truck, and he waved his hand at him—the driver was sitting and smoking in the cabin. "You should sit below," the corporal called out to Orshev. "Don't tempt fate—snipers!" Orshev shook his head no. "Fine, fine," the corporal said, casting a benevolent look at Orshev.

Rocking gently, the green armored transport was sailing along a wide main road lined with poplars and cedars. Passenger cars, buses, trucks, and cyclists were driving along the main road. The sides of the road were packed with *karachivals*—ragged-looking men with two-wheeled wooden handcarts loaded with bags, packs, and firewood: delivery vans for the poor. People were walking along the sidewalks: old men with white beards in relief against black European coats, officers and soldiers with assault rifles, bushy-haired youths in colorful shirts, jeans, and pants, dirt-caked naked children, women in chadors, and white-faced, black-haired girls in short denim skirts and light blouses. *Dukans* were screaming out their wares, store windows and restaurant signs were sparkling, shashlik was being grilled in the street, stray dogs were howling, children twittering, engines roaring, brakes squealing, the evening wind was stirring the poplar and plane-tree leaves, and high above the city the mountaintops were glowing red with the sun disappearing behind them.

The transit station, a tent camp surrounded by barbed wire, was on the other side of the city, not far from the airport. The night was still light when the armored transport stopped in front of the camp gates. Orshev said goodbye to the infantrymen and corporal and jumped to the ground. A sentry appeared at the gates.

Orshev didn't sleep but lay on his bare bunk, his case thrust under his head, smoking and staring at the ceiling. The recruits—the camp was full of them—were breathing and snoring in boyish concert. Orshev wasn't feeling good, his head was aching, the hand that Khmyzin had bitten was throbbing, and it seemed that his temperature had gone up. Orshev was thinking: Not well yet. He smoked and glanced at the glowing dial on his watch—time wasn't rushing by.

At one in the morning a bang broke the silence, then a shout and an explosion could be heard. A moment later there was the jerk of another, closer this time, and shrapnel whistled over the tents. The camp defenses opened fire with assault rifles and heavy-caliber machine guns. The recruits were leaping up and screaming at one another: Huh? What? Alert! What was that? They leaned out of their tents and saw black mountains and red tracer bursts. "They're bombarding us, they're bombarding us!" they had all begun yelling when a third shell exploded right nearby, some-where beyond the barbed wire. Orshev was lying down, smoking and thinking that this was how it would be, he had imagined it happening like this, at the very last curtain call.

"Are those shells?" they asked him. Orshev answered yes. The new recruits were crowding around the door and looking out the windows. Orshev suddenly saw it all very clearly. There they are in the blackness, one of them is shoving a cylinder with metallic feathers on its tail into the muzzle, leaping back, and the mortar hurls the cylinder. Whistling gently, hypnotically, it rushes through the night and plows into the top of the tent. Orshev could hear and see the recruits writhing, rolling, struggling to get out, choking, moaning, screaming, not believing that this could be happening on their very first day, and Orshev saw himself clutching a wet, burning, sticky hole in his stomach—now . . .

But the mortar wasn't firing anymore. The defenses were pouring bursts into the mountains. In half an hour everything was quiet. The camp was stirring, talking, lighting cigarettes; no more shouts could be heard, which meant that all the shells had fallen away into the spurge. Orshev smoked another cigarette and, lulled by the talking of the recruits, fell asleep. In his sleep he thought: The weather will be good, there will be an airplane, the weather will be good and there will be an airplane, weather, airplane.

The weather was good and there was an airplane. It was a transport craft from Bagram, loaded with coffins and their escorts, that was picking up something else in Kabul. Orshev found out that the first stop would be Orenburg, then Minsk and Moscow. That was fortunate. Demobilized soldiers were usually brought to Tashkent, from where it was left entirely up to them to get home—no problem in the winter, but in summertime, when the train station and airport were overcrowded, one was forced to loiter around in Tashkent for a few days. Orshev, who had to go to Moscow and then farther west, was in real luck.

Orshev settled himself on a folding seat in the tail section. It was stuffy. He ditched his jacket, pulled off his tie, unbuttoned his shirt.

167

The somber soldiers, in ironed and spotless field uniforms with snow-white undercollars, were looking at him sullenly—they had to escort the coffins home and say a few words at the funerals and memorial suppers. Among the escort were two officers, so there were officers in the coffins too. Long, matte metal coffins, roughly welded in the middle, were sitting two by two in the airplane. The officers were talking about this and that. The soldiers were silent.

At last the pilots in their light blue suits entered the airplane. The plane's tail doors shut tightly, it became murky, and the ceiling lights up above began to glow dully. The airplane whined its engines and started moving, taxied to the runway, picked up speed, and took off. Those sitting by the few windows pressed their heads against the thick glass. Orshev wanted to see Kabul one last time, but going up to someone and asking him to move aside for a minute—no, he couldn't do that. Orshev looked at the soldiers, at the metallic boxes, at the ceiling, at his feet. . . . He closed his eyes.

The airplane labored to gain altitude. It was hot. Sweat was running down their faces. He wanted to smoke. Orshev hadn't smoked in ages—while the transport was being loaded he had sat for an hour under the shade of its wings, but smoking wasn't allowed on the airfield. There was a weakness in his body. When he took a deep breath he felt an ache in his back around the top of the left lung. Or was that his heart? No, his heart was healthy, it had been quiet for two years, so it was working fine, even though they had run up and down the mountains like horses. No, it was his lungs. He hadn't been treated long enough, that was all. Or maybe Khmyzin had popped him a good one there, that was why it ached. But this damn weakness . . .

How long to the border—half an hour, an hour? Orshev was thinking. Until we cross the border it will be too early to say hurrah. But we've reached a decent altitude, they couldn't get us now, we're out of range. So—hurrah! Hurrah! Hurrah!

THE YELLOW MOUNTAIN

It was dry, warm, yellow. His body was light. A strange woman growing out of the earth was feeding him red berries from her hand. A downy white lump was pressing against his cheek, a warm, heavy lump.

And there was an explosion.

Pryadilnikov screamed and woke up. He sat up in his bed, rubbed his eyes, looked around, and realized that he had been asleep in his tiny apartment and that the ringing of his alarm clock had woken him. He stretched, set his feet down on the floor, walked toward the table, and switched on the tape deck. In the morning he always listened to rock. And this morning he listened to rock. It was invigorating, like strong Indian tea or rich Brazilian coffee. Pryadilnikov opened the blinds. The street was sunny. It was a warm, early Russian autumn.

Pryadilnikov walked barefoot to the toilet, then to the sink. After washing up he went into the kitchen, took three eggs out of the refrigerator, turned the gas on under the tea kettle and frying pan. When the frying pan was hot he dropped a bit of butter into it; the butter melted quickly, and into the yellow, foamy little pool he slipped three eggs, convex, white and yellow, covered with a transparent slime.

In nothing more than his shorts Pryadilnikov sat down at the table, ate the fried eggs and three slices of bread with butter, and drank two cups of bitter, ruby-colored tea. After breakfast he returned to his bedroom, grabbed an ashtray, matches, and cigarettes, lay down on the bed, struck a match, lit a cigarette.

171

Dove-colored locks and curls snaked down over his face.

The rock was rocking: Hey, come along with us, with us everything is simple, black is black, white is white, it's better to be lying back in a clearing with your girl and a can of beer than to play the games of adult idiots, it's better to be poor but lie to nobody, submit to nobody, give orders to nobody, we're telling you to love yourself, your girl, your beer, and not to stop anybody else from doing the same thing, it's better than preaching about love for all humanity, demanding people to love one another without loving themselves, to put idea and duty far above everything else—it's better than preaching, demanding, forcing, and time after time massacring for the sake of the triumph of your humanitarian ideals, you can't believe, no, can't believe anyone, anytime, anything, my friend, you can't believe.

The nicotine and the rock were dissolving in his blood, and Pryadilnikov was high.

You can't believe, no, can't believe. . . .

His mood was just fine. It wasn't good very often. Such a swollen head all the time—everything was always wrong, but today everything was all right. But why?

Had he dreamed something, maybe?

Yes, so it seemed.

Have to remember—but later, later. For now, rock.

Pryadilnikov looked at his watch. It was time. He got up, put on jeans, a black sweater, and light suede shoes. He glanced into the mirror. Not too bad. Healthier-looking. Limping, Pryadilnikov left the apartment.

His "armored car"—a Zaporozhets the color of sand—was parked near the entryway. Pryadilnikov wiped the fogged windshield off with a rag, got in, turned the key in the ignition, warmed the engine up, put the car into gear, and set out. The armored car wound through stone labyrinths, reached a broad street, and started gliding past bus stops and crowds, shops and restaurants. Pryadilnikov switched on the radio, twisted the tuner knob, and came across some rock. The rock was still rocking the same thing:

If the pot-bellied men in top hats haven't already led you astray with their speeches and slogans, come to us, we're not going anywhere since there's nowhere to go, and we won't tell lies about going somewhere and getting there in the end, we're just marking time, and we don't give a damn who you are—red or black, left or right, Christian or Buddhist, godless or anarchist—you're a human being, that's enough, that's all there is to say, you'll come to us because you're sick of humanitarian fables written in your blood and mine, let them smash in one another's top hats and heads, but we'll be looking at the sun, kissing our girls, and listening to rock, rock has united us, our ideology and our religion is rock.

That's great, Pryadilnikov thought. Only naive, kids. Those gentlemen in their top hats will suddenly start swearing, calling each other names, and send you your orders. And there won't be anywhere for you to run, you'll go off to defend the honor of those top hats, and you'll disembowel your brothers in rock.

He drove into the lot, thinking that he didn't really have to come here today, parked his car among the black and gray Volgas, and started limping toward the main entrance of the columned building. I shouldn't have come here, he thought again.

Sober-looking men in suits and ties were going into the edifice, nodding curtly and offering each other their soft white hands; women were going into the building too, all of them dressed the same way—à la Iron Lady of London.

On the fourth floor of the columned building, under the wings and indefatigable eyes of the district powers, were the editorial offices of two newspapers, one for the Party, the other for youth. It was in the latter that the lame, chain-smoking, sickly young person named Pryadilnikov was an employee. He had been coming to this building every morning for a year now. He should have become used to it. But he wasn't used to it at all. And this morning, finding himself in the spacious reception area with its mirrors, its shoe-shining machine, and its two militiamen behind

a small table covered with black and white telephones, Pryadilnikov felt awkward, like an uninvited guest at a party, and in fact
a party filled with complete strangers. He walked past the militiamen and looked the other way. He had never learned how to
nod to them baronially, and fraternally—he couldn't do it.

There were two elevators, one for those whose offices were
in the right wing, the other for the left-wing workers. He had to
take the left one, but among the left-wingers he spotted a familiar
round face and he swung to the right. Ah, him, that zavsepech.
A total bore. The zavsepech was the director of the press section,
and every newspaper in the district was under his control. He had
started out as the Party secretary at the Twenty Years Without a
Harvest kolkhoz, or something to that effect. Now he was the
zavsepech.

One time, on the eve of Red Army Day, the zavsepech had
proposed that Pryadilnikov say a few words at the ceremonial
assembly. Pryadilnikov had declined: I don't speak well, I don't
know what to say, no. The zavsepech started coaching him about
what was needed and how it was accomplished, and he got carried
away: Our people have lived so long under peaceful skies, but
you, on your generation it befell...um, um...it befalls...it
befell, that is, circumstances were such that your...you were
called by international duty to defend, guns in hand, the nascent
revolution of our fraternal brother to the south, and there you
rendered that help, couldn't you come with your medal so we
can admire it and know that our successors will be worthy successors, traditions, internationalism, Spain, heroes of the revolution, the southern borders, the Americans weren't dozing,
where there's trouble they're in like that—zap!—but you wouldn't
let those falcons and hawks rip the young revolution to shreds,
terror, bandits, intrigues, bravery, honor, Russian arms, to sunny
days—yes! yes! yes!—to nuclear explosions—no! no! no!

"My medal's being repaired," Pryadilnikov had said. His editor shook his fist at him behind the zavsepech's back. The zavsepech was taken by surprise: "How's that?" The editorial office

had fallen joyously silent. Behind the zavsepech, the editor was making terrifying faces. "It fell apart," Pryadilnikov said. "I've been wearing it around a lot." The editor cut in: "You'll speak without the medal. He'll speak, Demyan Vasilevich."

But on the following day Pryadilnikov wheedled a job out of his supervisor, the department head, and disappeared for the day. From that time on the zavsepech would stop Pryadilnikov whenever they ran into each other, clap him on the shoulder, and say:

"Young man, it seems to me there's something you don't quite understand. Of course, you did take, as they say, a direct part in it, but from the trenches you can only see one side of the fighting, and even if you could see every side of every battle—it isn't enough, because aside from the visible battles there are the hidden ones, imperceptible to a superficial glance, there are complexities inaccessible to superficial thinking . . ."

Pryadilnikov went into the elevator with two women and a gray-haired man. The elevator started to rise. The man looked disapprovingly at the journalist's well-worn jeans and was probably regretting that it was only women who were forbidden to come here in capitalistic pants. Pryadilnikov eyed the women in their severe suits. Dry water. Crooked straight line. Sweet lemon. But they're perfect for it, just perfect, he thought, looking at the woman officials. And it would be even more perfect if all the men were thrown the hell out of this building. The guys were pretty much just dead weight. But these women, shit.

He got out on his floor and started limping along the crimson-carpeted corridors to the left wing. When he passed by the door with OBLLIT written on it he recalled how one time the second page of the youth newspaper had been blocked out. In one sentence in a small article of literary criticism, the names of a well-known writer and Bulgakov had both appeared. The editor was telephoned and told that putting the well-known Soviet writer and Bulgakov in the same praiseful sentence was nonsense. The editor was an easygoing person. But sometimes his emotions got the better of him. He'd be working away, working away, not saying anything, doing what he was told, and suddenly he'd spot the latest red-calico watchword—"Trampling on headgear is strictly prohibited!"—and he'd tear off his shabby cap and start jumping up and down on it. And this time his emotions got him too. The editor replied that he, the whole editorial office, the author of the article, and intelligent people all over the planet saw no nonsense in it at all. But the person he had by implication ranked among the world's unintelligent people was beside himself and answered the following: Praising Whites plays into the hands of the enemy, malevolent nostalgia, decadent tone, the universal aims of socialist realism, a corrupting influence on developing hearts and minds, a perverted representation of reality, we, the Soviet people, who sense the greatness of the everyday, we declare a decisive no! This praiser, this slanderer, cannot stand beside a great Soviet writer!

But the editor was having none of it: "Then the newspaper won't run. The whole issue." "What? What is this? Sabotage?" "In a nutshell, yes," the editor replied, and hung up. Five minutes later he was summoned to the chief censor of OBLLIT. He heard the editor out and recommended resolving the question by having one writer appear in one sentence and the other in another. Solomon.

The student youth department was already smoky and smelling of coffee. The department director started clapping:

"Oh! Fedya didn't drink last night either!"

"He can't have any money," suggested the department's bearded correspondent, who was handsome and sad-looking as Garshin.

"Fedya, come over here," the department director called out.

Pryadilnikov walked over to her desk; she set her cigarette down on the edge of an ashtray, got up, firmly gripped his neck in her hand, pulled his head toward her, and kissed him on the lips. Encore, the bearded man said.

The other correspondent, just graduated from Moscow State University, a petite girl with big hazel eyes and curly hair, blushed and turned away.

"Okay, I won't do it anymore or Marina will end up pouring poison in my coffee," the director said, letting go of Pryadilnikov.

"Hah!" the young journalist said.

Pryadilnikov sat down at his desk.

"Marina, why don't you give him some coffee," the director said, then picked up her cigarette and pulled on it.

"You want some?" the petite journalist asked, looking at Pryadilnikov warmly. He nodded.

The girl stood up, gracefully walked over to the bookcase, picked up the pot of coffee, soundlessly and smoothly poured the brown liquid into a large cup, and brought it to Pryadilnikov. He thanked her and took the cup, his fingers brushing against her small ones. The director, a woman in her thirties who had already started the struggle against common sense and time, smiled thinly—her smiles had been infrequent and thin for some time, so the wrinkles would be smaller. The bearded man smiled too, but dreamily: what nice little legs.

"Fedya, is it true that you don't have any money?" the director asked.

"I do, I do," Pryadilnikov replied, and sipped his coffee. "I've just decided to be an angel."

"I'll give you some. Don't be shy," the director said.

"She'll give it to you, don't doubt it," the cartoonist and caricaturist Gostyev said as he came into the room. "Will you give it to me too, Louisa?"

Louisa—Liza, the director—was unfazed and answered:

"And you only have one thing on your mind."

"Yup. Freud said that it's on everyone's mind all the time."

"I wonder what's on the chief's mind today. Have you seen him? What side of the bed was he good enough to get out on?"

Gostyev was about to say something about the editor and his bed, but he didn't have the chance. The door opened and, puffing on a cheap cigarette, into the room came the editor, an imposing, big-eared man in glasses.

"Yegor Petrovich!" exclaimed Gostyev, standing at attention and thrusting out his chest. "Companee! Atten-tion!"

"Get out of here," the editor said, his large, tobacco-stained teeth showing when he smiled.

"Yessir!" Gostyev walked out in ceremonial step but immediately returned. "Permission to stand guard here!" he exclaimed by the door.

"Numskull," the editor said.

"Thank you, sir!"

"Good morning, Yegor," said the director.

The editor had passed the maximum Komsomol age limit ten years before, but he thought of himself as young and insisted on being called nothing more than Yegor, although, of course, only if there were no outsiders around.

"Morning," the editor replied. "You drinking coffee?"

"Coffee for the editor!" Gostyev bellowed, and rushed off to the bookcase to pour some in the editor's oversized baked-clay cup.

The editor chuckled and sat down on a free stool.

"So, Fedya, why are you looking so sad behind those deep blue pools?" the editor asked Pryadilnikov with a smile. He always asked the same question if he had woken up in a good mood. He had borrowed the deep blue pools from Esenin, his favorite poet.

"Fedya's looking well today," the director said.

"Yeah?" The editor looked him over. "What, no money? But I won't give you any, so don't even ask. If you turned your empties in you'd have enough for food. Dry yourself out."

"He needs to get married," the editor said, her eyes moving in the direction of Marina.

"Let's get him a wife," the editor said resolutely.

"Fast as we can," the Beard sighed. His own wife ran off to her mother's when he came home drunk and couldn't convince her that he had good reason to be so.

Their tongues thoroughly stretched, the journalists took up their pens.

Pryadilnikov was working on an article about military and patriotic instruction in the city schools. Pryadilnikov wrote. Marina glanced at him every now and then from the side. The Beard had left to interview someone. The director was looking for a book in the bookcase.

Pryadilnikov ran the tip of his pen across a piece of paper, and a flock of birds was slowly landing on the steppe before bare, soft hills; he and the other guards watched silently while the large black birds with small heads floated down toward the grass and flowers; it was early in the morning, quiet, the company was asleep in its armored transports; the birds were landing, folding their huge wings, cleaning their feathers with their beaks, looking around, wandering through the flowers; they had white stripes running from their beaks to their breasts and red crowns on their heads, and every so often they would stand still, turn their heads toward the column, and stare at it; the guards didn't budge and the birds probably mistook them for pillars, and the armored transports for shining green turtles; the white-necked birds were striding back and forth on the steppe, the birds were black, the steppe green, the bare hills and the herd of green turtles were asleep, there was already a crimson light in the sky to the east, and it was quiet, warm . . .

The door opened.

"I won't even give this to OBLLIT, Fyodor," the editor said, walking in and handing a manuscript to Pryadilnikov. "They'll tear it to pieces."

"That's what I thought too," Pryadilnikov replied.

"You understand . . ."

"I understand that I'm not really Soviet, I suppose."

"Come on, don't generalize. And don't take it to heart. That's all. And you know that for now you can write for the desk drawer. Sometime, perhaps . . . umm. But right now—alas!"

"Understood."

"And something else. You know, everything somehow turns out to be so subjective with you. Was it all really so gloomy? Nothing but negatives?"

"No, not at all. They gave us free cigarettes. You didn't have

179

to shave during operations. Well, actually you did, but the officers didn't look too closely at your stubble. What else? They shipped us vodka from the Union in tanker trucks."

"Ha ha." The editor laughed humorlessly.

"Thirty chits per bottle. But you could steal boots, gasoline, or heating fuel for the *dukans* and get enough to buy a bottle."

"Negatives, sheer negatives. A journalist has to be objective. In every article there has to be both negative and positive. That's what objectivity means."

"I can't. I'm blunt, unihemispherical."

"Why's that?"

"Only one hemisphere works, the pessimistic one; the optimistic one burst from dyspepsia."

"Don't talk nonsense. And try to be objective. Try, Fyodor," the editor said, then left.

"Memoirs?" the director asked coldly. She wasn't pleased that Pryadilnikov had given the manuscript to the editor and not to her.

"Yes, memoirs. And nothing to do with what our department does," Pryadilnikov said.

The director was silent.

"Fedya," Marina called out to him. "Can I please read them?"

"It's garbage."

"Come on, Fedya."

He shrugged his shoulders and handed her the manuscript.

AN ARMY ORATORIO

His name was Akimov. At the time in question he was a major, the regimental chief of staff. A stocky major of medium height with hard eyes, small hands, and boots that were always shiny. Close-shaved. Not a speck of dust on his uniform, although the place was dusty—in summer the djinns of dust would dance on the steppe around the camp, and from time to time they would band together and fall on it with a roar, and the sky would grow dark and the sun go dim, and a biblical haze would shroud our small tent city.

We four soldiers were detailed to the guard of the regimental CP. It was a long detail; it lasted five months. The command thought it more expedient to have a permanent guard for the regimental CP. And in fact it was better than rotating details that would carry out their duties in a less than meticulous way. So we, the permanent guard, cherished the life we were leading without the incessant surveillance of officers, training, drills, and marches, and we performed our duties eagerly. Everyone called the CP "the village" and envied us. The small stone house, actually more of a hut, stood a kilometer away from the camp on a road that led off into the steppe; this road and another road on the opposite side of the camp were the only unmined stretches of land—the camp was entirely surrounded by minefields, and the roads linked the camp to an alien, hostile world.

We watched the road around the clock. Two would sleep while two, in flak jackets, would be on guard. We had our meals with the battalion. Still, we did have, of course, a fireplace in a dugout, a tea kettle, and a bowl for pilafs. On the walls hung pictures cut from magazines, there were books on the table, and we had a shortwave radio hidden away. There was a deck of homemade cards. We didn't live badly.

Every night the duty officer would call on us, or sometimes Akimov or the camp zampolit.

Akimov loved Blok. The poet. Aleksandr Blok.

He came by one time to make sure that we hadn't been drinking liquor or smoking hash. We hadn't been smoking or drinking, and everything was in order; even our undercollars were clean. The major was satisfied with us. He spotted a little volume of Blok's poems on the table, asked whose book it was; I said I had borrowed it from the library, and he recited, in a melancholy voice, "At night, above the restaurants," said that Blok was his favorite poet, took the little volume, and allowed me to come see him in a week's time. A week later I went to camp and waited an hour for the major at headquarters; he appeared, invited me into his office, held the book out to me, and said: Poems of crystal. I answered yes, not steel. He looked at me closely. I broke into a sweat. Well, off you go, he said, and dismissed me.

Major Akimov put an end to our life at "the village."

It was evening. Snow was falling. We were stoking the stove. One man in a canvas cloak was pacing back and forth in front of the barricade in the road; sometimes he walked up to the window and looked in at us. It was hot, smoky, and noisy inside. We were baking flatcakes and roasting potatoes. We were celebrating someone's name day. A shy young boy, he was sitting, his arms folded, waiting for the presents and guests. The guests arrived soon. There were two of them, and they brought half a can of condensed milk and a pair of suspenders: suspenders were in fashion with us.

We sat down at the table, grape juice was poured into our cups, and I was getting up to make a speech when the sentry rapped on the snow-crusted window and said: A car! We were all suddenly terrified and started stashing the food under the bed, and the guests hurled themselves outside. I tried to stop them and said: But what's all this for if we're just celebrating a name day? But no one paid attention to me.

The car pulled up. We waited. A car door slammed. The muffled voice of our sentry could be heard reporting that since he had come on guard . . . and so on. The door opened and into the little house came Major Akimov, glowering, and the regimental duty officer, a lieutenant. Akimov looked around at our sweaty, cowering faces. From under the bed came the reek of flatcakes and potatoes, and on the table lay bread, jam, and a pile of sliced large onions.

"Get it out," Akimov said. "Everything."

We pulled the frying pan and the plate of cakes out from under the bed.

"I said everything," Akimov prodded.

"That is everything," our sergeant said.

"The liquor!"

We shrugged our shoulders.

"Lieutenant," Akimov called out.

The lieutenant rummaged through everything, looked under the pillow, then went outside.

"Comrade major," our sergeant began to explain, "we have a name day . . ."

The lieutenant returned with the two snow-covered guests.

"They were lying down in the trench."

"So," the major said, becoming animated. He took off his cap, smoothed his hair, and sat down at the little table.

"Where do you come from?" the lieutenant asked the guests. They fidgeted, hung their heads dejectedly, and said nothing.

"Where do you come from?" the major asked quietly, and the guests sighed, raised their heads, and stated their names and units.

"Unauthorized personnel are not allowed at the CP. Do you know that?" the lieutenant asked.

The guests said nothing.

"Do you know that?" the major asked, and the guests answered in chorus: Absolutely! Not at all!

One knew, the other didn't.

"So," the major said. "You don't know either, sergeant?"

"Yes, but it's a name day," our sergeant said, "and we're on permanent detail . . ."

"Permanent?" The major turned white. "Parasites," he said quietly.

He glanced at the table and suddenly struck the handle of the pan with the edge of his palm. The potatoes fell to the ground.

"A name-day party," the major said through his teeth, and stood up. "A name-day party! They're having a name-day party! Enemies all around just looking to cut everyone's throat! It's war, I tell you! And they're having a name-day party. A name . . . Why are you still sitting down?"

The boy whose name day it was leaped up off the bed and stood at attention.

"They're stuffing themselves, making pigs of themselves! Per-

183

ma-nent detail! I'll show you permanent . . . I'll teach you mothers
. . . the whole camp in zinc-lined boxes? In zinc, eh? . . . They're
having a name-day party! Yes, lieutenant, just look, just look at
these badgers in their hole! Permanent detail!"

Someone, I don't remember who anymore, giggled. No doubt
from nervousness. But it was enough to make the chief of staff's
eyes jump entirely from their sockets.

"Funny? You think it's funny?"

He grabbed the loaf of bread, heavy and brown, and swept
the cans, the salt, the flatcakes, the cups off the table. Terrified,
one of the guests rushed outside; the lieutenant sprang out after
him and dragged him back. He was holding him by the ear: What
were you doing, huh? What were you going to do? Where were
you going? To the *doukh*s, maybe?

The soldier started crying. The major turned even whiter and
frowned in disgust.

"Get rid of it all! Now!"

I grabbed a broom to sweep up the potatoes, flatcakes, salt.

"With your hands," the major said. "Your hands. Hands!
Come on!"

I stood there with my head bowed. My legs were trembling.

"Come on!"

I don't know. Maybe I bent down and started to pick the food
up with my hands. I don't know. I'm something of a coward.
But I didn't have time to make a complete coward of myself
because our sergeant suddenly made his move. He strode over
toward the pyramid of assault rifles and muttered, distinctly:

"We're in a combat post."

The oven singing. Snow outside the window. Silence.

The major glanced at the lieutenant.

"Whoa!" the lieutenant said and walked toward the sergeant.

The major burst out laughing.

"The movies! No, you won't die of boredom." He stopped
laughing. "Fine. Everyone will go to the cooler. The detail for
seven days, the guests for three. And you," he said to the sergeant,
"but you I . . ."

"Give him to Zhilmurdayev," the lieutenant suggested. "He likes hotheads like him."

Zhilmurdayev was the commander of the infantry battalion's third company, and "difficult cases" were sent to him for re-education. The "difficult cases" quickly turned tractable.

The major suddenly said:

"No. But you I congratulate."

No doubt the major thought himself a second Suvorov.

From that time there was a daily change of guard at the CP. Our "village" life came to an end. But that's beside the point.

In the summer a young soldier ran away from camp. For three days and nights soldiers scoured the steppes and *kishlaks*, but they never caught the deserter. The matter drew some attention, and an inquiry was launched. It became clear that the veterans... well, too many horrors, bestial, all kinds of inhumanities... and representatives of high command flew into camp. After investigating the matter they resolved to punish the guilty parties severely. Before returning to Kabul the officers called together the Komsomol activists from every unit for a discussion. My company sent me, although never in my whole life have I been an activist, especially not in the army—it was simply my idiotic habit at any gathering to pose the officers questions that would entertain a bored audience, and the officers considered me an activist.

The discussion took place in the regimental club. The club had neither walls nor a ceiling; there were rows of wooden benches, a semicircular stage, a huge, concave white screen, and sky and sun. On the stage were tables, and behind the tables sat majors and colonels in field uniforms: thick, distinguished mustaches, Roman chins, spectacles in thin frames, penetrating eyes, taut, close-shaved cheeks, snow-white undercollars, strong bald heads, and brows glistening with sweat.

The first to stand up was the chief of staff of our regiment, Major Akimov. He said: A peaceful foreign policy, but when things go badly for our neighbor we step in, tense days, imperialist machinations, undeclared war, losses, hardships, the glorious armed forces, trials by fire, traditions, great martial spirit, patriotism, superb military and political preparation, scores of successful operations, Orders of the Red Star, scores of decorations, three Heroes . . . Akimov poured some water out of the decanter into his glass and swallowed it in one gulp as though it were vodka. After a brief pause he continued: But notwithstanding glorious traditions, the legacy of our forefathers, notwithstanding the fact of superb military and political preparation, the three Heroes, the Orders of the Red Star, and all the efforts of the respective commanders and political workers, there are isolated shortcomings, although we are maintaining constant, painstaking work on them, that is to say, an unyielding and uncompromising struggle . . . And then what happened happened. Did what happened happen by chance? Both yes and no—a moral code, the great humanism of our ideals, the harmony of domestic and foreign cultures, but in our life there still persist ugly remnants of the past, hostile to socialism, like greed and corruption, the desire to take the most from society and give it nothing in return, mismanagement and waste, drunkenness and hooliganism, bureaucracy and the callous treatment of others, and thus there are isolated irresponsible elements, criminal elements, in fact, that allow themselves to physically and morally humiliate a human being!

I was sitting in the first row, listening. I thought: Just maybe, I . . . I still had a year to go until demobilization. I looked at the major's hard face, at his small, strong hands, at the faces of the staff officers who were listening with satisfaction to the major, and I thought: No.

I didn't stand up and didn't say anything. When the major was finished the staff officers stood up and spoke along the same lines as Akimov. After dinner the officers flew back to Kabul in helicopters. The veterans connected to the desertion of the young soldier were imprisoned. But for some reason the remaining old-timers did not listen to reason and continued to physically and morally humiliate the kids.

* * *

"Fedya, really, it's too much," Marina said when she handed the manuscript back.

"You think so too? Strange. But it's only half true. It was actually much worse."

"And why 'Oratorio'?"

"Nothing to do with music. It comes from the word 'orator.'"

"That's what I thought."

"Marina, I've been waiting half a week now for your article," the director Louisa-Liza said.

"I'll get it to you today," Marina muttered, and bent down over her papers.

"Your material is late too, Fedya."

"I hear you," said Pryadilnikov, picking up his pen.

He was writing about military instruction and learning aids, about the education of young people's sensibilities... traditions ...precepts... patriotism... we, youth, long-haired, our desires are straightforward, give us the vaults of heaven!... And the mountains were asleep, the herd of green turtles were asleep, it was quiet, warm. But a hatch cover creaked and a second lieutenant hauled himself out of an armored transport; he yawned, glanced around at the steppe, and froze when he spotted the black cranes; he vanished for a moment, reappeared, carefully climbed out of the machine, and, crouched low to the ground, walked across the steppe with an assault rifle, the guards following him with their eyes, and the birds caught sight of him, stretched their necks, stiffened, the lieutenant dropped onto one knee, raised the rifle butt to his shoulder, hunched his head, aimed, the birds ran off, bobbing up and down and flapping their wings, the flock took to the air, a pale red burst shot over the steppe and cut into the black flock. The guards watched in silence. It was Pryadilnikov's first operation, he was scared, not sure if, when he felt the crack of bullets around his feet or the whistle of shrapnel over his head, he would keep his composure and behave like a hardened soldier; he was afraid he would make a fool of himself and run away from the battlefield or do something else as shameful; he recalled all those hardened heroes from movies and books but it didn't help, he felt sick, he had lost his appetite and needed to piss all the time, but the raid was taking place peacefully, without any shooting, and only on this morning of the second day did Pryadilnikov hear any shooting or see any death: the second lieutenant dropped down to one knee, hunched his head, aimed, and a tracer burst, tracers . . . tracers . . . tracers . . . Where did I want to go this morning? Pryadilnikov thought. I dreamed of something and wanted to go. What could I have dreamed about? Tracers . . . trr . . . aa . . . ss . . .

"Louisa," Pryadilnikov said, "something isn't right at all with me."

"Fyodor." Louisa looked at him severely. "Don't be a jellyfish. Collect yourself. It has to be done today."

Pryadilnikov lit a cigarette.

"Well, children," Louisa said, "I'm off to the library. We don't have the book here. Behave yourselves." She walked over to the mirror on the wall, arranged her short dark hair, put lipstick on her large, pouty lips, took two steps backward to see the reflection of her legs, looked herself over, smiled to herself, and left.

Marina and Pryadilnikov were sitting at their desks and writing in silence. From time to time Marina would cast glances at Pryadilnikov. He seemed especially sick and exhausted today, and she wanted to feed him. She wanted to take his cigarettes away from him. She wanted to mend the faded, tattered, frayed cuffs of his jeans. She wanted to rub his lame leg.

The door opened.

"Oh! Pardon, pardon," Gostyev cried out, then vanished.

Some ten minutes passed and there was a knock on the door.

"Yes!" Pryadilnikov called out.

The door opened a crack. The zavsepech's eyeglasses were glowing white in the doorway. He seemed to be acting strangely.

"May I? I'm not bothering you too much?"

"Please," Pryadilnikov mumbled, puzzled. What did he want?

"Excuse me. Of course," the zavsepech said as he came in, "of course I understand humor, but . . . there's a time for fun and a time for work." He looked intently at Marina. "Good day, young person."

Marina raised her eyes from her article, glanced at him, blushed, and hastily said:

"Good day."

The zavsepech turned toward Pryadilnikov. "And good day to you, veteran, so to speak."

"We salute you, so to speak."

The zavsepech stared blankly at him: a little mockery from the puppy, eh?

"Might I please sit down?" the zavsepech asked with mock humility.

"Sit, sit, please, for the love of God who doesn't exist. Would you like some coffee? We'll make some."

"Please, no. But thank you. You're writing?"

"Yes."

"Business as usual, the bureau writing, ha, ha. And what, allow me to ask, is stirring your young hearts right now?"

"My young heart is racked with grief about imperfections in military and patriotic instruction in the city schools. And hers about drunkenness and all the other rashes and pimples from the bourgeois past that have arisen in the body of Soviet studentdom."

"The little students are drinking?"

Marina nodded.

"Good-for-nothings. But not the whole overwhelming majority?"

"No, no," Pryadilnikov answered instead of Marina. "It's atypical. She's describing a specific case. But Soviet students in general are very very."

The zavsepech narrowed his eyes.

"What?"

"Nothing. Just very very. Very very and most most."

189

"You criticize everything, Pryadilnikov," the zavsepech said with a smile. "Always with dark glasses planted firmly on your nose, always looking at the world from your trench. . . . Is your medal fixed?"

"Yes. Only there's a new problem. The color's chipped off. It has to be repainted, but I can't find the right color anywhere."

"Although," the zavsepech said, frowning, "you could think a bit before talking that way about a state decoration."

"We journalists talk first and think later, in the thick of it."

"And that's bad! Very bad! I would advise you to think first. Thoroughly. Tho-rough-ly!" the zavsepech exclaimed in an irritated voice. "Isn't it time to be serious? Why is it all such a big farce with you? Why be such a clown? I don't like that style at all. Granted, the youth press is a bit easygoing, which can be seen in the attitude of the editorial employees, but not to this degree! Journalism is a serious matter. There has to be a sense of responsibility. If you're not capable of feeling a sense of responsibility, then it's worth thinking about it very thoroughly: is this really the place for me?"

"I think about that all the time, Demyan Vasilevich. Is this the place for you? That's what I ask myself: Fedya, is this the place for you?"

The zavsepech fixed his eyes on Pryadilnikov. Marina smiled a startled smile and turned away toward the window. It didn't slip by the zavsepech.

"Where's the editor?" he asked quietly. He was still in control of himself.

"Probably in his office. I don't know," Pryadilnikov answered.

"Call him in."

Pryadilnikov looked darkly at the zavsepech and repeated:

"He's probably in his office."

The zavsepech stared at Pryadilnikov.

"Just a moment," Marina said, and stood up.

But the zavsepech had risen too and left without another word.

"You've lost your mind," Marina said.

"Yes, I have," Pryadilnikov agreed, and lit a cigarette.

Very soon the zavsepech's voice could be heard from the other side of the door:

"There, Yegor Petrovich, there, just look at those jokers. Huh? After all, it's an editorial office, not a circus. And what if it wasn't me but a visitor who'd seen it? What would he have thought of us? They write at the level of second-year high school students, but their ambitions—oh! Oh ho ho! You've let your gadflies get out of hand, Yegor Petrovich. No seriousness at all, no political maturity at all, just sarcasm. The Party and the government, you understand, have shown their concern for that, so to speak, veteran of yours, they've given him a car, they've given him an apartment—he's living off the fat of the land. What did you and I have at his age? Huh? And he mocks and scoffs at everything, he's always playing, you understand, the victim. He laughs at his state decoration! And so on and so on. We have to undertake a review. For a long time I've closed my eyes to your gadflies—but enough. You've collected, you understand, all sorts of underripe buffoons—clowns, you understand. But there are, we have at our disposal, competent, serious journalists. There are. They've been with the provincial papers for years. Experienced, mature. He writes like a dog, but his ambitions—oh! Oh ho ho! And on top of that I have some information . . ."

The door was thrown open and the knob slammed into the wall.

"Look at him!" the zavsepech demanded.

The editor glanced wearily at Pryadilnikov.

"Just look at his face. His place is in a detox clinic. I have verified proof."

Pryadilnikov was leaning back on his stool, smoking and staring at the ceiling.

The zavsepech couldn't stand the sight: he turned around abruptly and stalked off down the corridor. As soon as his steps had faded away everyone who worked in the area drifted into the student youth section, even the old typist. The editor sat down, took off his glasses, wiped them with his handkerchief, and lit a cheap cigarette.

"What on earth got into Demyan Vasilevich?" the gray-haired typist asked.

The editor showed her a sheet of paper. There was a heart pierced by an arrow drawn on it, with the words "Love break— 10:00–10:15."

"It was hanging on the door," the editor explained, "and then he walked by."

The old woman pulled out her glasses, held them up to her eyes, and looked at the piece of paper. She livened and glanced at Marina with interest. The director of the Komsomol life section stretched his lips into a deadened smile.

"Is this your work, numskull?" the editor gloomily asked Gostyev.

Gostyev lowered his eyes.

"Gostyev, we're going to have to do something about this," said the director of the Komsomol life section, a man in his thirties who drank a lot in his youth but had recovered from the fatal passion five years before. He didn't drink, was healthy and energetic, but for five years he had been smiling that dead Jesuit smile.

"I can explain," Gostyev said. "I suspect what this is all about."

"Shouldn't expect much of fools," the editor muttered.

"I suspect," Gostyev said, "that it wasn't the joke. Think about it. A heart's a heart. It's not a naked woman or something. I suspect what this is all about. It's something else."

"I'm dropping everything, fuck it all, and I'm moving to my in-laws' in the countryside, where I'm going to raise mad bulls," the editor announced.

"Simply put," Gostyev continued, "the zavsepech has feelings for Marina. The old man has a complex."

"I'm sick of you and your psychoanalysis," Marina said, and left the room.

"It's Freud, not me."

"Well, and you? Why do you always have to shoot off? Why did you have to shoot off to him like you were manning a machine gun? Fyodor—blue pools—you should hold your tongue," the editor said.

"I got sick of commanders and zampolits in the army."

The editor looked out the window at the sunlit street.

"In the country. Steaming milk, fishing," he muttered. "Rabbit hunting, a little bathhouse, a vegetable garden, a herd of mad bulls—joy."

Toward evening Pryadilnikov's head was roaring with tobacco and military-patriotic sentences like a stove full of pine logs, the only difference being that only he could hear it. He put the last touch on the article and handed it in. Louisa kissed him on the forehead. And he asked her for some money. But you said you had money, she replied. I'm just very shy, he said. And what will you buy? Milk and bread. Really? I swear. Well, just make sure it isn't anything flammable. Yes ma'am, I promise. He took the ten-ruble note and asked: Allow me to kiss your hand, mademoiselle? Better Marina's. Don't be a fool, Marina said to Pryadilnikov, who was heading toward her. Ah, Marina, you're no maker of your own happiness, Louisa said.

At ten to six everyone got ready to go home.

"Maestro, what plans do you have for the evening?" Pryadilnikov inquired of the Beard.

The Beard turned his sad, beautiful eyes to him and said in a melancholy voice: I'm going home. Come on, let's go to my place for a little bit, Pryadilnikov pressed. My wife will run to her mother's again, the Beard answered; I'll pass, but go ask Gostyev there. I'm sick to death of Gostyev, said Pryadilnikov. Well, I don't know then, but I'll pass, the Beard replied, then picked up his case, beat a hasty retreat, and even forgot to say goodbye to everyone.

"Fyodor! What did I hear?" Louisa shouted out.

"It was a joke."

"Well, watch out for this." Louisa threatened him with her fist. She said goodbye, then left.

Marina was slowly arranging pieces of paper on her desk. Pryadilnikov picked up the receiver, dialed the requisite number with his index finger. No answer. He drummed his fingers on the phone and dialed another number. Silence, or rather long rings. The pine logs were groaning and splitting, the pile of cinders crackling. Pryadilnikov rubbed his temples with his index fingers. He tried the two numbers again, hung up, said "Later" to Marina, and disappeared out the door.

Marina sat there, not moving, looking at the door.

He took the elevator down, passed by the militiamen without looking at them, went out onto the steps, limped between the à la Parthenon columns, walked to his armored car, unlocked the door, and climbed in. "Where to?" he asked the armored car.

Have to remember last night's dream, and then it will be clear where to go.

Pryadilnikov wrinkled his forehead. No, it was useless. He turned the ignition and drove out into the street. The armored car glided slowly through the autumn streets. Black birds settled onto the steppe. Then they flew away again, Pryadilnikov was thinking. Black birds settled onto the steppe. The mountains were asleep, the herd of green turtles was asleep, and it was quiet, warm, there were white flowers, the cranes landed, it was quiet and warm, there were white flowers, the flowers were white, whiteflowers, cranewomen, tankturtles . . . shit!

He braked by a liquor shop.

"Any wine?" he asked a shabby-looking man in sports pants and a blue jersey.

"Just vodka, but they say there's some at Jubilee. Mind taking me too?"

"Sure." The man climbed in next to him.

They stopped in front of the shop called Jubilee. Can I tag along with you? the man asked. Pryadilnikov shook his head no. Jerk, the man said, and got out of the car. Pryadilnikov climbed out after he did.

Two men were loitering by the shop door. They stopped a boy walking past and said something to him. The boy unhesitatingly reached into his pocket, gave them some change, and went on his way. The two spotted Pryadilnikov. One of them, jolly, brown-eyed, strode over toward him, smiled, and held out his hand: Hello! Pryadilnikov mechanically returned the handshake. The stranger squeezed his hand: Give me something, little brother, for a bit of wine, quick, quick. Pryadilnikov was no miser, but that "quick, quick" rubbed him the wrong way and he replied, pulling back his hand, "I'm a cheapskate."

He bought wine and cigarettes in the store and went back out into the street. Hey, cheapskate, what do you say we go have a little chat in the bushes? the jolly brown-eyed one said. No time for it. Come on, Silver, come on, let's go. But Pryadilnikov kept walking toward his armored car. Give it up, the second said to the first, it's a sin to beat up cripples. Pryadilnikov gritted his teeth but didn't stop. He opened the car door, got in, lay the plastic bag with the bottles in it on the seat, turned the key. The engine came to life. Pryadilnikov glanced out the window. The two were still loitering. What a lousy day, Pryadilnikov thought, and shut off the engine. He found his penknife in the mess in the car, pulled at the blade with his fingernail, and drew it out of its handle. He put the knife in his pocket. He unsealed the pack, took out a cigarette, lit it, and climbed out of the car.

"What do you want, Silver?" the jolly one asked, surprised. "Come on, let's go," said Pryadilnikov. "Ha! The little bull's blood is up!" the jolly one exclaimed. "We were joking, stay alive," the second one said appeasingly. "Let's go," Pryadilnikov repeated. "Listen, Silver, you'd better get away from here," advised the second one, "or you'll be limping on both legs."

"Hello, kids!"

All three turned around. Louisa.

"Hello, pussycat, if you're serious," the jolly one answered quickly, looking Louisa over.

"Out buying milk, Fedya?"

Pryadilnikov said nothing.

"Problems, kids?"

"Endless," the jolly one replied. "Never enough."

"There," said Louisa, taking a ruble coin out of her purse.

"It isn't fake?"

"So, any more problems?" Louisa asked.

"That's everything. No problems," the jolly one replied.

"Let's get home," Louisa said crisply, and pulled Pryadilnikov by the arm.

"You're late. Your man is already packing it in."

Louisa dragged Pryadilnikov away.

"Not bad, the little filly," the jolly one said.

"Let's get going," the second one said, and headed into the shop.

The armored car was rolling down the street. You really picked a pair to mess with, Louisa said. Pryadilnikov didn't answer. You really picked who to mess with. They would have killed you. Don't you know what kind of brutes they were? No doubt they both had knives in their pockets. Criminal mugs. They'd cut a sheep's throat or a man's with as much pleasure. And prison is home to them. So, what, you're going to drink all by yourself? No, Pryadilnikov answered, there are two guys I can always count on, classmates. Louisa didn't say anything for a moment. Can I keep you company? Pryadilnikov glanced at her. Sure, keep me company. Louisa smiled. I was joking. My husband's waiting for me; he's jealous as a bull. Why would bulls be jealous? I don't know, the word just popped into my head. Keep me company, Pryadilnikov said again. Louisa's eyes sparkled. It would be better if you asked Marina. Marina? Why Marina? Why? Why? Open your eyes and look at her, that's why. So, to my place then?

Pryadilnikov asked. You're cool, Louisa said, rolling her eyes languidly. Next time, Fedya. Today I can't.

The armored car came to a halt outside Louisa's building. Louisa picked up her handbag and opened the car door. Pryadilnikov looked at her sullenly. She lingered for a moment. Pryadilnikov looked at her. She said, quietly and firmly, "Next time," and got out.

He didn't look for his classmates. He didn't feel like it anymore. He would have to talk, listen, smile, and after a whole day of it he was tired of talking, listening, smiling. His tongue was heavy, his ears were hurting, and his flesh had turned to rubber from smiling. It was good to live alone: if he wanted company he could invite someone over, and if he wanted to be alone he wouldn't invite anyone. The worst thing about the army was that there had been nowhere to hide. Even in the latrines there was always someone grunting.

Only one person. Only one person had been always welcome, night and day, on duty or at home, when things were bad or good, one, only one, who could understand anything from just half a word. . . .

The recon company went out often. Yes, too often; they put on their combat gear and sneakers—like hikers—and slipped away from camp at night, and would return, just as suddenly, two or three days later, covered with dust, unshaven; the recon company would vanish and I would begin to wait, going to their tents every day to find out whether or not they were back. Then the company would return; I'd go to their tents, see the dirt-crusted boys cleaning their weapons; I'd crane my neck and try to spot the long, hook-nosed face, and sometimes I'd see it off in the distance, sometimes not; I would walk up to the boys: Well, guys, how did it go? They: The usual. Or: Lousy. And they would add: He went off to the weapons depot, or to the baths, or somewhere else. I would find him and ask: Like a smoke? He: Yes! I: But the Minister of Health warns against it. He: I want to be a human

being, and one learned old man has said: A human being is a
featherless biped that smokes! I: Well then, take this present from
Africa. I would give him a pack of cigarettes, much prized in the
army—Soviet or Bulgarian cigarettes, but our ritual was: A present
from Africa is a present from Africa! Beyond the firing range was
a hill that provided marble to build the baths, storehouses, and
toilets. The marble was white with sea-green stripes. Sometimes
we managed to escape there; we would settle down among the
sunlit slabs, the snow-white slabs. The snow-white slabs, the sun
shining, the marble painful to look at—he opens a book and reads
out loud from Baudelaire, Rimbaud the wanderer, Verlaine,
Bunin, Blok, Yevtushenko, I don't read because I'm awful at it,
but he reads wonderfully, he reads wonderfully because he writes
poems too. He reads, I lie back on the warm rocks, smoke a cheap
makhorka cigarette; I look down at the camp, the steppe, at the
distant southern mountains, they say it's already Pakistan there,
they say that cedars grow there, and to the west are the Iskapol
Mountains, was it the Greeks who named them that? Alexander
of Macedon waged war here once . . . The Iskapol Mountains are
bare, their peaks snowy; I look at the Iskapol Mountains, at the
cedar-covered mountains to the south, and far away on the steppe
I see a caravan: tiny camels, delicate white marching figures. . . .
But more often no one would be moving anywhere on the hot,
dusty, hard, bare land. "I am a man, like God I am condemned
to know the anguish of all nations and all times." I lie back on
the warm, brilliant rocks, looking at the sun through a chip of
white marble with a sea-green stripe, and I tell him that we should
be living on the shore of some ocean. He shuts the book, takes
the translucent chip from me, looks at the sun through the sea-
green wave, and agrees that we should live by the ocean when we
get out of the army. Every now and then he reads his own poems,
and that's better than Baudelaire, Blok, or Yevtushenko. The
recon company often went out on raids, too often; the company
would drive away and each time I would try to find out whether
or not it had returned. Then I would walk over and see, in the

distance, the blackened boys in their sun-faded fatigues: Hi, how did it go? The usual, and he's in his tent. Like a smoke? But the Minister of Health, take this present from Africa, you haven't read anything of yours for a long time. I'm not writing, nothing comes at all, Villon was a hopeless debauché but he still wrote, and I'm not that hopeless yet but nothing—or am I already hopeless? Don't worry, you'll still turn out an armor-piercing poem and the masters will all cry in envy. Hi, how did it go? Fine, and he's at the weapons depot. Hi, how did it go? Badly, and he's in the yard of the medical unit. The yard of the medical unit, at its center a canvas tent on four iron poles planted in the ground, and under the tent three humped sheets. A medic captain: Hey, don't go poking around there. I have to, captain, my comrade's there. Well, go ahead then. I drew the sheet away from the face, looked, left, came back, stuck a pack of cigarettes under the sheet, then stood there in the middle of the yard. It was hot and flies were flying over the sheets; I was standing in the sun in the middle of the scorching medical unit yard, the sheets were white under the tent, the yard was describing slow circles, rhythmic circles, in its center were the white sheets, motionless, dead sheets, sheets of stone, the yard was spinning around, the medical unit and the marble latrines were spinning around, the latrines stank of disinfectant, the sun was smeared with sticky brown disinfectant, the fetid liquid was running into the sky, spilling down to the earth, and flies were flying around the sheets: to and fro, fro and to . . .

Pryadilnikov poured from the bottle into his glass and thought: I'm sick of the editorial office. . . . He drank the glass, ate an apple and a piece of cheese. He lit a cigarette and thought: I'm tired of the colonnaded building, I don't want to see the zavsepech. And I'm bored with that kennel. But there's a good place somewhere. Cigarette smoke was curling coyly in front of his face. Too bad that Louisa didn't come. Louisa, Liza, liz-liz-liz. The black things landed. . . .

The birds with long white necks beat their wings soundlessly, stretched out their legs, alit on the earth. There were white flowers on the steppe—lumps of soapsuds floating low to the ground. The company was asleep in its armored transports. The guards saw the flock. It was early in the morning, warm and quiet. The birds landed, lowered their huge wings, cleaned their feathers with their beaks, and, peering around, wandered among the grass and flowers. They had white necks and red crowns, and every now and then they would stand still, turn their heads toward the column, and stare at it. The guards didn't budge and the birds probably mistook them for pillars, and the armored transports for shining green turtles. The white-necked birds were striding back and forth on the steppe, they were black, the steppe green, the hills and the herd of green turtles were asleep, there was a crimson light in the sky to the east. The guards looked at one another and smiled.

A hatch cover creaked and a second lieutenant hauled himself out of an armored transport; he yawned, glanced around at the steppe, and froze when he spotted the birds. He vanished for a moment, reappeared, climbed out of the machine, and, crouched low to the ground, walked across the steppe with an assault rifle in his hands. The guards followed him with their eyes. The birds caught sight of the lieutenant, stretched their necks, stiffened. The lieutenant raised the rifle, dropped to one knee, set the rifle butt against his shoulder, hunched his head, aimed. The birds ran off, flapping their wings. The flock took to the air. A pale red burst shot over the steppe and cut into the flock. One of the guards raised his rifle to his shoulder and fired a short burst without taking aim. A second and a third grabbed their rifles too and started shooting. And Pryadilnikov raised his rifle to his shoulder and fired two long bursts of tracers. First-second-third-fourth. First! Second! Third! Fourth!

Sleepy soldiers leaped, weapons in hand, out of the armored transports.

The cranes flew away. A few birds lay motionless on the steppe. Two, their wings broken, were flailing in the grass. The guards ran over, struck them with their rifle butts, and dragged them by their legs toward the column. The lieutenant and soldiers bent down over the tattered birds, looking for wounds and arguing about where the bullets had entered and exited. The captain appeared, furious. He yelled at the lieutenant and the guards and promised to give them all three days in the cooler for the false alarm. The lieutenant nodded toward the rising sun and said that reveille had been called in time. The captain didn't answer.

The soldiers climbed down onto the steppe and, yawning, urinated while watching the wine-colored sun rise over the green earth. Then they had breakfast—biscuits, cold tea, lumps of sugar, and canned fish in tomato sauce. The lieutenant was talking loudly about how he hunted geese in the tundra, gray, plump geese, delicious, fat, tender geese. The soldiers were swallowing wet, red pieces of fish and listening to him.

He had dreamed it again. Pryadilnikov woke up in the morning and the first thing he did was try to recall the dream. He dreamed of something yellow, dry, rustling, rounded. Yellow, dry, rustling, rounded, yellow, rustling, yellow—the mountain!

The mountain! Pryadilnikov got up and went to wash. He cupped cold water in his hands and splashed his face with it. The mountain! The mountain in autumn.

He washed up, dried his face with a towel, and went into the kitchen for some tea, strong tea, bitter, hot, sharp, dark, divine tea. On the mountain. Fifteen years ago there had been a mountain. Sharp, cherry-colored, no, peat-colored tea. Pryadilnikov wiped his sweaty face with his hand and poured a second cup. On the mountain. How could he have forgotten? There had been a mountain, and a rabbit. The rabbit had been white, with crimson eyes. He gave a rusty German bayonet to a small boy who lived in a one-family wooden house in exchange for it. The rabbit moved into their seventh-floor apartment. It lived in a suitcase under his writing desk. The rabbit was like a dog. When the boy came home from school the rabbit would leap out of the suitcase and hop along the walls to the boy across the room. The boy fed it cabbage and crusts of bread and carried it against his chest when he went for walks. His parents called the rabbit a pest and threatened to throw it outside or roast it in the oven with potatoes. The boy would say to the rabbit: Soon we'll run away. He wanted to run away into the woods with the rabbit, build a hut, and live off rabbit grass, nuts, and mushrooms. When the boy was given a D one day he showed the workbook to the rabbit and said: There, you see, it's terrible to be a human. The rabbit twitched its ears in agreement. His father had come home in the evening. He looked at the workbook and gave the boy a hiding. Sitting in its suitcase and hearing the wails of its master and friend, the rabbit knew for certain that it was better to be a rabbit. After the whipping the boy sat by his window. The rabbit crept up to him and began to lick his toenails. He liked that for some reason, licking toenails—could salt gather there from when the boy walked around?

His father said: Another D or C and the rabbit goes. On the very next day the boy was given a D even though he had learned the whole lesson—he hadn't been able, out of fright, to answer. He came home, put a blanket, bread, a little knife, salt, and matches into a backpack, hid the rabbit against his chest, reached the station by tram, climbed into a train to the city outskirts, saw a deserted stop through the window, and got out. He found an oak-covered mountain among the fields and spent two days there. During the second night the rabbit vanished. In the morning some peasants out mushroom hunting found the young boy. The rabbit had no doubt sensed that people would come in the morning. And it took off. And it did the right thing. Maybe to this day it's still free, if it hasn't been eaten by foxes. But the young boy hadn't sensed anything, he hadn't taken off, God only knows what was done to him.

On the mountain, on the mountain, on the mountain.

He put a kettle, two blankets, sugar, tea, and bread into a backpack and drove out of the city.

After yesterday's binge his head was spinning, his hands shaking, and his heart beating erratically. Pryadilnikov was sweating heavily.

He drove south along the highway for half an hour. He decided it was time and turned off onto a country road. The sand-colored armored car started to rock with the potholes.

There, the development. The railroad. Fifteen years before he had spotted this development from the window of the city train. The train had stopped here. Moved on. There had been another stop, and another. He had climbed out at the third. Or the fourth.

The armored car clambered up a hill. Beyond the railroad Pryadilnikov could make out hills and stands of trees. The mountain had to be somewhere around there. The armored car crossed the railroad and sailed onto bare gray fields covered with cobwebs.

The sand-colored armored car rumbled over the fields under a high empty sky.

There weren't any mountains anywhere. Maybe in fact it had never existed. Maybe he had dreamed it. And the white rabbit. And everything else.

His mouth was dry. His heart was beating too hard now, knocking against his shoulder blade. There were ponds and swamps, but clean water nowhere. He would have to head toward some village.

The car skirted a stand of trees. The houses of a village began to appear in silhouette straight ahead. Pryadilnikov drove a bit farther toward the village, then changed his mind and swung the armored car around. He didn't want to see people. It could have been peasants from this village who had gone out for mushrooms fifteen years before, caught the young boy on the mountain, and brought him to the militia.

His mouth was dry and bitter.

But had there been water on the mountain? No, not on the mountain. In a little gully, in the bushes. Yes, there's a little gully below the mountain . . . a spring there.

Just before evening Pryadilnikov realized that he wouldn't find it.

He pressed on the brake pedal and the armored car came to a stop. Pryadilnikov got out.

The sun was shining red and it was already hanging on the forested horizon.

Pryadilnikov looked around.

The land was flat in all directions. Green stands of trees everywhere. Red maples here and there. It was warm. Have to remember, Pryadilnikov thought, have to remember everything clearly. He sat down on the ground, his face to the sun.

And so there was a rabbit, white, crimson eyes, that loved watermelon rinds. And then the two of them ran away. A train to the city outskirts brought them south. After an hour, most likely, they got out. A railway stop.

He walked along a road. Fields all around. He saw the mountain. Swung toward it. It was yellow. Clusters on the lingonberry bushes were glowing a dull red below the mountain. The lingonberry nourished him with its fragrant fruit. On the mountain were yellow maples and oaks. Acorns were tumbling from the oaks. The acorns fell into russet ferns. He took off his cloth cap and stood under the biggest oak. The oak dropped a hard acorn onto the top of his head. It was funny. The rabbit was cautiously getting used to the smells. White in the russet ferns. We're going to live here. We'll build our hut right there. And that aspen will make a great spear to fight off wolves with. Acorns were falling. Everything was warm. Fat thrushes and bright jays were flying in and out of the trees. In the grass were boletus mushrooms. Full, yellow autumn. And not scared at all. The rabbit next to him. The lingonberry like a human being. The bush not quite human. But almost. Go on, I'll feed you with my berries, go o-o-on.

He took a load of hay from a stack in a field. He slept on the hay, covering himself with the blanket. He held the rabbit against his chest so it wouldn't get cold or scared. It was scary at night even though that auntie with her berries was somewhere close by. At night the moon shined. The leaves flew. They dropped, white in the moonlight, and he dreamed that it was snow falling, that snowflakes were settling on his face. He woke up and saw that it was leaves. Winter is still far off, and I'm still hoping to build a hut, warm and solid.

The morning was warm. The September sun shining in the sky. Yellow leaves were falling, yellow leaves quivering in the trees, yellow leaves lying on the blanket, the ground carpeted with yellow leaves, and down below, in the swamp, were yellow birches. He wandered around the mountain, came across the spring in the little gully, collected a panful of water. He made kasha. The rabbit breakfasted on a slab of bread. The rabbit hopped up the mountain and returned. The lingonberry watched from below. A magpie landed. It perched on a maple, examined the young boy and the rabbit, croaked "Watch it!" It flew off, returned soon after with three friends, and all of them fixed their black eyes on the young boy and the rabbit. He threw a stick at them and they cried, in chorus, "Watch it!" Then they flew away. Mice raced up and down the mountain. The mountain was rustling, the yellow, rustling mountain.

The jagged horizon had already cut off half the solar disk before the person sitting on the road by his car heard the flapping of wings. Shadows descended from above. They were black birds. They stretched out their legs and settled to the ground. The birds folded their wings. They had long necks with a white stripe from their beaks to their breasts and patches of red on their small heads. The birds paced around in the dry grass, pecking at its flowerlets with their beaks and picking the seeds from the ground. He put down his assault rifle, stood up, and walked away. He slowly climbed down the mountain. He smoothly descended from the mountain. He was walking downward, not making a sound. The white rabbit was hopping in front of him. The birds spotted them and froze.

They didn't fly away. Their heads turned toward him, the big black birds were waiting.

⇥ GLOSSARY OF RUSSIAN ⇤
AND AFGHAN TERMS

BMP *boevaya mashina pekhoty*, infantry combat vehicle

BTR *bronetransportyor dlya lichnovo sostavi*, armored personnel carrier

CP (in "The Yellow Mountain") *Kontrolnii punct*, checkpoint

CP (in "Winter in Afghanistan" and "Safe Return") *komandnii punkt polka*, regimental command post

doukh Afghan peasant; rebel

dukan small-scale Afghan merchant, most often on the black market

duval low mud wall in a *kishlak*

kiariz underground Afghan irrigation tunnel

kishlak mud-walled Afghan village

zampolit acronym for *zamestitel' komandira po polichasti*, (army) deputy commander for political matters

zavsepech acronym for *zavedouyoushchii sektora pechati*, (regional) director of the press section